A
KONKANI GRAMMAR

A
KONKANI GRAMMAR

ANGELUS FRANCIS XAVIER MAFFEI

GYAN

Published by

GYAN

Gyan Publishing House
5, Ansari Road
Daryaganj, New Delhi-110002
Phone: 011-47034999, 9811692060
E-mail: books@gyanbooks.com

Distribution Network
gyanbooks.com
India, USA, Canada, UK, Australia, France

ISBN : 978-81-212-4447-3 (PB)
First Published, 1882

2nd Impression 2020

Printed at: Gyan Press, Delhi.

A
Konkani Grammar
Author: Angelus Francis Xavier Maffei

A KONKANI GRAMMAR

BY

ANGELUS FRANCIS XAVIER MAFFEI

OF THE SOCIETY OF JESUS

MANGALORE

ON COMMISSION SALE AT THE

BASEL MISSION BOOK & TRACT DEPOSITORY

1882

CONTENTS

PART III. SYNETYMOLOGY

PART IV. SYNTAX

PREFACE

THIS Grammar was at first intended for private circulation among the Missionaries of this Vicariate. Hence there are many things which will probably be unintelligible to the general reader. It was only when a great portion had already passed through the press, that at the repeated request of friends it was thought not imprudent to present it to the general public.

This book in the main has been composed, on account of urgent necessity, within a few months, without any other assistance than what could be derived from a study of the spoken language in its many varieties, choosing the forms which seemed to be more exact and forming some general rules by way of induction, and this, after a year and half's acquaintance with English and Konkani. Hence the reader cannot expect either a perfectly English style or a masterly arrangement of the various parts of the Grammar, or a thorough accuracy in the formation of rules, or faultless purity in the Konkani language itself.

One word about the second appendix. After careful consideration the author has deviated from the common way, in writing Konkani with Kanarese characters, and this for the reasons touched upon in the *Parergon*. If this new way does not prove suitable, the common one can be kept.

In some secondary points, however, on account of hurry, a constant manner of writing in this new way could not be preserved.

Such therefore as this work is, it is offered first to the Missionaries, in the hope of its promoting God's glory, to whose help is due whatever good there is in this Grammar, and secondly to the Konkani public, in the hope of its stimulating the further study of their long neglected language.

Mangalore, January 1882. *A. F. X. M.*

A. M. D. G.

Advertisement

In order to have a more complete or exact notion of the various points of the Grammar, the corresponding pages of the *Parergon*, p. 395, must be consulted.

PART I. ORTHOGRAPHY

CHAPTER I. ALPHABET

The Konkani language was formerly written with the alphabet called Bālabōdha or Nāgar; sometimes it was written with the Mōḍi Alphabet, which is the Mahrāṭṭi Alphabet. Now the Kanarese Alphabet is generally used, and although it does not express all Konkani sounds, yet it is better adapted for this than the Latin Alphabet. But as the Kanarese Alphabet is not known to the greater part of my brethren, for whom I write, I shall use the Latin Alphabet, with the required modifications, which I am going to explain.

First of all, I premise that I pronounce and read all Konkani words written with Roman characters, as Latin is pronounced and read in Italy and more or less also in England by Catholics, with some few exceptions to be explained later on.

Now let us explain the Konkani Alphabet and the modifications to be introduced in the Latin Alphabet in order to make it express the Konkani sounds.

Although I am aware that many things should be said about this point of Orthography, yet I will limit myself for the present to the most essential observations.

The vowels are the same as in Latin, but each simple vowel has two sounds and in Kanarese two different characters: one sound is long, the other is short. The long vowels are pronounced slowly and have the stress of the voice upon them. The short vowels are pronounced quickly and have no stress of voice upon them. Thus the Konkani long and short vowels are not very different from the long and short Latin vowels. The short a is considerably different: it can be best learned from a teacher. The nearest approach to it is the short u in English, *e.g.* *but*, or the a in farō; although even this u and a are not the Konkani short a. In words of more than one syllable, this a short is pronounced almost as a short o.

I shall mark, *if required*, the long vowels by this sign ‑, placed above the vowel, the short vowels by this sign ˘.

Moreover some vowels may have an open or a closed sound as in Italian l'oro, loro. I shall use the sign ˋ to indicate the open, and the sign ˊ to indicate the closed sound, *when it may be required*.

Besides the usual full vowels a, e, i, o, u there is a half vowel; this is not an a, not an o, not an u: it is a middle sound similar to the half vowel which is added by the Romans to the words which end in a consonant. This sound is necessary, chiefly when a word ends in a double consonant; because without pronouncing this half vowel, the double consonant cannot be heard. Moreover there is a vowel, which may be called nearly u, because it sounds almost like u. It occurs in many words which have the accent upon the preceding syllable, *e.g.* kēsu̥=hair. It is similar to the preceding half vowel; yet there seems to be some difference.

As in Konkani no word can end in a pure full consonant, it will not be necessary to express this in writing, if this general rule be remembered, *i.e.* that no word can end in a pure consonant. Hence, if a word ends in a consonant in this Grammar and in the Dictionary, this half vowel must be always understood. It is true that there are degrees in the pronunciation of it, so that sometimes it is hardly heard, sometimes it seems to be half a, etc., yet for the present these niceties may be omitted. If it be required sometimes to indicate it, I shall write it ạ, as I write ụ the nearly u.

What I said, that no Konkani word may end in a pure consonant, is true if we write Konkani according to Kanarese. But if we do not take this into consideration, we may say that in Konkani words may occur ending in a pure consonant, as in European languages. Of course at the end of each word ending in a consonant, a kind of half vowel is, I may say, naturally pronounced; but this is not a thing peculiar to the Konkani language. This is one of the reasons why the Kanarese alphabet, following the Kanarese rules, is not perfectly suitable to Konkani.

The consonants are the same as in Latin, except that

1. d, dh, n, l, t, th may have two sounds, *i. e.* either as in Latin (about dh, th see below) or a sound which is got by turning the tip of the tongue upwards, so as to touch the roof of the mouth far away from the front teeth. For this reason they may be called cerebral consonants. I shall mark these cerebral consonants with a dot under them, *e.g.* ṭ. The best way to pronounce, at least approximately, the cerebral sound of ḍ and ḍh is to pronounce it like the English r, viz. not full as in Latin, but half only. Yet this ḍ and ḍh do not always take such a sound, *i. e.* of the English r. Use will teach you.

2. k or c hard, g hard (as g in gallus), g soft (as g in genus, or as the English j), ĉ soft (like c in cinis) t, ṭ, d, ḍ, p have two sounds, *i. e.* either as in Latin (and ṭ, ḍ, as explained above) or aspirated, as if there were an aspirated English or German h after the consonant, to be sounded distinctly from the preceding consonant, *e.g.* d'h. It is nearly expressed in the Irish pronunciation of the word *which.* I shall mark these consonants with an h written after them, *e.g.* th.

3. The Latin c and g may change in the same word, the soft sound into a hard sound: *e.g.* ager, agri; g, in the Nominative is soft, in the Genitive is hard. Not so in Konkani. If g in the Nominative has a soft sound, it keeps it in all cases; and if it has a hard sound, it keeps it in all cases. The same must be said of c hard or k and c soft. For the sake of dis-

tinction I shall write the soft g, j. But this j must be pronounced sometimes rather like č (which sound can be explained only orally) or thinner than the English j. The hard g I shall write g. For the same reason I shall write the soft c, č, and the hard c, k. So there is no necessity of a pure c; for its two sounds are expressed either by č or by k; yet, wherever c occurs it must be pronounced according to the Latin, namely before a, o, u as k, before e, i as č. To express, if required, the Latin j, I shall use the English y.

4. In Konkani there are five similar sounds, namely the first as a hard s (as in assis), the second a soft s (as in rosa), the third a hard z (as in Ital. sazio), the fourth a soft z (as in Zephirus or zio), the fifth a very strong z (as in German Zeit). The first and second sounds very seldom occur; but the others are very frequent. In order to simplify, I will not introduce signs for the first and second sound; where they occur, I shall mark expressely their sounds. I mark the hard z by s, the soft z by z only, the German z by tz or ts or tč.

This s may have many degrees, *i. e.*, from a sharp Latin s to the hard Italian z. For the sake of simplicity, I express all these sounds from the sharp Latin s to the hard Italian z by s, leaving those degrees to be learned by practice.

5. The Latin sound expressed by the Latin sc in scientia, and in English by sh, I will express by š.

6. In Konkani there occurs at every step the nasal sound expressed in Kanarese by ಂ. If this sound occurs in the middle of a word, it does not differ much from m or n. So in order to simplify, in the middle of a word I shall write it by m̲ or n̲. But at the end of a word, it has also the same sound, namely, of an indistinct m or n pronounced through the nose; but as in Latin a final m or n has not such a sound, I shall mark this nasal sound at the end of a word by m̃ or ñ.

7. The Latin compound consonant gn as in magnus, is usually pronounced, separating both consonants, as if it were written g-n or, as they pronounce it in German, *e.g.* Ig-natius. So in order to make this clearer, I write the two consonants

separately g-n. If the consonants gn are written united, then they should be pronounced as nh in Portuguese, viz. as one sound, and as in Italian is pronounced in the word mugnajo. This is chiefly the case in the Portuguese (or derived from the Portuguese) family-names, *e.g.* Norogna.

1. Often I write the family-names having this sound gn by nh in the Portuguese way, because this is the custom.

2. Moreover lh, occurring in the family-names is pronounced as in Portuguese, *i. e.* as gl followed by i in Italian, as in the word figlio; *e. g.* Coelho.

3. If sč occur, it cannot be pronounced as in Latin (scientia, scala), but the consonants must be pronounced separately as if it were written s-c; *e.g.* hăs-čem̃ = to laugh.

4. Some other sounds should be noticed, but for the present may be omitted. But exactness would require them, as also exactness would have required me to explain the above given sounds more distinctly, with some exceptions and niceties.

The following then is the Konkani alphabet written with Roman characters, modified:

ă, Ă = short a (often very near to ó)
ā, Ā = long a
a = common a
ạ = half a
am̃ *or* añ = nasal a
b = common b
bh = b aspirated
č = c soft
čh = the preceding aspirated
k = c hard, English k
kh = the preceding aspirated
d = common d
dh = d aspirated
ḍ = d cerebral
ḍh = ḍ aspirated
ĕ, Ĕ = short e
ē, Ē = long e
é = closed e
è = open e
em̃ *or* eñ = nasal e
f = common f
g = hard g, as gh in Latin
gh = g hard aspirated
j = g soft, as j in English
jh = the preceding aspirated
h = h aspirated as in English and German
ĭ, Ĭ = short i
ī, Ī = long i
im̃ *or* iñ = i nasal
i = Latin common i
l = common l
ḷ = cerebral l
m = common m
n = common n

ṇ =n cerebral
ŏ, Ŏ=short o
ō, Ō=long o
ó =closed o
ò =open o
o =common o
om̃ *or* oñ=nasal o
p =common p
ph =p aspirated, nearly f
q =as in Latin (qui)
r =common r
s =z hard, as in sazio, or as s in est
z =z soft, as in zio
š =sh in English
t =common t
th =t aspirated
ṭ =t cerebral
ṭh =ṭ aspirated
ŭ, Ŭ=short u
ū, Ū=long u
um̃ *or* uñ=nasal u
u̥ =half u *or* nearly u
v =v as in Latin, sometimes nearly u
y =y as in English
tz *or* ts=very strong z, as in German
kš =the Latin x
m̃ *or* ñ=nasal sound
" =sign of the accent (see below)

The signs of aspiration of the cerebral sound etc. will only be used when necessary. Sometimes by omitting some of these signs, the meaning is entirely changed; *e.g.* sōḍ=leave, sōd=seek, *etc.*

If we had to write Konkani with Kanarese letters, some other observations would be required, chiefly to show how pronunciation can agree with writing; *e.g.* what is written here e and ea should be written ye and ya; au should be written avu etc.

1. One consonant is often changed into another for the sake of euphony, *e.g.*

a) All Adjectives ending in so or zo in the Nominative Singular Masculine change the s or z into č or j in all other cases and genders; *e.g.* mozo=my; *fem.* moji.

b) A word ending in z or s in the Nominative Singular changes this s or z into j or č or š; *e.g.* sāns=evening, sanjer=in the evening; monis=man, monšāk=to the man.

c) S followed by another s or t becomes š, if the second s is changed into č on account of Declension; *e.g.* has-ta=laughs, hašcom̃=to laugh.

d) The nasal m̃ or ñ becomes a pure n, if by inflexion a word loses the consonant joined to ũ or m̃, so that ñ be followed by a vowel, or by another n; *e.g.* burgeanō=O children!

e) The nasal sound ñ which is hardly heard at the end, is very distinctly heard if, by adding some letter, it becomes medial; *e.g.* atañ = now, atāñts = just now; saddāñ = always, saddañts = always (emphatic).

f) The half vowel ạ, which, if final, is hardly heard in many cases, is very distinctly heard if by adding a syllable it ceases to be final; *e.g.* apun = himself; a is not heard, although if we write it in Kanarese, we should put the semi-vowel a. But if we add to apun the emphatic tz, that a appears = apunătz.

g) Common people often pronounce *h* instead of s; *e.g.* aha, *instead of* asa; kăhălo *instead of* kăssălo.

2. I said above that the Kanarese alphabet is not quite suited to the Konkani language, because there are some sounds which cannot be expressed exactly by the Kanarese alphabet. They are chiefly these: the hard Latin s, the soft Latin s, z, tz, ụ. Moreover many names have the half vowel in such a slight degree, that they seem to end in a consonant. But in Kanarese we cannot express this exactly.

3. The sound expressed by tz sometimes seems to be rather tċ, sometimes ts; hence sometimes it may be found written tz, sometimes tċ or ts. The sounds tz or ts are almost the same; tċ inclines a little to ċ, preceded by t; nay sometimes it is not clear whether it is ċ or tċ or tz.

4. Finally, the compound vowels (as all others) ei, ai, au, oi, ou, etc., as hinted, are pronounced in the Latin way; hence, *e.g.* baunta is pronounced not as in *taught* but as ou in *house*: ou is not pronounced as in *house*, but with the sound of o in *note*, followed by the sound of u in *rule* etc.

CHAPTER II. ACCENT

In order to enable ourselves from the very beginning to read correctly we must know something about the accent.

As a general rule all Konkani words have the accent on the last syllable.

1. I do not reckon as a syllable that which ends in ạ or ụ. Hence the accent falls upon the preceding syllable, because the preceding syllable is truly the last full syllable.

2. If the last syllable is a diphthong, usually the first vowel has the accent, although there are some exceptions; *e.g.* ui″ = yes; kai″ = when; khai″ = where; tăi″ = there.

3. I shall mark in the Dictionary the accent in doubtful cases. If nothing is noted about diphthongs, it must be understood that the accent is on the first vowel.

Exceptions

1. The cardinal numbers from 11 to 18 inclusive, (according to low castes), and

2. Raja, sade and a few other words have the accent upon the penultimate.

3. Foreign words adopted, chiefly family-names, retain their original accent, although common people are very fond of making even these follow the general rule, especially Portuguese words; thus they say: Soz, Coel, Pint etc. instead of Suza, Coelho, Pinto.

N. B. When it is necessary the accent will be shown by this sign ″ put after the vowel which has the emphasis.

APPENDIX

about long and short vowels

Great care is to be taken in pronouncing the vowels according to their quantity. The quantity is often indicated in the Dictionary. Moreover note this: a is long in the termination of the 1st Declension, o and eñ are always long in the 3rd Declension. Further e, the termination of the cases in some declensions, is open. Generally speaking, I think that if a word ends in a full vowel, it is long.

PART II. ETYMOLOGY
or Parts of Speech

CHAPTER I. SUBSTANTIVES

The chief things to be considered about Substantives are Declension and Gender.

Art. I. Declension

A. General Observations

The Declensions may be arranged more or less as in Latin; thus I shall simplify this apparently hopeless task. It is true, there may be some exceptions, but what language is there without exceptions?. This happens even in the most cultivated languages; much more then must this happen in Konkani, which is an assemblage of dialects rather than a formed language. Moreover consider, that I am writing the Grammar for the districts in which we are living; perhaps going further north, some difference, though not a substantial one, may be found.

How then can we arrange Konkani words in Declensions so that they may be distinguished one from the other? In Latin we distinguish five Declensions, because there are five different ways of modifying a word in the different cases. Thus any Latin word is inflected in the different cases either as *rosa* or as *ager*, or as *homo*, or as *spiritus*, or as *dies*. Moreover one Declension is distinguished from another by the Genitive Case which is different in each Declension; whereas some other case of one Declension may be the same as some other case of another Declension. In a similar way in Konkani there are five different ways of modifying a word in the different cases; and as in Latin, we know the Declension of a Noun from the Genitive, so in Konkani we may know the Declension of a Noun not from the Genitive (as there is no Genitive, usually), but from the case which is different in each Declension, which consequently might be called the Characteristic. This case is the Original. Thus some Nouns have the Original ending in e or je, some in a not preceded by e, some in a preceded by e (ea), some in i, some in u. I could not find another termination; hence there are five Declensions. I said now the Original in Konkani may be used as the Genitive in Latin, in order to distinguish the Declensions. But this Original in Konkani has an additional advantage over the Latin Genitive; for it is at the same time the stem from which all other cases may be formed. And what I say, must be understood also of the Original Plural, namely from the Original Plural we can form all other cases; yet the Declension is known only from the Original Singular. The Original Singular is always given in the Dictionary. The Original Plural will be given below. There are therefore five Declensions. In each Declension there are two Numbers, Singular and Plural.

In Konkani eight Cases may be distinguished; namely, Nominative, Original, Dative, Accusative, Vocative, Instrumental, 1st Locative, 2nd Locative. The cases which require an explanation are Original, Instrumental, 1st and 2nd Locative. Instrumental and Locative are used also in Kanarese and Tulu. That case which is used to indicate instrument, cause, manner, is called Instrumental from the chief meaning which it has; Locative is that which indicates chiefly place and time, and is called Locative, because it is mostly used to indicate place. I must subdivide this Locative into 1st and 2nd Locative, because there are two different ways; the first corresponds to the English Preposition *in*, the 2nd to *on* or *upon*.

The Original Case does not exist in Kanarese and Tulu. This case usually has the same form as the Vocative, just as in the Latin 2nd Declension, Dative and Ablative have the same form, yet the meaning is very different; hence I cannot include it in the Vocative. This case is called Original, not from the chief meaning as the other cases, but from the chief use of it; that is, this case is nothing else but the pure stem from which all other cases (which have not the same form as the Nominative) are derived by adding some terminations. Therefore, I call it Original; it might be called also stem or crude form. The use of it will be indicated in the Syntax; for the present it is enough to know, that usually this case is used with nearly all Postpositions. What I say here, must be understood also of the Adjectives; because even these have their Original Case; nay sometimes the Original Case of the derived Adjective is used with some Postpositions instead of the Original Case of the corresponding Substantive.

There is no pure Genitive Case, because the Genitive Case is changed into an Adjective; *e.g.* the "love of God" is changed into "Divine love;" this will be explained below more distinctly. But in order to meet the objection that there is a Genitive, I answer that the Genitive in Konkani follows in every thing the rules of the Adjective: it has three terminations, like the Adjective; it agrees with the governing noun in gender, number, case etc. Yet, if even this does not satisfy, let us at least suppose the Genitive to be an Adjective; because thus it becomes very easy: else, it becomes very difficult and, I may say, inexplicable. Nevertheless I grant that a pure Genitive sometimes occurs (see below). Now I explain each Declension in particular: first I will try to give a general rule for all Declensions, then I will explain the rule of each Declension or rather apply the general rule to each Declension. This general rule may render this point much easier; it should be read again after having learned the five Declensions.

1. I call *stem* that form of the noun from which all other cases may be derived. This form is usually found in the Original Case, and is given in the Vocabulary.

2. I call *characteristic* the last vowel or diphthong of the stem, viz: e for 1st Declension, a for the 2nd, ea for the 3rd, i for 4th, u for the 5th.

3. I call *root* what remains after having taken away the characteristic from the stem; *e.g.* in mōg = love, *mōg-a* is the stem, *a* the characteristic, *mōg* the root. Often the root is found in the Nominative, but not always; *e.g.* in the 3rd Declension, the Nominative is not the root.

How are Nouns to be declined? *Singular:* The Nominative and Original are given in the Dictionary; the Dative is formed by adding k to the stem, the Accusative in animate objects is usually equal to the Dative; in inanimate objects, it is equal to the Nominative; Vocative is equal to the Original; the Instrumental is formed by adding n to the stem. The 1st Locative is formed by adding nt to the stem. The 2nd Locative is formed by adding r to the stem, (or sometimes gér. See below) in the inanimate objects, or čer with animate objects, (or we may say also by adding r to the stem of the feminine-derived Adjective). In Latin the Instrumental should be expressed by the pure Ablative or by the Preposition a, per etc., with the required case. The Locative in Latin should be expressed by the Preposition *in*....*supra*....followed by the required case. The Latin cases preceded by some Prepositions, which are not to be translated with the Instrumental or Locative, are not expressed in Konkani by a peculiar case, but by the Original followed by the Postposition required by the meaning; *e. g.* bāpā višiānt = about the father, *de patre*. Even the Instrumental and Locative sometimes may be expressed by the Original, followed by the Postpositions required by the meaning; *e.g.* instead of bāpān = through the father, we may say bāpā vorvi; instead of mezār, mezā voir.

Plural: For the Nominative I could not find any general rule; because this as well as the Original differs in the different Declensions. About the Original I can only say that it is always nasal; and this must be borne in mind, as it must be known in order to form the other cases of the Plural. Nevertheless I put here the characteristics of the Original Plural which might be called the stem of the Plural; for, from this the other cases are formed. 1st Declension añ, 2nd Declension añ, 3rd Declension eañ, 4th Declension iñ, 5th Declension uñ.

The sign ñ has to be considered as an indistinct n which at the end of a word is not so distinctly heard; but if a consonant follows, it sounds more distinctly like n.

In order to form the other cases of the Plural proceed in the same way as in the Singular, remembering that you have to take as the fundamental form the stem of the Plural, *i.e.* the Original Plural given above; whereas, in the formation of the Singular, we take as the fundamental form the stem of the Original Singular.

Here it must be observed about all or, at least, about some Declensions, that, as in Greek, there are in Konkani many contracted Nouns. It seems to me, that this general rule might be laid down regarding this point. In Nouns of more than one syllable in the Nominative singular, the vowel before the last syllable of the other cases is usually dropped, if the nature of the consonants allows it, or, more clearly, if the word can be easily pronounced without a vowel. (It is understood that if the Accusative is equal to the Nominative, the vowel is not dropped.) Thus pātak=sin, in the Dative becomes pātkāk, shortened from pātakāk. The same rule is to be observed in the Plural. Thus here pātkāñ=sins. This contraction is generally indicated in the Dictionary; and it takes place chiefly in the 2nd Declension and also in the 1st Declension and in the 4th.

Usually the omitted vowel is a and by this omission the Noun has as many syllables as in the Nominative. Yet sometimes, this omitted vowel is also u or i; *e.g.* zulum=violence; Ablative: zulmen; vonad, vondi=wall.

1. I said above that in Konkani a contraction takes place as in Greek: there is some difference; for in Greek more usually the vowels are contracted; but here a vowel is simply omitted.

2. Sometimes I found inanimate objects having the Accusative in k, and animate objects having the Accusative equal to the Nominative. Nevertheless I think that the above general rule is always right, viz. in animate objects to make the Accusative equal to the Nominative.

3. Though no general rule can be given for the formation of the Original Plural, yet we may obtain its stem in the first three Declensions by changing the characteristic of the Singular into -añ (except the Original of the 3rd Declension which is -eañ), and in the 4th and 5th Declensions by making the characteristic of the Singular nasal.

4. As in Latin so in Konkani there are Nouns which seem to follow one or the other Declension *ad libitum*. Those Nouns will be put in the Dictionary.

5. Names of measures seem to be used in the Singular with Plural meaning; *e.g.* tīn vār = three yards. Yet this is not so fixed, and I have heard also tīn vāri.

6. Nouns have no determinate article like the English *the*.

Tō, tī, teñ = is, ea, id, or o, i, eñ = hic, hac, hoc, may be used for it; yet it does not correspond exactly to the English *the*. The undeterminate article corresponding to the English *a* or *an* is yek. (See below.)

There occurs often a case in r not according to the above rules, viz. at the nuns = mādringér; at our house = ămgér; at Coelho's house = Coelhiger. This form seems to be used only to show place in a house, as in the given examples, as in English: at Robertson's. This irregularity may be explained either by saying that that 'gér' is a corruption of gǎr = house, so that ămgér would be the same as amčo garǎr, or by saying that the postposition suffix čer is changed into gér, if the meaning is as given above, *i. e.* to live in the house of.....

Now having already given the general rule for the Declensions, we may add some general observations about them.

1. I said that Postpositions are often added to the Original, *e.g.* bāpāvorvi. If the Postposition begins with a vowel, this is omitted to prevent two vowels coming together.

2. Some Postpositions are simply added to the affected Noun in a separate word, some are joined to it in one word: these are the Postpositions, which have been given above as terminations of the Instrumental and Locative. Probably, formerly they were true Postpositions; now they are used only as terminations, except r, which perhaps is shortened

from "voir"=upon, which voir is even now used as a true Postposition.

3. It is allowed very often to add the Postpositions to the stem of the derived Adjective instead of adding them to the stem of the Substantive; *e.g.* "bāpāče višiānt"= about the father, instead of "bāpā višiānt". Yet use sometimes may require the one rather than the other form. Usually the shortened Postposition r of the 2nd Locative, is added to the stem of the Noun with inanimate objects, to the stem of the Adjective with animate objects; but in the Plural it is always added to the stem of the Adjective. So "rukānčer"=on the trees; "porvotānčer"=on the mountains.

4. There are only a few (perhaps only one) Postpositions which are added to the Nominative, not to the Original; this is "paryant"=till, in Latin *usque; e.g.* găr paryant=till to the house. Few others govern the Dative Singular Postpositions.

5. Some suffixes, if added to the Plural, undergo a little change; *e.g.* -nt in the Plural becomes -niñ, r becomes sometimes ri; namely, r becomes ri in the Plural, if it is added to the stem of the Noun, and poetically sometimes ri is used also in the Singular, added to the stem of the Noun, but this is also poetical. So "garānt"=at the house, "garāniñ"=in the houses. Nevertheless this change of Postposition in the Plural seems not to be so strictly demanded; for, I have sometimes heard also "garānt"=in the houses.

6. If the English Preposition "from" in the meaning of "out of" is to be translated into Konkani, the Noun affected by that Preposition seems to become an Adjective in lo, li, leñ; hence this will be better explained in the paragraph on the Adjective, *e. g.* "J. C. delivered us from hell". This "from hell" is changed into an Adjective: "yemkaṇḍāntlo."

7. The Nouns in a are seldom used in the Plural form; although the concord may be Plural, if the meaning is Plural; I say they are not used in Plural form, but they may be used

with Plural meaning: "kurpa, or krupa"=grace and graces; "čintna"=thought and thoughts.

8. There are some Nouns in which the stem seems to be derived from the Nominative by adding a whole syllable; *e.g.* "dū"=daughter, stem: "duve"; but this is not really so, for that v of the stem exists in the Nominative also, but not distinctly. Yet there are Nouns in which the stem is formed by adding two letters.

9. If many Nouns, one after the other, which should be put in the Genitive, Dative or Accusative, belong to the same thing, only the last Noun receives (or may receive) the full termination; the others are put often in the Original; *e.g.* "Somia Jezu Kristāk namaskār kār"=adore the Lord Jesus Christ; "Sargā āni souñsārāso ratznār"=Creator of Heaven and Earth.

10. As in Latin, so in Konkani, there are some Nouns used only in the Singular or only in the Plural; *e.g.* "aṭeviṭe"= agony, is only Plural; "lōk"=people, is used more commonly in Singular etc.

11. There are some indeclinable Nouns; they will be given in the Dictionary.

After these general considerations, each Declension is now to be explained.

B. Declensions in particular

§ I. First Declension

Stem in e *or Characteristic* e

The Nouns of this Declension are usually feminine, as in Latin. The Nominative may have different terminations, namely i, a, u, or a consonant. Of these terminations only the 2nd is peculiar to the 1st Declension, viz. a. If you find a Noun ending in the Nominative Singular in a, you may say it is of the 1st Declension; whereas the other terminations may be *found* in other Declensions also. In order to decline a Noun of this Declension, the above rule (A.) is applied. To know whether a Noun belongs to this Declension, see in the Vocabulary whether it has the stem in e. It might be known also by the meaning and termination, but not so certainly and easily by a beginner. To determine by the meaning and termination whether a Noun belongs to the 1st Declension, this rule may be laid down:

1. Nouns ending in a in the Nominative Singular are of the 1st Declension. There are only a few Nouns ending in a, which do not belong to this Declension; *e.g.* "kuḷḷa" = dwarf, and "loṭṭebira" = quack, which belong to the 2nd Declension.

2. Nouns ending in i or in a consonant of the Feminine Gender are mostly of the 1st Declension. Those in i of Feminine Gender, if not of the 1st, are of the 4th Declension.

3. If you find a Noun having e before the termination of the oblique cases, or if you find an Adjective derived from the Noun, having e before the termination of the Adjective (so or lo), that Noun is of the 1st Declension; *e.g.* kuśālaieso = pleasant, from kuśālai, -e = pleasure.

4. Nouns ending in ai of the Feminine Gender usually follow this Declension; *e.g.* laḍai = war.

The Nouns of this Declension are thus declined:

Singular.

Nominative, as given in the Dictionary.
Original, as given in the Dictionary.
Dative, add to the Original k.
Accusative, in animate objects as the Dative, in inanimate objects as the Nominative.
Vocative, as the Original.
Instrumental, add n to the Original.
1st Locative, add nt to the Original.
2nd Locative. add r. or ḍer. as it has been explained above.

For the other Latin cases which cannot be translated by one of these eight Konkani cases, use the Original, followed by the Postposition required by the meaning; *e.g.* Dēvā višiānt = about God; šārā thāun = from the town; bāpā lāgiñ = with the father; Dēvā thāiñ" = in God; māye kāḍe = close to the mother, *etc.* The required Postpositions may be found in the Dictionary. Moreover sometimes instead of using the Instrumental, 1st and 2nd Locative, the Original may be used, followed by the required Postposition; *e.g.* kurpen *or* kurpe vorvi = by the grace. (See A. General Observations.)

The things said here about Original followed by a Postposition must be understood also of the Plural.

Plural.

Nominative, add to the root o (is pronounced nearly yo sometimes).

Original, add to the root āñ (stem).

Dative, add to the stem k.

Accusative, in animate objects equal to the Dative, in inanimate objects as the Nominative.

Vocative, as the Original.

Instrumental, add niñ.

1st Locative, niñ.

2nd Locative, šer *etc.* as in the Singular.

Examples.

1. Animate object: Rāṇi = queen; *stem:* Rāṇi-e (or Rāṇiye).

	Singular:	*Plural:*
Nominative	Rāṇi	Rāṇi-o
Original	Rāṇi-e [1]	Rāṇi-āñ
Dative	Rāṇi-e-k	Rāṇi-āñ-k (= Rāṇiāṅk) [2]
Accusative	Rāṇi-e-k	Rāṇi-āñ-k (= Rāṇiāṅk)

[1] Exactly Rāṇiye, and so in the other cases.

[2] This ṅ, which has not been put in the I. Chapter (as it is a nicety) should be pronounced as *ng* in "singing". The beginner may pronounce it as *n*, in order not to increase the difficulties.

	Singular:	*Plural:*
Vocative	Rāṇi-e	Rāṇi-āñ (Rāṇiā-no, *or* Rāṇiānu, *with the suffix*)
Instrumental	Rāṇi-e-n	Rāṇi-āñ-niñ (=Rāṇiāniñ)
1st Locative	Rāṇi-e-nt	Rāṇi-āñ-niñ (=Rāṇiāniñ)
2nd Locative	Rāṇi-e-čer	Rāṇi-āñ-čer
Original followed by Postpositions	Rāṇi-e pāsun *etc.*	Rāṇi-āñ pāsun *etc.*

I write this example with the hyphens only in order to show the formation of the different cases; but usually the words are written without any hyphens.

2. Inanimate object: vāṭ = way; *stem:* vāṭe.

Nom.	vāṭ	vāṭ-o
Orig.	vāṭ-e	vāṭ-āñ
Dat.	vāṭ-e-k	vāṭ-āñ-k-(= vāṭāṅk)
Accus.	vāṭ	vāṭ-o
Voc.	vāṭ-e	vāṭ-āñ (*or* vāṭāno *with the suffix*)
Instrum.	vāṭ-e-n	vāṭ-āñ-niñ (= vāṭāniñ)
1st Loc.	vāṭ-e-nt	vāṭ-ā-niñ
2nd Loc.	vāṭ-er	vāṭ-āñ-čer
Orig. followed by Postpositions	vāṭ-e lāgiñ *etc.*	vāṭ-āñ lāgiñ *etc.*

1. What has been said about the Accusative equal to the Dative for animate objects, and equal to the Nominative for inanimate objects, is not so certain: Hence the above general rule must be modified according to the use. Moreover this word "animate object" must be understood of *subsistent* animate objects (*subsistent* in the philosophical meaning); hence čintna = thought, has the Accusative equal to the Nominative, as it is not a subsistent animate object. Ātmo = soul (of the 3rd Declension) is an animate object, but not a subsistent animate object; hence Accusative ātmo equal to the Nominative. The names of God and of angels follow the rule of animate objects. The plants and trees have a vegetative life; hence they could have the Accusative equal to the Dative; yet as they cannot be called "animate objects" in the same way as animals and men, it seems that we may make their Accusative equal to the Dative or to the Nominative. So we say "ruk *or* rukāk poḷeitā" = (he) sees the tree.

2. As it appears from the Declension, the nasal ñ is sometimes changed into a common n: exactly it should be written double; *e. g.* vorsāñ-niñ = vorsānniñ; yet, as it seems to be pronounced simple, I do not write two n. (See Part I. Ch. I.)

These two Remarks belong to the following Declensions too.

Exercises
on the First Declension.[1]

podvi, -ve = power
kurpa, -pe[2] = grace
duv, -e = daughter
vāṭ, -e = way
sikša, -še = punishment
gărječi = necessary (*fem.*)
moji = my
assāñ *or* zaun assāñ = am
assai = art
assā = is
zatāñ = I become
zatai = thou becomest
zatā = he becomes

čintna, -ne = thought
kumok, -mke = help
măy, -e = mamma *or* mother
păṭṭi, -e = list
bori = good (*fem.*)
sobit = necessary
săma = right
assauñ = are (we)
assāt = are (you)
assāt = are (they)
zatauñ = we become
zatāt = you become
zatāt = they become

poḷei = see

Singular:
poḷei-tāñ = I see
poḷei-tai = thou seest
poḷei-tā = he sees

Plural:
poḷei-tauñ = we see
poḷei-tāt = you see
poḷei-tāt = they see

māg = ask *or* pray
Pl. māgā = ask

gāl = put
motint = in the mind

---

[1] The following Substantives are all feminine. The vowel put after them indicates their Original Case, which is obtained by adding the vowel to the Nominative. Sometimes the vowel is not added to the pure Nominative; a little change is to be made, *e. g.* the last vowel of the Nominative is cut off before adding the Characteristic; in these cases, usually, I write also the last letter to which the vowel is to be added; *e. g.* "vāṭ, -e" means vāṭ, vāṭe; "kurpa, -pe" means kurpa, kurpe; "kumok, -mke" means kumok, kumke.

[2] Or kṛupa, as Hindu Brahmins pronounce.

Kurpa gărječi (assā). Māy duvek poḷei-tā. Bori čiutna bore vāṭer gal-tā. Pāṭṭi sāma zāun assā. Vāṭ bori zāun assā. Duv māye lāgiñ kumok māgtā. Kurpen duv sobit zatā. Kurpā motint bori čintna gal-tā. Bori duv bore vāṭer assā. Moje māyek bori duv assā.

§ II. Second Declension

Stem in a, *or Characteristic* a

The Nouns of this Declension are very numerous. As far as I can learn, only Masculine and Neuter Nouns follow this Declension. I found only two Substantives, which, according to some persons, would follow this Declension, and are said to be Feminine. But this is not certain; for some other persons told me the contrary. These two Substantives are "kuli" = tribe, and "kurāḍ" = axe. If these two Substantives are truly used as Feminine, they follow another Declension, as I think; so I heard "kurāḍin" (of the 4th Declension) = by the axe.

The termination of the Nominative Singular varies, *i. e.* the Nominative may end in any consonant and vowel, except a, which is a sign of the 1st Declension, and o or eñ, which is a sign of the 3rd Declension; yet it is true that a full u very often is a sign of the 5th Declension; and i is a sign of the 1st or 4th Declension in the Nouns of Feminine Gender. Consequently the chief terminations of the Nominative are a consonant (sometimes with ạ, half vowel) or i, iñ, ai, u, uñ.

The Nouns of this Declension are known by the characteristic a given in the Vocabulary. They may be known also by the termination and by the meaning, but not so surely. Namely, the following Nouns follow this Declension, although not exclusively.

1. All Nouns of Masculine or Neuter Gender ending in the Nominative Singular in a consonant. There may be perhaps a few Nouns of Masculine Gender ending in a consonant (or in ụ) belonging to the 5th or to the 4th Declension.

2. The Nouns in uñ, pon, ap (which always, or almost always are Neuter). Nouns in iñ of Neuter Gender follow this Declension, Nouns in iñ of Feminine Gender follow mostly the 4th Declension; *e.g.* "dudiñ, -n" = pumpkin, is of the 2nd Declension; whereas "buiñ," *f.*, is of the 4th Declension.

3. Mostly also, the Nouns in auñ or aoñ (which usually are of foreign origin).

4. Finally a Noun having in the Oblique Cases a before the termination, or Adjectives derived from Nouns having a before the termination, belong to this Declension. Hence, no Noun ending in o, eñ, and no Feminine Noun of any termination follows this Declension.

In order to decline any Noun of this Declension, the above (A) rule is applied.

Singular.

Nominative, as given in the Dictionary.

Vocative and *Original*, as given in the Dictionary or as known by the above given rules.

Dative, add k to the stem.

Accusative, in animate objects as the Dative, and in inanimate as the Nominative.

Instrumental, *Locative etc.*, as in the 1st Declension.

Plural.

Nominative, Masculine equal to the Nominative Singular, in the Neuter add añ to the root.

Vocative and *Original*, (Masculine and Neuter), add añ to the root.

Dative, add k to the stem.

Accusative, in animate objects as the Dative, in inanimate objects as the Nominative.

Instrumental, *Locative etc.* as above.

Example of an animate object

Putrụ *or* pūt=son; *stem:* putr-a *or* pūt-a.

	Singular:	*Plural:*
Nom.	putrụ	putrụ
Orig.	putr-a (*or* pūt-a)	putr-añ
Dat.	putr-ā-k	putr-āñ-k (=putrāṅk)
Accus.	putr-ā-k	putr-añ-k (=putrāṅk)
Voc.	putr-ā	putr-āñ (*or* putrānu)
Instrum.	putr-ān	putr-āñ-niñ (=putrāniñ)
1st Loc.	putr-ā-ṅt	putr-āñ-niñ (= „)
2nd Loc.	putr-ā-čer	putr-āñ-čer
Orig. followed by Postpositions	putr-ā lāgiñ *etc.*	putr-āñ lāgiñ *etc.*

Example of an inanimate object of Neuter Gender

Vórs=year; *stem:* vors-a.

Nom.	vors	vors-āñ
Orig.	vors-a	vors-āñ
Dat.	vors-ā-k	vors-āñ-k (=vọrsāṅk)
Accus.	vors	vors-āñ
Voc.	vors-ā	vors-āñ (*or* vorsānu)
Instrum.	vors-ā-n	vors-āñ-niñ (=vorsāniñ)
1st Loc.	vors-ā-nt	vors-āñ-niñ („)
2nd Loc.	vors-ā-r (vorsā-čer)	vors-āñ-čer
Orig. followed by Postpositions	vorsā lāgiñ *etc.*	vorsāñ lāgiñ *etc.*

Remember that the Suffix in the 2nd Locative Singular can be added to the stem of the Adjective; so, instead of vors-ā-r, we may say vorsā-če-r. (See below Adjective, and above General Observations.)

Observations. 1. Kāšṭ=pain is Neuter in the Singular and Masculine in the Plural; consequently the Nominative Plural is "kāšṭ". Yet many say that "kāšṭ" is Masculine also in the Singular.

2. Contracted Nouns (see above A.) belong chiefly to this Declension.

3. In this Declension there are many Nouns ending in u in the Nominative, which u disappears in the stem. There are other Nouns which end in u and keep this u in the stem.[1] The Dictionary will show whether they keep or lose this u. But Nouns in auñ or aoñ change usually the uñ (or oñ) in a v; *e.g.* "sermauñ"=sermon, has in the stem: "sermav-a", and so many other Nouns like this; very few Nouns in auñ follow the 5th Declension; *e.g.* "kordauñ" = string. Moreover those Nouns which end in a nasal sound in the Nominative Singular lose it in the Declension, *e.g.* tāntiñ=egg; *Original:* tāntia; although in the 4th Declension the nasal sound of the Nominative is sometimes kept also in the other cases; *e.g.* bhuiñ = earth.

4. Some Nouns of this Declension change the closed é of the stem of the Singular into an open è in the Plural; *e.g.* "késu̥"=hair; *plural:* "kès".[1] Moreover this u̥ disappears in the Plural.[1]

5. In this Declension chiefly, (or perhaps exclusively) there occurs sometimes a kind of Ablative in iñ; it is an old form, used chiefly to show manner, place, time.....*e.g.* "āntāskarṇiñ"=heartly, from "antaskārṇ"=heart, instead of "antaskarṇān"; "veḷiñ", instead of "veḷār"=at the time; "St. Mark pustakiñ"=in the gospel of St. Mark, instead of "..... pustakānt"; "Bāpāče nāviñ", instead of "Bāpāče nāvān"= in the name of the Father *etc.* Yet in these cases the common form too, might be, and is really, used sometimes.

6. There are a few irregular Nouns; *e.g.* bāpui=father, is declined as if the stem were bāpai *or* bāpā: those Nouns will be indicated with their irregularity in the Dictionary.

---

[1] About these points a general rule cannot at present be formed.

Exercises
on the Second Declension.

găr, -a = house (*n.*)
kaliz, -lza = heart (*n.*)
bāgil, -gla = door (*n.*)
bāu, -ava = brother (*m.*)
āz = today
kăr = do
khăiñ" = where?
thăiñ" = there
dis, -a = day (*m.*)
monis, monša = man (*m.*)
akmān, -a = offence (*m.*)
mozo = my
āmso = our
tāso = his
tānso = their
kumgār, -a = Communion (*m.*)
pāḍ = bad
ašir = narrow
kiteñ = what, which?
inām, -a = prize (*n.*)
kūḍ, -a = room (*n.*)
mez, -a = table (*n.*)
kām, -a = business (*n.*)
ò (*pron.* uò) = this (*m.*)
tò = that (*m.*)
mārόg, mārgā = road (*m.*)
Deu, -eva = God
vóḍ = big
lān = small
tuzo = thy
tumso = your
dī = give
rūnd = broad
ukto = open
gī = (an interrogative particle)

Găr vòḍ zāun assā. Mezār yek buk assā. Bāgil ukteñgī? Kūḍ lān zāun assā. Mārόg ăšir zāun assā. Āz boro dis assā. Moji māy khăiñ assā? Tuji māy thăiñ assā. Vāţ ašir zāun assā. Ī vāţ rūnd. Ò monis boro, tò monis pāḍ. Deu boreañ āni pāḍ monšānk upkārañ kartā. Bāglār yek monis assā. Tuja bāvāk vóḍ găr assā, moja bāvāk lān găr. Tujeñ kām kiteñ? Deu monšānk bore dis ditā; monis Devāk akmān kartāt. Āz Pādri kumgār ditāgī? Monis pāḍ: tančeñ kaliz vāiţ. Kumgārān monis boro zatā.

It has been said above (p. 22, n. 2) that Nouns in uñ are Neuter and follow this Declension. This must be understood thus: Nouns in uñ *not preceded by* a *or* o are Neuter and follow this Declension; because if uñ is preceded by a or o (auñ, ouñ), those Nouns may be Masculine or Neuter (and then they follow usually the 2nd Declension), or seldom Feminine (and then they follow usually the 1st Declension); *e.g.* Irmaũ, -ava = confrier (*m.*); māṭṭoũ, -ova = = shed (*m.*); karoũ, -ova = crown (*n.*); loũ, love = wool (*f.*); māũ, māve = scar or crust (*f.*).

§ III. Third Declension.

Stem in ea, *or characteristic* ea.

This is the most regular Declension and contains mostly, if not exclusively, Nouns of Konkani origin; whereas the other Declensions contain many foreign Nouns.

Only Masculine and Neuter Nouns belong to this Declension. The terminations of the Nominative Singular are only two ò for the Masculine, èñ for the Neuter, and are peculiar to this Declension.

To determine whether a Noun belongs to this Declension, consult the Dictionary, or observe these rules:

1) Nouns having o or eñ in the Nominative, or (if the Nominative is not known) having the termination ea in the oblique cases, belong to this Declension.

2) When an Adjective derived from a Noun has ea before the termination of the Adjective (lo or so), that Noun belongs to this Declension; *e.g.* "burgeānu" = O children, is known to be of this Declension by that ea; again, in "vāṇṭeāso" = partial, that ea before so indicates that its original Noun must be of this Declension.

3) All Participles and Adjectives ending in o in the Nominative Singular, if used as Pronouns in Masculine or Neuter Gender, follow this Declension; *e.g.* kello = done, kelleānt = in doing; boro = good, boreānk = to the good.

4) Finally, as the English Genitive is changed into an Adjective of three terminations, and as the Adjectives of three terminations follow, at least partially the 3rd Declension (see below, Adjectives), so we may say that the Konkani Genitive (as also the other Adjectives and Participles of three terminations [o, i, eñ] not used as Pronouns) follows, at least partially, the 3rd Declension.

What is here said, will be better understood below Ch. II.

The Declension is formed according to the above given (A) general rule; viz.

Singular.

Nominative, as given in the Dictionary (o or eñ).
Original, ea for both genders (as given in the Dictionary), stem.
Dative, add k to the stem, or Original.
Accusative, as the Dative in animate objects, as the Nominative in inanimate objects.
Vocative, as the Original.
Instrumental, add n to the stem.
1st Locative, add nt to the stem.
2nd Locative, add r or ðer to the stem.
Original followed by *Postpositions*, lagiñ, kăḍe *etc.* (as above explained, 1st Declension).

Plural.

Nominative, add to the root e for the Masculine, iñ for the Neuter.
Original, add to the root eañ for both genders.
Dative, add to the stem k.
Accusative, as the Dative in animate objects, as the Nominative in inanimate objects.
Vocative, as the Original.
Instrumental, add to the stem niñ.
1st Locative, add to the stem niñ.
2nd Locative, add to the stem ðer.
Original followed by *Postpositions*, lāgiñ, pāsun *etc.* (as above explained, 1st Declension).

1. *Example of an animate object of Masculine Gender.*
"Burgo" = boy; *stem:* "burgea."

	Singular:	*Plural:*
Nom.	burgo	burg-e
Orig.	burg-ea	burg-eañ
Dat.	burg-eā-k	burg-eāñ-k (= burgeāṅk)
Accus.	burg-eā-k	burg-eāñ-k (= burgeāṅk)
Voc.	burg-eā	burg-eāñ (*or* burgeāno)
Instrum.	burg-eā-n	burg-eāñ-niñ
1st Loc.	burg-eā-nt	burg-eāñ-niñ
2nd Loc.	burg-eā-čer	burg-eāñ-čer
Orig. followed by Postpositions	burg-eā lāgiñ *etc.*	burg-eāñ lāgiñ *etc.*

2. *Example of an inanimate object of Neuter Gender.*
"Foḷeñ" = plank; *stem:* "foḷ-ea."

Nom.	foḷeñ	foḷiñ
Orig.	foḷ-ea	foḷ-eañ
Dat.	foḷ-eā-k	foḷ-eāñ-k
Accus.	foḷ-eñ	foḷ-iñ
Voc.	foḷ-eā	foḷ-eāñ (*or* foḷeānu)
Instrum.	foḷ-eā-n	foḷ-eāñ-niñ
1st Loc.	foḷ-eā-nt	foḷ-eāñ-niñ
2nd Loc.	foḷ-eā-čer *or* foḷ-eā-r	foḷ-eāñ-čer
Orig. followed by Postpositions	foḷ-eā kāḍe *etc.*	foḷ-eāñ kāḍe *etc.*

3. *Example of an animate object of Neuter Gender.*
"Burgeñ" = child; stem: "burg-ea."

Nom.	burgeñ	burg-iñ
Orig.	burg-ea	burg-eañ
Dat.	burg-eā-k	burg-eāñ-k (= burgeāṅk)
Accus.	burg-eā-k	burg-eāñ-k
Voc.	burg-eā	burg-eāñ (*or* burgeāno)
Instrum.	burg-eā-n	burg-eāñ-niñ

	Singular:	*Plural:*
1st Loc.	burg-eā-nt	burg-eāñ-niñ
2nd Loc.	burg-eā-čer	burg-eāñ-čer
Orig. followed by Postpositions	burg-eā lāgiñ *etc.*	burg-eāñ lāgiñ *etc.*

Observations:

1. The termination ea, characteristic of the 3rd Declension, chiefly in speaking, is not to be confounded with ia of the 2nd Declension; that is to say, many Nouns in i follow the 2nd Declension; hence they have in the stem ia by adding the characteristic a to the Nominative; *e.g.* "pātki" = sinner; "pātkiāk" = to the sinner, is similar to "burgeāk" = to the boy, as regards termination. We can easily avoid this mistake of confounding the termination ia of the 2nd with the termination ea of the 3rd, if we recollect that all Nouns of this Declension must end either in o or in eā in the Nominative Singular. Although there is the above difference, as regards spelling in Latin letters, between Nouns in i of the 2nd Declension and Nouns of the 3rd Declension in the oblique cases, yet the pronunciation is nearly the same (and in Kanarese they would be written in the same way); because that ea, characteristic of the 3rd Declension, is pronounced not distinctly ea but as a sound between ea and ia, like ya. Nevertheless I prefer to write ea instead of ia, because thereby we distinguish it better from the 2nd Declension. At all events we must make the above difference, if not in pronunciation and writing, at least in our mind; because on it their different Declension depends.

2. The above 1st and 2nd rule (p. 26), *i.e.* that, if the oblique case or the derived Adjective has the termination ea, that Noun is of the 3rd Declension, cannot be taken *exclusively*, that is to say, cannot be understood thus: "whenever the desinence ea occurs, only and always the 3rd Declension is thereby indicated. The reasons of this limitation are three: viz.

a) The termination ia occurs also in the 2nd Declension (see Observation 1.), and in the oblique cases of the Plural of the 1st Declension, if the Noun ends in i in the Nominative Singular: but this ia can be easily confounded with ea, nay, some might perhaps write both terminations by ya.

b) The termination ea (or ya) occurs also in the oblique cases of some Nouns of the 1st Declension; *e. g.* "čintna = thought; čintneāniñ = by thoughts. (See p. 18, Declension of the Plural.)

c) The Adjectives of three terminations have ea in the oblique cases of the Plural Feminine and sometimes also of the Singular (see below, Adjectives); *e.g.* boreañ ăstriānk = to good women.

3. From this Declension chiefly, it appears that the Characteristic of the Declension is not always added to the pure Nominative. Sometimes the last vowel of the Nominative is changed before adding the Characteristic. Moreover a contraction often takes place before adding the Characteristic to the root (see p. 20, Note 1. and A. General Observations). The Dictionary shows, whether the Characteristic is to be added to the pure Nominative or whether a change is to be made. This second observation regards the other Declensions too.

4. In this Declension chiefly, attention is to be paid to the nasal sound; else the Gender is easily mistaken. Thus, if you do not pronounce the nasal sound of the Neuter Nominative Singular, they would think that it is Nominative Plural (e) etc.

Exercises

on the Third Declension.[1)]

burgo = boy	nākāzāllo = nonsense
bēñ = fear	kāido = duty
māg-ņeñ = prayer	hageñ = hatred
vāṇṭo = part, division	suņeñ = dog

1) The Gender and the Original of the following Nouns may be known by the above rules.

beḷeñ = crop
ušār = clever
auñsāraso = hasty
āltzi = lazy
mogāḷ = dear, merciful
sāddāntz = always
sāng = say
kātār = cut
puṇ = but
distā = appears
boreñ = well
meḷtā = is found
dovor = keep
līp = be concealed

Tuzo bāu ušār burgo; puṇ mozo bāu āltzi. Suṇeāk beñ distā. Tò monis hageñ kārtā. Auñsāraso burgo kām boreñ kartāgī? Āltzi monis beḷeñ kātartāgi? Ye burge sāddāntz nākāzālle sāngtāt. Ò mozo vāṇṭo, tò tuzo vāṇṭo. Ušār burgeānk inām meḷtā: āltzi burgeānk šikšā meḷtā. Bore burge monšānk mogāḷ; vāiṭ burgeānčer monis hageñ dovortāt. Māg-ṇeā vorvi monšānk kurpā meḷtā. Devā lāgiñ māg: tukā (*to you*) boro vāṇṭo meḷtolo (*fut.*). Tò burgo beān liptā. Burgeānu, āplo (*own*) kāido kārā: āuñ inām ditoloñ.

§ IV. Fourth Declension.

Stem in i, *or characteristic* i.

This Declension contains chiefly Nouns of the Feminine Gender.[1] The termination of the Nominative is i (especially in Masculine Nouns), but it may be also a consonant. The termination i in the Nominative is found also in the 1st and 2nd Declension. Consequently there is no termination exclusively belonging to this Declension, as is the case in the 3rd and partially in the 1st Declension.

To know whether a Noun belongs to this Declension there are two ways: 1) the Vocabulary, 2) meaning and termination. As to the 2nd way, these rules may be laid down:

1. All Feminine Nouns ending in i, if not of the 1st Declension (as mostly), are of the 4th.

2. All Masculine Nouns ending in i, if of foreign origin, seem to follow more frequently this Declension; if of Kon-

[1] Nouns of males, of occupations proper to men etc. are Masculine. I do not recollect now any Noun of Neuter Gender belonging to this Declension.

kani origin, more frequently follow the 2nd Declension; *e. g.* "Pādri" = father, and "mutsudi" = treasurer (Hindustāni word), are of the 4th Declension; "pātki" = sinner, is of the 2nd Declension. (The Masculine Nouns of this Declension end, usually, in i).

3. Feminine Nouns in iñ and n (by which termination n many Masculine Nouns are made Feminine) mostly follow this Declension; *e. g.* buiñ = earth, năiñ = river, băiñ = well, gărkārn = house-wife.

4. All Feminine Nouns ending in a full consonant (without u and a), if not of the 1st, are mostly of the 4th Declension (very seldom of the 5th); *e. g.* ākānt = distress.

In this Declension (as in the 5th) the stem of the Singular is kept also in the Plural, except that it is made nasal.

This Declension is formed according to the general rule (A) namely:

Singular.

Nominative, as given in the Dictionary.
Original (stem ending in i), as given in the Dictionary.
Dative, add k to the stem.
Accusative, in animate objects as the Dative, in inanimate as the Nominative.
Vocative, as the Original.
Instrumental, add n to the stem.
1st Locative, add nt to the stem.
2nd Locative, add r *or* ěr to the stem.
Original followed by *Postpositions*, as above.

Plural.

Nominative, add 'i' to the root.
Original, make nasal the characteristic, *i. e.* iñ.
Dative, add k to the stem of the Plural.
Accusative, in animate objects as the Dative, in inanimate objects as the Nominative.
Vocative, as the Original.

Instrumental, add niñ to the stem.
1st *Locative*, add niñ to the stem.
2nd *Locative*, add čer to the stem.
Original followed by *Postpositions*, as above.

1. *Example of an animate object.*
"Pādri" = father; *stem*, "Pādri".

	Singular:	*Plural:*
Nom.	Pādr-i	Pādr-i
Orig.	Pādr-i	Pādr-iñ
Dat.	Pādr-i-k	Pādr-iñ-k (= Pādrink)
Accus.	Pādr-i-k	Pādr-iñ-k (= Pādrink)
Voc.	Pādr-i	Pādr-iñ (*or* Pādrinu)
Instrum.	Pādr-i-n	Pādr-i-niñ
1st *Loc.*	Pādr-i-nt	Pādr-i-niñ
2nd *Loc.*	Pādr-i-čer	Pādr-iñ-čer
Orig. followed by Postpositions	Pādr-i lāgiñ *etc.*	Pādr-iñ lāgiñ *etc.*

2. *Example of an inanimate object.*
"Vāt" = candle; *stem:* "vāt-i".

Nom.	vāt	vāt-i
Orig.	vāt-i	vāt-iñ
Dat.	vāt-i-k	vāt-iñ-k
Accus.	vāt	vāt-i
Voc.	vāt-i	vāt-iñ (vātinu)
Instrum.	vāt-i-n	vāt-i-niñ
1st *Loc.*	vāt-i-nt	vāt-i-niñ
2nd *Loc.*	vāt-i-r (vātičer)	vāt-iñ-čer
Orig. followed by Postpositions	vāt-i kāḍe *etc.*	vāt-iñ kāḍe *etc.*

Observations: 1) In this Declension in the Nouns ending in i in the Nominative Singular, this i is to be cut off before adding the terminations i, ik etc. in order to avoid two i.

2) The Nouns of this Declension ending in iñ retain mostly the nasal sound also in the other cases, much more distinctly than the nasal sound; *e. g.* of "burgeāñ" is kept in the Dative "burgeāṅk". Hence, if we wish to comprehend all cases, we must say, that the characteristic of this Declension is i or iñ.

Exercises

on the Fourth Declension.[1]

āvoi[2] = mother	kuḍ = body
boiṇ[3] = sister	ākānt[4] = distress
pādri = father	yēk = a, an, one
saserdot = priest	bāgivont = holy
čiṭ = note	vātz = read
zār = fountain	āpoy = call
kāls = chalice	piḍest = sick

Āvoik dogi boiṇi (*or* boiṇeo) assāt. Moja gārā lāgiñ yēk sobit zār distā. Āmči kuḍ kumgārā vorviñ bāgivont zatā. Moji čiṭ khāiñ assā?—Tuji čiṭ tuje āvoi kāḍe assā. Ākāntint (*or* ākāntānt) Devā lāgiñ māg-ṇeñ kār, ani tukā ādhār (*help*) meḷtolo. Pādrik āpoy, moji āvoi piḍest. Saserdot Igārjent čiṭ vātztā. Devāso (*divine*) móg yeke zāri bāri (*fontis instar*). ātmeā bitór (*in the soul*) zatā. Kuḍik tel lāi (*oil apply, anoint*). Bisp saserdotink benjer (*holy*) tel lāitā, ani Pāp Sāib Bispānk benjer tel lāitā. Āvoi duvek āpoitā; puṇ tikā (*to her*) beñ distā. Deu monšāṅk sābār pauṭi (*many times*) āpoitā, puṇ monis tāčeñ uttar (*his word*) āikanānt (*do not hear*).

---

[1] All these Nouns are of the 4th Declension and their Original is formed regularly. The Gender is Feminine, unless the meaning requires Masculine Gender.

[2] Āvoi follows the 1st Declension in the Plural. Pronounce v almost like u. See P. I.

[3] Some decline it according to the 1st Declension in the Plural.

[4] Some decline it according to the 2nd Declension.

§ V. Fifth Declension.

Stem in u, *or characteristic* u

A few Nouns belong to this Declension.

As far as I know, the Nouns belonging to this Declension, usually, are Feminine, unless the meaning requires the Masculine Gender; *e.g.* guru = priest; bāppu = paternal uncle.

The usual termination of the Nominative is u or ụ; but this ụ or u may be found also in other Declensions. Moreover there may be a few Nouns ending in a consonant, of this Declension. It seems to me that Feminine Nouns ending in u or ụ are of the 4th Declension, or sometimes, of the 1st; Masculine Nouns in u belong to the 2nd, sometimes to the 4th. I do not recollect any Neuter Noun following this Declension.

To determine whether a Noun belongs to this Declension, we may lay down these rules in addition to what is given in the Dictionary.

1. The Feminine Nouns ending in u or ụ follow sometimes the 1st, more frequently the 4th Declension; *e.g.* "sūrụ, -re" = toddy; "suru, -ruve" = beginning, are of the 1st, "vāstụ" = thing, is of the 4th Declension.

2. Among Masculine Nouns ending in u or ụ some follow the 4th, some the 2nd Declension; *e.g.* "bāppu" is of the 4th, "duḍḍu" is of the 2nd Declension.

Perhaps no Masculine Noun ending in "ụ" follows this Declension.

3. Neuter Nouns ending in ụ or uñ follow the 2nd Declension, not the 4th.

This Declension is formed according to the general rule (A), except that in Nouns ending in u or ụ before adding the characteristic u, the u or ụ of the Nominative is cut off in order to avoid uu or ụu, for the sake of euphony.

Singular.

Nominative, as given in the Dictionary (usually u or ụ).
Original, u (given in the Dictionary).

Dative, add k to the stem.
Accusative, in animate objects as the Dative, in inanimate objects as the Nominative.
Vocative, as the Original.
Instrumental, add n to the stem.
1st Locative, add nt to the stem.
2nd Locative, add r *or* čer to the stem.
Original followed by *Postpositions*, "lāgiñ" *etc.*, as above.

Plural.

Nominative, add u to the root.
Original, make nasal the characteristic of the Singular.
Dative, add k to the stem of the Plural.
Accusative, equal to the Dative or to the Nominative, as above.
Vocative, as the Original.
Instrumental, and *1st Locative*, add niñ to the stem.
2nd Locative, add čer to the stem.
Original followed by *Postpositions*, as above.

1. *Example of an animate object.*

"Guru" = priest (pagan); *stem:* "guru".

	Singular:	*Plural:*
Nom.	gur-u	gur-u
Orig.	gur-u	gur-uñ
Dat.	gur-u-k	gur-uñ-k
Accus.	gur-u-k	gur-uñ-k
Voc.	gur-u	gur-uñ, (guruno)
Instrum.	gur-u-n	gur-uñ-niñ
1st Loc.	gur-u-nt	gur-uñ-niñ
2nd Loc.	gur-u-čer	gur-uñ-čer
Orig. followed by Postpositions	gur-u lāgiñ *etc.*	gur-uñ lāgiñ *etc.*

1. *Example of an inanimate object.*

"Văstu̥" = thing.

	Singular:	*Plural:*
Nom.	văstu̥	văstu
Orig.	văst-u	văst-uñ
Dat.	văst-u-k	văst-uñ-k
Accus.	văst-u	văst-u
Voc.	văst-u	văst-uñ, (văstuno)
Instrum.	văst-u-n	văst-u-niñ
1st Loc.	văst-u-nt	văst-u-niñ
2nd Loc.	văst-u-čer	văst-uñ-čer
Orig. followed by Postpositions	văstu kăḍe *etc.*	văst-uñ kăḍe *etc.*

In this Declension there are many Nouns ending in "u̥" in the Singular and "u" in the Plural; consequently those Nouns have different accent in the Singular and in the Plural. See P. I. Ch. II.

Exercises

on the Fifth Declension.

guru = priest (*m.*)
kāzu̥ = cajou (*f.*)
văstu̥ = thing (*f.*)
hostu̥ = host (*f.*)
boṭăi = offer
kharo (kharots) = true
foṭkiro = deceiving
foṭăi = deceive
lók, -a = people (*m.*)
săkăṭ = all

Annas Judevānso guru zāun vortavatalo. Konsekrār kelo hostunt ani konsekrār kelo kalsint săg̣lo Somi Jezu Krist assā. Devā thăiñ (*in God*) săkăṭ boreo" văstu assăt. Dayā kărn (*please*) makā yēk kāzu̥ dī.. Kharots saserdot lókā pāsun sakrifis beṭăitā ani Devā lāgiñ māgtā: foṭkiro saserdot lókāk foṭăitā.

§ VI. Declension of Proper Nouns.

The Declension of Proper Nouns is not different from the Declension of Common Nouns; for, all Proper Nouns are declined according to one of the given Declensions. But this is peculiar to them, that some Proper Masculine Nouns follow the 1st Declension, whereas Common Nouns of the 1st Declension are Feminine; moreover many Masculine Proper Nouns follow the 4th or 5th Declension, and a few Feminine Proper Nouns follow the 2nd Declension; whereas no Feminine Common Noun follows the 2nd Declension.

To determine to which Declension a given Proper Noun belongs, we may say thus:

I. **Baptismal Names.**

1. *Names of Males.* The greatest part of them follow the 2nd Declension, or more distinctly, if they end in e, they follow the 1st Declension, *e.g.* Zoze = Joseph, if they end in o, the 3rd, *e.g.* Lorso = Lawrence; if they end in i, mostly the 4th, *e.g.* Joki = Joachim; if they end in u, the 5th, *e.g.* Gabru = Gabriel; as, often, also if they end in auñ, *e.g.* Juāuñ = John. The others seem to follow the 2nd Declension; yet there are some, among these, which do not follow the 2nd; *e.g.* Mingel, Mărtin, Anton, Manuel, are of the 4th Declension.

2. *Names of Females.*

a) *Names of married or grown up females.* The greatest part of them follow the 1st Declension, or, more distinctly, those in a or e follow the 1st; of those in i some follow the 4th, some the 1st, those in u follow mostly the 5th; those in auñ seem to follow more frequently the 2nd, those in eñ, follow the 3rd Declension; of those in a consonant, some follow the 1st, some the 4th (seldom the 2nd).

b) *Names of girls.* As girls are considered in grammar as Neuter, hence also their Christian names are considered as Neuter, and mostly follow the 2nd Declension. Thus "Mări" = Mary, if used for a woman, is of the 1st Declension, if used for a girl, is of the 2nd; *e.g.* O Mary = "Mărie" in the 1st case, "Măriă" in the 2nd. There are a few names of girls not according to this rule. In the Dictionary the most common baptismal names are put with the sign of their Declension.

II. Family-Names.

1. The (Portuguese) family-names, used now among natives here, generally follow the 2nd Declension; *e.g.* Suz, -a, Brit, -a, etc. A few names are not of the 2nd Declension; *e.g.* "Koelh" (or better "Kuel") is of the 4th.

Moreover in familiar conversation family-names applied to women take the termination of the Feminine **ăn** or **in** or **n**; *e.g.* Suzin, Kuelin *etc.*

2. Foreign family-names (not Portuguese) follow, it seems to me, more frequently, the 2nd Declension. Yet analogy with the Declension of Common Nouns and euphony may require another Declension. Thus "Pagăni" is of the 4th, according to the rule laid down in the 4th Declension.

If the Christian and family-names are joined, only the 2nd is declined; *e.g.* "Pedru Souzāk". The same happens, if the family-name is preceded by some title, *e.g.* Pādri Pagănik = "to Fr. Pagani"; so also in other names, *e.g.* Šesar Augustăčeñ forman = the order of C. Augustus.

Finally in Christian and also family-names we must distinguish the full pronunciation and writing from the vulgar and shortened pronunciation, *e.g.* Bonaventur, shortened Intru.

III. Names of Towns, Villages *etc.*

These Nouns more commonly are not declined; *e.g.* "auñ Koḍiāl vetāñ = I go to Mangalore. Yet if the Proper Nouns of places do not end in u or i (perhaps ăi), it seems allowed also to decline them; *e.g.* "auñ Koḍiālak vetāñ" = I go to Mangalore. But it does not seem usual to say: auñ Bombăiak vetāñ or Jeppuak vetāñ.

IV. Names of Mountains, Rivers, Kingdoms *etc.* seem to be declined according to the general rules of Declensions; yet about this point a more particular rule cannot at present be formed. *Examples:* Europānt = in Europe, Indiānt = in India, Himālayăčer = on the Himalaya.

Names of places are very often followed by "moḷḷo = said", (so called); *e.g.* "Rom moḷḷea ṡerānt" = in the town called Rome, instead of "Romā ṡerānt." If

they are followed by ïer or gãuñ and the like, it seems allowed to put the Proper Noun of place in the pure Original, *e.g.* "Roma ïerãnt," and so also in other examples, if euphony allows it; or more generally, if a Proper Noun is followed by an apposition, this only may be declined, and the Proper Noun left in the Original, or simply, in its primitive form; *e.g.* "Israel, moje porjecer, raevoṭkãi kãr" = reign upon my people Israel.

C. *Observations about Declensions.*

1. Omitting the minute things said in each Declension, we may now by one general rule know which Nouns chiefly belong to each Declension.

a) Feminine Nouns ending in the Nominative Singular in a or ai are of the 1st Declension.

b) Nouns in ap and pon are of the 2nd Declension.

c) Nouns in auñ or ouñ are mostly of the 2nd, seldom of the 1st or 5th Declension.

d) Feminine Nouns in i are of the 1st, or of the 4th Declension.

e) Masculine Nouns in i are of the 2nd or of the 4th Declension.

f) Neuter Nouns in iñ are of the 2nd Declension.

g) Feminine Nouns in iñ are of the 4th Declension.

h) Feminine Nouns in u (or ụ) are of the 1st or of the 5th Declension.

i) Masculine Nouns in u (or ụ) are of the 2nd or of the 5th Declension.

j) Neuter Nouns in uñ, preceded by a consonant, are of the 2nd Declension. Nouns in uñ, preceded by a vowel, may be of any Gender and of the 1st, 2nd, or 5th Declension.

k) Nouns in o are of the 3rd Declension.

l) Nouns in e (Proper Nouns) are of the 1st Declension.

m) Nouns in eñ are of the 3rd Declension.

n) Nouns ending in a consonant are, if Feminine, of the 1st, or of the 4th, seldom of the 5th; if Masculine, mostly of the 2nd; if Neuter, of the 2nd Declension.

o) Nouns having in the termination of the oblique cases or in the derived Adjectives **e**, are of the 1st; having **a**, of the 2nd (or also of the 3rd, as sometimes **ea** is pronounced as **a**); having **ea**, very often of the 3rd; having **i**, of the 4th; having **u**, of the 5th.

2. The nasal sound **n** which is found in many Nouns in the Nominative (and Accusative, often), undergoes many changes in the oblique cases; the chief changes are these: in Neuter Nouns in **uñ**, or **iñ**, this **ñ** is lost; in Feminine Nouns of the 4th Declension it is kept; in Nouns ending in **auñ** or **ouñ** of the 2nd Declension it is changed into a **v**; in Nouns in **auñ** or **ouñ** of the 1st Declension it is changed sometimes into **v**, sometimes into **n**. *Examples:* goruñ, gorua (or goruva) = cattle (*n.*); dudiñ, dudia = pumpkin (*n.*) (but Plural Nominative, of course, dudiāñ); nāiñ, nāyñ = river (*f.*); devăsāuñ, devăsāva = devotion (*n.*); māṭouñ, māṭava = shed (*m.*); māuñ, māve = scar; dāuñ, dāune = running, turn (*f.*). Many other things to be said about this **ñ** will be explained more conveniently elsewhere.

3. The Latin Prepositions are not all translated in the same way: some are translated by Konkani suffixes, some by true Postpositions. The first are *per*, *in*, *super* and similar Prepositions having about the same meaning as these three. The 1st is translated by **n** (*Instrum.*), the 2nd by **nt** (*1st Loc.*), the 3rd by **r** (*2nd Loc.*). Probably, that **n** formerly was a true Postposition "**an**", that **nt** also was "**ant**"; the 3rd is shortened perhaps from "**voir** = upon". These two **an** and **ant** joined to the Noun, lost the vowel and became **n**, **nt** (see page 14 *n.* 1 of the text). Only these Postpositions (which might be better called suffixes as forming a peculiar case) drop the initial vowel (**an** = **n**, **ant** = **nt**), if joined to the Original or pure stem; so, "mezā-ānt = mezānt *etc.* (See *ibid.*) The Postpositions which are added as a separate word, do not drop any vowel; *e. g.* yēkavorsā ādiñ = before one year.

The second kind of Prepositions are all other Prepositions different from these three. Nay, even these three may be translated by some true Konkani Postpositions to be written as a separate word. (See pp. 12 and 18.) The Postpositions of the 2nd kind are chiefly these: vorvi = by; lāgiñ, *or* kăḍe = close, at; pāsun = on account of, for; ādiñ = before; višiānt = about, (Lat. *de*); mukār = in face, before (Lat. *coram*); săkăl = under; voir = upon; pāṭleān = behind, *etc.*

4. As in Latin, there are some irregular Nouns; some used chiefly or only in the Singular, *e.g.* "kurpā = grace", "lók = people"; some used only in the Plural, *e.g.* "kărkăr", some heteroclite, *e.g.* āvoi of the 4th Declension in the Singular, of the 1st in the Plural; some declined a little irregularly, *e.g.* māḷăi, māḷi = story; but as I do not recollect them all at the present, they will be put in the Dictionary, as they occur. Here I put down only those which now occur to my mind besides the indicated ones.

a) Nouns of the 1st Declension ending in a are seldom used in the Plural (see p. 15, para. 7); yet some of them may be used, at least, in some cases of the Plural; *e.g.* "čintna = thought" is not used in the Nominative Plural, but is used in the Dative and Instrumental: "čintneānk, čintneāniñ".

b) "Monis = man (*homo*), if used for a woman is Neuter; then, commonly, it is joined to "bāil = woman", bāil-monšañ = women (low expression).

c) Some other Nouns used only or chiefly in the Plural are "dăgd, -añ = sufferings" (*m*); "dăg, -añ = vaccine matter" (*m*) *etc.*

d) Some may be declined according to one or according to another Declension; *e.g.* "kīḍ = insect" is of the 2nd, "kīḍo" of the 3rd Declension. Some say that "kīḍ" means a smaller insect, and "kīḍo" a bigger one. So also "ākānt = distress" is of the 4th or of the 2nd Declension, *ad libitum.*

e) Some Nouns form the Original from the Nominative in a rather different from the common way: these are chiefly some

Nouns ending in ăi; *e.g.* "māḷăi = story" and "vaḷăi = white ant"; Original: "māḷie, vaḷie". Moreover "vaḷăi" means one white ant or more; it has no Plural form. Bāpui, if applied to God is changed into "băp." It may be declined in two ways, *i.e.* "bāpa, bāpāk" *etc.* or "bāpai, bāpaik", *etc.*

5. There are some Nouns which may be applied to males and females together, as in Latin *homo; e.g. primi homines* (Adam and Eve). Those Nouns, if used to signify males and females at the same time, are often put in the Neuter Gender, although generally used as Masculine. These Nouns seem to belong only or chiefly to the 2nd Declension; *e.g.* "monis", *pl.* "monšañ"; although, if used in a general meaning, it has "monis" (*m.*) also in the Plural.

6. As regards accent, the terminations **ia, ea, eo, io** (or **ya, yo**) which occur in the Declensions have the accent upon **a** and **o**, although diphthongs: if written with Kanarese letters, they would not be diphthongs, because they should be written **yo, ya**; but **y** is not a vowel. This must be understood also of such terminations of the Adjectives. (See following Art. 2.) Thus: "burgea", pātkia", rāṇio", boreo"" etc.

What has been said above, (Observation 1), that *e.g.* Feminine Nouns in i are of the 1st or of the 4th, must not be understood thus: "it is free to decline them according to the 1st or according to the 4th," but thus: "some are of the 1st, some of the 4th Declension."

Art. II. Gender of Nouns

There are three Genders in Konkani viz. Masculine, Feminine and Neuter.

The Gender may be known either by the termination or by the meaning.

I. From the meaning:

Masculine

1. All names (Proper or Common) of men and of offices peculiar to men are Masculine.

Exceptions: *a*) Small children are considered as Neuter; so also the Noun "Burgeñ" = child.

b) If the Noun expressing some office of man, is used figuratively and it was originally Neuter, it remains Neuter, also if it is used figuratively; *e.g.* "Pāp sāib amčeñ mostak" = *Pontifex est nostrum caput.*

2. The names of male animals are Masculine.

Exceptions: *a*) If sex is not taken into consideration, animals are considered as Neuter.

b) The names of some animals are always Feminine or Neuter. (See below *Notes* 3-4, pages 46, 47).

3. Names of hills, mountains, seas, months and days of the week are also Masculine.

4. Nouns of false gods, of devils and of heavenly bodies are Masculine.

Exception: Neketrų = star, is Neuter.

Feminine

1. The names (Proper or Common) of women and of offices peculiar to women are Feminine.

Exceptions: *a*) Names of women in speaking to them, or of them, by those who consider themselves equal or in some way superior to them, are considered as Neuter. Thus a boy says of his small sister "teñ khāiñ geleñ? = where did it go?" So a man speaking of a Paria woman, uses the Neuter Gender.

b) Nouns of women before puberty or marriage, are Neuter; but if they speak of themselves in First Person, they use the Feminine Gender.

c) Čeḍuñ = girl, is always of Neuter Gender.

2. Nouns of female animals are also Feminine.

Exception: There are some names of animals which are always of Masculine or Neuter Gender. (See below *Notes* 3-4, pages 46, 47).

3. Names of rivers are also Feminine.

Neuter

1. Names of kingdoms, cities, winds, ships, are Neuter. Also
2. The above exceptions;
3. Names of fruits (with many exceptions);
4. The diminutives (in er and ăt).

II. From the termination:

Masculine

1. All Nouns ending in the Nominative Singular in o are Masculine.

2. Nouns in ai or i having the characteristic a (2nd Declension), are Masculine.

Feminine

1. Nouns ending in the Nominative Singular in a, are Feminine, provided they are of Konkani origin.

Exceptions: "vora = four Rupees"; "loṭṭebīra = quack"; "kuḷḷa = dwarf", and perhaps a few others are Masculine.

2. Nouns ending in ai, i, u, ụ or in a consonant, with the characteristic e, are also Feminine.

Neuter

1. Nouns ending poṇ are always Neuter.

2. Nouns ending in ap, iñ and uñ preceded by a consonant, are also mostly or always Neuter, at least, if they have the characteristic a, *i. e.* if they are of the 2nd Declension.

Exceptions: "santap, -a = affliction"; "gusăp, -a = confusion", and perhaps a few others are Masculine.

3. Mostly also, foreign Nouns not inflected according to the idiomatical Konkani sound, chiefly if they end in a consonant, are Neuter.

4. All Common Nouns ending in eñ, (which may be true Nouns or the Infinitives of Verbs used as Substantives) are Neuter.

As it appears from the above rules, the Gender of many Nouns may be known also by the characteristic alone, *i. e.* the characteristics e, i, u (1st, 4th and 5th Declension) are, mostly, a sign of Feminine Gender, if meaning does not require another Gender; the characteristics a and ea (2nd and 3rd Declension) are a sign of Masculine or Neuter Gender.

If we consider the characteristics a and ea together with the termination of the Nominative, then we may say thus: as to a, if the Nominative ends as above (*n.* 2. Neuter), a is a sign of Neuter Gender; if it ends in ai and i, mostly is a sign of Masculine Gender; if it ends in some other vowel or in a consonant, that Noun having the characteristic a may be still Masculine or Neuter. As to ea, if the Nominative ends in o, it is a sign of Masculine Gender; if in eñ, Neuter Gendor is indicated.

The characteristic can be easily known considering the termination of any oblique case of the Singular, as regards 1st, 2nd and 3rd Declension, and in the 4th and 5th Declension, considering also the oblique cases of the Plural; because the characteristic of one Declension appears different from all characteristics of the other Declensions in the Singular of the 1st, 2nd and 3rd Declension; as to the Plural, it appears different only in 4th and 5th Declension; because in these two Declensions the characteristic of the Singular is kept also in the Plural.

The Accusative sometimes is equal to the Nominative; then it cannot be considered, in order to find the characteristic.

1) If the meaning requires Masculine Gender, as shown before, the termination cannot be taken into consideration; *e. g.* Zose = Joseph, is Masculine; although it has the characteristic "e".

2) In this matter of Gender the chief difficulty regards only the 2nd Declension. For, the first Declension has only Feminine Nouns, the 3rd only Masculine in "o", and Neuter in "eñ", the 4th and 5th mostly Feminine Nouns.

3) Although the above rules about male and female animals is right, if we consider the matter generally and "in abstracto", yet in particular cases it may be exposed to many objections. Hence we might perhaps say better so: Male animals have often a name of Masculine termination, female animals have often a name of Feminine termination; *e g.* "bokḍo" = mutton; "bokḍi" = sheep; in this case there is no difficulty. Often there is also a name used both for

male and female; such a name is often of Neuter Gender; *e.g.* "suņeñ = dog" (male or female); but sometimes the names of male or female animals have a termination not agreeing with their natural Gender; *e.g.* "kolgeñ = bitch" (*n.*), and then their Grammatical Gender follows the termination, although meaning would require another Gender. Sometimes animals have a name, the termination of which does not require a certain Gender; in this case, more commonly those names are Neuter. If in this last case, you want to express male or female, I would add "daḍleñ" or "bāileñ".

Examples: "gōḍo = horse" (*m.*), "gōḍi = mare"; "suņeñ = dog" (*n.*), "peṭo = male dog" (*m.*), "kolgeñ = female dog, bitch" (*n.*); "māzar = cat" (*n.*), "bokul = male cat" (*m*); "asvel = bear" (*n.*), "daḍleñ asvel = male bear", "bāileñ asvel = female bear". See also the following Observation:

4) There are some names of animals, (as stated above) which have only one termination for the different genders, as in Italian "*oca*" which may mean either male or female. Among these Nouns some have the termination of the Masculine Gender, and are considered as Masculine; some have the termination of the Feminine, and are considered as Feminine, and some have the termination of the Neuter Gender, and are considered as Neuter. In order to distinguish male from female the words "daḍlo = male", and "bāilo = female" are prefixed to those Nouns, as in Italian we say *oca maschio*, *oca femmina*, with the difference that in Konkani the words daḍlo and bāilo take the terminations of the Adjective and agree with the corresponding Noun; *e.g.* "pārvo = pigeon" has the termination of Masculine; hence "cock-pigeon = daḍlo pārvo"; "hen-pigeon = bāilo pārvo". So: "girboji = sparrow", this is Feminine; hence "cock-sparrow = daḍli girboji", "hen-sparrow = bāili girboji"; "ḍònk = crane," is Neuter; hence: "male crane = daḍleñ ḍònk", "female crane = bāileñ ḍònk." These names are called Epicene, *i. e.* common to both sexes.

5) There may be some exceptions more against the above rules of the text. Only here must be well remarked, that, as the meaning sometimes must be considered in order to establish the Gender, and not the termination (see *Note* 1); so on the other hand sometimes the termination must be considered, not the meaning. Thus, although, *e. g.* names of kingdoms are usually of Neuter Gender (see above), yet if the name of the kingdom has a termination and a characteristic of Feminine Gender, *e. g.* of the 1st or of the 4th Declension, that Noun is Feminine; thus "India, -die = India" is of the 1st Declension; "Itali", is of the 4th, consequently they are Feminine. So also there are some diminutives ending in "ki", or "i"; *e.g.* "pāḍki" = small cow; "guḷo = ball", "guḷi = small ball (shot)"; those Nouns are not Neuter, but Feminine. With this limitation the above rules must be understood.

CHAPTER II. ADJECTIVES

I divide this chapter into three articles: 1) Adjectives in general; 2) Adjectives in particular; 3) Degrees of Adjectives.

Art. I. Adjectives in General

§ I. Common Adjectives

There are two kinds of Adjectives in Konkani.

1. Some have three terminations o, i, eñ for the three Genders in the Nominative Singular, viz. o, i, eñ, as in Latin *us, a, um; e.g.* boro, bori, boreñ = *bonus, bona, bonum.*

2. If the Adjective terminates with a consonant or with any other vowel than o, it has only one form in the Nominative Singular.

The first kind of Adjectives is easy and fixed; but the second kind seems to be still vague.

Let us now see how they are declined. In order to learn this, we have to distinguish the first kind from the second kind of Adjective, and again in each kind we have to distinguish the case in which they are true Adjectives from the case in which they are like Pronouns; *e.g.* in the sentence "God is good", *good* is a true Adjective. In the other sentence: "God gives reward to the good" *good* is like a Pronoun, namely instead of *good man.*

The first kind of Adjectives, if they are true Adjectives, are declined as follows: in the Masculine, they have only two cases, viz. Singular Nominative o, oblique cases ea; Plural Nominative e; oblique cases eañ, just according to the 3rd Declension. In the Feminine, as in the Masculine, they have only two cases, viz. Singular Nominative i, in the oblique case change that i into e; Plural Nominative change i into eo or yo in the oblique cases eañ, namely almost according to the 1st Declension, except that instead of ie there is e, and instead of e there is eo.

This rule is to be applied whether the Adjective be attribute as "the *merciful* God has forgiven you" or predicate as "God is merciful".

If the Adjectives are used as Pronouns, then they are declined like Nouns of the 3rd Declension.

Usually if the Adjectives are used as Pronouns, they are used in the Masculine Gender; hence they are declined as the Masculine of the 3rd Declension. Yet if they be used, (1) in the Feminine, or (2) Neuter Gender, then they should be declined in the first case as Nouns of 1st Declension, and in the second case as Neuter Nouns of the 3rd Declension.

The second kind of Adjectives must be subdivided into Adjectives 1) ending in a consonant, or 2) ending in a vowel, except o.

The Adjectives ending in a consonant, if they are used as true Adjectives, seem to be declined only in the oblique cases, namely they take a for the Masculine and Neuter; e for the Feminine in the Singular; and añ for the Plural in all Genders.

1. Sometimes people use 'ea' in the Feminine Singular instead of 'e', and 'e' instead of 'ea'.

2. It seems to be allowed to use the Adjectives ending in a consonant as indeclinables.

3. Some Adjectives, *e.g.* "bhăgivónt = holy", take 'i' in the oblique case of the Feminine instead of 'e'; *e.g.* "bhăgivónti Mărie = holy Mary".

The Adjectives ending in a vowel, except o, are not declined at all.

If these second kind of Adjectives are used as Pronouns, then the Adjectives ending in a consonant are declined like Nouns of the 2nd Declension. If they end in a vowel, except o, they are not declined at all.

Exception. The Neuter Nominative Plural, which should be añ, in this last case, (viz. if the Adjectives ending in a consonant, are used as Pronouns), is often equal to the Masculine; *e.g.* "săkăṭ = *omnes et omnia.*" Yet we could say also "săkṭāñ = *omnia.*" Nay it seems better.

These rules are to be applied also to the Adjective, corresponding to the Genitive (see below).

Examples.

1. *a*) First kind of Adjective: boro = good, *bonus*.

	Singular:	*Plural:*
Nom.	boro monis	bore monis
Orig.	borea″ monša	boreañ monšāñ
Dat.	borea monšāk	boreañ monšāṅk
Accus.	borea monšāk	boreañ monšāṅk
Voc.	borea monšā	boreañ monšānu
Instrum.	borea monšān	boreañ monšāniñ
1st Loc.	borea monšānt	boreañ monšāniñ
2nd Loc.	borea monšāčer	boreañ monšāñčer
Orig. followed by Postpositions	borea monšā lāgiñ *etc.*	boreañ monšāñ lāgiñ *etc.*

b) Bori = *bona;* bori ăstri = good woman.

Nom.	bori ăstri	boreo″ ăstrio″
Orig.	bore ăstrie	boreañ ăstreañ
Dat.	bore ăstriek	boreañ ăstreāṅk
Accus.	bore ăstriek	boreañ ăstreāṅk
Voc.	bore ăstrie	boreañ ăstreānu
Instrum.	bore ăstrien	boreañ ăstreāniñ
1st Loc.	bore ăstrient	boreañ ăstreāniñ
2nd Loc.	bore ăstriečer	boreañ ăstreāñčer
Orig. followed by Postpositions	bore ăstrie kăḍe *etc.*	boreañ ăstreāñ kăḍe *etc.*

c) boreñ = *bonum;* boreñ balseñ = good baby.

Nom.	boreñ balseñ	boriñ balsiñ
Orig.	borea″ balsea″	boreañ balseañ
Dat.	borea balseāk	boreañ balseāṅk
Accus.	borea balseāk	boreañ balseāṅk
Voc.	borea balseā	boreañ balseānu
Instrum.	borea balseān	boreañ balseāniñ
1st Loc.	borea balseānt	boreañ balseāniñ
2nd Loc.	borea balseāčer	boreañ balseāñčer
Orig. followed by Postpositions	borea balseā lāgiñ *etc.*	boreañ balseāñ lāgiñ [*etc.*

2. Second kind of Adjectives

Vōḍ = large; vōḍ găr = large house.

	Singular:	*Plural:*
Nom.	vōḍ găr	vōḍ gărāñ *or* vōḍañ gărāñ
Orig.	vōḍa găra	vōḍañ gărāñ
Dat.	vōḍa gărāk	vōḍañ gărāñk
Accus.	vōḍ găr	vōḍ gărāñ *or* vōḍañ gărāñ
Voc.	vōḍa gără	vōḍañ gărānu
Instrum.	vōḍa gărān	vōḍañ gărāniñ
1st Loc.	vōḍa gărānt	vōḍañ gărāniñ
2nd Loc.	vōḍa gărāčer	vōḍañ gărāñčer
Orig. followed by Postpositions	vōḍa gără kāḍe *etc.*	vōḍañ gărāñ kāḍe *etc.*

In this example in the Singular Accusative, I put "vōḍ" not "voḍa", though it is an oblique case, because, if the Accusative of the Noun is equal to the Nominative, the Adjective too must be equal to the Nominative.

In a similar way you may decline "săkăţ vāţ = all way," of Feminine Gender, namely: *Nom.* săkăţ vāţ; *Orig.* sakţe vāţe, *etc.*

There is no need of putting an example of an Adjective ending in a vowel different from o, as it does not undergo any change, nor is there need of putting an example of the Adjective as a Pronoun, as there is no difficulty.

How to form Adjectives, will be shown in the Appendix to this II. Part; now it is enough to say that a great many Adjectives are derived from Nouns by adding to the stem so, čiñ, čeñ, (*us*, *a*, *um* of the Latin) *or* lo, li, leñ; *e. g.* souñsăr = world, souñsărāso = worldly; mōg = love or charity, mōgāso = charitable (*fem.* mōgāči, *neutr.* mōgāčeñ).

§ II. Adjectives corresponding to the Genitive.

The most simple way of making this Adjective or Genitive is this: Make of the English Genitive an Adjective of three terminations by adding to the stem of the Singular, if the Genitive is Singular, or to the stem of the Plural, if the Genitive is Plural, so, či, ce (or seldom, lo, li, leñ), and let this new Adjective agree in gender, number, and case with the Noun governing the English Genitive; *e. g.* the Love of God = "Devāso mōg = Divine Love"; "the stones of the house = gărăčo fātor", "the stones of the houses = garānče fātor"; "the master of the boys = burgeāñso mēstri", "the masters of the boy = burgeāče mēstri" *etc.*

Observations.

1. If the Genitive is a Noun with an Adjective, the Noun only takes the terminations so, či, čeñ and the accompanying Adjective is to be put in the case required by the concord (Vide Syntax). Yet, if the Noun governing the Genitive is in the Nominative, and, consequently, the Noun in the Genitive is to be changed into an Adjective of Nominative Case, the accompanying Adjective, if it is an Adjective of three terminations, must be put in the oblique case of the Singular, if the Genitive converted into Adjective was Singular; Plural, if the Genitive was Plural; of the Masculine or Neuter or Feminine Gender, according to the Gender of the Noun, Genitive converted into Adjective; *e. g.* "the custom of all good men = săkṭañ boreañ monšānči dastur"; here, grammatically we should say: "bori monšānči dastur"; yet such is not the custom. For the same reason we must say "aḍvarlelea rukāčiñ foḷañ = the fruits of the prohibited tree", instead of "aḍvarleliñ rukāčiñ foḷañ". In this point the Genitive follows the rule of the Substantives more than the rule of the Adjectives; because if we consider "monšāñči" and "rukāči" as Nouns in the oblique case, we should say truly "boreañ" and "aḍvarlelea." It seems to me that this rule is in some way to be observed also with Adjectives of one termination; *e.g.* "sămestañ rukānčiñ foḷañ = the fruits of all trees"; "sămestañ" is an oblique case.

2. If the Adjectives are used like Pronouns, and they are put in the Genitive, then they take the terminations so, či, čeñ, just as if they were Substantives; *e. g.* "the way of the wicked = koṭṭepoṇāñso mārog".

3. Sometimes the Genitive is not changed into an Adjective, but the pure stem is used; in this case, it seems, that the stem should be put before the governing Noun; *e.g.* "Devā (*or* Devāči) kurpa = the grace of God". This is the pure Genitive of which I said above, that it occurs sometimes.

4. If there are many Genitives, then, if they are, I may say, parallel, viz. all governed by the same name, only the last Genitive usually is changed into an Adjective, though it is no mistake if you change all into Adjectives; *e.g.* "the duty of the mother and father = āuoi bāpāso kāido", instead of "āuoiso ani bāpāso kāido". If only the last Genitive takes the terminations of the Adjective, usually the Conjunction "ani = and" is omitted.

If the Genitives are subordinate one to the other, *i.e.* if the 1st Genitive is governed by a word, the 2nd Genitive is governed by the first *etc.*, usually all are changed into Adjectives, although sometimes only the last Genitive is made Adjective; *e.g.* "the Feast of the Sacred Heart of Jesus = Somia Jezu Kristāčeñ Kalzāčeñ fest", *or* "Somia Jezu Kristā Kalzāčeñ fest"; or, as some people say: "Somia Jezu Kristāča Kalzāčeñ fest".

5. What I said above, (p. 49) viz. that the Adjectives take sometimes 'e' or 'ea' indifferently in the oblique cases, is to be applied to these Adjectives too. So "Devāčea Māyek" or "Devāče Māyek = to the Mother of God", "mōgāče burgeāk" or "mōgāčea burgeāk = to the dear child."

6. Many Verbs are compounded with a Substantive and a Verb, which consequently require the Genitive; *e.g.* "love = mōg kăr = make charity, make love"; hence "love God" is translated as if it were in English "make the love of God = Devāso mōg kăr". But not all Verbs compounded of a Verb and a Substantive require the Genitive. The meaning must be consulted, or better, translate literally in English the Konkani Verb, and then see whether it would require the Genitive; *e.g.* "molāk kāṇe = buy," literally: "take at

price"; it does not govern the Genitive; because, we should say in English: "take at price a book", *not* "take at price of a book". In the Dictionary it is shown whether a Verb governs this Genitive, by the sign *G.* = Genitive, with *m.* or *f.* or *n.* (=*masculine*, *feminine*, *neuter*) joined, to show the gender of the Noun, united to the Verb; because the Genitive must agree in gender etc. with the Noun. Yet in many cases this rule, *i.e.* of these Compound Verbs, is not observed; *e.g.* "to pātkāñ kumzār zatā = he confesses his sins", instead of "pātkāñčeñ kumzār zatā".

7. This Genitive or Adjective in so, či, čeñ is not only used in cases in which in English there would be a Genitive, but also in many other cases, as use will teach you; *e.g.* "dusreāñso-rāg āilā = "anger against others came", literally: "anger of others came" *etc.* (See Syntax.)

§ III. Adjectives derived from the Postpositions tāun, voir, *etc.*

If the English *from* means distance of place or of time, it is translated regularly by tāun; *e.g.* "Europā tāun āilo = (he) came from Europe"; "from 10 to 12 = dhā tāun bārā pāriānt"; or "dārn = taking" sometimes is used; "dhā uorañ dārn bārā pāriānt = from (*lit.* taking) 10 till 12". But if it means *out of*, or better, if it means *going out from inside*, as in the sentence "Jesus Christ delivers us from sin", then the Nouns governed by *from* or a similar particle, is changed into an Adjective, namely, that Noun is put in the 1st Locative nt, and to it lo (or li, leñ for Feminine and Neuter) is joined in one word. But, with which word must it agree? This is not so easily known. Yet I think, we may say that this new Adjective must agree with the Noun which is meant to go out of *etc.*; *e.g.* "Jesus Christ delivers us from sin"; "us" is the thing which goes out of "sins", figuratively; hence = "Jezu Krist amkāñ pātkāntle soḍaitā"; as appears from this example, the Adjective in lo does not agree in Case, but only in Number and Gender with the corresponding Noun. (See Syntax.) Sometimes, chiefly when there is no Noun with which this -ntlo should agree, it is put in the Instrumental Case; *e.g.* "it comes from the cloud = kupāntleān yetā", from "kup, -a = cloud".

A similar construction takes place with "voir = up", "bităr = within", "lāgiñ = close", "pois = far" *etc.*; they are changed into Adjectives "voilo, bitărlo, lāgso, poislo" and agree with the governed Noun; *e.g.* "porvatā voilo deuñlo = he descended from the mountain"; "Jezu Krist Saitānāk monšāvoilo soḍaitā = Jesus Christ expells the devil from man"; "kōṇ tumče bitărlo = who among you?" "vōtz moja lāgso = go far from me", literally: "go from my neighbourhood"; "moja poislo vōtz = go far from me".

Exercises on §§ I, II, and III.

durbaḷo = poor
porno = old (*of things*)
mātāro = old (*of person*)
dusro = other
tāmḍo = red
dovo = white
kāḷo = black
nilso = blue
pātzuo, *or* tarno = green
ălduvo = yellow
ubār = high
moṭvo = short
moṭṭo = fat
vōḍ = large *or* great
toḍo = few
săbār = many
ital, -tla = garden (*n.*)
piko = ripe
bāpui, -pā, *or* -pai = father (*m.*)
lēsu̥, -a = handkerchief (*m.*)
răng = colour
zanel, -a = window (*n.*)
foḷ, -a = fruit (*n.*)
rūk, -a = tree (*m.*)
vāiṭ = evil (*n.*)
besṭeñ = in vain
kāḍ = take away *or* draw
nāuñ, -āva = name (*n.*)
sikoi = teach
mān, -a = honour (*m.*)
dī = give
uttar, -tra = word (*n.*)
aika-tā = (he) hears
mor-tā = dies

adar = commit
lāgtā = is attached [m.)
mōg kār = love (make love G.
yemkanḍ, -a = hell (n.)
soḍāi = deliver
atāñ or atāntz = now or just now
vondautā = is inclined

Mozo porno buk khāiñ assā? To moje lāgiñ assā. To mātāro monis mozo bāpai. Mojo boiṇik sobit tāmḍeñ lugaṭ, moja bāvāk nilso lēsu assā. Mezār doveñ lugaṭ galā. Moja gārāčiñ zanelañ patzuiñ; tuja gārāčiñ zanelañ kāḷiñ. Teā rukāčiñ foḷañ pikiñgī? Nāiñ, ani tarniū assāt. Moje gār ubār. Mozo bāpai moṭvo monis; tujo bāpai moṭṭo monis. Tuja itlānt sobār rūk assātgī? Nā, toḍe rūk assāt. Pedruso burgo boro, Paulaso burgo pāḍ. Sāmestañ monšānčiñ kalzañ vāiṭāk vondautāt. Monis sābār pauṭi Devāčeñ nāuñ besṭeñ kāḍtāt. Ya burgeačā bāpaičeñ nāuñ Pedru. Somia Jezu Kristāčeñ kaliz āmso mōg kartā. Moja išṭāso bāu āz gārā (or gārānt) assā. Āmčañ burgeāñso mestri boreñ sikoitā. Voḍānk mān diā. Voḍānčeñ uttār aikā. Sāmestañ pātkāñ sāng (*say all sins*). Sāmest monis mortāt. Sāmestañ monšānk Deu kurpā ditā. Sāmestānk kumok dī. Sākāṭ monis pātak aḍartāt. Sākṭāñ monšānk pātak lagtā. Bore monis Devāso mōg kartāt, pāḍ monis pātkāso mōg kartāt. Burgeāno, āuoi bāpāso (or bāpaiso) mōg kārā. Somi Jezu Krist monšānk yemkanḍāntle ani pātkāntle soḍaitā. Šerāntlo kōṇ āilogi? (*Is somebody come from the town?*) Vōi, Pādri ātāntz ailā. Vo porno soro (*wine*): tò novo soro. Tāmḍeñ lugaṭ mezār boreñ distā. Tuje lāgiñ (*with you*) dusreñ lugaṭ assāgī? Rukānčeo kollio tarneo. Tuje kāḍe yēk āldovo lēsu assāgī? Durbaḷeānk aikā: Deu tumkā (*you*) aikatolo (*will hear*). Mātāreānči dastur siṇ uleuñso (*custom of old men is to complain*). Tea ubār porvotār (*mountain*) yēk nāḍ (*village*) assā. Ubār porvotānčer dov (*snow*) assā. Sezāričea (*of the neighbour*) itlānt yēk sorōp (*snake*) distā. Kāssālo (*which*) rāng tukā boro distā? Adāuñ aḍvarlelea (*prohibited*) rukāčeñ fōḷ khātā (*eats*) ani āče vorvi (*hereby*) pātak aḍartā; Devāči kurpā bāir galtā (*puts out, loses*), ani nirbhāgi (*wretched*) zatā. Toḍe monis sărgār (*into heaven*) rigtāt (*enter*), săbār monis yemkaṇḍānt rigtāt: asseñ (*thus*) uleitā Somi Jezu Krist. Sămestānk saimbāčeñ pātak lāgtā, baptism kāṇeuñčea ādiñ, [*to all, of nature sin* (*original sin*) *is attached before receiving baptism*, (*of desire at least*)].

Art. II. Adjectives in particular

Numeral Adjectives

Now I will speak of the Adjectives in particular, but not of all kinds; about the Adjectives which are derived from the Pronouns, it is better to speak in the chapter on Pronouns. In this article I speak only of Numerals.

§ I. Cardinal Numbers

First I put down the chief numbers; because they cannot be put easily in the Dictionary.

1 = yēk
2 = dòn *or* dòg; dòni *or* dogi = both
3 = tīn *or* tèg
4 = čār *or* čoug, *or* tčóug
5 = pānz *or* pānč
6 = să
7 = sāt (*pronounced quickly*)
8 = āṭ
9 = nóv *or* nóu
10 = dhā
11 = ïkrā
12 = bārā
13 = tèrā
14 = čoudā
15 = pondrā
16 = sòḷā
17 = sotrā
18 = ăṭrā
19 = yēkuṇīs
20 = vīs
21 = vīs ani yēk, *or better* yēkvīs
22 = vīs ani dòn *or* băvīs
23 = tēvīs *or* vīs ani tīn
24 = vīs ani čār, *or* čovīs
25 = vīs ani pānč *or* pončis *or* panČvīs
26 = vīs ani să *or* sovīs
27 = vīs ani sāt *or* sattāvīs
28 = vīs ani āṭ *or* ăṭṭāvīs
29 = yēkuṇtīs
30 = tīs
31 = tīs ani yēk *or* yektīs

32 = tīs ani dòn *or* bottīs
33 = tīs ani tīn *or* tettīs
34 = tīs ani čār *or* čoutīs
35 = tīs ani pānč *or* pāntīs
36 = sättīs [1]
37 = sättīs
38 = aṭtīs
39 = yēkuṇečāḷis
40 = čāḷis
41 = čāḷis ani yēk *or* yēke-čāḷis
42 = bāvečāḷis
43 = tečāḷis *or* tevečāḷis
44 = čāḷis ani čār *or* čove-čāḷis
45 = pončvečāḷis *or* pānčve-čāḷis
46 = sovečāḷis
47 = sättečāḷis
48 = äšṭečāḷis
49 = yēkuṇeponās
50 = ponās
51 = yēkpan *or* yēkāon
52 = baupan *or* bāon
53 = tevepan
54 = čoupan
55 = pančāvan
56 = soupan
57 = sättāvan
58 = äṭṭāvan
59 = yēkuṇesāṭ
60 = sāṭ (*pronounced slowly and cerebral*)
61 = yeksäsṭ
62 = besäsṭ *or* beasäst
63 = tresäsṭ *or* treasäsṭ
64 = čousäsṭ
65 = pāñsäsṭ
66 = sousäsṭ
67 = sātsäsṭ
68 = äṭsäst
69 = yēkuṇesättär
70 = sättär
71 = yēkasättär
72 = beästär (*shortened from* bāve sättär)
73 = treasättär *or* treas-tär
74 = čóveastär
75 = pončästär, *or*, *more commonly*, pauṇseñ = ¼ less hundred (100 – 25)
76 = sóastär *or* syastär
77 = sätte-ästär *or* sat-tyästär
78 = äṭṭe-ästär *or* aṭṭya-ästär
79 = yekuṇe-äišiñ
80 = äišiñ
81 = yekkyā-äišiñ
82 = beāšiñ *or* beāišiñ
83 = teāšiñ *or* treāišiñ *or* teaišiñ
84 = čove-aišiñ
85 = pončve-aišiñ
86 = sā-aišiñ

[1] The common way of forming numbers by "ani", *e.g.* here "tīs ani sā" must be understood, although it is not always put.

87 = săttya-aišiñ
88 = aṭṭya-aišiñ
89 = yēkuṇe-nóvód
90 = nóvód
91 = yēkanóvód
92 = beanóvód *or* beannói
93 = treanovoi
94 = čouveanovoi
95 = pančanovoi
96 = sóvanovoi
97 = săttyanovoi
98 = ăṭṭyanovoi
99 = yēkuṇesembor *or* novanói
100 = señ *or* sembor
101 = sembor ani yēk
102 = sembor ani dòn *or* dòg *etc.*
110 = sembor ani dhā
111 = „ „ ïkrā *etc.*
120 = „ „ vīs
121 = sembor vīs ani yēk *or* sembor ani yēkvīs
130 = sembor ani tīs *etc.*
150 = deḍseñ
151 = deḍseñ ani yēk *or* sembor ponās ani yēk *etc.*
160 = deḍseñ ani dhā *or* sembor ani sāṭ *etc.*
200 = donsiñ
250 = ăḍeñsiñ
300 = tinsiñ
350 = tinsiñ ani ponās *or* sāḍetinsiñ *etc.*
1,000 = hazār *or* sās
1,500 = deḍ hazār
2,000 = dòn hazār *or* dòn sās
2,500 = ăḍez hazār
10,000 = dhā hazār
100,000 = lāk

Observations:

1. Up to 20 there is no general rule for forming numbers, which consequently must be learnt by heart; from 20 it is enough to know the beginning of the decade; for the other numbers are formed, more usually, by putting the larger number before and the smaller one after it, separated by "ani = and". So "26 = vis ani so", *literally:* "twenty and six". Another way is to put the smaller number before, the larger one after it without any Conjunction. So "yēkvīs = 26", "pančvis = 25 (*vulgar:* pončis)". Moreover to say 22, 23, 32, 33, *etc.*, the words **bāve, teve** (or shortened **bā, te**) are prefixed to the larger number. This way of forming the numbers now indicated by **bā** and **te** is commonly understood up to 33 in-

clusive. Further, probably common people would not understand this way of counting by bā and te, nay many can count not only the numbers formed thus, but also all numbers higher than 33, and they count by doubling or by adding lower numbers. The numbers higher than 33 are not commonly used, nay not even perhaps understood, except the decades, *i. e.* 40, 50, 60, 70 *etc.* Or better we may say so: the numbers lower than 33 are known generally (although there are some, who know only till 25), they may be formed in any of the given ways. The numbers higher than 33 may be formed in two ways, *i. e.* either by adding the lower number from 1 to 9 inclusive to the decade; *e. g.* "tīs ani čār, tīs ani pānč" *etc.*, and this way, although not generally used, at least above 40 or 50, might perhaps be understood; or they may be formed by joining the lower number to the decade (usually prefixing the lower number) as one word; this way is not used and not even understood, at least by common people. I did not learn this 2nd way from common people, but I took it from the Mahrātti; yet also the numbers formed in this 2nd way are Konkani words and should be used in order to make them common, and to raise a little this neglected Konkani language.

19, 29, 39 *etc.* are expressed, saying "one minus twenty" *etc.* so "yēkuṇīs" is shortened from "yēkuṇeñ vīs = one minus twenty"; but for 29, 39 *etc.* "yēkuṇeñ" is used instead of "yēkun."

To say 150, 250, 1500, 2500 *etc.* (in this order only) there are peculiar forms as shown above, namely they are converted into mixed numbers: So 150=one hundred and a half, $100+\frac{100}{2}$, and then expressed "deḍseñ" *etc.* (deḍ = $1\frac{1}{2}$, ăḍez = $2\frac{1}{2}$).

To say 100 only, "sembor" is more commonly used instead of "señ". In the Plural "sembor" cannot be used; hence the plural of "señ" (3rd Declension) must be used "donsiñ = 200", "tinsiñ = 300" *etc.*

2. The second form of 2, 3, 4, is used only when speak-

ing of persons or irrational animals. Sometimes a third form occurs of these three numbers, but seldom.

3. Are the Cardinal Numbers declined? All may take an **añ** in the oblique cases, at least if they are joined to a Substantive; but the numbers 2, 3, 4 have a peculiar Declension, *i. e. Nom. Masc.* "dòn, dòg, tīn, tèg, čār, čoug"; *Fem.* as the Masculine, or "dòni, dògi, tīni, tegi, čāri, čougi"; *Neuter:* "dònañ, dògañ, tīnañ, tegañ, čārañ, čougañ". *Oblique Case:* all take **añ** in all Genders, *i. e.* "dònañ, dògañ", *etc.*

4. Common fractions are expressed in this way: "$\frac{1}{4}$ = yēk pāu" *or* "yēk kaldo", this second is used as Adjective of three terminations agreeing with its Noun; "$\frac{1}{2}$ = ărdo", used also as Adjective of three terminations (Lat. *dimidius, a, um*); "$\frac{3}{4}$ = pāuṇo", literally: "(one) quarter less", also declinable as Adjective of three terminations. They use also "mukāl" for $\frac{3}{4}$, and "tīn vaṇṭe = three parts". To express $1\frac{1}{4}$, $2\frac{1}{4}$ *etc.* the literal translation is used, viz. "yēk ani yēk kāldo" *etc.* Yet for $1\frac{1}{4}$ there is another form, viz. "sovai" indeclinable, or, more clearly: "sovai" alone means $1\frac{1}{4}$; "sovai" prefixed to a number means $\frac{1}{4}$, *e.g.* "sovai ikrā = $11\frac{1}{4}$". To express $1\frac{1}{2}$, $2\frac{1}{2}$, there are peculiar forms, viz. "dēḍ = $1\frac{1}{2}$", "ăḍēz = $2\frac{1}{2}$". Yet the ordinary form would also be understood. From $3\frac{1}{2}$ upwards the word "sāḍe" is prefixed to the inferior number: so "$3\frac{1}{2}$ = sāḍe tīn" *etc.* To say $3\frac{3}{4}$, $4\frac{3}{4}$ *etc.* we may prefix "pāuṇeñ" [*lit.* (one) quarter less] to the whole number; *e.g.* "pāuṇeñ tīn = $2\frac{3}{4}$, *lit.* (one) quarter less three"; "pāuṇeñ čār = $3\frac{3}{4}$" *etc.*; or we might also affix, as a separate word, "ani tīn vaṇṭe = and three parts" to the whole number; *e.g.* "dòn ani tīn vaṇṭe = two and three parts". This second way is not so exact as the first.

My present circumstances do not allow me to explain ulterior fractions.

1. As it has been already observed, "dēḍ" and "ăḍēz" are used also to express 150, 250, 1500, 2500 *etc.*, by prefixing them to the number which re-

mains after having taken away 50, 500, 5000 *etc.*; if the remainder begins with 1, "dēḍ" is prefixed; if it begins with 2, "ăḍēx" is prefixed.

2. "Pāu" means a quarter, not of this or that kind, but generally; hence it must be joined to a Substantive; *e. g.* "yēk pāu uṇḍo; yēk pāvu ser tanduḷ" *etc.* "yēk pāvu" without a Substantive (expressed or understood) means $\frac{1}{4}$ absolutely.

3. "Kaldo = $\frac{1}{4}$" may be used for time, *e. g.* "kaldeñ uor = $\frac{1}{4}$ of an hour"; for money, *e. g.* "kaldo Rupoi = $\frac{1}{4}$ Rupee" *etc.*; it must be joined as an Adjective to the affected word.

4. "Pāuṇo" may be used either as a Noun or as an Adjective; in the 1st case, it is used commonly only for $\frac{1}{4}$ of an anna or 3 pies, (i. e. $\frac{3}{4}$ of one "poiso = 4 pies"); if it is used as Adjective, then it is joined to a Substantive in this way; "pāuṇeñ yēk moṇ = $\frac{3}{4}$ of a maund" *lit:* "one quarter less one maund", "pāuṇeñ yēk rātlu = one quarter less one pound" *etc.*

5. "Mukāl = $\frac{3}{4}$" is also a general Adjective, which consequently must be joined to a Noun; this Noun (expressed or understood) often expresses time; yet it may express also some other thing; *e. g.* "mukāl ser tanduḷ = $\frac{3}{4}$ seer of rice", "mukāl uor = $\frac{3}{4}$ of an hour".

§ II. Ordinal Numbers

These are formed from the Cardinal Numbers by adding vo (vi, veñ), and are declined as Adjectives of three terminations; so "pāns-vo = fifth", "sovo = sixth" *etc.*

The three first numbers are irregular, "1st = poilo (-i, -eñ)", "2nd = dusro", "3rd = tisro".

§ III. Distributive Numbers

These correspond to the Latin: *singuli*, *bini*, *etc.* They are formed by doubling the first syllable of the Cardinal Number; thus: "yēyēk = one by one"; "dògdòg = *bini*" *etc.*

§ IV. Reduplicative or Multiple Numbers

They correspond to the Latin *duplex*, *triplex etc.* They are formed in the same way as the Distributive Numbers. The context must decide. Yet, more usually, these are formed also in another way, namely, *duplex* or double = "doḍo" (-i, -eñ) *or* "dubāri"; "threefold = tidoḍo"; "single = yekoḍo"; from *quadruplex* to higher numbers we may say "čārdoḍo, pānčdoḍo" *etc.* or, better "čār tarāniñ (*or* čār jinsāniñ) vóḍ=large in 4 ways". Instead of "vóḍ" we have to put the Adjective required by the meaning. It is more common, instead of "čārdoḍo *or* čār tarāniñ vóḍ", to say "čār pāuṭi tzăḍ=four times greater" *etc.*

§ V. Repetitive Numbers

They signify the repetition of a thing at certain intervals; *e.g.* once every tenth year. These are formed by doubling the first syllable of the Cardinal Numbers, and consequently are declined; *e.g.* "dādāvea vorsa=every tenth year" *or* "dādāveañ vorsāniñ" in the Plural.

§ VI. Numeral Adverbs

For convenience, these Adverbs are inserted here, though their proper place would be elsewhere. These Adverbs correspond to the Latin *semel*, *bis* *etc.* They are formed by translating literally, "one time, two times=yēk pāuṭi, dōn pāuṭi, tīn pāuṭi" *etc.*

Exercises
on the Numeral Adjectives.

vār, -i = a measure nearly equal to a yard (*f.*)
uṇḍo, -ḍea=bread or loaf (*m.*)
dūdu̥, -da = milk (*n.*)
mās, -a = meat or flesh (*n.*)
molāk kāṇe=buy (take for price)
zāi = is required
kitlo = how much?
kuṭṭeñ, -ea = (a measure equal to ½ [or sometimes ¼] seer) (*n.*)
témp, -a = time (*m.*)
uor, -a = hour (*n.*)
zālo = became
uprānt = after
sumār = about
zūz, -a = war (*n.*)
soḷḷo, -ḷea = peace (treaty of peace) (*m.*)
suru zatā=begins (*principium fit*) G. *f.*
isvi, -ve = year (date) (*f.*)
pāuṭi=time (*e.g.* four times)

tzăl = walk	monšākul, -a = mankind (*n.*)
sūru̥, -re = toddy	bădăl = different, changed
vetā = goes	bogăr = but
šeār, -a = town (*n.*)	nǎints = not only
mol̥l̥o = called	bokši = forgive

Yēk pāu uṇḍo molāk kāṇe. Tuja bāpaik kitleñ dūdu̥ zāi? Bāpaik dēḍ kuṭṭeñ dūdu̥ zāi. Boiṇiči nessoṇ karunk kitleñ lugaṭ zāi? Ăḍez vāri zāi. Băvāso kutāuñ karunk kitleñ lugaṭ zāi? Pāuṇeñ čār vāri zāi. Atañ kitleñ uorañ zāliñ? Sovāi ikrā zāliñ. Kitlo témp zāi tujeñ kām karunk? Kaldeñ uor zāi. Pedručeñ kām karunk kitlo témp zāi? Ărdeñ uor, yā mukāl. Ātañ tzălči (*current*) isvi kitli? Yēk hazār āṭsiñ āiši ani yēk isvi. Konstantin rāy zālea uprānt sumār dēḍ hazār vorsāñ zāliñ. Deḍ-šeñ (*or* deḍsea) vorsāñ ādiñ yēk vóḍ zūz zāleñ. Sumār ăḍéz seañ vorsāñ ādiñ Vesṭfālyo sol̥l̥o zālo. Dhā ani mukāl zāliñ. Sovāi zāleñ (1¼ *o'clock*). Kitleañ uorāñčer mis suru zatā? Sāḍe dhā uorāñčer. Tukā kitlo uṇḍo zāi? Makā yēk pāu zāi, moja voḍa bāvāk ărdo, boiṇik yēk pāu, ani moja bāpaik yēk rātlu̥. Yēk moṇ tandul̥ molāk kāṇ-geunčeāk kitle rupoi lagtāt? Toḍe pāuṭi sāḍo čăr rupoi, toḍe pāuṭi čăr, toḍe pāuṭi sāḍe tīn, toḍe pāuṭi tīn ani uṇeñ (*and less*). Kristāvāñso poilo Pāp Sāib Sañ Pedru assullo, dusro Sañ Lin, tisro Sañ Klet, čouto Sañ Klement, pānsvo Sañ Anaklet. Dog-dog Igarjent tzălā. Pončisvea vorsa Pāp Sāib jubileu ditā. Nāiñtz sāt pāuṭi, bogăr săttăr ani sāt pāuṭi tujā bāvāk bokši.

Art. III. Degrees of Adjectives

§ I. Comparative

There are three kinds of Comparative: of Superiority, of Inferiority, and of Equality.

1. Comparative of Superiority.

a) This is formed in a similar way to the Kanarese, that is to say, the Adjective has no proper Comparative form, but it is as if we had to say in Latin: *sapientia bona est quam divitiae*, or, literally: *divitiae quam sapientia bona est*, with the difference that the word which follows *quam*, viz. *divitiae*, in Konkani is to be put in the pure stem or Original Case. "*Quam*" is expressed by "präs" or "päräs", put after the Noun which it modifies, like the Kanarese "inta"; *e.g.* "grestkaic präs zaṇvai bori = riches than wisdom good (is)". Instead of "präs", some other particle may be used; *e.g.* "vorn" or "ki" or, sometimes "mukär". Thus "grestkaie vorn zäṇvai bori = riches above wisdom good". If ki is used, the affected Noun is, more commonly, put in the Original of the derived Adjective, Masculine or Feminine according to the Gender; *e.g.* "Pedručea ki" instead of "Pedru präs"; "Märioče ki" instead of "Mărio präs". "Mukär", literally means: *in the face;* hence the sentence must be changed a little sometimes.

b) Another way of making this Comparative, corresponds to the English "more" and to the Latin *magis*, but it is not often used: this 2nd kind of Comparative is formed by prefixing "ădik = more" to the Adjective and then putting "präs" or "vorn", as before. Thus the Adjective itself becomes truly Comparative; *e.g.* "Antoni präs Pedru ădik boro = Peter is better (more good) than Antony".

c) There are some other ways, less obvious, of forming this Comparative; *e.g.* sometimes the pure Positive Degree is used without any sign of comparison: only the context can show the Comparative. So, to express: "Which is the shorter way of these two?" we may simply say "konči väṭ moṭvi? = which way is short?" So also "tsăḍ = much *or* more". The context must decide about the meaning; *e.g.* if you ask a penitent "Did you commit this sin about a hundred times?" if he answers: "tsăḍ zäit", the meaning is "*more* than a hundred times".

2. Comparative of Equality.

It corresponds to the English "Peter is as good as Antony". This Comparative may be expressed *a*) with "bări = as" (Latin *instar, sicut*) put after the stem or Original of the affected Noun; *e.g.* "Ankuār Māri māye bări kākuļtiči = the Virgin Mary is merciful as a mother".[1]

b) This Comparative may be expressed very often with the Correlative Pronouns, as *qualis talis* (see below ch. III.); *e.g.* "zăsso Pedru tăsso Anton = as Peter so Antony".

3. Comparative of Inferiority.

This does not seem to be very common, at least in this form. It is as the Latin: *Petrus minus bonus est quam Paulus.*

a) The easiest way to translate this Comparative is to change it into a Comparative of Superiority; *e.g.* "*Paulus est melior quam Petrus* = Paul Pedru prăs boro".

b) Another way is to change the sentence, so as to get a Comparative of Equality with negative form; *e.g.* "Peter is less good than Paul", change it thus: "Peter is not so good as Paul = Pedru Paulā bări boro năiñ".

c) This Comparative may be expressed also by "titlo" *or* "itlo" = such (Latin *talis* or *tam*) chiefly if in the sentence the Noun of comparison is understood; *e.g.* after having spoken of a good person, you say of another: "N. is not so good as he = N. titlo boro năiñ". A literal translation of the English "less good" is possible, but would not be according to the nature of the Konkani language, although it occurs sometimes, *e.g.* "uņ boro = less good" (instead of "ūņo boro").

Exercises

on the Comparatives.

bud, -i = wisdom (*f.*)
duḍḍu, -ḍua = money (*m.*) (*not to be confounded with* dūdu, -da = milk *n.*)
moladik = precious
sompūrn = perfect
piḍā, -ḍe = sickness (*f.*)
durbaļkai, -e = poverty (*f.*)
grest *or* grestăso = rich
găuñ, -āva = country (*m.*)

Bombăi, Koḍiāla (*Mangalore*) prăs rūnd assā. Bud duḍḍuā vorn moladik. Sămestañ văstu prăs Deu boro ani sompūrn.

[1] Instead of "bări" we may use "póri", but this is not so common as "bări."

Pātak piḍe ani durbaḷkaie vorn vāiṭ. Pedru Paulā[1] prăs boro, puṇ Paulu Pedru prăs grest. Konči vāṭ moṭvi, īgi, tī? Tī vāṭ moṭvi, puṇ bori năīñ. Amso gāuñ tumčoa gāvā prăs ădik sobit. Pedru bări, Paulu sikpi, puṇ Pedru bări bhăgivănt (*holy*) năiñ. Ankuār Mărie bări āmčeo sauñsārāčeo (*or* sauñsārāntleo) māiyo amso mōg kartātgī? Nā, Ankuār Māri sauñsārāčeañ māiyañ prăs ădik kākultiči ani mogāḷ. Kăsso bāpui, tăso pūt, ani kăssi āuoi tăssi duv. Santānči kuši Devāk kalti assălli, amči kuši titli bori năiñ.

§ II. Superlative

There are two kinds of Superlatives: 1) Absolute, 2) Relative Superlative.

First kind. This is very easy: it is obtained by prefixing "bhou *or* tsăḍ = much" to the Positive Degree of the Adjective; *e.g.* "vōḍ = great", "bhou vōḍ = very great"; "tsăḍ piḍest = very sick". By prefixing "bhou tsăḍ", the Superlative is still higher; *e.g.* "to bhou tsăḍ piḍest = he (is) sick in the highest degree".

Second kind. This is formed *a*) in a similar way to the Comparative, except that besides "prăs" *etc.* "bităr" may be used as in Latin *inter* or *super*; *e.g.* "Antony is the most clever boy = Anton săkṭañ burgeāñ bităr ušār"; we may say also: "Anton săkṭañ burgeāñ prăs (*or* vorn) ušār".

b) Another way is to prefix "ădik = more" to the Adjective, putting then, if required, "vorn" or "bităr"; *e.g.* "the Himalayas are the highest mountains = Himālaya ădik ubăr porvot".

There are, besides these, some other ways of forming both Superlatives; *e.g.* "pois pois = far far (very far)" *etc.*; these may be learnt by practice.

Adverbs have no proper form of the Comparative and Superlative; they follow the rule of the Adjectives, except that sometimes to form the Comparative, "tsăḍ" is prefixed, if the Adverb is the Instrumental of the Substantive; *e. g.* "Peter walks more slowly than Simon = Pedru Simava prăs soukās tsăltā"; "he talks Konkani more easily = to Konkani bhās tsăḍ sasārāyen ulaitā", *literally:* "he speaks Konkani with greater facility".

[1] Or "Paulu"; for this word may follow the 2nd or 5th Declension, *ad libitum*.

§ III. Irregular Comparatives and Superlatives

Lān = little	*Comp.* uṇo (-i, -eñ).
Bhou = much	*Comp.* tsăḍ.
Boro = good	*Superl.* bhou boro (*reg.*) *or* uttăm *or* uttim: the 2nd form, *i.e.* uttim, is more common.
Pois = far	*Comp.* mukār = before, or further.

§ IV. Augmentative and Diminutive[1)]

They correspond to the Italian *libriccino* and *librone* as regards Substantives, to *piccolino* and *riccone* as regards Adjectives.

1. Very often there is no proper form for these degrees. Hence if it is required to use them, two or more words must be used; *e.g.* *a*) sometimes the Augmentative is made by repeating the Adjective or Substantive; so "pois pois = far far"; "fulañ fulañ = many flowers", as in the Bible: *tribus tribus;* but this is rather a Superlative, as regards the Adjective; *b*) often the words "illo (-i, -eñ)" or "toḍo (-i, -eñ)" or "tikeñ" indeclinable (which all mean "a little"), can be prefixed to make the Diminutive both of Substantives and Adjectives; *e.g.* "illo boro, *or* tikeñ boro = somewhat good"; "illeñ udak = a little water".

2. Sometimes the Diminutive of Substantives has a proper form; *h. e.* *a*) the Substantives are formed diminutive by adding the termination -er or -aṭ, and then they are, mostly, of the Neuter Gender; *e.g.* "rāuḷ = palace (*m.*)", "rāuḷ-er = small palace (*n.*)" (a part of a large palace); "kauḷo = crow (*m.*)", "kauḷer = small crow (*f.*)"; "vāg = tiger (*m.*)", "văgăṭ = small tiger (*n.*)"; but this form of Diminutive is used only with a few Nouns. *b*) With some other Nouns the Diminutive is formed by adding -i or -ko, (-ki for the Feminine) or -geñ; *e.g.* "ghāṭ, -a = hill (*m.*)", its diminutive is "ghāṭi = hillock (*f.*)"; "pāḍo = little bullock,"

---

1) For the sake of convenience I speak here also of Substantives.

"pāḍko = very little bullock"; "pāḍi = small she-calf", "pāḍki = very small she-calf"; "rāṇḍ = widow", "rāṇḍgeñ = small widow (*n.*)"; ("rāṇḍ" and "rāṇḍgeñ" are very low, and rather offensive words). The terminations -i and -ki mostly are a sign of Feminine Gender, -ko of Masculine Gender, -geñ of Neuter Gender. Before adding these terminations, euphony may require to cut off the last vowel, as the above examples show.

Besides the above given forms of Diminutive and Augmentative, there are some others, *e.g.* by prefixing "dakto = little", "sumār = moderate"; as these are very easy, I leave them to the private diligence.

Exercises

on the Superlatives

kotṭeponāso = wicked
rāz, -ja = kingdom (*n.*)
sōḍ = leave
ubir, -bra = mud (*m.*)
yer = other
dhairyavont = courageous
sukh, -a = happiness (*n.*)
gārmi, -me = heat (*f.*)
sāsārāi, -e = facility (*f.*)
khāro = true
dukh, -i = sorrow (*f.*)
reuñ, reve = sand (*f.*)
bangār, -a = gold (*n.*)

Deu bhou boro: monśāčeñ kaliz bhou koṭṭeponāčeñ. Sārginčeñ rāz bhou moladik: tāče pāsun sākāṭ vāstu sōḍ. Sāmestañ vāstuñ prās Devāso mōg boro: tāče mukār bangār reve bāri ya ubra bāri. Khāri pātkānči dukh sāmestañ yerañ dukhiñ vorn vōḍ. Sākṭañ vāiṭāñ bitār pātak bhou tzāḍ vāiṭ. Pedru yerañ burgeāñ mukār ādik dhairyavont burgo. Lān lān sukh toḍe pāuṭi vōḍ vāiṭānči suru zāun assā. Pedru Paulu vorn tsāḍ sasārāyen siktā. Pedruso duḍḍu uṇo zatā. Atāñ gārmi tsāḍ (*or* vòt tsāḍ); toḍeañ disāñ uprānt uṇi zāteli. Lādru (= *Lazarus*) uttim (*or* uttām) burgo. Goyiñ pois assā: Bombāi ani mukār assā.

CHAPTER III. PRONOUNS

§ 1. Personal Pronouns

Āuñ = I

	Singular:	*Plural:*
Nom.	āuñ	amiñ
Dat.	makā	amkāñ
Accus.	makā	amkāñ
Instrum.	āuveñ	amiñ
1st Loc.	*not used*	*not used*
2nd Loc.	mojer	amčer
Orig. followed by Postpositions	moje kāḍe *etc.*	amče kāḍe *etc.*

Tūñ = thou

Nom.	tūñ	tumiñ
Dat.	tukā	tumkāñ
Accus.	tukā	tumkāñ
Instrum.	tuveñ	tumiñ
1st Loc.	*not used*	*not used*
2nd Loc.	tujer	tumčer
Orig. followed by Postpositions	tuje kāḍe *etc.*	tumče kāḍe *etc.*

To = he

Nom.	to	te
Dat.	takā	tankāñ
Accus.	takā	tankāñ
Instrum.	taṇeñ	taṇiñ
1st Loc.	tantu	tantu
2nd Loc.	tačer	tančer
Orig. followed by Postpositions	tače pasun *etc.*	tanče kāḍe *etc.*

Tī = she

Nom.	tī	teo
Dat.	tikā	tankāñ
Accus.	tikā	tankāñ
Instrum.	tineñ	taniñ
1st Loc.	tantu	tantu
2nd Loc.	tičer	tančer
Orig. followed by Postpositions	tiče kāḍe *etc.*	tanče kāḍe *etc.*

Teñ = it

Nom.	teñ	tiñ
Dat.	takā	tankāñ
Accus.	takā (*seld.* teñ)	tankāñ
Instrum.	taṇeñ	taṇiñ
1st Loc.	tantu	tantu
2nd Loc.	tačer	tančer
Orig. followed by Postpositions	tače kāḍe *etc.*	tanče kāḍe *etc.*

Instead of to, remote Pronoun, o (uo) may be used, which is approximate Pronoun. It is declined almost in the same way; but as there is some difficulty in the pronunciation, I put its Declension too. According to the Kanarese, it should be written o, i, eñ but pronounced uo, i, yeñ. I will write it as it is pronounced in order to remove this difficulty.

	Singular:			*Plural:*		
	m.	*f.*	*n.*	*m.*	*f.*	*n.*
Nom.	uo	i	yeñ	ye	yeo	iñ
Dat.	akā	ikā	akā		ankañ	
Accus.	akā	ikā	akā		ankañ	
(*seld.*)	uo	i	yeñ	(*seld. as the Nomin.*)		
Instr.	aneñ	ineñ	aneñ		aniñ	
1st Loc.	antu				antu	
2nd Loc.	ačer	ičer	ačer		ančer	
Orig. with Postp.	ače	iče	ače kāḍe *etc.*		anče kāḍe *etc.*	

Observations:

1. The pure Genitive does not exist; if required, the corresponding Adjective Possessive is used, just as I have shown above, of the other Genitives. So "*amore tui*=tujea mogān=*amore tuo*". Vocative and Original do not seem to be used. If the Vocative be really required, the Nominative perhaps might be used, although I have never found such an example; *e.g.* "O thou, man of God!=ye, tūñ, Devāgelea monšā!" Instead of the Original of the Pronoun, the Original of the derived Possessive Adjective may be used.

2. If a Preposition in English be joined to the Personal Pronoun, it is translated into Konkani by the Adjective Possessive in the oblique case, followed by the Konkani Postposition; *e.g.* "Pray for me=moje pāsun māg"; "the book is with you=livrụ tuje lāgiñ assā" *etc.* Yet, see 7th Observation.

3. The Pronoun to, ti, teñ (as also o, i, eñ) may be used either as a Pronoun (*he*, *she*, *it*) or as a Demonstrative Adjective (*ille*, *illa*, *illud*). If it is used as a Pronoun, it is declined as above; if it is used as a Demonstrative Adjective, it is declined like an Adjective of three terminations; *e.g.* "give that book to him=to livrụ takā dī"; "give the book to that man=to livrụ tea monšāk dī".

4. The Pronoun tūñ is used in speaking with others, but to show respect in speaking to a person "tumiñ" is used, and the Pronouns of the 3rd Person Plural, speaking about a respectable person; *i.e.* te for a man, tiñ (neuter) for a woman. (See Syntax.)

5. Chiefly the Personal Pronouns are sometimes used in the second form of the Locative (-ger instead of -čer or -jer) as has been explained (page 14).

6. Instead of the 1st Locative, which is not used, we may use the Original of the derived Adjective followed by "bitār=within" or "thāiñ=in"; *e.g.* "moje bitār=in me", *or* "moje thāiñ".

7. Instead of "tače" followed by the Postpositions "pasun, vorviñ" *etc.* we may use "tea" followed by the same Postposi-

tions, if "tače" has reference to things; *e. g.* "tea pasun" instead of "tače pasun = therefore". The same must be said about -ya instead of -ače.

8. We meet sometimes another case of the Pronouns to and o; *h. e.* "tantlean = from that", "antlean = from this." This case is the Instrumental formed from the derived, but unused, Adjectives in -lo, "tantlo" and "antlo". This case will be better explained in the Syntax. Some say "tantlu" and "antlu" instead of "tantleān" and "antleān"; yet the first form is more common.

9. Instead of the given form of the Instrumental of the Pronouns we meet sometimes another form in -ān; *e.g.* "mojān, tujān". This form is used with "nozo = it is impossible". It is not peculiar to the Pronouns, we meet it also with the Substantives; *e.g.* "bāpāčān nozo = it is impossible to the father". It is the Instrumental of the derived Adjective in zo or so. This form will be explained in the Syntax.

10. The Instrumentals "antu" and "tantu" are not used speaking of animate subsistent objects: instead of them, the Original of the derived Possessive Adjective, followed by "thaiñ", is used; *e.g.* "tī moji māi, tiče thaiñ mogāḷ kaliz assā = that is my mother, a good heart is in her".

Adjectives derived from the Personal Pronouns.

These are the Possessive Adjectives.

From	āuñ	*comes*	mozo,	(moji,	mojeñ)
"	tūñ	"	tuzo,	(tuji,	tujeñ)
"	to *or* teñ	"	taso,	(tači,	tačeñ)
"	tī	"	tiso,	(tiči,	tičeñ)
"	amiñ	"	amso,	(amči,	amčeñ)
"	tumiñ	"	tumso,	(tumči,	tumčeñ)
"	tē *or* tīñ	"	tanso,	(tanči,	tančeñ)
"	teo	"	tinso,	(tinči,	tinčeñ)

Here you see a change of z into j, of s into č, i. e. the Possessive Adjectives which have z in the Masculine, change z into j; those which have s, change s into č. *Cf.* Part I. Ch. I. *Prope finem.*

There is some difficulty about the use of the Possessive of the 3rd Person. In English the Pronoun changes according to the Gender of the possessor, so we have *his*, *her*, *its;* the same in Konkani, "taso = his", "tiso = her", "taso = its". But besides this, in Konkani this Pronoun must agree in Number and Case with the thing possessed, in Gender with the possessor, or, more clearly, the terminations (-o, -i, -eñ *etc.*) of these Possessive Adjective must agree with the thing possessed; the vowel of the stem (*e. g.* a in taso) must agree with the possessor. So, *e. g.* speaking of a boy, you say: "taso bāp, tači bóin, tačeñ găr = his father, his sister, his house"; speaking of a woman you say: "tiso dadlo, tiči duv, tičeñ găr = her husband, her daughter, her house", and so on.

I put here all these combinations.

[*Abbreviations: Ps.* = possessor; *pd.* = thing possessed; *sn.* = singular; *pl.* = plural.]

If *ps.*	*sn.*	*m.*,	*pd.*	*sn.*		
"	"	"	"	"	"	*m.* = taso
"	"	"	"	"	"	*f.* = tači
"	"	"	"	"	"	*n.* = tačeñ
"	"	"	"	"	*pl.*	*m.* = tače
"	"	"	"	"	"	*f.* = tačeo"
"	"	"	"	"	"	*n.* = tačiñ
"	"	"	"	"	"	*m.* = tanče
"	"	"	"	"	"	*f.* = tančeo"
"	"	"	"	"	"	*n.* = tančiñ

The same things are to be said about "aso, ači, ačeñ", *etc.* which come from o, i, eñ. The difference between "to" and "o" is as in Latin between *ille* and *hic.*

§ 2. Demonstrative Pronouns

As in Latin *hic* and *ille*, so in Konkani "to, tī, teñ, *or* uo, ī, yeñ" may be 1) Personal Pronouns, or 2) Demonstrative Pronouns, or 3) Demonstrative Adjectives. In the 1st and 2nd case they are declined just as given above, in the 3rd case they are declined as Adjectives of three terminations. (See p. 72, *n.* 3.)

Adjectives derived from the Demonstrative Pronouns.

Two Adjectives are derived from **to** and **o**, *i.e.* "tăssălo *and* ăssălo = such"; the first is remote, the second proximate; so "tăssălo = like that", "ăssălo = like this"; perhaps "tăssălo" is shortened from "tea kăssălo = like that", and "ăssălo" shortened from "ya kăssălo = like this". Moreover from **to** and **o** some other compound words are derived, but shortened; *e.g.* "yeusin = in this side", instead of "ya kusin"; "teusin" instead of "tea kusin = in that side". Finally from **to** and **o** "tăsso" *and* "ăsso" (used more frequently in the neuter) are derived: "tăsseñ = in that way"; "ăsseñ = in this way".

§ 3. Relative Pronouns

	Singular:			*Plural:*		
	m.	*f.*	*n.*	*m.*	*f.*	*n.*
Nom.	zo	ji	jeñ	je	jeo	jiñ
Dat.	zakā	jikā	zakā		zankañ	
Accus.	*as the*	Dat.,	*seld. as the*	Nominative		
Instrum.	zaneñ	jineñ	zaneñ		zaniñ	
1st Loc.		zantu			zantu	
2nd Loc.	začer	jičer / zičer	začer		zančer	
Orig. follow. by Postp.	zače	jiče / ziče	zače kăḍe *etc.*		zanče kăḍe *etc.*	

Observations:

1. The Genitive is formed according to the general rule, viz. "zaso, zači, začeñ", if the Noun to which this Pronoun refers is Singular; "zanso, zanči, zančeñ", if it is Plural. The observation about "taso" made on p. 74, is to be applied also to "zaso": the table about "taso" likewise is to be applied to "zaso".

2. Though the full Declension of the Relative Pronouns has been given, yet it is seldom used. In familiar language

they use rather the participle obtained by omitting the Relative Pronoun or "taso = his". (See Syntax.)

3. "Zo, ji, jeñ" may sometimes be used as Adjective, namely if it is joined with a Noun; and then it is declined as an Adjective of three terminations; *e.g.* "jea monšăk tũñ guṇăzo zači, ăuñ takă guṇăzo zatoloñ = *cui homini tu propitius fueris, ci ego propitius ero*"; "jea sakramentă vorviñ = by which sacrament".

4. The Original of this Pronoun, as also of the Demonstrative Pronouns, does not exist; unless we take as Original "zea" *or* "jea" for the Relative and tea *or* ea for the Demonstrative Pronoun. Indeed zea and tea *or* ea are sometimes found as Pronouns after Postpositions in the same way as we have seen in the Nouns; *e.g.* "tea pasun" instead of "tače pasun"; "jea vorviñ" instead of "zače vorviñ". It seems to me, that "tea pasun, jea pasun" *etc.* are used only for things; whereas "zače pasun, tače pasun" *etc.* are used for persons and for things. Instead of the Original of the Pronoun, the Original of the derived Adjective may be used; *e.g.* "zače vorviñ = by which".

5. Instead of "zantu" the Original of the Adjective, "zače" followed by "bităr" may be used as has been said about the Personal Pronouns. We might say also "jea" or "zea bităr."

6. If a Preposition be joined to the Relative Pronoun, it is translated by the Original of the derived Adjective followed by the Konkani Postposition; *e.g.* "for which = zače pasun"; sometimes the Original of the primitive Adjective (zea) is used, instead of the Original of the derived Adjective. This 6th observation, of course, supposes that the Konkani Postposition governs the Original; if the Postposition governs the Dative or the Nominative, then the Dative or the Nominative of the Pronoun is used. This limitation is to be applied also to the 2nd observation, p. 72.

7. The observations 8 and 9 about Personal Pronouns, p. 73, *mutatis mutandis*, are to be applied also to the Relative Pronouns and will be explained in the Syntax.

Adjective derived from "zo".

From zo is derived "zăsso", in Latin *qualis*, and it requires a Correlative Pronoun; because its exact meaning is "in that way, which, or that which" and the like; *e.g.* "zăsso ailo, tăsso yeundi=let him come, as he came, or in the very state in which he came".

§ 4. Pronoun "apuṇ"

The Latin *ipse* as in this sentence: *ipse faciam*, or *ipse facias*, etc. is somewhat similar to this Pronoun. It may be used in all persons, and in both numbers. There is some other form of this Pronoun, but this is the most common. It is declined like a Noun of the 2nd Declension. In the oblique cases it is like the Latin *sui ipsius*, *sibi ipsi etc.*

	Singular:	*Plural:*
Nom.	apuṇ	apuṇ
Dat.	apṇāk	apṇānk
Accus.	apṇāk	apṇānk
Instrum.	apṇeñ, āpṇāpeñ	apṇeñ
1st Loc.	apṇāpent	apṇāpent
2nd Loc.	apṇāčer	apṇānčer
Orig. followed by Postpositions	aplea kăḍe *etc.*	apleañ kăḍe *etc.*

Observations:

1. The Genitive is formed as usually, namely "apṇāso" *Sing.*, "apṇānzo" *Plural.*

2. Not all cases of this Pronoun are used, at least, commonly.

3. It seems to be used only for persons.

4. The pure Original or stem does not seem to be much

used; instead of it the stem of the derived Adjective "aplo" is used: yet sometimes "apṇa" as Original of "apuṇ" occurs. *Examples:* "to aplea kăḍe uleitā=he speaks with himself"; "apleā pasun to vāur kartā=he works for himself", or "apṇa pasun to vāur kărtā".

Adjective derived from "apuṇ".

This is "aplo" corresponding to the English *his own*, to the Canarese "tanna". It is very frequent; and is declined like an Adjective of three terminations. It is also used as Adjective of 1st and 2nd Person "apliñ pātkañ sāngtañ = I say my sins", although more commonly both Pronoun and Adjective are used only for the 3rd Person.

§ 5. Interrogative Pronouns

1. Kōṇ = who? *quis?*

Nom.	kōṇ	kōṇ
Dat.	kōṇāk	kōṇānk
Accus.	kōṇāk	kōṇānk
Instrum.	kōṇeñ	kōṇeñ
1st Loc.	*not used*	*not used*
2nd Loc.	kōṇāčer	kōṇānčer
Orig. followed by Postpositions	kōṇa lāgiñ *etc.*	kōṇāñ lāgiñ *etc.*

Observations:

1. The Genitive is formed as usually; "kōṇāso" *Singular*, "kōṇāñso" *Plural.*

2. Instead of the 1st Locative, we may use the Original followed by "bităr".

3. This Pronoun is used sometimes in the Plural when we should use the Singular; *e.g.* "găra kōṇ natelle". [Perhaps in this example it is not Plural, but the Neuter Singular (natelleñ), as this kōṇ comprehends both men and women, consequently Neuter Gender]. (See p. 43, *n.* 5.)

4. All the above cases, chiefly in the Plural, are not common; on the contrary its Original "kōṇa" occurs sometimes, although not often.

2. Kiteñ = *quid*, what?

It is declined according to the Neuter of the 3rd Declension.

Stem "kitea".

Nom.	kiteñ	*Instrum.*	kiteān
Dat.	kiteāk	*Orig.* followed by Postpositions	kitea pasun *etc.*
Accus.	kiteñ		

3. Kōṇ to *etc.* = which?

To express the English "which", Lat. *uter* or *qualis*, "kōṇ", above given, may be used, or "kōṇ to" literally = *quis iste* or kōṇso (shortened from kōṇāzo) which seems to be different from "khainso = of what origin", derived from "khaiñ" = where"; it may be derived also from "khaiñ? = what?" and then it means *qualis*.

The Declension of "kōṇ" is as above; of "kōṇ to" the compound of the Declension of "kōṇ" and "to"; the others are declined as Adjectives of three terminations.

There are other Interrogative Pronouns; they may be found in the Dictionary, with their irregularity, if there be any.

§ 6. Indefinite Pronouns

1. I put first those which correspond to the Latin Adjective in *libet* or *vis*. These Adjectives may be formed

a) By doubling the first syllable of the original connected Pronoun; *e.g.* "yeyeklo = every one"; "yeyek = every", from "yeklo *and* yēk = one"; or

b) By adding "ei" or "i"; so from "kōṇ = *quis*", we get "kōṇei = *quilibet*", or "kōṇi". These Pronouns compounded with "ei" or "i" are declined only in the first part; "ei" remains always the same. So "kōṇākei = *cuilibet*" *etc.*

c) The word "khaiñ = something" gives also an indefinite meaning to the word to which it is added; *e.g.* "to khaiñ pātak kărinā = he does not commit any sin at all"; "tuveñ titleñ khaiñ poḷeunk nā = you did not see such a thing"; "khaiñ beaña = no fear at all"; "khaiñ yēk = any (*qualsiasi*)"; "khaiñ illeñ = any little thing".

There is no real negative Pronoun as in Latin *nemo* etc., but if required, the affirmative Pronouns are used with the negative particle joined to the Verb; so instead of making the Pronouns negative, they make the Verb negative; *e.g.* "*nemo venit* = kōṇ yeunk nā", literally = *aliquis venit non.*

2. Other Indefinite Pronouns are:

"Kōṇ = *aliquis*", declined, as above; "kōṇ nā ('nā' particle to be joined to the Verb, if expressed) = *nemo* (*aliquis non*)"; "khaiñ *or* kiteñ = *aliquid*, something"; "khaiñ nā = nothing (*aliquid non*)"; "yēklo = a man, *aliquis*, *unus*"; "kōṇyēklo = somebody"; "ariyēklo = every one"; "fālano *or* ămko = a certain man", in Latin *quidam.*

Adjectives connected with the Indefinite Pronouns.

These are: "kōṇyēk *or* ariyēk = *aliquis*", "yēk = a, an, some"; *e.g.* "yēke pauṭi = sometimes". From "khaiñ" are derived the two very common Adjectives "kăsso (*or* khăsso)" and "khaiñso" the first = "how", but it is used as an Adjective; again, from "kăsso" is derived another Adjective, "kăssālo = which, *or* how". The second, "khaiñso", corresponds to the Latin "*qualis* = of what quality or of what origin". They are used as Adjectives of three terminations. (*Cf.* p. 75.)

The Declension of the Adjectives, compounded with "yēk", is as the Declension of "yēk", viz. Singular Number "yēk" in all genders, oblique case *m.*, *n.* "yēka"; *fem.* "yēke", but "kōṇyēk" and "kōṇyēklo" decline also the first part, *i.e.* they add a to "kōṇ" in the oblique cases thus: "kōṇayēka, kōṇayēkleak", *etc.* The Pronouns in o are declined as Nouns of the 3rd Declension; the others have been given above. The Adjectives in o are regular.

§ 7. Reflexive Pronouns

They are like the English "myself" *etc.*

These Pronouns are formed by adding to the original Pronoun in each case the compound letter -ts or -tz. So, "āuñts = myself", "makāts = to myself", "tūñts = thyself", "tukāts = to thyself".

If this -ts is to be joined to a word ending in ạ or ụ, by the addition of -ts, this ạ or ụ appears, although perhaps the word before the addition of -ts, was written without ạ, ụ, as not necessary[1]. Nay, this ạ or ụ seems to become sometimes ā, or, at least, ạ and ụ, by the addition of -ts are heard more distinctly; *e.g.* "apuṇ" should be written "apuṇạ", although it has been written "apuṇ", in order to avoid unnecessary niceties. By adding -ts it becomes "apuṇạts" or "apuṇāts". This ạ or ā might perhaps be inserted before adding -ts, also in words ending in a pure consonant (see p. 8, *note*), if euphony requires it. This -ts is nothing else than the emphatic -ts I am going to speak of.

§ 8. Emphatic Pronouns

I call Emphatic Pronouns those which add a peculiar strength or emphasis to the original Pronoun. Thus *nos ipsi* would be emphatic of *nos*. This emphasis seems to be a Konkanism, because it is used very often, and gives sometimes to the affected word a meaning which can scarcely be rendered in English. So "to = he" by -ts becomes "tōts = he truly", or the same (Latin *idem*). This -ts is added in all cases ("āuñts, makāts" *etc.*) to the above given terminations of the Pronouns without making any other change. This -ts is added to the affected word: if this word is compounded of two words, *e.g.* of a Substantive and an Adjective, it may be added to either of them; *e.g.* "teāts uora *or* tea uorāts = at the same hour"; "Devā pasuntz = for God".

---

[1] ạ and ụ are not always written by me, but only or chiefly, if by not writing them some ambiguity might arise. (See Part I. ch. I.)

This -ts, emphatic, is added not only to Pronouns, but also to all other parts of speech, except perhaps Interjections.

The right use of this -ts is to be learnt only by great practice. In Italian it corresponds to *giusto*, *propriamente*, *esattamente* etc., "săg̦lo = whole", "săg̦lōts = *tutto quanto*". *Examples:* "Pedru văur kartătz = Peter works truly"; "tuje pasuntz o livrụ = this book is just for you"; "tuveñ makā āpoilo dekunạtz āuñ ailoñ = I came just because you called me"; "tăssentz = just so (Ital. *proprio così*), or in the same way"; "Ankuăr Mări borits = the Virgin Mary is *truly* good"; "uo āmbo tarnōts = this mango is truly green or perfectly green"; "atāñ = now"; "atănts = just now"; "kāiñ nā = nothing"; "kāints nā = nothing at all"; "Jezu = Jesus"; "O Jezuts = O my Jesus".

1. Another meaning which this "-ts" gives to the original word is "only"; *e. g.* "toḍcā = a little", "toḍents = only a little"; "gără bitărạts = only at home"; "gărjecĭ văstụ = necessary thing"; "gărjecits văstụ = only necessary thing"; "no = this"; "nots = only this". Even common people use this "-ts" in cases in which it seems to be out of place.

2. Now I should speak of Pronouns quite contrary to the Emphatic Pronouns, *i. e.* of the quasi Diminutive Pronouns; it will be better to speak about them later on.

§ 9. Correlative Pronouns

These are like the Latin *talis*...*qualis*, *tantus*...*quantus*, and also *sicut*...*ita* and the like, because these *sicut ita etc.* are translated by Pronouns or Adjectives. The following are the chief Correlative Pronouns.

kósso...tósso = *sicut*...*ita*, as...so (more exactly "kăsso, tăsso, zăsso)"

zósso...tósso = *qualis*...*talis*, from "zo" = *qui*, and "to = *is*"

kitlo...itlo = *quot*...*tot* (proximate)

kitlo...titlo (remote)

kedo...yedo = *quantus*...*tantus* (proximate)

kedo...tedo (remote)

zo...to = *qui*...*is*

zo kōụ...to = *quicumque*...*is*, or *quisquis*...*is*.

Observations:

1. "Kedo...yedo" and "kedo...tedo" are seldom used.

2. Some of these Pronouns may be used also absolutely; *e.g.* "kitle?=*quot?*" "kăsso?=how?", or "kăssăleñ?".

3. Very often only the 2nd Correlative is expressed, the 1st is left out and understood; *e.g.* "Jezu Kristān kelañ teñ kăr=(what) Jesus Christ has done, do it". Nay, this is the more common way of using "zo...to" *i.e.* to leave out "zo".

4. All except the last, are used as Adjectives of three terminations, usually in the Nominative; but sometimes also in the oblique cases.

5. If they are used absolutely and as Pronouns, they are declined as Nouns of the 3rd Declension.

6. Of "zo kōṇ" only the first part "zo" is declined as the Relative "zo"; it can be used in the Plural also. But in the oblique cases, it seems better to omit "kōṇ" and to use only the 1st part. Yet sometimes the Genitive is used; *e.g.* "Zo koṇāso Deu mōg kartā, takā šikšā ditā=*Quem Deus diligit corripit*". Moreover "zo kōṇ" always requires a Correlative Pronoun as in Latin *quisquis*.

7. Sometimes they are united with another Adjective; *e.g.* "kedo" with "vōḍ"="kedo vōḍ?=how great?" *fem.* "kedi vōḍ?" *neut.* "kedeñ vōḍ?"

8. "Kăsso=how" is declinable and follows the rules of concord (see Syntax); *e.g.* "kăsso assai?=how are you?" (speaking to a man), "kăssi assai?=how are you?" (speaking to a woman).

9. The difference between the proximate and remote Pronouns is the same, *servata proportione*, as the difference between o and to.

Exercises on Pronouns

Personal Pronouns.

nozo = is impossible
kărizăi = must do (= must be done)
šivai = except, (*praeter*)
kărni, -e = action (*f.*)
zătān kāṇe = take care

äskät = weak
viṇe = without
jiṇi, -e = life (*f.*)
jie = live
sämbäḷ = keep [(*m.*)
upadés, -a = commandment
päu = reach
aḍar = commit (*v.*)

Äuñ tukä, Deva, mojeñ kaliz ditäñ, tüñ makä tuji kurpä dī. Anton ani Mingel moje bäu: to uššr, o ältzi burgo; takä inäm, akä šikšä diä. Yeñ käm karunk mojän nozo: tuveñ yeñ käm kärizäi. Monis Deväči ratčna: taṇeñ Deväso mōg kärizäi: Deväče kurpe šiväi boreo kärneo aḍarunk tačeän nozo. Tī amči äuoi: tineñ moji zätän käṇeizäi. Säkäṭ monis äskät: tankäñ Deväči kumok zäi: Deväče kumke viṇe bori jiṇi jieunk tančeän[1] nozo. Moje lägiñ yëk buk assä; to tuje pasun assä. Mojä vorviñ Deväk akmän zälo. Moje višiänt lók kiteñ uleität (*speak*)? Moje särsi (*with*) käiñ nä. Tuje käḍe käiñ assägī? Moje lägiñ käints nä. Särgär päunk äuveñ kiteñ kärizäi? Sämbäḷ upadés.

Demonstrative Pronouns

kākult, -i = mercy (*f.*)
utar, -tra = word (*n.*)
räk = keep
voḍil, -a = superior (*m.*)
suät, -e = place (*f.*)
piso = foolish

Deu amso bäpui. Täso mōg, täči käkult ani täčeñ utar amkäñ sämbäḷtät. Deväči mäi amči mäi, tiso mōg ani tiči käkult amkäñ säddänts meḷtät. Särgär amčeñ gär, tačeñ bägil ani tači tčävi Sañ Pedru räktä. Amče voḍil Jezu Kristäče suäter assät. Amiñ tančiñ utrañ aikazäi. Äuoio apleañ burgeänso mōg kartäṭ, puṇ toḍe päuṭi tinso mōg foṭkiro, tinčiñ utrañ pisiñ.

Relative Pronouns

päḷ, -a = root (*n.*)
yetä = comes

(Zo) atañ vetä, to mozo bäu. (Zakä) tüñ boksitai äuñ takä boksitäñ. Rukäk, zäčiñ päḷañ lämb, väḍäso rūk (*banyan*

[1] This form in "an" is found in all or in nearly all Pronouns: it is declined; consequently here we have "tančeän" instead of "tačeäñ".

tree) moṇṭāt. To zo ataṅ yetā, mozo bāu. Devāče upadés sāmbāḷtolo Devāso mōg kartā (*or* Devāče upadés sāmbāḷtā, to Devāso mōg kartā; *or* Devāče upadés sāmbāḷtāt, te Devāso mōg kartāt).

Pronoun "apuṇ"

vaḍai = educate
birānt, -i = fear (*f.*)
kiteāk moḷeār = because

Kōṇ Pedručeṅ gār raktā? Āpuṇ raktā. Zo kōṇ apṇāk jiuvsi martā, to Devāk akmān kārtā. Yeṅ kāsseṅ zāleṅ? Apṇāpentz (*or* apseṅtz) zāleṅ. Mozo buk koṇā lāgiṅ assā? Tuzo buk apṇā lāgiṅ (*or* tuje lāgiṅ) assā. Āuoi bāpaino, tumiṅ tumčeaṅ (*or* āpleaṅ) burgeānk Devāče birāntint vaḍaiyā; kiteāk moḷeār, tanče pasun tumiṅ Devāk lek dīzāi. Yeṅ koṇāčeṅ gār? Yeṅ moja bāvāčea putāčeṅ gār. Kitea pasun to dusreānčea gārānt rautā? To āz aplea iśṭāk beṭṭā. Konso iśṭ? Pedru. To kāssālo iśṭ? To boro monis. Pedru kōṇ to? Gār bānḍaitālo. Uṇḍo khainso? Gauṅso uṇḍo. Gauṅso uṇḍo kāssālo? To boro rutztā.

Indefinite and Interrogative Pronouns

dótórn, -i = doctrine (*f.*)
zaṇā = knows
tank-tā = can
āilo = came

Devāče kurpen koṇāki boreo kārneo aḍarunk tank-tā. Tumče bitār kōṇ dótórn zaṇā? Kāseāloi burgo zaṇā. Yeyēklo apṇāso mōg kartā. Yeyēk monis apleaṅ vāstunči zātān kāṇeitā. Baglār kōṇ assā? Kōṇ nā. Tukā kiteṅ assā? Makā kāiṅ nā. Tukā ani kāiṅ assāgī? Ani khaiṅ (*or* kiteṅ) assā? Baglār yēklo (*or* yēk monis) assā; poḷe, kōṇ assā. Fālāno sākāl assā, takā āpoi. Ariyēklo pātkaṅ aḍartā. Ariyēkleāk Devāči kākult zāi.

Reflexive and Emphatic Pronouns

āstri, -e = woman (*f.*)
beṭai = offer

Kōṇ yetā mojā sangatā? Āuntz, saibānu. Koṇāk āpoitāt,

makāgī? Ui tukātz āpoitañ. Āpuṇatz yetāñ. Somi Jezu Kristatz sārgārtāun āilo amče pasun. Tī āstri tuji āuoigī? Titz (*proprio quella*). Yōkātz (*only one*) dis sāgleñ kām pāḍ kārtā. Tuji āuoi borigī? Borītz (*truly good*). Kōṇso bānk tukā zāi? Uōtz (*proprio questo or questo solo*). Moja Devā, āuñ tukā makātz sāglōtz (*tutto quanto*) beṭaitāñ.

Correlative Pronouns

Rupoi, -a = Rupee (*m.*)

Kitle rupoi makā title tukā assāt. Kedeñ vōḍ mojeñ gār, tedeñ vōḍ tujeñ gār. Zo kōṇ pātkānt mortā, to yemkaṇḍānt (*hell*) vetā. Zāssi tuji kuši sārgār zatā, tāssi sauñsārānt zāuñ (*be done*). Kāsso to tāssi tī

CHAPTER IV. VERBS

Art. I. Verbs in general and their Conjugation

§ 1. Preliminary Observations

1. We may reduce all Conjugations to one; because we may find a paradigm, according to which all the different kinds of Verbs are modified, except a few irregular Verbs.

2. The different Tenses and Moods will appear from the Conjugation itself. I was obliged to introduce or rather to give a name to Tenses or Moods, which do not exist in English and Latin.

3. Some Tenses have in some persons three terminations according to the gender. These Tenses are chiefly those which end in the 1st Person Singular in oñ. I say chiefly, because sometimes also Tenses ending in añ have three terminations for one person.

4. There is not a perfectly passive form; but, on the contrary, there are two forms, one for the affirmative, the other for the negative Verb; *e.g.* I say, I do not say.

5. The First Person Singular, if it ends in a vowel, is nasal. The Neuter is nasal in all persons ending in a vowel.

6. The forms ending in **-ea, -eat, -eo,** (or **-ya, -yat, -yo**) have the accent upon the last vowel (**a, o**), the forms ending **-ai, -auñ** (or **aoñ**) have the accent upon **a**, *i. e.* upon the penultimate vowel. If there be any exception, it will be indicated.

§ 2. Formation of Tenses

First find the root, namely that part of the Verb from which all Tenses may be derived by addition, and which, consequently, remains in all Tenses. This root usually is found pure in the 2nd Person Singular Imperative. The root is given in the Dictionary; to it add the following terminations[1]:

I. *Affirmative form*

A. Indicative Mood

Present.	*Sing.*	1) -tañ	2) -tai	3) -tā
„	*Plur.*	1) -taoñ[2]	2) -tāt	3) -tāt
Imperfecte.	*Sing.*	1) -taloñ (*m.*)	-taliñ (*f.*)	-taleñ (*n.*)
„	„	2) -taloi (*m.*)	-talī[3] (*f.*)	-taleiñ (*n.*)
„	„	3) -talo (*m.*)	-tali (*f.*)	-taleñ (*n.*)
„	*Plur.*	1) -taleaoñ	2) -taleat	
„	„	3) -tale (*m.*)	-taleo (*f.*)	-taliñ (*n.*)[4]

---

[1] These are the ordinary terminations; yet euphony may require some change; *e. g.* "rau" does not require "unk" in the supine as other Verbs, having already "u", but only "nk" *etc.*; "di" has "din" *not* "diin" in the Contingent Future.

[2] Or "tauñ", and so whenever this termination "aoñ" of the 1st Person Plural occurs, and this consequently must be understood, although not written expressly.

[3] This "ī" is pronounced nearly "ii"; we might write also "ii", and so whenever this termination "ī", 2nd Person Feminine, occurs.

[4] The three terminations of the 3rd Person are, according to the Adjectives, so "o" (*m.*), "i" (*f.*), "eñ" (*n.*) in the Singular, "e" (*m.*), "eo" (*f.*), "iñ" (*n.*) in the Plural.

Past. (in Latin: *amavi*, in Italian: *amai*)
" *Sing.* 1) -loñ (*m.*), -liñ (*f.*), -leñ (*n.*)
" " 2) -loi (*m.*), -lī (*f.*), -leiñ (*n.*)
" " 3) -lo (*m.*), -li (*f.*), -leñ (*n.*)
" *Plur.* 1) -leauñ, 2) -leat
" " 3) -le (*m.*), -leo (*f.*), -liñ (*n.*)
Perfect. ("I have loved" in English, *ho amato* in Ital.)
" *Sing.* 1) -lañ (*m.*), -liañ *or* -leañ (*f.*),[1] -lañ (*n.*)
" " 2) -lai (*m.*), -liai *or* -leai (*f.*), -laiñ (*n.*)
" " 3) -la (*m.*), -lia *or* -lea (*f.*), -lañ (*n.*)
" *Plur.* 1) -leauñ *or* -leaoñ 2) -leat
3) -leat (*m. f.*), -leant (*n.*)

Past Perfect. (Latin *amaveram*). Usually this Tense is made by doubling the l of the Past; *e.g.* "zalo, zallo; kelo, kello"; and then it is conjugated just as the Past. If this cannot be done on account of the nature of the consonants, o is inserted between the two l; *e.g.* "tsăl = walk"; *Past* "tsallo"; *Past Perfect* "tsal-o-lo"; others, chiefly Brahmins, in this case instead of inserting o between the two l, add to the root "ụlloñ" *or* "ạlloñ" *etc.*, *e.g.* "nid-ụlloñ = I had slept". The Conjugation of "ụlloñ" in the different persons is the same as the Conjugation of "-loloñ"; so we get

Sing. 1) -loloñ, -leliñ, -leleñ[2] *or* -ụlloñ, -ụlliñ, -ụlleñ
" 2) -loloi, -lelī, -leleiñ *or* -ụlloi, -ụllī, -ụlleiñ
" 3) -lolo, -leli, -leleñ *or* -ụllo *etc.*
Plur. 1) -leleaoñ, 2) -leleat, 3) -lele, -leleo, -leliñ *or* -ụlleauñ *etc.*

1st Fut. Absol. Sing. 1) -toloñ, -teliñ, -teleñ[2]
" " 2) -toloi, -telī, -teleiñ
" " 3) -tolo, -teli, -teleñ
" *Plur.* 1) -teleaoñ, 2) -teleăt, 3) tele, -teleo, -teliñ.

---

1) Both "liañ" and "leañ" etc. may be used: in Kanarese it should be written "lyañ", which may be rendered either by "leañ" or "liañ".

2) The first "o" is changed into "e" in the Feminine and Neuter Singular, and in the Plural for all three Genders.

2nd Fut. Seldom used, yet if required, is thus:

Sing. 1) -an[1] (sometimes "-in"), 2) -či (*or* -ši), 3) -it (*or* "-at" if the 1st Person is "-an").

Plur. 1) -uñ, 2) -čat (*or* -šat), 3) -tit.

Sometimes the Future Contingent followed by "zaleär", may be used instead of this form; *e.g.* "märit zaleär = *si percusserit*"; sometimes, though very seldom, the following form is used, namely the Past Participle of the Verb followed by the 1st Future of the Verb "assä = is", just as in Italian in some Verbs; *e.g. sarò andato* = gelo astoloñ.

Contingent Future, very frequently used, has the same form as the 2nd Future in an.

B. Imperative Mood

Sing. 1) -uñ, *or* -ungi (*rare*)
" 2) *the pure root*
" 3) -undi, *or* -uñ
Plur. 1) -yañ, (-iañ") *or* -uñ
" 2) -a *or* -ya (-ia")
" 3) -undit, *or* -uñ

C. Optative Mood

Present. "-uñ" in all persons; *e.g.* "Deu boreñ käruñ = *Deus faciat bonum*". This very form is sometimes used as a pure Subjunctive.

Imperfect. The 1st Conditional (see below) with "puro", or with "boreñ assälleñ" or sometimes only the Conditional is used; *e.g.* "to aileär puro = *utinam is veniret*" *or* "to aileär! = *si veniret!*"

Past. (Corresponding to the Latin *utinam hoc fecissem!*). The Past Conditional is used; *e.g.* "öh to ailo asleär! = *utinam venisset!*"[2] "Puro" *or* "boreñ assäleñ" may be added.

---

[1] Some castes pronounce "-än" in the 1st Person, "-ät" in the 3rd Person.

[2] "Ailo" is declined as an Adjective of 3 terminations, "asleär" is indeclinable.

D. Subjunctive Mood

Present. "-uñ" in all persons. It is very seldom used as a pure Subjunctive; instead of it the Indicative Present is used, or the Gerund, or some other Tense.

Imperfect. Corresponding to the Latin *ut amarem* (*ut* expressing *aim*, Ital. *affinchè*).

Sing. 1) -soñ (*m.*), -siñ (*f.*), -señ (*n.*)
3) -so (*m.*), -si (*f.*), -señ (*n.*)
Plur. 3) -se (*m.*), -seo" (*f.*), -siñ (*n.*)

The 2nd Person Singular and 1st and 2nd Plural are not used. An euphonical a or i is usually inserted between the root and these terminations.

Past and Perfect. I do not remember to have ever heard it. It is expressed by the Indicative or by the Past Participle *etc.*; yet for this Perfect sometimes the Future Contingent may be used, followed by the Conditional Tense; *e.g.* "sikat zaleār = *si didiccrit*". (See the Appendix to the Grammar.)

First or Present Conditional, "-leār" in all persons.

Second or Past Conditional is formed by the Past Participle in lo, followed by the First Conditional of "assā" or of "zatā".

First Conditionatum, (as the 2nd part in the sentence "if you studied, *you would learn*") the form of the 2nd Future in -an, -īt *etc.* is used.

Second or Past Conditionatum, (as the 2nd part in the sentence "if you had studied, *you would have learnt*",) is formed by the Present Participle in -tolo (or, shortened, in -to) and the *Past* of "assā".

Instead of the given form of the Present Conditional sometimes some other form is used; *e.g.* instead of "sikleār = if I learnt", the 2nd Person Plural Imperative with the Conditional of "assā" is used: "sika zaleār", and instead of the Past Conditional as above given, the termination "-loleār" is used, *etc.* but the above given forms are the most common.

E. Potential Mood

It expresses possibility, probability *etc.*

Present. There are three forms: 1) "-iye", *or* "-iyet", *or*

2) "tank-tā = is possibile" added to the Supine, *or* 3) "puro" added to the Supine.

Past. Add to "-iye" *or* "-iyet"[1] the Past of "assā" *i.e.* "assolloñ", *or* we may also add the Past of "tanktā" to the Supine.

Future. 1) the Present is used also for the Future, *or* 2) the same terminations as in the 2nd Future in "an", *or* 3) add to the Present (-iyet) the Future of "zatā" *or* of "assā", *or* 4) add the Future of "tanktā" to the Supine.

F. Necessary Mood

It expresses the necessity of doing something.

To express necessity zāi is used: zāi alone means "is necessary"; *e.g.* "I am in need of the grace of God = makā devāči kurpā zāi".

To show a particular necessity, this zāi is added to the root of the required Verb after having inserted sometimes, on account of euphony, an a or i between the root and zāi. This is for the Present and Future. For the Past it seems that the Past of the Potential Mood, which should have also the meaning of necessity, is used by some. Yet I doubt about it. I would rather use the Future Gerund Passive, given above, called in Latin *Gerundivus* with the Past of "assā"; *e.g.* "karčeñ assalleñ = *faciendum erat* or *fuit*". See below the Periphrastic Conjugation. This periphrastic form, to express necessity, can be used also in the Present and Future. Or we may express the Past by adding the Past of "zatā" or of "assā" to the Present; *e.g.* "kārizāi assalleñ"; the Future may be expressed also by adding the Future or "zatā" or of "assā" to the Present of this Mood.

G. Indefinite or Infinitive Mood

About this Mood it is difficult to speak, if we keep the denominations of the Latin or English Grammar, as there is a great difference between the English and Konkani Indefinite; nevertheless, for the present, I think we may say thus:

[1] We might say also "-iyeto, -ti, -teñ".

Absolute Indefinite. I call by this name the Infinitive which we would express in Latin saying: "*to legere* = *il leggere*" as in the sentence *ridere* (or *risus*) *abundat in ore stultorum.* These are the terminations: -so (*m.*), -či (*f.*), -čeñ (*n.*), or -unso, -unči, -unčeñ[1].

The form in -unso is used chiefly for Causati e Verbs and for those which, although not Causative, have a similar form in ai or ei; *e.g.* "ulei = speak"; "uleunčeñ = to speak," or end in a vowel.

Supine. I call Supine the Infinitive preceded by the Italian *per* (to show aim) or the Latin *ad amandum, ut amarem*, or the true Supine, (*eo ambulatum*), though sometimes it has the same meaning as the Absolute Indefinite. The termination of the Supine is -unk, and is not declined. Sometimes instead of the Supine in "-unk", the Dative of the Absolute Infinitive is used, *e.g.* "ulounčeāk āilo = he came to speak".

All these are Present Infinitives: there is no Past Indefinite Mood, nor a pure and simple Future Infinitive Mood, though this can be expressed by some periphrasis, chiefly by resolving the Infinitive into a Finite Mood by "-moṇ = that", as in Latin; *e.g. spero eum venturum esse* may be resolved into *spero quod ipse veniet.*

H. Participles

Present. (*-ns* in Latin). 1) "-tolo (*m.*), -teli (*f.*), -teleñ (*n.*)"; 2) "-ta to, -ta ti, -ta teñ". This is not a true Participle, but the 2nd part of a correlative sentence in which the Relative Pronoun is simply omitted, without changing the construction: hence that -ta of "-ta to" is the termination of the 3rd Person Singular Present Indicative; hence in the Plural 2nd and 3rd Person it becomes "-tat te", not "-ta te". See below in the Syntax a more distinct explanation; 3) "-so, -či, -čeñ", the same as the Infinitive; or "-unso, -unči, -unčeñ," if the Infinitive

[1] More exactly "-tso, -tči, -tčeñ" and "-untso, -untči, -untčeñ" in order not to confound this termination with "-so" *quasi* Diminutive.

has this termination; 4) "-ta" used chiefly in composition with "astanañ = being", to form the Gerund.

Past. 1) "-lo, -li, -leñ"; 2) "-un", if the root ends in u or uñ, or if euphony requires, only n is added.

Future. "-so, -či, -čeñ" (or "-unso, -či, -čeñ", for the Verbs which have the Infinitive in "unso").

I. Gerunds

Present. -tanañ *or* -tastanañ.

Imperfect. -un (or n, see above).

Past. 1) -täts.

„ 2) -un (or n, see above).

Future (passive) -so, -či, -čeñ in Latin *amandus, -a, -um* (or -unso as before).

II. Negative form

There are many ways of expressing a Verb in the negative form. I give that which is more common here in Mangalore and the neighbourhood.

A. Indicative Mood

Present. It is formed by adding to the root [after having inserted sometimes (see below) a or i] the negative particle na, giving to it the termination of the affirmative form of the Present.[1] Thus we get:

Sing. 1) -näñ, 2) -nai, 3) -nä

Plur. 1) -näoñ, 2) -nänt, 3) -nänt (instead of -nät).

Imperfect. Insert na between the root (with the euphonical a or i, if required) and the terminations of the affirmative form, with some modifications which will appear from the paradigm of the Imperfect to be given now.

Sing. 1) -natloñ, -natliñ, -natleñ; *or* -natuloñ, -nataliñ, -nataleñ.

---

[1] For the sake of brevity I call *negative root*, the root of the affirmative form followed by "na" with the insertion, often, of the euphonical "a" or "i".

Sing. 2) -natloi, -natlī, -natleiñ, *or* -natuloi, -natạlī, -natạleiñ; 3) -natlo, -natli, -natleñ, *or* -natulo, -natạli, -natạleñ;

Plur. 1) -natleauñ, *or* -natuleauñ (*m.*), -natạleauñ (*f. n.*);
2) -natleāt, *or* -natuleāt (*m.*), -natạleāt (*f. n.*);
3) -natle, -natleo, -natliñ, *or* -natule (*m*), -natạleo (*f.*), -natạliñ (*n.*)

Past and Perfect. Add na to the Supine giving to it the terminations of the affirmative form (but Plural 2nd and 3rd Person "-nānt").

Past Perfect. Add "-natullo", *or* "-natlo" *or*, better, "-natụllo" (conjugated as the Imperfect) to the Supine.

Contingent Future. Add the Contingent Future affirmative of "zatā" to the negative root. Sometimes the negative form of the Absolute Future is used also for the Contigent Future negative.

1st and 2nd Future. Add to the root -so, -či, -čeñ (according to the gender), and after it the negative "-na" giving to it the terminations of the Present. If a Verb has the root ending in a vowel, then in the Negative Future it takes "-uñsonā", "-unčinā", "-unčenā", instead of "-sona, -čina, -čena"; but if this Future means a resolution of the will, such a Verb takes "-sonā" *etc.* as the others; *e.g.* "pīe = drink", "pieunsonāñ = I shall not drink", "piesonāñ = I will not drink", (although I were compelled to drink); "ye = come", "yeuñsonāñ = I shall not come"; "yesonāñ = I will not come".

B. Imperative Mood

Sing. 1st Person may be expressed by the negative form of the Potential or Necessary Mood (see below), or add "zauñ" to the negative root.

2nd Person, add "naka" to the root.

3rd Person, as the 1st Person, or add to Negative root "zāundi" *or* "zāuñ" (Imperative of "zatā"), inserting, if required, a or i.

Plur. 1st, As the 1st Person Singular.
„ 2nd, Add "nakãt" to the root.
„ 3rd, As the 1st Person, or add to the negative root the Imperative of "zatã" (zãundit *or* zãuñ).

C. Optative Mood

Present. Not commonly used. If really required, I would add "zãuñ" to the negative root in all persons, *i. e.* as one of the forms of the Negative Imperative. Also the Imperfect Optative might be used for the Present.

Imperfect. The same as the 1st Conditional Negative (see below) followed by "puro" *or* "boreñ assãlleñ".

Past. The same as the Past Conditional Negative (see below), followed by "boreñ assãlleñ", *or* "puro", or only the Past Conditional Negative.

D. Subjunctive Mood

Present seems not to be used; if it occurs in English, some other Tense is used in Konkani. Perhaps "zãun" added to the negative root may be used.

Imperfect is formed by adding the terminations of the affirmative form to the negative root.

1st Conditional. Add the 1st Conditional of "zatã" to the negative root.

2nd Conditional. Add to the Present Participle Negative the Conditional of "zatã" (zaleãr).

1st Conditionatum, as the 1st Future Negative or as the Contingent Future Negative.

2nd Conditionatum, add to the root "tonã" (in one word), and, if you like, besides "tonã" add the Past of "assã"

Perfect. Sometimes it may be expressed by the negative root, followed by "zaleãr"; yet this is rather a particular case than a Perfect, corresponding generally to the Latin Subjunctive Perfect: hence, if required, some other tense must be used. (See Appendix.)

E. Potential Mood[1)]

Pres. There are three forms: 1) "naye" (with the euphonical a or i); 2) "tankanā" added to the Supine affirmative; 3) "nozo" added to the Supine.

Future. 1) Add to the negative root the Potential Future of "zatā (zāin)," or 2) add "nozo zateleñ" to the Supine, or 3) add the Future of "tankanā" to the Supine.

Past. 1) Add the Past of "assā" to the first form of the Present Potential Mood, or 2) use the Past "nozo" (nozo zaleñ) added to the Supine, or 3) add the Past of "tankanā" to the Supine.

F. Necessary Mood

This Mood is not exactly Necessary Mood, in the negative form, but the contrary or quite opposite to the Necessary, *i. e.* Impossible; hence it should be called Impossible Mood, yet in order not to multiply Moods, I retain the same word "Necessary."

Pres. "Nozo" added to the Supine, or sometimes to the pure root. For the other tenses, I think, we might use the "gerundivus" with the required tense of "assā"; or also we may add the required Tense (Past or Future) of "assā" or of "zatā" to the Present Negative of this Mood.

G. Indefinite Mood

Absolute Indefinite is not commonly used; if required, the Negative Present Conditional might be used; sometimes the Negative form of the Supine (see hereafter) may be also used. Very often a periphrasis may be used; *e.g.* "not to sleep = nidanāstanañ rāunčeñ", *lit.* "to remain without sleeping."

Supine. 1) Add na to the Affirmative Supine, or 2) add "zāunk" to the negative root.

---

1) The negative form of the Potential coincides mostly with the negative form of the Necessary Mood, as will appear from the paradigm.

H. Participles

Pres. -natlo, -natli, -natleñ, *or* -natulo, -natạli, -natạleñ.
Past. -natullo, -natạlli, -natạlleñ.
Fut. -sonā, -činā, -čeññā, *or* -uñsonā *etc.* (see above).

I. Gerunds

Present "nastanañ (after having inserted the euphonical a or i, if required).

Imperfect. There is no proper form; if required, resolve it into the Past Participle or some other form, chiefly into the Negative Present Gerund in "nastanañ".

Past. Add "zatāts (Affirmative Past Gerund of "zatā") to the negative root.

Future. -sonā, -činā, -čenā, *or* -uñso *etc.* as above, declined as the Affirmative Gerund: ("nā" indeclinable).

1) Besides the given Tenses or forms of Tenses there are some other, not so important Tenses or forms: they may be indicated, some at least, in the examples of the Conjugation or in the following observations.

2) Under certain Tenses or Moods I have put some forms, which seem not to belong properly to that Tense or Mood; *e. g.* "tanktā" preceded by the Supine is called Potential. I did so, in order not to multiply Moods and Tenses without an urgent necessity.

§ 3. Conjugation of the Auxiliary Verbs "zatā" and "assā"

As in the Conjugation, the two Verbs "zatā" and "assā" are required, I put first these two Verbs, though they are irregular: "zatañ = I become"; "assañ = I am".

"Z a t ā"

I. Affirmative form

A. Indicative Mood

Present. Sing. 1) zatañ, 2) zatai, 3) zatā;
Plur. 1) zatauñ, 2) zatāt, 3) zatāt.
Imperf. Sing. 1) zataloñ, zataliñ, zataleñ;
„ 2) zataloi, zatalī, zataleiñ;
„ 3) zatalo, zatali, zataleñ.

Plur. 1) zataleaoñ, 2) zataleãt,
„ 3) zatale, zataleo, zataliñ.
Past. Sing. 1) zaloñ, zaliñ, zaleñ;
„ 2) zaloi, zalī, zaleiñ:
„ 3) zalo, zali, zaleñ.
Plur. 1) zaleaoñ, 2) zaleãt, 3) zale, zaleo, zaliñ.
Perfect. Sing. 1) zalañ, zaleañ, zalañ;
„ 2) zalai, zaleai, zalaiñ;
„ 3) zala, zalea, zalañ.
Plur. 1) zaleaoñ, 2) zaleãt,
3) zaleãt (*m. f.*), zaleãnt (*n.*)
Past. Perfect. zalloñ (*conjugated as* "zaloñ").
1st Fut. Absol. Sing. 1) zatoloñ, zateliñ, zateleñ;
2) zatoloi, zatelī, zateleiñ;
3) zatolo, zateli, zateleñ.
Plur. 1) zateleaoñ, 2) zateleãt,
3) zatele, zateleo, zateliñ.
2nd Future and Conting. Future:
Sing. 1) zãin, 2) zãči, 3) zãit;
Plur. 1) zauñ, 2) zaããt, 3) zatit.
Another 2nd Absol. Future is this: zato, (-i, -eñ) assoloñ (-i, -eñ) *etc. as the Past of* "assã", *and* "zato" *as an Adjective of three terminations.*

B. Imperative Mood

Sing. 1) zauñ,
„ 2) zã,
„ 3) zauñ *or* zaundi;
Plur. 1) zauñ,
„ 2) zayã,
„ 3) zauñ *or* zaundit.

C. Optative Mood.

Pres. zauñ! *or* zata zauñ, *in all persons.*
Imperf. zaleãr puro!
Past. zalo zaleãr! *or* zalo zaleãr puro!

D. Subjunctive Mood

Pres. zauñ, *or* zata zauñ, *in all persons.*

Imperf. Sing. 1) zaissoñ, zaissiñ, zaisseñ; 3) zaisso, zaissi, zaisseñ.

Plur. 3) zaisse, zaisseo, zaissiñ.

1st Conditional. zaleär.

2nd „ zalo asleär, or zalo zaleär, zali asleär *etc.*

1st Conditionatum. Sing. 1) zain, 2) zači, 3) zait.

Plur. 1) zauñ, 2) začat, 3) zatit.

2nd „ *Sing.* 1) zatoñ, zatiñ, zateñ;

2) zatoi, zatī, zateiñ;

3) zato, zati, zateñ.

Plur. 1) zateaoñ, 2) zateät,

3) zate, zateo, zatiñ.

E. Potential Mood

Pres. 1) zaviet, *or* 2) zaunk puro (=*it may be*), *or* 3) zaunk tanktä.

Past. 1) zaunk puro assąleñ, *or* 2) zaunk tank assąli, *or* 3) zaviet assąleñ.

Future. 1) zaviet, *or* 2) zain, zači *etc.* (*as the Cont. Fut.*) *or* 3) zaviet asteleñ, *or* 4) zaunk tank asteli.

F. Necessary Mood

Pres. zäizäi (compound of "za" root of "zatä" the euphonic "i" and "zäi = it is necessary").

Past. zäizäi zaleñ.

Future. zäizäi zateleñ.

G. Infinitive Mood

Absolute. zäiso, zäisi, zäiseñ *or better*, zauñso, zaunči, zaunčeñ.

Supine. zaunk.

H. Participles

Pres. | *Future.* } zatolo, zateli, zateleñ, *or* zauñso, zaunči, zaunčeñ.

Imperf. zatalo, zatali, zataleñ.

Past. zalo, zali, zaleñ.
„ *Perfect (or also emphatic).* zallo, zalli, zalleñ.

I. Gerunds

Pres. zatanañ. *Imperf.* zaun. *Past.* zatüts.

II. Negative form

A. Indicative Mood

Present. Sing. 1) zainañ, 2) zainai, 3) zainā.
„ *Plur.* 1) zainaoñ, 2) zainānt, 3) zainānt.
Imperf. zainatuloñ *etc., as the Imperfect Negative of* "assā".
Past & Perfect. zaunknāñ, zaunknai *etc.* (*as the Present*).
Past Perfect. zaunknatulloñ *etc.* (*as the Imperfect.*)
1st & 2nd Future Sing. 1) zasonāñ, začināñ, začeññāñ;
2) zasonāi, začināi, začeññāi;
3) zasonā, začinā, začeññā.
Plur. 1) začenāuñ, začeonāuñ, začiññāuñ;
„ 2) začenānt, začeonānt, začiññānt;
„ 3) „ „ „
or zauñsonāñ, zaunčināñ zaunčenāñ, *etc. as explained above.*

Another 2nd Future is this: "zatonā (zatinā, zatenā) assoloñ" *etc. as the Past of* "assā", *added to* "zato" *declinable.*

Fut. Cont. 1) zainā zaiu; 2) zainā zači, *etc.* only the 2nd part is conjugated, *h. e.* as the Affirm. Cont. Future.

B. Imperative Mood

Sing. zauññakā, *Plur.* zauññakāt, *or* zainā zauñ, *in all persons,* (*or* zainā zaundi, zainā zaundit, *in the 3rd person*).

C. Optative Mood

Pres. zainā zauñ, *in all persons.*
Imperf. nāzaleār puro!
Past. zaināṭullo zaleār! zainatulli zaleār, *etc.*

D. Subjunctive Mood

Pres. zaunnā, *or* zainā zaunā.
Imperf. zaironāñ, zaisināñ, zaisenāñ *etc.* (*as the Affirm. Imperfect with the addition of* "na").
1st Conditional. nāzaleār.
2nd " zainātullo zaleār.
1st Conditionatum. zaunso nā (*as the Future*).
2nd " *Sing.* 1) zatonāñ, zatināñ, zatenāñ,
2) zatonai, zatinai, zatenai *etc.*
(*as the Affirm. 2nd Condit. with the addition of* "na").

E. Potential Mood

Pres. 1) "nozo" (the same as the Necessary Negative), *or*
2) the Present Indicative Negative "zainā", *or*
3) zaunaye, *or* 4) zaunk tankanā, *or* 5) zaunk nozo.
Past. 1) zaunaye assạleñ, 2) zaunk nozo assạleñ,
3) zaunk tank natạli.
Future. 1) as the Conting. Fut. *or* 2) zaunaye zateleñ, *or*
3) zaunk tank aščinā.

F. Necessary Mood

Pres. nozo, *or* zaunk nozo.
Past. nozo zaleñ, *or* zaunk nozo zaleñ.
Future. nozo zateleñ, *or* zaunk nozo zateleñ.

G. Infinitive Mood

Absolute. zaunsonā, zaunčinā *etc.*
Supine. zaunknā.

H. Participles

Pres., *Past*, *Future*: zaunknatulo *or* zaunso nā, zaunknatạli *etc.*

I. Gerunds

Pres. zainastanāñ.
Past. nā zatāts[1].

---

[1] There are three other Auxiliary Verbs, viz. "zāi, nozo, tanktā". "Zāi" and "nozo" have no proper Conjugation; the required Tense of "assā" or "zatā" is added to them (see § 7 of the 2nd Art); "tanktā" is regular, except that it is often resolved chiefly in the Past and Future into "tank assā etc.=power is etc."

"Assā"[1]

I. *Affirmative form*

A. Indicative Mood

Present. Sing. 1) assañ, 2) assai, 3) assā;
Plur. 1) assauñ, 2) assāt, 3) assāt.

Imperfect[2] *Sing.* 1) astaloñ, astaliñ, astaleñ;
„ 2) astaloi, astalī, astaleiñ;
„ 3) astalo, astali, astaleñ.
Plur. 1) astaleauñ, 2) astaleāt,
3) astale, astaleo, astaliñ.

Past Sing. 1) assoloñ[3], assạliñ, assạleñ;
„ 2) assoloi, assạlī, assạleiñ;
„ 3) assolo, assạli, assạleñ.
Plur. 1) assạleauñ, 2) assạleāt,
3) assạle, assạleo, assạliñ.

Perfect: not used.

Past Perfect. asloloñ *or* assolloñ, assolliñ, assạlleñ *etc. as the Past.*

1st Absol. Future Sing. 1) astoloñ, asteliñ, asteleñ;
„ 2) astoloi, astelī, asteleiñ;
„ 3) astolo, asteli, asteleñ.
Plur. 1) asteleaoñ, 2) asteleāt,
„ 3) astele, asteleo, asteliñ.

2nd Absol. Future and Conting. Future
Sing. 1) assan, 2) aščí, 3) assat;
Plur. 1) assuñ, 2) aščāt, 3) astit.

---

[1] According to the Kanarese we should write "asa"; in order to prevent a wrong pronunciation of the s, I prefer to write "assa".

[2] This Tense is not often used; instead of it, the Past is used.

[3] *or* assạle. The pronunciation of the 2nd vowel (also in the other persons) is not settled: we might perhaps write "ă *or* e" instead of "ạ". The most simple way would be to write the 2nd vowel of Perfect Past and Simple Past, always "ạ".

Another 2nd Future is this:

Sing. 1) asto (-i, -eñ), assoloñ (-iñ, -eñ),
2) „ „ assoloi (-I, -eiñ),
3) „ „ assolo (-i, -eñ);
Plur. 1) aste (-eo, -iñ) assąle (-eo, -iñ),
2) „ „ assąleāt,
3) „ „ assąle (-eo, -iñ).

B. Imperative Mood

Sing. 1) assuñ, 2) ās, 3) assundi;
Plur. 1) assuñ, 2) assa (*not often used*),
3) assundit,
or astañ zauñ, *in all persons.*

C. Optative Mood

Pres. assuñ, *or* astañ zauñ.
Imperf. asleār puro.
Past. assolo (assąli, assąleñ) zaleār puro.

D. Subjunctive Mood

Pres. assuñ, *or* astañ zauñ *in all persons.*
Imperf. *Sing.* 1) assassoñ assassiñ, assasseñ,
3) assasso, assassi, assasseñ,
Plur. 3) assasse, assasseo, assassiñ.
1st Conditional. asleār.
2nd „ assolo, (assąli, assąleñ) zaleār.
1st Conditionatum. assan *etc.* (*as the 2nd Future*).
2nd „ *Sing.* 1) astoñ, astiñ, asteñ,
2) astoi, asti, asteiñ, *etc.* (*as* zatoñ).

E. Potential Mood

Pres. 1) assayet, *or* asuyet 2) assunk tanktā,
3) assunk puro.
Past. 1) assunk tank assąli, 2) assunk puro assąleñ.
Fut. 1) asayet, 2) assan (*as the Cont. Fut.*)
3) assayet asteleñ, 4) assunk tank asteli.

F. Necessary Mood

Pres. assazäi.
Past. assazäi asşlleñ.
Fut. assazäi, *or* assazäi asteleñ.

G. Infinitive Mood

Absolute Infinitive. asso, aš-či, aš-čeñ.
Supine. assunk.

H. Participles

Pres. 1) astolo, asteli, asteleñ, 2) astuñ.
Imperf. astalo, astali, astaleñ.
Past. assolo, assşli, assşleñ.
Past Perfect. assollo, assşlli, assşlleñ.
Fut. as-so aš-či, aš-čen, *or* astolo, asteli, asteleñ.

I. Gerunds

Pres. astanañ *or* astañ.
Imperf. assun.
Past. astäts.

II. Negative form

A. Indicative Mood

Present. There are two forms, *i. e.* if it means 1) to be in a place, or 2) simple existence, the form is thus:

Sing. 1) näñ, 2) näi, 3) nä.
Plur. 1) näuñ, 2) nänt, 3) nänt.

If it means quality, *e.g.* "Peter is not good", the form is thus:

Sing. & Plur. näiñ" *or* niñ.

Imperf. Sing. 1) natuloñ, natşliñ, natşleñ, *or* natloñ, natliñ, natleñ;
„ 2) natuloi, natşli, natşleiñ, *or* natloi, natlī, natleiñ;
„ 3) natulo, natşli, natşleñ, *or* natlo, natli, natleñ.

Plur. 1) natąleaoñ, 2) natąleät, 3) natąle, natąleo, natąliñ; *or* 1) natleaoñ, 2) natleät, 3) natle, natleo, natliñ.

Past & Perfect. asunknäñ *or* assoñnäñ, assunknai *etc.* (*as the Present*).

Past Perfect. assunknatụlloñ *etc.* (*as the Imperfect*).

1st Absol. Fut. Sing. 1) assoñnäñ (*m.*), aščiñnäñ (*f.*), ašče ñnäñ (*n.*)[1]

„ 2) assonai (*m.*), aščinai (*f.*), aščeñnai (*n.*)

„ 3) assonäñ (*m.*), aščinäñ (*f.*), aščeñnäñ (*n.*),

Plur. 1) aščenäoñ, (*m.*), aščeonäoñ, (*f.*), aščiñnäoñ (*n.*)

„ 2) aščenänt (*m.*), aščeonänt (*f.*), aščiñnänt (*n.*)

„ 3) aščenänt (*m.*), aščeonänt (*f.*), aščiñnänt (*n.*)[2].

2nd Fut. astonäñ (astinäñ, astenäñ) assoloñ *etc.* as the 2nd Future Affirmative, except that you add -nañ to the first part.

Conting. Future. assanäñ zäin, assanäñ zäči *etc.* (*as the Conting. Future of* "zatä").

B. Imperative Mood

Sing. 1) assanäñ zäuñ, 2) assanakä, 3) assanäñ zäundi.

Plur. 1) assanäñ zäuñ, 2) assanakät, 3) assanäñ zäundit, *or* aščeñ nä, *in all persons;*

or *Sing.* 1) assuñ nakä,

„ 2) assa nakä,

„ 3) assuñ nakä, *or* assundi nakä.

Plur. 1) assuñ nakä,

„ 2) assa nakät,

„ 3) assuñ nakä, *or* assundit nakä.

---

[1] This "š" followed by "č" is pronounced like a Latin hard *s* as in *assis;* I use "š", because this letter "š" renders this hard "s" better than s, or any other letter. (See p. 4.)

[2] This form is used sometimes also as 2nd Future.

C. Optative Mood

Pres. assanāñ zāuñ, *in all persons and numbers.*
Imperf. nāñ asleār *or* assanāñ zaleār.
Past. natullo (-i, -eñ) zaleār.

D. Subjunctive Mood

Pres. assanāñ zāuñ, *or* "assuñ nāñ" *in all persons.*
Imperfect. Sing. 1) assanāsoñ, assanāsiñ, assanāseñ;
„ 3) assanāso, assanāsi, assanāseñ.
Plur. 3) assanāse, assanāseo, assanāsiñ.
1st Conditional. nāñ asleār, *or* assanāñ asleār.
2nd „ natullo (-i, -eñ) zaleār.
1st Conditionatum. Sing. 1) assoññāñ, aščiññāñ, ašceññāñ *etc.* (*as the Future*).
2nd „ *Sing.* 1) astoññāñ, astiññāñ, asteññāñ.
„ 2) astonai, astinai, asteñnai,
„ 3) astonāñ, astināñ, asteññāñ.
Plur. 1) astenāoñ, asteonāoñ, astiññāoñ,
„ 2) astenānt, asteonānt, astiññānt.
„ 3) astenānt, asteonānt, astiññānt.

E. Potential Mood

Pres. 1) asunaye, 2) assunk tankanāñ, 3) assunk nozo.
Past. 1) assunaye assąleñ,
„ 2) assunk nozo zaleñ,
„ 3) assunk tank natąli.
Fut. 1) assanāñ zāin, assanāñ zači *etc.* (*see Cont. Future* of "zatā"), *or*
2) assunk nozo zateleñ, *or* 3) assunk tank aščināñ.

F. Necessary Mood

Pres. nozo, *or* assunk nozo.
Past. nozo assąleñ, *or* assunk nozo assąleñ.
Fut. nozo zateleñ, *or* assunk nozo zateleñ.

G. Infinitive Mood

Absolute. assunknāñ, *or* assonāñ, aščināñ, aščeññāñ.
Supine. assunknāñ.

H. Participles

Pres. natlo *or* natulo, natali, nataleñ.
Past. natlo *or* natullo, natalli, natalleñ.
Fut. assonāñ, aščināñ, aščeññāñ.

I. Gerunds

Pres. nastanāñ.
Past. nāñ astāts.
Fut. assonāñ, aščināñ, aščeññāñ (*if used*).

§ 4. Conjugation of a Regular Intransitive Verb "Nid = sleep".[1]

I. *Affirmative form*

A. Indicative Mood

Present. Sing. 1) nid-tañ,[2] 2) nid-tai, nid-tā = I sleep *etc.*
" *Plur.* 1) nid-taoñ (*or* nid-tauñ), 2) nid-tāt, 3) nid-tāt.

Imperf. Sing. 1) nid-taloñ (*m.*), nid-taliñ (*f.*), nid-taleñ (*n.*)[3] = I was sleeping *etc.*, Lat. *dormiebam.*
" 2) nid-taloi, nid-talī, nid-taleiñ.
" 3) nid-talo, nid-tali nid-taleñ.
Plur. 1) nid-taleauñ, 2) nid-taleāt, 3) nid-tale, nid-taleo, nid-taliñ.

Past. Sing. 1) nid-loñ, nid-liñ, nid-leñ = I slept *etc.*, Lat. *dormivi.*
" 2) nid-loi, nid-lī, nid-leiñ;
" 3) nid-lo, nid-li, nid-leñ;

---

[1] This "n" is pronounced nearly "gn".

[2] I write these hyphens only to show more distinctly the formation of the tenses. In other cases they are omitted.

[3] And so whenever three terminations occur in one person, they are for the three genders, although *m.*, *f.*, *n.* are not written.

Plur. 1) nid-leaoñ, 2) nid-leāt, 3) nid-le, nid-leo, nid-liñ.

Perfect. Sing. 1) nid-lañ, nid-leañ, nid-lañ = I have slept *etc.*
„ 2) nid-lai, nid-leai, nid-laiñ;
„ 3) nid-lā, nid-leā, nid-lāñ.
Plur. 1) nid-leaoñ, 2) nid-leāt, 3) nid-leāt (*m.f.*), nid-leānt (*n.*).

Past Perfect. Sing. 1) nid-ullоñ, nid-ulliñ, nid-ulleñ = I had slept *etc.*;
„ 2) nid-ulloi, nid-ullī, nid-ulleiñ;
„ 3) nid-ullo, nid-ullī, nid-ulleñ.
Plur. 1) nid-ulleaoñ, 2) nid-ulleāt,
3) nid-ulle, nid-ulleo, nid-ulliñ,
or the form nid-loloñ, nid-leliñ, nid-leleñ *etc.* *p.* 88.

1st Future Sing. 1) nid-toloñ, nid-teliñ, nid-teleñ = I shall sleep *etc.*
„ 2) nid-toloi, nid-telī, nid-teleiñ.
„ 3) nid-tolo, nid-teli, nid-teleñ.
Plur. 1) nid-teleaoñ, 2) nid-teleāt, 3) nid-tele, nid-teleo, nid-teliñ.

Conting. Future Sing. 1) nid-an = I may sleep, I shall perhaps sleep *etc.* 2) nid-či, 3) nid-at.
Plur. 1) nid-uñ, 2) nid-čat, 3) nid-tit.

2nd Future. 1) as the Contingent Future, *or*
2) *Sing.* nid-lo astoloñ *etc.*, (*as the Future of* assā *and* nidlo *as an Adjective of three terminations*) *the meaning is:* I might have slept, *as in Ital.* "*avrò dormito;* or, *può essere che abbia dormito*";
or 3) *Sing.* 1) nid-to assoloñ *etc.* (*as the Past of* assā *and* nidto *as an Adjective of three terminations*) *the meaning is:* I shall have slept.

or 4) *Sing.* nidun astoloñ *etc.* (*only* astoloñ *is declined, as the Future of* assā) *the meaning is* I shall have slept, *as the preceding one, for which it can be used.*

B. Imperative Mood

Sing. 1) nid-ungi = let me sleep, Lat. *dormiam.*
2) nid,
3) nid-undi.
Plur. 1) nid-iañ,
2) nid-ā *or sometimes* nidiā,
3) nidundi;
or niduñ *in all persons*, in Lat. *dormiam,*
or nid-tañ zauñ *in all persons* = get sleeping, Lat. *fiam dormiens,*
or nida-zāi (*in all persons*) = I must sleep *etc.*

C. Optative Mood

Pres. nid-uñ! *or* nid-tañ zaun![1] = Lat. *utinam dormiam!*
Imperf. nid-leār puro! = Oh if I could sleep.
Past. Sing. nid-lo, (nidli, nidleñ) asleār! (boreñ *or* puro!)
Plur. nid-le, (nidleo, nidliñ) asleār „ „ „
= Oh if I had slept! (it would be good).

D. Subjunctive Mood

Pres. nid-uñ (*rare*), *or* nid-tañ zauñ = that I sleep.
Imperf. Sing. 1) nid-a-soñ, nid-a-siñ, nid-a-señ = that I may sleep.
3) nid-a-so, nid-a-si, nid-a-señ.
1st Conditional (*present*). nid-leār = if I slept.
2nd „ (*past*). nid-lo asleār, nid-li asleār, nid-leñ asleār *etc. as above* = if I had slept.

---

[1] Vulgar people use also this form: "nidundi-gā, Devā! viz. "-gā Devā (O God!)" is added to the 3rd Person of the Imperative: but this form seems to be too low.

1st Conditionatum (*present*). nid-an, *etc.* (*as the Cont. Fut.*) = I would sleep.

2nd „ (*past*). *Sing.* 1) nid-toñ *etc.* (*as* zātoñ *page* 99) = I would have slept; *or this form Sing.* 1) nid-toñ assoloñ, nid-tiñ assąliñ, nid-teñ assąleñ; 2) nid-to assoloi *etc. conjugating* "nid-to" *as an Adjective of three terminations and* assoloñ *as the Past of* assā.

E. Potential Mood

Present. 1) nid-iyet = it is possible *or* allowed to sleep.
2) nid-unk tanktā *or* nid-unk tank assā = there is power to sleep.
3) nid-uñ (*or* nid-unk) puro = may sleep, perhaps he sleeps.

Past. 1) nid-iyet assąleñ = it was possible *or* allowed tosleep.
2) nid-unk tank assąli = there was power to sleep.

Future. 1) nid-an *etc.* (*as the Contingent Future*) = perhaps I shall sleep.
„ 2) nid-iyet,
„ *or* nid-iyet asteleñ = it will be possible *or* allowed to sleep.
„ 3) nid-unk tank asteli = there will be power to sleep.

F. Necessary Mood

Pres. 1) nid-a-zāi = I must sleep *etc.*
„ 2) nid-čeñ assā = Lat. *dormiendum est.*

Past. 1) nid-unk zāi assąlleñ = it was necessary to sleep; *or*
„ 2) nid-čeñ assąleñ, *or* 3) nida-zāi assąleñ.

Fut. 1) nid-a-zāi, 2) nid-a-zāi asteleñ,
„ 3) nid-čeñ asteleñ = it will be necessary to sleep.

G. Infinitive Mood

Absolute. nid-so, nid-či, nid-čeñ = to sleep;
some say: nid-uñso, nid-unči, nid-unčeñ.

Supine. nid-unk (*sometimes* nid-unčeāk) = in order to sleep.

H. Participles

Pres. 1) nid-tolo, nid-toli, nid-toleñ = he who is sleeping, (*or* nid-toli, nid-teli, nid-teleñ);
2) nid-so, nid-či, nid-čeñ;
3) nid-tā to, nid-tā tī, nid-tā teñ = (who) was sleeping, that; 4) nid-tañ.

Imperf. nid-talo, nid-tali, nid-taleñ = he who was sleeping[1].

Past. nid-lo, nid-li, nid-leñ = he who slept.

Past Perfect. nid-ullo (*or* nid-lolo, nid-leli, nid-leleñ) = he who had slept.

Fut. nid-so, nid-či, nid-čeñ = he who will sleep.

I. Gerunds

Pres. nid-tănañ, *or* nid-tastănañ, *or* nid-tañ astănañ = while sleeping.

Imperf. nid-un.

Past. 1) nid-tăts, 2) nidun = having slept.

Fut. nid-so, nid-či, nid-čeñ = to be slept.
Lat. *dormiendum* (*est*).

II. Negative form

A. Indicative Mood

Pres. Sing. 1) nid-a-nāñ = I do not sleep. 2) nid-a-nāi, 3) nid-a-nāñ.

Plur. 1) nid-a-naoñ, 2) nid-a-nānt, 3) nid-a-nānt.

Imperf. Sing. 1) nid-a-nātuloñ, nid-a-natliñ, nid-a-natleñ = I did not sleep, Lat. *nondormiebam.*
2) nid-a-natuloi, nid-a-natlī, nid-a-natleiñ;
3) nid-a-natulo, nid-a-natli, nid-a-natleñ.

Plur. 1) nid-a-natuleaoñ (*m.*), nid-natleaoñ (*f. n.*),
2) nid-a-natuleāt (*m.*), nid-a-natleāt (*f. n.*)
3) nid-a-natule, nidanatleo, nidanatliñ.

---

[1]) This Participle, not given § 2, is formed by adding the terminations of the Imperfect to the root.

Instead of "natullo" *etc.* we may use the other form "natloñ" *etc.* (See page 93.)

Past. Sing. 1) nid-unk-nāñ, 2) nid-unk-nāi, 3) nid-unk-nāñ = I did not sleep, Lat. *non dormivi.*

Plur. 1) nid-unk-nāoñ, 2) nid-unk-nānt,
3) nid-unk-nānt.

Perfect: as the Past.

Past Perfect Sing. 1) nid-unk-natulloñ (-iñ, -eñ) = I had not slept [1].
„ 2) nid-unk-natulloi (-ī, eiñ),
„ 3) nid-unk-natullo (-i, eñ);
Plur. 1) nid-unk-natuleaoñ,
„ 2) nid-unk-natuleāt,
„ 3) nid-unk-natule (-eo, -iñ).

1st & 2nd Fut. Sing. 1) nid-soñ-nāñ, nid-čiñ-nāñ, nid-čeñ nāñ = I shall not sleep, I shall not have slept.
„ 2) nid-so-nai (-či-nai, -čeñ-nai),
„ 3) nid-so-nāñ (-či-nāñ, -čeñ-nāñ).
Plur. 1) nid-če-nāoñ (-čeo-nāoñ, -čiñ-nāoñ),
„ 2) nid-če-nānt (-čeo-nānt, -čiñ-nānt),
„ 3) *as the 2nd Person.*

Conting. Future. Sing. 1) nidanāñ zāin, 2) nidanāñ zači,
3) nidanāñ zāit;
Plur. 1) nidanāñ zāuñ, 2) nidanāñ začat,
3) nidanāñ zatit.

Another 2ndFuture is this: nid-tonañ assoloñ (*conjugated as* zatonañassoloñ, *p.* 100.)

B. Imperative Mood

Sing. 1) āuveñ nidanaye, *or* mojān nidunk nozo *or* nidanañ zauñ; *the 1st form means* "it is not allowed to me to sleep," *the second about the same*, *the 3rd* "get not sleeping".

---

[1] "u" of "natullo" becomes "a" in the Feminine and Neuter, in all persons.

2) nid-a-nakā, 3) tāṇeñ-, tineñ nid-a-naye, *or* tačān-,[1] tičān nidunk nozo, *or* to-, tī-, teñ nidanāñ zāundi *or* nidanāñ zāuñ.

Plur. 1) amiñ nid-a-naye, *or* amčeān nidunk nozo, 2) nid-a-nakāt, 3) taṇiñ nid-a-naye, *or* te-, teo-, tiñ nidanāñ zāundit, *or* tančān nidunk nozo.

More simple forms of the Imperative are these:

1) nid-čeñ nakā, *in all persons.*

2) nidanāñ zāuñ = get not sleeping, *in all persons.*

3) *Sing.* 1) nidanāñ zāuñ, 2) nid-a-nakā, 3) nidanāñ zāuñ; *Plur.* 1) nidanāñ zāuñ, 2) nid-a-nakāt, 3) nidanāñ zāuñ.

In the 3rd Person Sing. and Plur. we may say "zāuñdi" (*Sing.*) and "zāundit" (*Plur.*), instead of "zāuñ".

C. Optative Mood

Pres. nidanāñ zāuñ! = may I become not sleeping, *in all persons*[2].

Imperf. nidanāñ zaleār (purō) = Oh if I could get not sleeping (enough)!

Past. nidanatullo zaleār! *or* nidanatullo zaleār boreñ! = Oh if I had been not sleeping (it would be good)!

D. Subjunctive Mood

Pres. nidanāñ zāuñ = that I may not sleep, *in all persons.*

Imperf. Sing. 1) nidanāñ-soñ, nidanāñ-siñ, nidanāñ-señ = that I might not sleep.

3) nidanāñ-so, nidanāñ-si, nidanāñ-señ;

Plur. 3) nidanāñ-se, nidanāñ-seo, nidanāñ-siñ.

1st Conditional. nidanāñ zaleār = if I became not sleeping.

2nd „ nidanatullo (-i, -eñ) zaleār = if I had become not sleeping.

---

[1] Or "tačeān"; and so whenever this form occurs in any Gender, Number, Case or Person.

[2] Vulgar people say "nidanāñ zāundi-gā Devā"; viz. they add "gā, Devā" to the negative root; but this form seems to be too low, as I said of the similar affirmative form.

1st Conditionatum. nid-soñ-nāñ *etc.* I would not sleep (*as the 1st Fut. Absol.*), *or* nidanāñ zāin, *etc.* = I might become not sleeping, (*as the Conting. Future of* zatā *added to* nidanāñ).

2nd „ nid-toññāñ, nid-tiññāñ, nid-teññāñ *etc.* (*as* zatoññañ, *p.* 101) = I would not have slept; *or* nid-toññāñ assolloñ *etc.* (*conjugating* nid-toññāñ *as an Adjective of three terminations with the addition of* nāñ *and* assoloñ *as the Past of* assā.)

E. Potential Mood

Pres. 1) nid-a-naye = is not allowed to sleep,
2) nidunk nozo = it is not possible to sleep,
3) nidunk tankanāñ = there is no power to sleep.

Past. 1) nidanaye assạleñ = it was not allowed to sleep;
2) nidunk nozo assạleñ = it was impossible to sleep;
3) nidunk tank natạli = there was no power to sleep.

Fut. 1) nidanaye-, *or* nidanayet asteleñ = it will not be allowed to sleep;
2) nidunk nozo zateleñ = it will be impossible to sleep;
3) nidunk tank aš-čināñ = there will be no power to sleep;
4) nidanāñ zāin *etc.* = perhaps I shall get not sleeping.

F. Necessary Mood

Pres. nidunk nozo = it is impossible to sleep.

Past. 1) „ „ assạlleñ = it was impossible to sleep;
2) nid-čeñ natạlleñ = Lat. *dormiendum non erat* (or *non fuit*).

Future as Pres. or nidunk nozo zateleñ = it will be impossible to sleep.

G. Infinitive Mood

Absol. nidanastanāñ raunčeñ = to remain without sleeping.

Supine. nidanāñ zāunk = in order not to sleep.

H. Participles

Pres. 1) nid-a-natulo, nid-a-natạli, nid-a-natạleñ = not sleeping, he who does not sleep;
2) nidanāñ = not sleeping (*used with an Auxiliary Verb*);
3) nid-so-nāñ, -či-nāñ, -čeñnāñ (*seldom used*).

Past. nidunk-natullo *or* nid-a-natullo = he who did not sleep.

Fut. 1) nid-a-natulo = he who will not sleep,
2) nid-so-nāñ, -či-nāñ, -čeñnāñ (*seldom used*),
3) nid-to-nāñ, -ti-nāñ, -teñnāñ (*used with an Auxiliary Verb.*) Some might consider this last Participle as a finite Mood: yet the construction and form of it is similar to the form and construction of other Participles; hence I put it as a Participle.

I. Gerunds

Pres. nida-nāstanañ *or* nidanañ āstanañ = without sleeping *etc.*

Past. nidanāñ zatātz = not having slept.

Futur. nid-sonāñ (-čināñ, -čenāñ), *or* nidanāñ zāuñso Lat. *non dormiendum.*

Although the Verbs having the root ending in a vowel follow mostly the above given paradigm, yet, as in some small things, they have some peculiarity, an example of these Verbs also should be given: but it will be more convenient to insert it when I speak of the Irregular Verbs.

§ 5. Observations on Verbs.

Before explaining the different kinds of Verbs, let us make some important observations, reserving others for the Syntax. I put them down as they come in my mind without order.

1. In the paradigm I have put all the persons, and, as far as possible, also the most common Tenses. Yet, in particular cases, certain Persons and Tenses are often either not used or only seldom; *e.g.* the 1st Person Neuter never or almost never occurs; for the ordinary case in which it should

be employed is if a girl (Neuter) speaks; but although nouns of girls are Neuter, yet when girls speak, they use the Feminine Gender for themselves. For this reason, I think, some told me, when I asked about the 1st Person Neuter, that it was like the 1st Person Feminine. I have tried also to supply the deficiency of some Tenses by other forms, chiefly by Periphrastic Conjugation.

2. As hinted at in the paradigm, an a or i, for the sake of euphony, is often inserted between the root and the terminations. This happens chiefly in the negative form and in the Necessary Mood with "zāi". This a or i is usually inserted if the root ends in a consonant, and the termination to be added begins with a consonant. Yet, if the root end in n or ṇ and the termination begins with n, euphony does not require any insertion of vowel; *e.g.* "moṇ = say", "moṇṇānt = (they) do not say", but "moṇazāi"; so also if it ends in l, it does not require any a or i; *e.g.* "kaṇṭāḷnā = he does not hate", from "kaṇṭāḷ", and so perhaps some other termination may not require any insertion. If the root ends in i, u, e, o, mostly no euphonic vowel is inserted; because then euphony does not require it. If it ends in a, it seems to be more common not to insert any vowel; yet there are exceptions. I say a or i, but not indifferently: in certain cases a is more euphonic; in certain other cases i is more euphonic,—practice will teach you. So "khā = eat" requires i, because two a are not euphonic; "khāinā = (he) does not eat".

If the root ends in u, or uñ, or au, or auñ, this u is changed (in the above said cases, in which a or i must be inserted) into v, and then the euphonic vowel is inserted: "rāu = remain", "rāvāzāi = it is required to remain"; "rāvanā = does not remain". Again, if the root ends in a, one v is inserted in the Potential Mood: "khā = eat", "khāviyet"; "zā", "zāviyet".[1] Moreover, if

[1] The same happens, often at least, with the above said Verbs in "u", "uñ" etc.; *e.g.* "rāviyet", from "rāu"; or better we may say so; they change the "u" into "v".

the root ends in a or e, for the sake of euphony i is inserted between the root and the termination of the 2nd Person Plural Imperative: "poḷe = see", *Plur.* "poḷeiā"; "khā = eat", *Plur.* "khāiā"; "zā = become", *Plur.* "zāiā". Finally, the Verbs ending with a in the root lose this a in the Infinitive, and sometimes also in the 2nd Person Singular Imperative: "aikatāñ = I hear", "aik = hear". Yet the pure form "aik" is not often used: some affix is added; *e.g.* "aik-re" speaking to a boy; so also "voḷkatāñ = I know" should make "voḷk". Yet this is used commonly with the affix, *e.g.* "voḷk-re", "voḷk-ago". The gist of this 2nd observation is this: a or i or v is inserted, as euphony requires.

3. The Future Potential, as also the Contingent and 2nd Future, end sometimes in an, sometimes in in. Perhaps the following may stand in the place of a rule.

a) All Causative Verbs have in, although the original Verb, from which the Causative is derived, was neuter; thus "tzălain = I may rule (cause to walk)"; but of the two i, one of the termination, the other of the root, only one is kept. (See below *d*.)

b) Generally, the Transitive Verbs, whether Causative or not Causative, have in; *e.g.* "măr-in = I may beat"; "kăr-in = I may do".

c) The Neuter Verbs, whether they have a corresponding Causative one or not, have an; *e.g.* "poḍ-an = I may fall"; "tzăl-an = I may walk".

d) Verbs having the root ending in e or i, and mostly also in a, add only n; *e.g.* "gē = receive", *Sing.* "gēn, geši, gĕt"; *Plur.* "geuñ, gešăt, getit".

4. The 1st Person Singular of the Absolute Future, if interrogative, is uñ, as in the Present Subjunctive; the reason may be, because if the Future is interrogative, it becomes doubtful.

5. The use of the different Tenses, except perhaps the Present, Imperfect and Past, is very different from the use of

Tenses in our languages, as will be explained in the Syntax; *e.g.* some Tenses have a passive meaning: what has been put as 1st Person, is often 3rd Person etc.

6. There is no passive form, at least not such as in our languages. In the Syntax I will say how the passive meaning may be expressed. For the present, if the passive meaning occurs chiefly in the Past Tense, or in Tenses derived from the Past (see 7), make the construction as if the above given forms of those Tenses were truly Passive; and in the other Tenses change the English Passive sentence into the Active and then translate it.

7. In the formation of Tenses some are derived from the Present, some from the Past. In the regular Verbs this scarcely appears; but it appears clearly in the irregular Verbs. The Tenses derived from the Past, I say from the root of the Past (which is found by cutting off the above terminations of the Past) are the Perfect, Past Perfect, 1st Conditional (and 2nd Conditional, if the form "-leleăr" is used. See p. 90), Past Participles in lo, and the Tenses formed with these Participles, or, shorter, the Tenses formed by a termination which begins with l or ųl. The others are formed from the root of the Present, (viz. from the Imperative 2nd Person Singular, in which the pure root is found); *e.g.* "kăr=do", *Past* "ke-lo", *Perfect* "ke-lă", *Past Perfect* "ke-llo", *1st Conditional* "ke-leăr", *Participle* "ke-lo". Hence also the *2nd Conditional* is "kelo asleăr". What I say must be understood of the affirmative form.

8. Now in order to say something more in particular, the Absolute Future differs from the Contingent Future in this, that the first expresses, as the word *absolute* shows, that a thing will happen without fail; the second shows that a thing may happen. Exactness would have required me to put the Contingent Future only in the Potential Mood: yet by putting it close to the Absolute Future their difference may

appear more distinctly. What I call 2nd Future might be called Past Future.

9. As 2nd Future I have put down the form of the Contingent Future, because many use truly the Contingent Future also as a 2nd Future. Yet I think that this is not quite correct. I think that the real 2nd Absolute Future of the affirmative form is that which is compounded of the Participle in "tolo" and "assoloñ". The form given as another 2nd Future, viz. "nidlo astoloñ" might be considered as 2nd or Past Future of the 1st Contingent Future. Again, I have put down the form of the 1st Absolute Negative Future, as 2nd Future for the same above-said reason; yet here too, I think that the exact form of the 2nd Absolute Future (or Past Absolute Future) is the other, viz. "nidtonāñ assoloñ". As 2nd Future of the 1st Contingent Future I would use the form "nidtonāñ assolo zāin, nidtināñ assoli zāin, nidteññāñ assoleñ zāin" *etc.* conjugating "nidtonāñ" as given on p. 112, and "zāin" as the Contingent Future of "zatā", and "assolo" as an Adjective of three terminations.

10. The Participles are a difficult part of the Verbs; even their spelling is complicated. As to the spelling, it seems first that whenever they are used for the first Person Singular, if they end in a vowel, they are nasal, although in the paradigm this has not always been observed, as this point as yet is not quite settled. Now, in order to say something more in particular about them, two forms have been given for the Present Participle, *h. e.* "nidtolo, nidteli, nidteteñ", *or* "nidtolo, nidtoli, nidtoleñ". Perhaps the first of these two forms might be better used as Future Participle, for it has the terminations of the Future; at any rate it can be used as Future Participle, although not given on page 111 and § 2. But I say besides this, that it is perhaps more exact to use the first of the now given forms only as Future. Another Participle has not been given, as it occurs only in composition with another part of the Verb; this is the Participle in "toñ"

in the affirmative, and "tonāñ" in the negative form (nidtoñ, nidtonāñ). The Participle Present in "-tañ" (nidtāñ) is used with the Gerund in "tanañ", shortened; "kărtanañ = kărtañ astanañ"; it is used moreover in the Periphrastic Conjugation; many Tenses have been formed by this Participle and an Auxiliary Verb. What is "nidtāñ" for the affirmative form, "nidanāñ" is for the negative form; this Negative Participle likewise has not been put down in § 2, for it occurs very seldom out of the Conjugation; *e. g.* "mortañ monis = decrepit man". In the paradigm only one Past Participle has been put (-lo); but we may subdivide this into two, *i. e.* into a simple Past Participle which would correspond to the Past Tense; and this has been put down in the § 2; another would correspond to the Past Perfect, and has the same form as the simple Past, except that it doubles the l, or if this is not possible, by inserting one o, or by adding to the root ullo, just as we have seen in the Past Perfect. A Participle corresponding to the Perfect seems not to be used, at least as a real Participle, although it might be used as second part of a correlative sentence, as I said of "-ta to". About this last Participle in "-ta to" it must be observed, that as it is not a real Participle, it may become "-talo to", "-tolo to", "-lo to" *etc.* according to the Tense of the Verb of the corresponding relative sentence; *e.g.* "yetā to monis mozo bāu = the man who comes is my brother"; "fāleā yetolo to monis mozo bāu = the man who will come to-morrow is my brother"; "kāl ailo to monis mozo bāu = the man who came yesterday is my brother" *etc.*

11. Another difficult point is the Conditionatum. As the 1st Conditionatum (§ 2, p. 90) I have put down the form of the Contingent Future; because this is really used in many cases. Yet I think that this form is neither general nor the most exact one. As this Contingent Future always includes some doubt, it may be used as 1st Conditionatum only or chiefly when the Conditionatum includes some doubt: if no doubt is

expressed or understood, the form of the 1st Conditionatum, is, as far as I can judge, the form in "toñ" ("nidtoñ"), given §4, as 2nd Conditionatum. Then, what remains for the 2nd Conditionatum? This very form ("nidtoñ") or better, "nidtoñ assoloñ", which 2nd form is, it seems to me, the exact form of the 2nd Conditionatum, although the first is also used sometimes. If the 2nd Conditionatum implies some doubt, we might use the 2nd Contingent Future ("nidlo astoloñ"). The same, *servata proportione*, is to be said of the negative form, *i.e.* the real 1st Conditionatum should be "nidtonãñ", if no doubt is implied, "nidanãñ zãin", if doubt is implied; the 2nd Absolute Conditionatum should be "nidtonãñ", or better, "nidtonãñ assoloñ"; the doubtful 2nd Conditionatum exactly is this "nidtonãñ assolo zãin"; yet "nidtonãñ assoloñ" seems to be often used also as doubtful 2nd Conditionatum. As to the 2nd Conditional Negative, besides the given form ("nidanatullo zaleãr"), we might use, nay, we should use the other form "nidunknatullo zaleãr"; yet as "nidanatullo" is commonly used also for the Past Participle, the form given in §3 and §4 may pass. As these things as yet are not quite settled, I prefer to put them in the observations rather than in the paradigm.

12. Some Tenses or some forms of Tenses have been formed by borrowing the forms of some other Tense; *e.g.* in the Imperative, besides the proper forms, I have put also some forms of the Potential; because the meaning allows it; of course in this case the borrowed forms follow the rules of the Tenses from which they have been borrowed.

13. In the formation of Tenses the reader might have remarked that the Imperfect Negative of "assã" is used also as Perfect, and Past: yet we could use also "assunknãñ" and "assunknatulloñ" instead of "natulo" if the meaning requires it. The same must be said of "tanktã" if resolved into "tank assã"; *e.g.* "tank natḁli", used for the Past.

14. As to the Infinitive, I said that some use "niduñso"

instead of "nidso, (and so also in the Participles of the same form): but although we may use it, we must not confound it with the almost equal Infinitive of the corresponding Causative Verb; *e. g.* "nid=sleep", "nidai=cause to sleep"; the first has or may have "niduñso", the 2nd has "nidouñso", although in the pronunciation these two forms can be scarcely distinguished. (See below Art. II., Causative Verbs).

15. As regards the spelling of the preceding -so or -uñso, it has been observed already that its exact pronunciation seems to be "-tzo, -tŏi, -tŏeñ, rather than "-so, -ŏi, -ŏeñ"; consequently this s *or* ŏ must be pronounced somewhat sharp; we might have written also "-tzo, -tŏi, -tŏeñ." This 16th observation regards not only the termination of the Infinitives, but also all other terminations ending in "-so, -ŏi, -ŏeñ," or "-so, -si, -señ" as *e.g.* the Imperfect Subjunctive; nay, it regards also the Adjectives in "-so, -ŏi, -ŏeñ", as I shall say later on.

16. The Gerund in "-tastanañ" is as much used as the Gerund in "-tanañ". As to the Gerund in "un", we shall see in the Syntax that our Present Gerund is often translated by this Gerund, although it is used chiefly as Imperfect and Past Gerund, for which reason I did not put it also among the Present Gerunds. Moreover the Gerund in "un" is used sometimes as a Participle, although for the reason just now indicated, I do not put it among the Participles.

17. In the Compound Tenses the meaning may require "zatā" instead of "assā" and *vice versa*, although in the paradigm usually only one of these two Verbs has been put. About this point I shall speak hereafter.

18. As to the modifications of the above forms, generally speaking only the forms ending in o or oñ are conjugated, *i. e.* they take i in the Feminine, eñ in the Neuter; if they happen to be used in the oblique cases, the rule of the Adjectives of three terminations is applied to them. Ordinarily only the Participles are sometimes to be used also in the oblique cases

(see Syntax). As to the forms in "a" or "añ", the paradigm itself indicates the changes to be made.

This observation regards chiefly the compound Tenses and the periphrastic Conjugation, which will be explained more distinctly hereafter. Examples: "poḷeiyet assolo = *conspici potuit*"; the 1st part indeclinable, (but if we give to it the terminations in o, declinable), the 2nd part declinable: "kărtolo assolo = *facturus erit*", both parts declinable; "nidun = having slept, or sleeping", indeclinable, *etc.*

19. As regards the declension of the parts of which the Verb is compounded, we must consider separately and distinctly another point. In some Tenses there is a double conjugation; *e. g.* in the Conditional Past, "zalo asleăr" the first part "zalo" is not only declined according to the genders, (-i, -eñ, -e, -eo, -iñ) but can be also conjugated; so in the 2nd Person you may say: "zaloi (-i, -eiñ) asleăr", and a similar form may be used, I think, whenever we have a compound form, the first part of which ends in o in the Masculine Singular.

Moreover in the Future Absolute Negative we have another kind of Conjugation, because the first part takes the terminations of the Adjectives according to gender and number, and the second part, *i. e.* the negative particle, takes the terminations of the Verb.

20. The Potential, formed with "puro", is pronounced by some in such a way that it seems to end not in unk but in uñ; and zăi of the Necessary Mood is pronounced by many as je.

21. The different forms put under one Tense are not all equal, *h. e.* we must not think it allowable to use them indifferently; they will be explained in the Syntax. Moreover if of some form in § 4 no translation is given, we must apply to it the translation of the form which is in the same sentence; one form has not been translated at all (p. 112) "nidanăñ zăin = perhaps I shall be not sleeping".

22. nāñ is changed into nakā in the Imperative, as in Latin *non facis*, *ne facias*. This nāñ is always nasal.

23. As hinted in the paradigm, if a form is to be changed from the Masculine into the Feminine or Neuter, some euphonical changes take place: the principal changes are of o or u into ẹ or ă or e; these changes take place not exclusively but chiefly in the Participles in lo.

24. As regards the double consonants, although exactness in this point was not so necessary throughout the Grammar, yet in the matter of Verbs more exactness is required: thus in some Verbs or Tenses, if you write a Participle with one l, it is Present; if with two l, it is Past Perfect; *e.g.* "natulo, natullo *or* natụllo". About this double l it must be well observed, that it has very often an emphatic meaning; nay, this is the chief meaning of the double l in the Conjugation. (See Syntax).

25. Sometimes to the given forms chiefly in the Imperative, an Interrogative or other particles are added as one word to the termination, so that it seems to have another termination, as we have seen in the Vocative of the Substantives, to which no or nu is added. This change of termination is only apparent; just as the change of the termination by the adddition of the particle "nāñ" in the negative form is only apparent and not real. Examples: "kărtāigī? = do you do....?" "kăr-re = do" (*or* "kăr-go" speaking to a girl); "kărta-so = he seems to do", "kărtā-tz = he truly does" *etc.* These particles will be explained later on. But as to "nāñ", it apppears from the paradigm, that in some way the termination of the affirmative form goes over to "nāñ", with some little changes.

26. In order to make still easier to remember and to learn the above apparently difficult Conjugation, let us make the following remarks: In the above paradigm in some Tenses two or more forms are given; one is, very often, simple, another or the others are, mostly, compounds, chiefly of the

periphrastic Conjugation. For the present let us put aside these secondary forms and keep in view only one form, the principal and more common one. Then, after having made this separation, we may again distinguish the Tenses into Simple and Compound; but the Compound Tenses usually are compounds of Simple Tenses; consequently we may limit our attention only to Simple Tenses. Now these Simple Tenses may be divided into two classes, viz. into declinable, *i. e.* modifying the termination according to the Gender, and indeclinable. The indeclinable Tenses are these: in the Indicative, Present, 2nd Future (in "an"), Contingent Future; moreover the Imperative; in the Optative, Present, Imperfect (-leār puro), one part of the Past (-leār); in the Subjunctive, Present, 1st Conditional, one part of the 2nd Conditional (-leār), the 1st Conditionatum; in the Potential the forms in **yet**, in **an** and with **puro**; and if these two forms are joined to another declinable part, they remain indeclinable; in the Necessary Mood the forms with "zāi", if joined to a declinable part, they remain indeclinable; in the Infinitive, the Supine; in the Participles, only those in **tañ** and in **un**[1]; all Gerunds except the *Gerundivus*, which, properly speaking, is the Future Participle Passive. As to the Negative form, the reader himself can easily find out the declinable and not declinable Tenses. All other Tenses are declinable; some even have a full declension also in the oblique cases, as the Participles in **o**; some have only different terminations according to the Gender, as the Imperfect, Past, Perfect, Past Perfect etc.; moreover all or nearly all simple finite Tenses have the first Person nasal, if it ends in a vowel. Further, in the declinable Tenses the 1st Person Singular usually ends in **oñ, iñ, eñ,** *or* **añ, yañ, añ**; the 2nd Person ends in i (oi, i, eiñ *etc.*); the 3rd Person ends in **o, i, eñ** *or* **a, ya, añ**. The 1st Person Plural ends in **uñ** *or* **auñ**, the 2nd mostly in **at**; the Plural is not declined (at least fully). Finally the termi-

[1] About this Participle in "un", not put down, § 4, see observation 16.

nation of the Neuter Gender is commonly nasal, if it ends in a vowel, in any declinable Tense (*i.e.* having different terminations for the different Genders).

27. As to the quantity of o and e, viz. whether closed or open (see Part I. Art. I.), the final o and e in the Verbs are open according to the rule laid down in the Appendix to the Part I.; so "marlò, marlè, marlòñ, marlèñ" *etc.* not "marló, marlé, *etc.*

28. As regards the formation of the Past Perfect, I said that o is inserted between the two l (see p. 88); because the most common case in which this o is inserted is when we have a Verb ending in l, as the example given (p. 88) shows; yet if we have a Verb ending in another consonant, which cannot be pronounced easily with l, of course then also o is inserted, not between the two l, but between l and the last consonant of the root.

29. Although the use of each Tense will be explained later on, yet for the present we may say that the first form, if more than one form is given in one Tense, is more common; hence the beginner had better to take the first, although in some cases it may not be the most suitable.

30. A peculiar explanation is required for the Potential and Necessary Moods, as they do not exist in our European languages. First about their Conjugation. As the paradigm shows, there are not two full Numbers, and three Persons unless the Tense takes the form of another Tense, *e.g.* of the Contingent Future. Sometimes the whole form is not conjugated at all, *e.g.* the form in "-iyet"; sometimes only one part is conjugated, *e.g.* "kariyet assạleñ". Although one part is conjugated, the conjugation consists mostly in changing the terminations according to Gender and Number, unless, as I said, a conjugated form of another Mood be used for the Potential, *e.g.* the Contingent Future. Which are those forms to be partially conjugated? It appears from the above observation 26, and from the paradigm. Finally in these two Moods many

forms given in the other Tenses do not exist, *e.g.* the Gerund of the Potential. Yet some Participles exist, which have not been put in the paradigm in order not to terrify my readers with so many forms; but I must put them here.

Potential. The first Participle of this Mood is formed by adding "assollo" to the Present in "-iyet"; thus we get, *e.g.* from "poḷeiyet = it may be seen", "poḷeiyet assollo = which can be seen, worthy to be seen". The second Participle is formed by adding the Future Participle of "assā" or of "zatā" to the same form in "-iyet"; so we get, *e.g.* "poḷeiyet astolo = which will be to be seen". In a similar way we may form the Negative Participle "poḷeiyet natullo = not to be seen".

Necessary. By analogy with the Potential, we may form a Participle by adding "assolo" to the form in "zāi", *e.g.* "kărizāi assọleñ kām = the business which is or was to be done" and "kărizāi asteleñ kām = the business which will have to be done". The Negative Participle would be "kărizāi natullo"; but it seems not to be used. Some other forms might be formed in these two Moods; they may be indicated, some at least, in the Syntax, if it be found necessary. As to the termination "-iyet", given in the paradigm, I must say that although I do not recollect now any Verb taking "-ayet" instead of "-iyet", for which reason I have put down "-iyet"; nevertheless I think safer to say that the termination is "-yet" with the euphonical vowel inserted before "-yet" which vowel is mostly i.

31. Chiefly in this point of Verbs, the reader may remark some inconsistencies, more than in other parts. The reason is (besides the great hurry, which does not allow me to go again and again through the *MS.*) the state of this uncultivated language; there is nothing completely settled. Consequently the same thing may be written in many ways, or one way seems sometimes the right one; at other times another way seems to be the right one. Little by little these things may

be settled, chiefly if we begin to write Konkani with Kanarese or, still better, with Mahrātti characters, which are the proper characters of the Konkani language.

Exercises on Verbs

kiaḷ = play	jīk = gain
sōd = seek	ulei = speak
tūk = weigh	bānd = bind or tie
mār = beat	formai = command
obolsi = praise	pōḷ = flee
fūnk = blow	lačil, -a = meadow (*n.*)
sār = start	rāgat, -gta = blood (*n.*)
ghe = receive	saukār, -a = merchant (*m.*)
ub = fly	fāleā = to-morrow
gāme = sweat	usko, -kea = lap (*m.*)
rāḍ = weep	āsro, -rea = refuge (*m.*)
pōs = feed	sukneñ, -ea = bird (*n.*)
tzōr = steal	vāreñ, -ea = air or wind (*n.*)
īk = sell	uzo, -jea = fire (*m.*)

Present, *Imperfect*

Burge lačilānt keḷtāt. Moje kāḍe līvrụ nā. Mozo bāu tukā sōdtā. Amso saukār sākār tuktā. Pedru uzo funktā. Fāleā mozo bāpui angā tāun bāir sārtā ani Bombāi vetā. Zokōṇ Devāk obolsitā, takā Deu obolsitā. Ankuār Māri āuoi bāri amkāñ aplea uskeār getā ani amso āsro zatā. Sukniñ vāreānt (vāreār) ubtāt. Somi Jezu Krist Olivet moḷeānt rāgat gāmetalo, ani amčeañ pātkañ pasun rāḍtalo. Zāssi yēk āuoi apleñ burgeñ (aplea burgeāk) postā, tāsso Somi Jezu Krist aplea kuḍi ani aplea rāgta vorviñ amkāñ postā. Zokōṇ tzortā ani Devāk akmānāčiñ utrañ moṇṭā (*says*) ani yerañ mahā pātkāñ (*mortal sins*) aḍartā, to yemkaṇḍānt vetā.

Past, *Perfect*

Alexandrān sauñsārāso voḍlo vāṇṭo jiklo. To kiteñ uleilo? To nakāzalle uleilo. Judevāniñ Somia Jezu Kristāk bāndlo ani mārlo. Pilātān Jezu Kristāk mārunk niāṭurāyen formaileñ (*or only* māreilo=*caused to be beaten*). Somia Jezu Kristāčea paisāvānt Apostolāniñ takā sānḍlo.

1st Future Absolute

bós = sit, seat	borei = write
mōḍ = break	dākei = show
bouñ = walk	fūṭ = crack, break
pie = drink	nītidar, -a, = judge (*m*).
khā = eat	aidān, -a = vessel (*n*.)
póḍ = fall	siāsan, -a = seat (*of a bishop etc*.) [*n*.

Nītidar siāsanār bostolo phaisāl (*sentence*) utzārunk (*pronounce*). Somi Jezu Krist yeunčea veḷār (*when Jesus Christ will come*) monis pietele ani khātele. Koinča disā Paskānčeñ fest poḍteleñ? Āṭṭrāve tārker (*day*) poḍteleñ. Jezu Kristāso Vanjel sāgḷea sauñsārānt pārgāṭ zātolo.

Imperative Mood

tzukoi = avoid	pāṭlauñ, -ava = following (*m*.)
dék, -i = example (*f*.)	pelo, -lea = neighbour (*m*.)

Jezu Kristāso pāṭlauñ kār, ani sasnāči jin tukā meḷteli. Āuveñ Somi Jezu Kristāči dék kāṇezāi.[1] Monis pātak tzukoundi. Amiñ yēka mekāso (*each other*) mōg kariāñ. Tumiñ, monšāno, Jezu Kristāči kuḍ seuā; Jezu Kristāčeñ rāgat pieyā; ače vorviñ tumče ātme posā. Tumiñ tumčeā peleāso mōg kāriā. Sākor apleñ kām kārundit. Atañ māg-ṇeñ[2] kārizāi. Āuñ nidānañ zāuñ. Foḷañ pikanāñ zāundit. Sākor yeundit (*let the servants come*). Mosor kārināñ zāundi (*he must not hate*). Atañ mojān kéḷunk nozo, iskulānt votzazāi.

Optative Mood

Deu boreñ kāruñ. Devāči kuši zāuñ. Tūñ sārgār pauleār boreñ! Tūñ sābār pauṭi vago raulo asleār (boreñ): (vago rāu =

[1] *Or* kāṇeizāi.

[2] About this hypen see p. 4, n. 7.

be silent.) Ye, Somi Jezu Krist moje kāḍe aileār! (*utinam veniret Dominus J. C. ad me!*)

Subjunctive Mood

Makā kurpā meḷazāi zaleār[1], kiteñ āuveñ kārizāi? Māg-ṇeñ kārizāi. Amčeñ voḍilāniñ amkāñ uleileār, amiñ kalteponān (*humbly*) aikazāi. Tuveñ lesāoñ sikleār, āuñ tukā yēk inām dīn. Āstrie, tuveñ tujā daḍleāk mān dillo zaleār, tuji duv tuji kuši kārti assalli. Devāso ādhār amkāñ meḷasso kiteñ kāruñ?

Infinitive Mood

bōg = enjoy
bòḷ -a = violence (*n.*)
rīg = enter
čintna, -ne = thought (*f.*)
ničeu, -eva = resolution (*m.*)
dosmānkāy, -e = enmity (*f.*)

Suk bogunk Devāči kuši kārizāi. Sārgārājānt rigonk[2] amiñ amkāntz bòḷ kārizāi. Tzāḍ česṭāi kārči bori nāiñ. Čintna sāmestañ vāstuñ thāiñ Devāči kuši kārunk Devāgeli čintna. (*The thought of doing in everything the will of God, is a divine thought.*) Ničeu dosmānkāy dorči, saitānāči (*or* ničeu dosmānkāy dorso saitānāso).

Participles

mosor, -sra = hatred (*m.*)
kaṇṭāḷ = abhor
tān, -i = moment (*f.*)
nimāṇo = last
zārti, -e = judgment (*f.*)

Pātak aḍartā to monis, āplo ātmo kaṇṭāḷtā. Monšāñso mosor kārtolo (monis) Devāk akmān kārtā. Mosor kārso monis Devāk ani monšānk kāṇṭāḷso. Kāl keḷtalo burgo āz mornāče tānir assā. Nimāṇea disā yeuñso nītidar sāmestāñči zārti kārtolo. Devān rātzullo souñsār Devāče podveso gurtu zāun assā. Monšāniñ aḍarleliñ pātkañ buḍtugalāčeñ kāraṇ

[1] About this Tense, see the Appendix. It means: "If you wish to receive the grace."
[2] Some pronounce "onk" instead of "unk".

zāun assąlliñ. Yeñ gār bāndlo monis ušār ani zaṇto monis. To tzallo mārog boro nāiñ, āuñ gello mārog bhou boro. To burgo zaso bāpui gelea vorsānt mello, vo. (*This is the boy, whose father died last year.*)

Gerunds

argañ = thanksgiving[1] tčaḍ = ascend

Deų amkāñ upkārañ kārtanañ amiñ takā argañ dīzāi. Somia Jezu Kristān Apostolānk ani disipulānk soukāsaiečiñ utrañ sāngtātz, sārgār tčaḍlo. Amčāñ gārzaniñ kiteñ kārčeñ? Tuveñ karčeñ kām kiteñ? Igarjent votzun pātkāñso ugḍās kār (*make examination of conscience*). Devāk poḷeun bhou kušālai bogtaoñ. Devāči sākri kārn, amkāñ soukāsai meḷtā.

Potential Mood

pāus, -a = rain (*m.*) bāipāṭ = by heart
pēṇṭ, -e = market (*f.*) borei = write
rasim, -smi = silk (*f.*)

Bore kušien ani zāgrutāyen sābār vāstu kāriyet. Motin Devāk uoḷkunk amkāñ tanktā. Tuzo bāu falea yetologī? Yeunk puro. Pāus poḍatgī? Poḍunk puro. Peṇṭent rasim meḷtāgi? Meḷat. Kumsār zāun kitlo temp zālo? Tīn moine zatit. Tumiñ sangšāt: tukatz boro kār; āuñ tumkañ sangtañ: Kāssoloi profet aplea gāvānt manuonā.

Necessary Mood

Mestri, iskulnatąllea disāniñ amiñ kāsseleñ kām kārizāi? Rajā" assąleañ disāniñ āveñ tumkāñ dileñ lesaoñ bāipāṭ kārizāi, lek kārizāi ani vātzizāi. Āveñ yeo vāstu moja burgeapoṇātaun keḷeāt; ani kiteñ karčeñ? Sompurṇ zāizaleār, votzun ani sāmest vāstu ikun, moje paṭlauñ kār ani tukā sārgār yēk bāṇḍār meḷteleñ.

---

[1] Nominative Plural Neuter, used only in the Plural.

Negative form.

Sānganakāt: mojān nozo; kiteāk moḷeār, Devān tumkañ kumok dileār, sārvụ vāstu tanktāt. Amiñ amkañ bòḷ karināñ zaleār ani amkāñ āḍ yenāñ zaleār (*if we do not deny ourselves*), sārgarājānt rigunk nozo. Amiñ pātkañ nizzāun kaṇṭāḷḷeār, yeā mukār itleñ sompeñ pātkañ kārčenauñ. Tāṇeñ aplo kāido kello zaleār, āuñ takā sikšā ditonāñ (*or* ditonāñ assoloñ).

Pātak kārināseñ pātkiāk būd sāngizāi. Mestri sikoitanañ tāṇeñ aikunk natụlleñ: ače pasun to atañ neṇār. Āuñ sāngtaloñ: tumiñ aikalleñgī?—Amiñ teo vāstu aikunk natạlleò.

Tumiñ yemkaṇḍānt poḍṇañ zāunk Deu tumkañ kāšṭ ditā. Boreñ sikleār, Devā ani monšāñ mukār tukā ānānd meḷtā. Sikanāñ zaleār tukatz ākmān zatā. Aḍvarlelea disāniñ mās khāinaye (*or* mās khāunk nozo). Zārtār tūñ atañ veḷ pāḍ kārtāi, māgir luksān sāma kārunk nozo zāit. Zōkōṇ pātkānt dhārun mortā, takā benjerkarnatulle suāter purtāt (*in not consecrated place bury*). Dhāirān lāḍāi kārsonāñ to sojer kāšṭ bogtolo. Sipoiyānčeñ mostāk beān aplo kāido kārinastanañ sipoi beān dāuntāt. To apli suāt soḍit zaleār, tākā inām dīnaye.

Art. II. Different kinds of Verbs

§ 1. Causative Verbs

In Konkani, as in Kanarese and Tulu, almost all Verbs, Neuter and Transitive, can be made Causative. Some examples will explain what I mean by Causative Verbs. "Tzāl = walk", "tzālai = cause another to walk"; "hās = laugh", "hāsai = cause to laugh"; "pāu = reach", "pāuoi *or* pāvai = cause to reach"; "kār = do", "kārai = cause to do". Yet, use does not allow us to make all Verbs Causative, although in itself it might seem right.

How are the Causative Verbs formed? Generally speaking they are made Causative by adding ai to the root of the Verb. Sometimes ai or i or oi, or ei is added; *e.g.* "por-tañ = I turn, go around"; *Causat.* "portitañ = I move around".

Exceptions: 1) Verbs ending in u, before adding ai, mostly change u into v; *e.g.* "rāu = remain", "rāvai = cause to remain"; yet some of those Verbs might be made Causative also by adding oi; *e.g.* "rāu" has also "rāuoi".

2) Of the Verbs ending in ñ some are made Causative by adding -dai and changing the ñ into n (which in Kanarese would be written nasal as before); *e.g.* "dāuñ = run", "dāuṇḍai = cause to run"; yet some say also "dāvoi". Some others are made Causative by adding oi, or ai and changing uñ into v, or rather by omitting ñ and changing u into v; *e.g.* "deuñ = descend", "devoi = cause to descend".

Their Conjugation is regular, although the original Verb be irregular; *e.g.* "kărai" has in the Past "kărailo", although "kăr" has "kelo". They have few irregularities or rather euphonical changes, which will be shown in § 6.

If we consider not the root of the not Causative Verb but the root of the primitive word, we must say that not only those words which end in ñ but others also are made Causative by adding "dai"; *e.g.* "gusap = confusion", *root:* "guspa"; Causative Verb: "guspadai". Moreover some other Verbs take "dai" instead of "ai".

§ 2 Reciprocal Verbs

These are like the English "love each other". These Verbs are formed by "yĕkameka (= one another)" joined to all persons of the Verb; *e.g.* "yĕkameka keḷtāt = they play among themselves". But if the Verb governs the Genitive (as the Verbs compound with "kăr" and a Noun), then this "yĕkameka" takes the termination of the Genitive or Adjective which must agree with the governing Substantive; *e.g.* "yĕka mekăso mōg kără = love (make love) each other".

§ 3 Reflexive Verbs

They are like the English "he beats himself". These Verbs may be formed in three ways:

1. By adding "itleāk" to the stem of the Feminine Possessive Pronoun corresponding to the person of the Verb; *e.g.* "āuñ

moje itleăk mārtāñ = I beat myself"; "tūñ tuje itleăk mārtai = thou beatest thyself", etc.

2. By adding "apuṇ = *ipse* (put in the required case) to the different persons; *e. g.* "to apṇāk mārtā = he beats himself".

3. There is also a 3rd way, viz. by taking away from the Causative Verbs the Causative sign (ai or i); this way is not suited to all Verbs, but only to some, chiefly to those which from Neuter have been formed Causative; *e.g.* "paloai = quench", "paloa-tā = is quenched or quenches itself". These Verbs should rather be called "Neuter". Their Conjugation is regular or irregular according to the primitive Verb.

4. There is another way but suited only to a few Verbs; this way is to change the o into u; *e. g.* "soḍlo = has been left", "suḍlo = he got rid of, he left himself"; "foḍlo = has been broken", "fuḍlo = broke"; "soḍtā = he leaves", "suḍtā = he gets rid of"; "foḍtā = he breaks", "fuḍtā = he gets broken." These also are rather Neuter Verbs than Reflexive.

§ 4. Verbs excluding Companionship (perhaps Solitary Verbs)[1]

There is another kind of Verbs which imply exclusion of companionship or assistance; *e.g.* "I do this work by myself, alone, without being assisted or helped by any one; I live alone". These Verbs are formed by adding "itleăk" to the oblique case of the Feminine Possessive of the corresponding person of the Verb; *e. g.* "āuñ yeñ kām moje itleăk kărtāñ = I do this work by me alone"; "tūñ yeñ kām tuje itleăk kărtai = thou doest this work by thee"; "to yeñ kām aplea itleăk kărtā", *etc.* Their Conjugation appears to be regular or irregular according to the Verb to which "itleăk" is joined. If the Verb is irregular, you may find its Conjugation hereafter.

---

[1] This expression "solitary" is not quite suited; but I cannot find a better one for the present.

§ 5. Compound Verbs

The Konkani Compound Verbs do not present such difficulties as other languages; for the sake of brevity I shall speak of them in the Part III. Only the Verbs compounded of the Gerund in un are a little difficult; about these I speak in Part III. and in the Syntax; yet their construction is not difficult. Here I mention a vulgar manner in which some Verbs are used which seem to be Compound Verbs. Instead of saying: *e.g.* "āuveñ takā mārleñ", they say: "āuñ takā mārun geloñ = I went to beat him"; viz. they add the corresponding tense of "vetañ = I go" to the Participle in un of the principal Verb; but the meaning is the same as if I said "I have beaten him", except that this manner of speaking implies a resolution of not doing it any more.

§ 6. Periphrastic Conjugation

This is just like the English "I am writing, I was writing" *etc.*, or like the Latin "*amaturus sum, amandus sum*" *etc.;* by its aid we may supply the apparent deficiency of many Tenses. This Conjugation is formed in a similar way to the Latin, viz. by joining the Verb "assā *or* zatā" to the Participle or Gerund Present, or Past, or Future, according to the meaning; this Verb "assā *or* zatā" is put in the Tense required by the meaning. So "mārun assā = he is beating"; for *venturus est*, you must use the Future Participle, for *faciendum erat* you must use the Passive Future Participle (Gerundive). "He is beating" could be translated by the Present Participle in "-tolo", yet the Participle in un seems to be more in use for this Periphrastic Conjugation, if the meaning requires the Present Participle.

Another more common way of making this Periphrastic Conjugation is to add "thāiñ = there" and "assā" in the required finite Tense to the Participle in -tañ of the principal Verb; *e.g.* "āuñ mārtāñ thāiñ assañ = I am beating, *lit.*

(where) beating there I am"; "mārtāñ thaiñ astoloñ = I shall be beating"; "mārtāñ thaiñ assoloñ = I was beating" *etc.*

To this paragraph of the Periphrastic Conjugation some Tenses can be reduced, which are compounded of the principal Verb in a finite Mood, and of the Auxiliary Verb also in a finite Mood; *e.g.* "kărin zaleār = *si fecero*"; "kărināñ zāin = *non fecero* or *non faciam*" (Future Potential Negative); here the Conjunction "moṇ = that" is omitted, yet the whole construction is as if it had been put. So it is not difficult to understand the above examples. Thus "kărin zaleār" may be literally translated thus by supplying the omitted "moṇ" = *si fiat (ut) ego faciam* (-*si fecero*) "kărināñ zāin = *potest fieri (ut) ego non faciam*".

§ 7. Irregular Verbs

They are very few in number, and even these few are not entirely irregular; for, usually only the Past and the Tenses derived from the Past are irregular. Hence we may say that only the Past, for the most part, is irregular; for, the other Tenses are derived from the Past regularly (see above). Hence I will not write the whole Conjugation of these Verbs, but only what is required. But remark that the irregularity is only in the affirmative form for the greatest part; if there be irregularity also in the negative form, it will be indicated.

The two first Irregular Verbs are the Auxiliary Verbs "assā" and "zatā", given above.

3. "nozo" which may be considered as another Auxiliary Verb for the Negative Necessary Mood, means "it is impossible". This form in itself has no Conjugation; if other Tenses are required, the corresponding Tense of "assā" *or* "zatā" is added to "nozo"; *e. g.* "nozo zaleñ, nozo assalleñ, nozo zateleñ" *etc.* Perhaps this "nozo" is shortened from "nā za(tā) = does not become, does not suit".

4. Another Auxiliary Verb is "zāi", for the Affirmative Necessary Mood; "zāi" means "it is necessary"; it has no Con-

jugation in itself, but the required Tense of "assā" or, better, of "zatā" is added to "zāi", just as with "nozo"; *e. g.* "zāi zateleñ, zāi zaleñ, zāi zataleñ, zāi zāit *etc.*

5. Finally "tanktā", another Auxiliary Verb, is regular, except that it governs the Dative of the person, and is often resolved into the Noun "tank = power" and the Verb "assā"; the Past Negative has also "tanklenāñ", and the Imperfect "tank natẹli" is used also for the Past.

6. kăr = do. *Past.* ke-lo. *Neg. Past.* kărunk-nāñ.
7. khā = eat. *Past.* khe-lo.
8. ye = come. *Past.* ai-lo. *Supine.* iunk (*vulg.*), *or* yeunk (*reg.*)
9. ve-tāñ = I go. (*In North Canara and by Hindus* voi-tāñ).
Past. gelo. *Imperative.* vôtz (2nd pers. Sing.).
Supine. votzunk, but *Abs. Inf.* votzo *or* veso.
Conting. Future. votzan. *Neg. Abs. Fut.* vetsonāñ.
Neg. Imperf. votzanātlo. *Pres. Neg.* votzanāñ *etc.*

Hence of this Verb there are three roots or fundamental forms ve, ge, votz; the 1st is for the Present, Imperfect, Absolute Future, Absolute Infinitive, Participles (except "votzun", and "votzuñso"; see p. 121, observation 14), Gerunds; the 2nd is for the Past and for the Tenses derived from the Past, (see above Art. I. § 5); the 3rd is for the Negative Form, and for the Imperative, Optative Present, Subjunctive Present, Supine, Potential and Necessary Mood, Contingent Future, Participle in -un and -uñso of the Affirmative Form. As perhaps some might think this too difficult to be retained, I put the full Conjugation.

Affirmative form

A. Indicative Mood

Pres. vetāñ *etc.* *Imperf.* vetāloñ *etc.* *Past.* geloñ *etc.* *Perf.* gelāñ *etc.* *Past Perf.* gelloñ *etc.* *Fut. Abs.* vetoloñ *etc.* *2nd and Contingent Fut.* votzan *etc.*

B. Imperative Mood

vótz, *etc.*

C. Optative Mood

Pres. votzuñ! *Imperf.* geleãr puro! *Past.* gelo asleãr puro!

D. Subjunctive Mood

Pres. votzuñ. *Imperf.* votzasoñ. *1st Condit.* geleãr. *2nd Conditional.* gelo asleãr. *1st Conditionatum.* votzan. *2nd Conditionatum.* vetoloñ assoloñ.

E. Potential Mood

votzãyet.

F. Necessary Mood

votzazãi.

G. Infinitive Mood

Absol. veso *or* vetzo. *Sup.* votzunk.

H. Participles

Pres. vetolo. *Imperf.* vetalo. *Past.* gelo.
Past Perf. gello. *Fut.* vetzo.

I. Gerunds

Pres. vetanañ. *Imperf.* votzun. *Past.* 1) votzun, 2) vetatz.

Negative form.

"votzanãñ *etc.*" from the root "votz" except "vetzonãñ" and "vetonãñ".

After the Conjugation of "vetã" I put also an example of the full Conjugation of another Irregular Verb, to show more distinctly how the Tenses of the Irregular Verbs are either derived regularly from the Past or Regular

Kãr = do

Affirmative form

A. Indicative Mood

Pres. kãrtãñ *etc.* *Imperf.* kãrtaloñ *etc.* *Past.* keloñ *etc.* *Perfect.* kelañ *etc.* *Past Perfect.* kelloñ or keloloñ *etc.*

1st Fut. Absol. kărtoloñ *etc.* *2nd and Conting. Fut.* kărin *etc.* Three other *2nd Futures*: 1) kărun astoloñ *etc.*, 2) kărtoñ assoloñ *etc.*, 3) keloñ astoloñ *etc.*

B. Imperative Mood

kăruṅgi *etc.*

C. Optative Mood

Pres. kăruñ *or* karundigă, Devă! *etc.*
Imperf. keleăr puro! *Past.* kelo asleăr puro!

D. Subjunctive Mood

Pres. kăruñ *etc.* *Imperf.* kărisoñ *etc.*
1st Conditional. keleăr. *2nd Conditional.* kelo asleăr.
1st Conditionat. kărin *etc.* *2nd Conditionat.* kărtoñ *etc.*, *or* kărtoñ assoloñ *or* kărtoloñ assoloñ.[1]

E. Potential Mood

Pres. 1) kăriyet, 2) kărunk tanktă, 3) kărunk puro. *Past.* 1) kăriyet assąleñ, 2) kărunk tank assąli, 3) kărunk puro assąleñ. *Future.* 1) kăriyet, 2) kărin *etc.*, 3) kariyet asteleñ, 4) kărunk tank asteli.

F. Necessary Mood

Pres. 1) kărizăi, 2) kărčeñ assă. *Past.* 1) karizăi assąleñ, 2) kărčeñ assąleñ. *Future.* 1) kărizăi. 2) kărčeñ asteleñ. 3) kărizăi asteleñ.

G. Infinitive Mood

Absol. kărso *etc.* *Sup.* kărunk.

H. Participles

Pres. 1) kărtolo. 2) kărso. 3) kărtă to. 4) kărtañ. *Imperf.* kărtalo. *Past.* kelo. *Past Perf.* kello, *or* kelolo. *Fut.* kărso, *or* kărtolo.

I. Gerunds

Pres. kărtanañ. *Imperf.* kărun *or* kărn. *Past.* kărtătz.

---

[1] This form, i. e. to use the Participle in "-tolo" instead of the Participle in "-to", with "assolo", is as common as the other form put in the Paradigm, i. e. as "-to" or "-to" with "assolo". (See 2nd Conditionatum §§ 2 and 4.)

Irregular Verbs (*continued*)

10. Mór = die, *Past.* melo (*different from* mello *and* mhèḷo, *and* mór *different from* móḍ).

11. Văḍ *or* văr = carry. *Past.* velo.

12. Moṇ = say. *Past.* moḷo. *Participle Imperf.* moṇ, *besides* moṇun.

13. Ubza = proceed. *Participle.* ubzono.[1]

14. Bos = seat. The regular *Past.* "boslă" seems to be used also for the Present (*vulg.* boholă).

15. Ge = receive. *Past.* getlo; but the compound "kăṇge" has "kăṇgelo *or* kăṇgetlo".

16. "Aik = hear" forms the Tenses regularly, but as if the root were "aika", when it would be too hard to pronounce the Tense formed from "aik"; so we have *Pres.* aikatăñ *etc.*, but *Imperat.* "aik, aikă", *Subj.* "aikuñ" *etc.*, as there is no cacophony in saying "aikă" *etc.*

Besides these single Verbs, there is a whole class of Verbs which properly are not irregular, yet require some euphonical changes, I mean the Verbs having the root ending in a vowel. But here again we have to remark:

a) The Verbs ending in u or uñ change in the Contingent (and Potential, equal to the Contingent) Future u and uñ into v whenever the termination to be added to the root begins with a or u (which u sometimes is pronounced by some o). The same change takes place if "zăi" is to be added to them; thus "rău = remain", has "răvan, răuši, răvat, răvuñ (răvo), răušăt, răutit, răvazăi (some castes say "răbazăi"): "dăuñ = run", "dăvan" *etc.*, "dăvazăi"; "deuñ = descend", "devan", "devazăi".

b) The Verbs having the root ending in a vowel except a, take in the Absolute Infinitive and equal Participle and Gerundive, "-uñso (*or* -untzo)" instead of "-so (-tzo)". But if the root ends in ăi, ai, oi, i, ei, as all Causative and some other Verbs, the terminations "-uñso" and "-unk" are added to the root omitting

---

[1] Some do not admit as Konkani this "ubzono", they always say "ubzalo".

the i, as if the root ended in a, or e, or o; *e.g.* "poḷei, poḷeunk, poḷeuñso"; "kărai, kărauñso, kăraunk *or* kărounk". As I see that there is some difficulty about these Verbs ending in a vowel, I shall put hereafter an example.

c) Verbs ending in a, add in the Absolute Infinitive only "-ñso." as also in the Future Negative Absolute.

d) If the root ends in u or uñ, then euphony requires us to add nk, instead of unk in the Supine, n instead of un in the Gerund in un.

Some other changes, which are not put down here, may be required by euphony. See also p. 94, Future Tense.

Conjugation of Verbs ending in a vowel

"Pie = drink" [1]

Fut. Cont. Sing 1) pien, 2) pieši, 3) piet.
Plu. 1) pieuñ, 2) piešăt, 3) pietit.
Imperat. Sing. pie, *Plur.* pieyā.
Supine. pieunk (*vulg.* piunk).
Infin. Absol., *Particip.*, *Gerundive* } pieuñso (*vulg.* piuñso).
Fut. Neg. Abs. 1) pieuñsonāñ *etc.* = I shall not drink;
2) piesonāñ = I will not drink.

"Dăuñ = run"

Future Cont. Sing. 1) dăvan, 2) dăuši, 3) dăvat;
Plu. 1) dăvuñ, 2) dăuñšăt, 3) dăuntit.
Imperat. Sing. dăuñ,
Plu. dăuñā *or* dăvā,
Caus. dăuṇḍăi.

---

[1] The Tenses not put down here are regular throughout.

Conjugation of a Causative Verb and of its corresponding Non-Causative Neuter Verb

"Paloăi = quench"

Fut. Cont. paloăin *etc.*
Supine. paloăunk (*vulg.* palounk).
Infin. Abs. / *Particip.* / *Gerundive* } paloăuñso (*vulg.* palouñso).
Pres. Neg. paloăinăñ *etc.*
Fut. Neg. 1) paloăuñsonăñ (*vulg.* palouñsonăñ) = I shall not quench.
2) paloăisonăñ = I will not quench.

"Paloa-tă = is quenched"

Fut. Cont. Sing. 1) paloan, 2) paloaši, 3) paloat;
Plu. 1) paloauñ, 2) paloašăt 3) paloatit.
Supine. paloaunk.
Infin. Abs. / *Participle* / *Gerundive* } paloañso.
Pres. Neg. paloanăñ.
Fut. Neg. paloañsonăñ.

In a similar way to the above Causative Verb are conjugated also those Verbs, which although not Causative, have a similar termination; *e. g.* "poḷei = see"; "borei = write"; "kărtči = expend"; so "kărtzounk, kărtzouñso" *etc.*

From the given examples we may see the difference between the Causative and the Non-Causative (Neuter) corresponding Verb. I say "Neuter", because if it is not Neuter, *per se* it has no peculiarity.

In order to make still easier the Conjugation of these Verbs, let us put together all different things said in different places about Verbs ending in a vowel, and frame a rudimental rule. The general rule can be expressed thus: The Verbs ending in a vowel either insert some consonant, or change some letter or do not take the full termination whenever euphony requires that; or, more distinctly,

1. Verbs ending in a insert v in the form "-iyet" of the Potential; ending in a and e insert y in the 2nd Person Plural Imperative.

2. Verbs ending in u or uñ change u or uñ into v in the form "-iyet" of the Potential; the same happens also in the Contingent Future whenever the termination to be added to the root begins with a vowel, and when "zāi" is added.

3. Verbs ending in a, e, i, mostly omit the initial vowel of the termination in the Contingent Future, and those in a omit also the vowel a of the termination -uñso, and those in u or uñ omit u of the termination -uñso and -unk, or, we may say, omit u and uñ before adding -uñso and -unk.

4. Verbs ending in any vowel usually take -uñso (and -uñsonāñ in the Negative Future, see p. 94) instead of -so (and -sonāñ the Negative Future. See *ibid* a limitation); but if the last vowel of the root is i (ăi, ai, ei, oi, i preceded by a consonant), they add the terminations -uñso and -unk to the root, either omitting this i, if it is preceded by a, e or o, or changing it into ă or o, if it is preceded by a consonant. There may be a few exceptions, which practice will teach you.

What has been said (*n.* 3) must be limited thus: Verbs ending in "a", drop the initial vowel of the termination of the Contingent Future, if this is "-an", as this is usually the case; because mostly this "a" is a sign of a Neuter Verb derived from its corresponding Causative Verb in "ăi", by omitting "i"; consequently it takes "an" not "in" (see p. 117, *n.* 8, *d.*); but sometimes Verbs ending in "a" are transitive; *e. g.* "khā=eat" has "khā-in". For this reason I say (p. 117. *l. c.*) mostly, not always, Verbs ending in "a" take only "n".

What to say if the Verb ends not in "a, e, i," but in "u" and "o"? If this "u" is preceded by "e" or "a", *e. g.* "rāu, jou, seu," then see above *n.* 2. If this "u" is preceded by a consonant, first I say that I do not recollect now any Verb ending in such a way; yet with analogy to other cases, if such a case happens, I would change this "u" into "v", or add to "u" the terminations without the initial vowel; *e. g.* suppose that "māru-tā" be a Konkani Verb: then I would say "mārvan *or* mārun".

If the Verb ends in "o", if such Verbs exist and this "o" be not a short "a (ă)", then if it is transitive, it seems more euphonical to add the full terminations "-in" *etc.*; if it is Neuter, it does not seem prohibited *per se* to add the full terminations "an" *etc.*, chiefly if this "o" be preceded by a consonant; yet, as in this matter, use is the rule, practice will teach you what is the best way. I said above, "unless this 'o' be not 'ă'," because these two letters can be exchanged very easily; so "mānuă-tā=pleases" seems to be pronounced by many "mānuo-tā". This Verb has "mānuan" in the Contingent Future.

What I said in this matter about Verbs ending in a vowel, (as also in many other cases) supposes that we write Konkani with Roman letters; because some of these rules would be useless, if we had to write it with Kanarese letters.

These little irregularities might perhaps induce some to put at least two Conjugations, *i.e.* one of the Verbs ending in a consonant, the other of the Verbs ending in a vowel. Yet, as both Conjugations are mostly the same and the small differences between them are euphonical rather than grammatical, so for the sake of simplicity I thought it better to put only one Conjugation.

§ 8. Defective Verb

The following Verbs, though a little irregular, may be called Defective Verbs, because all the Tenses are not used.

1. Zāṇañ=I know. *Present*. zāṇañ, zāṇai *etc.* (regularly). The other Tenses which can be used are formed by adding to "zāṇa" the required Tense of "assā". Thus "zāṇañ assoloñ= I knew", *or* "zāṇañ zāun assoloñ".

2. "Neṇañ[1)]=I do not know" may be considered as the negative form of "zāṇañ"; its Tenses are formed just as the Tenses of "zāṇañ".

Moreover "nozo" and "zāi" may be considered as defective (see above).

Exercises on Verbs (*Continued*)

Causative Verbs

hās=laugh

Burgeā, kiteāk iskul karčea veḷār hāstai? To makā hāsaitā. Āuveñ sāngleñ, kēlāingī? Āuveñ kārunknāñ. Pedrun

1) Pronounce nearly "neaṇañ", passing over "nea" very quickly.

kăraitañ. Burgeñ tzăltăgī? Nāñ; āuoi takā tzălaitā. Mēz porti. Mēz vareān portatā. Āuoi băpaino, tumiñ tumčeañ burgeānk Devāče birāntint vāḍaiyā. Burgeñ khāinăñ zăi zaleār, āuoi takā khāuoitā[1]. Devāči kurpā amkāñ Devāk mānuāitā[2]. Takā boreunčeāk lăi[3].

Reciprocal Verbs

Băvānu, yēkamekāso mōg kărā; yeñ Somia Jezu Kristāčeñ formān dekun. Burge lačilānt yēkamekā kel̥tāt. Monis peleāso mōg kărčea suāter săbār păuṭi yēkamekā zagaḍtāt ani lăḍăi kărtāt. Băp ani āuoi khāiñ assāt? Yēkamekā gazāli mārtāt (*have a chat*).

Reflexive Verbs

Sañ Luis apleā itleāk mārtālo, zăritār tāṇeñ vōḍ pātkañ kedintz aḍarunknatul̥liñ. Tuje itleāk boreñ čintun niščcsi. Sañ Frančis Zaver Meliapurānt astanañ, vigārāčea gārā lāgiñ assal̥lea itlānt aplea itleāk ratir (*or* ratzo) băuntālo ani niāl kărtālo.

Verbs excluding Companionship

Āuñ moje itleāk čintāñ: meleā uprānt dusri jini mel̥năzaleār amiñ sămestañ monšăñ prăs nirbhăgi. Monis apleā itleāk săbār păuṭi Devān keliñ upkārañ niāl̥l̥eār, dubāu nastanañ Devāso tzăḍ mōg karit. Tūñ koṇāger rāutai? Āungī? Āuñ aplea itleāk jietāñ. Āuñ kāl tăḍir moje itleāk băuntanañ ani utzambol dărio pol̥eitanañ, Devāčea rāgāčeñ sarkeñ makā distāleñ.

---

[1] Causative Verb from "khā"; it is formed irregularly.

[2] Causative Verb from "Mānuă-tā = pleases"; as the primitive Verb ends in "ă", only "i" is added; so also in other similar cases; *i. e.* if the Verb (primitive) ends in a consonant, the Causative Verb is formed by adding "ăi" (sometimes "ai, ei, oi"); if it ends in a vowel chiefly in "a", then very often only "i" is added, or "a" is changed into "i" ("portatăñ, portităñ") or, seldom, "uoi" or other irregular termination is added. See moreover the exceptions § 1.

[3] By "lăi = apply", many Verbs which cannot be formed Causative by "ăi" etc., take a causative meaning.

Verbs compounded of the Gerund in un

Pedru khāiñ assā? Āpoun āḍtāñ. Moji pēṭ koṇā lāgiñ assā? Anton kāṇeun (*vlg*. kāṇ) yetā. Mukār vótz: āuñ tuzo livrụ kāṇ yetāñ. Saibānu, tumiñ kāgad boreyā; āuñ dāṇditāñ (dāḍun ditāñ). Kārt (*master*) apleā kuṭmāk khāṇ aṇditā (āḍun ditā). Rāyān aḍli hukum kāḍun galleā. Pal (*canopy*) ukoln dorā.

Irregular Verbs

kēḷeñ, -ea = plantain (*n*.)

Tuveñ tuzo vāur keloiṅgī? Āveñ yedoḷ kārunknāñ, fālea kārtāñ. Tuveñ kiteñ khelaiñ? Āveñ dōn kēḷiñ kheleānt. Tuveñ kelleā kām boreñ natụlleñ, tea pasun teñ portun kārčeñ assạlleñ. Mozo livrụ bhāir poḍlo, tukā meḷḷāgī? Makā meḷunknāñ. Tuzo bāpui melogī? Morunknāñ, assā. Yā bāint mhēḷeñ[1] udāk assāgī? Ui, yere bāink votzazāi.

Periphrastic Conjugation

Āuñ boreun assāñ. Āuñ yetanaā to nidun assolo. Tūñ zāun vortautāigī to zo yeunzo assā? Povitrụ pustakānt kiteñ boreun assā? Devāčeñ utar boreun assā. Āuñ ataā boreitāñ thāiñ assāñ, makā kārkar kār nakā. Zōkōṇ khālto zatā, takā Deu vorto kārtolo; zōkōṇ vorto zatā, to khālto kelo zatolo. Tūñ yeunčea veḷār, āuñ siktoloā astoloā. Monšāñ kāḍe ādhār meḷnatụllea veḷār, Devā thāiñ āsro kāṇeuñso assā.

Verbs ending in a Vowel

Zōkōṇ Devāče kurpe bitār rāvanāñ[2] to apṇāk luksān,

---

[1] This "m" which neither in Kanarese, nor in Marāthi is reckoned among the aspirated letters, becomes aspirated by adding "h" just as in Kanarese, by adding ꠸; or rather there are two different letters "m" and "h".

[2] "U" of "rāu" becomes "v" not only when "zāi" is added, but also in the Negative form when "nāñ" is added. See Art. I. § 5 *n*. 2. p. 116.) The above rule (p. 148) in order to be complete must be compared also with § 5 *l. c.* chiefly *nn*. 2, 3.

Devāk akmān kārtā. Somia Jezu Kristāči kuḍ seuñso Devāči jini jietā. Aple dis tzāḍ jeun ani pieun kārtsouñso monis Devāso santos. boganāñ. Tsāḍ ulounčeānt āib tzukčeñuāñ, sangtā povitrụ pustak.

CHAPTER V. ADVERBS

About the Adverbs many questions might be put. The chief ones are these: 1) Which are the principal Adverbs? 2) How are they formed? 3) How are they used?

1. *a*) Principal Adverbs of Place with the derived Adjectives

"angā = here"—angāso (angāsār = here above)
"thāiñ" = there, thither"—thāiñso
"khāiñ" = where, whither"—khāiñso
"sāgḷean" = everywhere"—*Instr. of* sāgḷo
"sārvụthāiñ" = everywhere" *used chiefly in religious matters*
"lāgiñ = close"—lāgšilo
"sārsi = close"—sārsilo
"pois" = far"—poislo *or* poisilo
"voir = above, up stairs"—voilo
"sākāl = down, below"—sāklo
"pāṭi (*or* paṭleān) = behind"—pāṭlo
"mukār = before, in face"—mukāvelo
"teusin = in that side", *shortened from* tea kusin—teakusilo
"yeusin = in this side," *shortened from* yea kusin—yeakusilo
"bitār = inside"—bitārlo
"bhāir = outside"—bhāilo

***b*) Principal Adverbs of Time with the derived Adjectives**

"āz = to-day", —āiso
"fāleā, *or* phāleā = to-morrow"—fāleāso
"kāl = yesterday"—kālso
"poir = the day before yesterday" *or* pōr—porso
"porvāñ = after to-morrow"—porvāñso

"poruñ = last year"—poruñso
"disā'dis = every day"—disādisāso
"sakāḷiñ = early"—sakāḷiñso
"phanteār = at daybreak"—phanteāparāso
"sakāḷiče = in the morning"
"sānjer *or* sānječe = in the evening"—sānjeso
"bhou sakāḷiñ = early in the morning"
"toḍou = late"
"vegiñ = early, in time"—vegiñso
"ādiñ = before"—ādlo
"māgir = afterwards"—māgirlo *or* māgirso
"atāñ = now"—atāñso
"purviñ *or* ādiñ purviñ = in ancient times"—purviñlo
"voḍól = lately"—voḍolso
"yedóḷ pāriant = up to this"—yedolso
"sāddañ (*emph.* saddants) = always"—sāddantso
"kedints...nāñ = never"—kedintso...nāñ
"tovoḷ *or* teaveḷār = then, at that time"—tovoḷso
"khāiñ" = when (*low castes say* khoiñ)"—khāiñso
"seki
"kaḍek } = finally"—kaḍieso
"yea fāde = afterwards (in future)"
"poilentz = already (first)"
"sove = at the same time"
"aprup = seldom"—aprupso, *or* aprupaso

c) **Principal Adverbs of Quantity with the derived Adjectives**

"bhou
"sābār } = much"
"illo (-i, -eñ)
"toḍo (-i, -eñ)
"tikeñ (*or* čikeñ) } = a little"
"sumār = moderately, neither very much nor very little"—sumārso
"uṇo (-i, -eñ) = less"

"tsăḍ = much, more, too much"
"ani = still, more", *e.g.* ani dòn = two more
"puro = enough"

d) Principal Adverbs of Manner with the derived Adjectives

"boreñ = well" (*or* boro, -i, -eñ)
"pāḍ = badly"
"tzukon = wrongly"
"sompeñ
"sompeponān } = easily"—sompo, sasārāyeso
"sasārāyen
"kăšṭān = with difficulty"—kăšṭāñso
"tzăḍ uṇeñ = nearly, about" (Latin *circiter*)
"lāgiñ lāgiñ = almost" (Lat. *paene*), *e.g.* "lāgiñ lāgiñ tīs = almost 30 (less than 30)"
"tzăḍāvotzăun = generally, usually"
"kapas! = very well! perfectly!" (*used often ironically*)
"aučit
"yekăts pharā } = suddenly"
"čintinastanāñ
"portun = again"
"neaṇārpoṇān = ignorantly"—neaṇārpoṇāso
"besṭeñ = in vain"—besṭo
"asseñ = in this way"—asso
"tasseñ = in that way"—tasso
"viñgăḍ = separately"
"sañgatā = together"
"voṭṭu = altogether"
"kăsso (-i, -eñ) = how"
"kăssălo (-i, -eñ) = how"
"vegiñ = fast"—vegiñso
"soukās = slowly"—soukāsāyeso *or* soukāsaiso
"nizzăun
"dubăunăstanañ } = certainly"
"drăḍzăun

"yekādevēḷā = perhaps"
"zāit = well (yes)"
"ui" = yes"
"niñ
"nāiñ" } = no"
"nāñ
"puṇi *or* puṇ = at least".

Besides these, which I may call primitive or original Adverbs, (except very few, which are not primitive, *e.g.* kāšṭān) there are many derived Adverbs; of these I shall speak in the III. Part, about Derivations.

2. See Part III.

3. I answer for the present (reserving the more exact explanation for the Syntax) that they are not declined, except the Adverbs of Place; and even these are not declined when used absolutely. We must except the Adjectives which are used also as Adverbs, as we shall see in the Syntax; those Adjectives agree with the corresponding Noun; *e.g.* among the above Adverbs "kāsso, kāssalo, poilotz" *etc.* These Adjectives may be recognized by the termination "o (otz) *or* eñ". But if they are used to show some peculiar relation of place, they are declined according to meaning, after being changed into Adjectives, viz. after having given to them a form of Adjective in so *or* lo; *e.g.* "angā = here", "angāčeān = through here", Instrumental from "angāso"; "modeñ = in the middle", "modleān = through the middle", Instrumental from "modlo".

If "-so, -či, -čeñ" were to be taken as signs of the Genitive, we should say also that the Adverbs of time etc. are declined; so "āiso = of to-day"; "angāso = of here". But, as I consider "-so, -či, -čeñ" to be signs of the Adjective, or at least I am allowed to suppose it, I will speak of them in the Chapter on Adjectives in the Syntax, if possible.

Exercises on Adverbs

Āz Pedru āučit melo. Kāl Lorso čintinastanañ tzārlo. Poir Simāuñ piḍent poḍlā. Poruñ kumsār zālloigī? Āuñ kumsār zāun tintz moine zāḷe. Fāleā yā porvañ āuñ tumger rāutoloñ. Fāleā Āitārā paisāvāso sermauñ astolo; kālčeā Āitārā sermauñ nātullo. Khăiñ vetāi? Gărā vetāñ. Angāčeān votziyetgī? Geleār, zăgo pāḍ zatā. Tujeñ găr khăiñ assā? Vāḍeāčā modeñ assā. Gāḍiegārā, gāḍi modlean vór. O monis konso? To angāso. Ani to monis? To porgāvāntlo. Āiso vānjel kāssālo? Āiso vānjel paisāvāso. Mōgān sămestañ kăḍe ulei. Grest monis kăšṭān sărgār pāutāt. Făvoṭe jinsiñ kumgār kāṇeitoleānk Devāči jiṇi meḷtā. Mēstri sāngtā, teñ čiṭ diun aikāzāi. Mojeñ kām boreñ kărn kărunknāñ. Tūñ khăiñ vetoloi? Āuñ Bombāi vetāñ. Kăiñ Bombăi vetāi? Fāleā.

CHAPTER VI. POSTPOSITIONS

1. Under this name are included what we call in our languages *Prepositions*, because in Konkani all such words are put after the affected part of the speech.

2. Postpositions which govern the Nominative:—

pāriant }
moṇasor } = till

Postpositions which govern the Dative:

āḍ }
porte } = against
viródh }

Postpositions which govern the Original:

ādiñ = before
mukār }
hujir } = in face, at the presence of
phāḍeñ = before, after (see Dictionary)
uprānt }
magir } = after
paṭleān = behind, Lat. *retro*
voir = above, upon

sākāl
khāl } = under
talā

pois = far

lāgiñ
kāḍe } = close
sārsi

thāiñ' = in, as regards, towards, *e. g.* "Devā thāiñ = in God"

bitār = in, within

bhāir = out, without, beyond

viṇe *or* vin = without (Lat. *sine*)

sangatā = with

vingāḍ = separately from

pasun *or* pasvot
khatir } = for, on account of

pārmaṇe = according to

bāuntaṇeñ = around

veslean *or* dikān = in the direction of

thāun = from, *e. g.* from Calicut to Mangalore, from 3-4

poltoḍi = beyond (*ultra*)

āltāḍi = on this side (*citra*)

vorviñ = through

šivāi
karit } = beside (Lat. *praeter*)

bādlāk = instead of

suater = in the place of.

From some Postpositions are derived some Adjectives; these mostly have been given in Ch. V., because those Postpositions are also Adverbs.

3. Are the Postpositions declined? If we consider the true Postpositions, not the derived Adjectives, I answer, no; yet in some cases they seem to be declined, for they change according to the Number and Gender; *e. g.* "from hell = emkaṇḍāntlo": "gārānt = in the house"; "gārāniñ = in the houses". Yet this is only an appearance, because in the first case, as we

have seen above, the Substantive with the Postposition is changed into an Adjective. The 2nd example would show only that -nt is not used in Plural; yet we have seen that we can say also "gărānt = in the houses", though not so well as "gărāniñ".

4. What case do they govern? This appears from the given list.

5. The change of Postpositions into Adjectives is very remarkable, chiefly of the Postpositions "bităr, voir, lāgiñ", (see above Chapter II. Art. I. § 3); *e.g.* Among the Chapters of the Canticle, this is the 3rd." That "Among...Canticle" is considered as an Adjective of "Chapter"; hence it takes the terminations of the Adjective; "Kantiklea avesvără bitărlo vo tisro avesvăr"; we might translate it literally into bad Latin, thus: *existens intra capita Cantici hoc Caput tertium*. So also: "St. Paul is one of the Apostles = Apostalāntlo St. Paul yeklo". It seems that if there is in the sentence, besides the word governed by the Postposition, a Substantive or Pronoun with which the Postposition has some connexion, the Postposition is changed into an Adjective. About this later on.

6. Sometimes two Postpositions are joined in a similar way as in the Latin sentence: "*De sub cujus pede fons vivus emanat*"; *e.g.* "sărgār thāun = from heaven"; "sărgārānt = above in heaven"; *i.e.* they wish to express at the same time two ideas: 1, that heaven is *above*, 2, that *in* this high place, *e.g.* happiness is found.

7. Some Postpositions, if joined to Participles, prefer to be joined to the Past rather than to the Present Participle, *e.g.* "uprānt = after"; others on the contrary prefer to be joined to the Present or Future Participle; *e.g.* "adiñ = before". There are some which seem to be joined indifferently to the Past or Present Participle according to the meaning.

8. The use of the Postposition in Konkani is much more frequent than in our languages; many Tenses, which in English or Latin are not preceded by any Preposition, are trans-

lated by a Postposition with the Participle, as will be shown in the Syntax.

9. But on the other hand, some English or Latin Prepositions are not translated at all in Konkani. This is the case chiefly with so many Verbs compounded with Prepositions; often the English Preposition is omitted, because the simple Konkani Verb renders the meaning of the English compound Verb; yet sometimes the English Preposition gives quite a different meaning to the Verb; then, of course, either a Konkani Postposition or Adverb must be used, or a simple Verb which corresponds to that changed meaning; *e.g.* "*call on*" is not translated by "voir apoi", but by "bet = visit". Moreover although the English Preposition (or Adverb) does not change much the meaning, sometimes we may use in Konkani the corresponding Postposition (or Adverb).

Excercises on Postpositions

Kodiāla thāun mojeñ gār pāriant tīs kòs assāt. Šerāntlo kòṇ ailo? Kòṇ yeunknāñ. Devā thāiñ kitle zóṇ assāt? Devā thāiñ teg zòṇ. Amčea ātmeā thāiñ Deu kiteñ kārtā? Ajapāčeo vāstu kārtā, amiñ takā kābul dileār. Gārā bitār kòṇ assā? Gārā bitār kòṇnāñ; bāgil dāmpun assā. Igarje bāir votzun tumiñ āikalleñ vitzārnakāt. Pedru Simāvāk āḍ yetā, tače pasun (tea pasun) Simāuñ Pedruk viródh yetā. Tumče bitārlo kòṇ yemkaṇḍāntli kešṭ sosit? Somi Jezu Krist saitānāk monšāñ voilo soḍounčea veḷār, saitān bōb mārn sāngtālo: "Kiteāk amkāñ kāšṭ diunk ailāi?" Somi Jezu Krist nimāṇea disā koṭṭeānk sāngtolo: "Moje lagše votzā, maldisāoñ poḍleleāno.

CHAPTER VII. CONJUNCTIONS

1. In Konkani there are not so many true Conjunctions as in English, because many English Conjunctions are translated by Correlative Pronouns; *e.g.* "as = zosso—tosso"; sometimes they are translated by an Adjective, *e.g.* *quam magnus*, which

quam is translated by an Adjective (kitlo *or* kedo), though we may say also that they are Conjunctions, but declined. Some others are translated by Postpositions, *e. g.* "because = pasun"; some others are omitted, *e.g.* "either or" are translated by one Conjunction.

2. Principal Conjunctions:

kiteāk – kiteāk moḷeăr = why—because
dekun = because, therefore
tăr = therefore
puṇ, puṇi = but
bogăr = but (*in opposition, e.g.* not only....but also)
tări, zaleări = nevertheless, yet
ī = although, also
zărităr *or* zăritări = although
zărtăr = if
ki, moṇ = that
vo *or* uo, yā = or
muṇčeñ *or* muṇjeñ = that is to say
săit", legun = also, even
tače šivai = besides, moreover
ani = and

Negative Conjunctions, *e. g.* "neither nor", are formed by adding the negative particle to the affirmative. (See Part III. Chapter IV.)

3. Among them there are some which may be divided, *e. g.* "zărtăr = if", which can be divided in such a way that zăr is put in the beginning of the conditional sentence, and tăr in the beginning of the 2nd part, *e. g.* "zărtăr te bhāgevănt, săргār vetăt = if they are holy, they go to heaven", or we may say also "zăr te bhāgevănt, tăr săргār vetăt"; so also "zărităr = though", compound with "zărtăr = if", and "i = also" may be separated so as to put this i joined to the Verb, *e. g.* "zărităr yēk ānj aileăr = though an angel would come", or "zărtăr yēk anj aileări".

4. Some Conjunctions are put after the affected word, as in Lat. *enim*. So "puṇ", if it means "at least", is placed after the affected word—"vorsāk yēk pāuṭi puṇ kumzār zāizāi = once a year at least we must confess". Moreover "legun, sait, i", which all mean "also", are placed after the affected word, as in Latin *quoque:* i is not only placed after, but also joined to the word, *e. g.* "keleāri = though you did".

5. Many English Conjunctions cannot be translated literally, but by some circumlocution, as the Syntax and use will teach. Something more about Conjunctions will be said in the Syntax.

CHAPTER VIII. INTERJECTIONS

About these here I have nothing to say, but to put a list of the most common of them.

"ayo, kaṭā, yē" expressive of sorrow, pain.

"ah, āh, ahaha" expressive of surprise, pleasure, jest, reproach.

"āñ? = what?"; some use it also for "yes".

Our "o" of the Vocative is expressed by "ye"; *e.g.* ye Fraskā = O Francis!

"o *or* vo? = what?" in asking to repeat words not understood.

"čhi!" expressive of disgust.

PART III. SYNETYMOLOGY

In this part I treat of certain points, which belonging to some, if not to all, the Parts of Speech, may very appropriately be classed under the head of Synetymology. They are distinct both from Etymology properly so called, and from Syntax.

CHAPTER I.

Words used in speaking to or about persons

This chapter is almost a continuation of the Chapter VIII. of the II. Part; for, these words I speak of, are in some way Interjections, although not in the common meaning: and so this chapter may be the link between II. and III. Part.

1. We have already seen that no *or* nu is the Interjection added to the Vocative Plural; *e.g.* "bāvāno! = O brethren!"

2. To show respect to a person the Plural is used not only in addressing, but also in speaking of a person; *e.g.* "Sāibānu! = Oh lord!" "khāiñ gele? = where is he (the lord) gone?"

3. The second degree of honour is, when a man addresses another superior in age or in some other respect, to affix to the proper name the word or syllable "mā" for a man, and "māmie" for a woman; *e.g.* "Antoni mā! = Oh Antony!" "Mārie māmie! = Oh Mary!" This "mā" seems to be an abbreviation of "mamā, vocative of "mām = uncle", and "māmie" is the vocative of "māmi = aunt". If a more than common superiority is to be expressed, instead of "mā" they use "agā" for a man, "age" for a woman; if a still higher superiority is meant, they use "babā" (vocative of "bāb") for a man, "bāye" (vocative of "bāy") for a woman: finally the highest degree is "Sāib

or Somi *or* Suāmi" for a man, "Sāibiṇ" for a woman; although this last, "Sāibiṇ" among Christians is used almost exclusively for the blessed Virgin Mary. Note that by joining "age" and "bāye" you have a smaller degree than by using only "bāye=O lady".

4. Speaking to a boy, are is prefixed or re is added not only to their proper name, but also to the Verb, to the Pronoun *etc.;* speaking to girls and figuratively also to women, ago is prefixed or go placed afterwards.

5. As a term of endearment towards children or young persons amā *or* bāḷ is used.

6. If they have not to address but to speak of other superior persons, the above words, in the Nominative, are used; but mā is often changed into am or m; *e.g.* "Anton-ām". It is almost like our *Mr.*

Some examples will show the use of the above words.

"Pedru mā, Sāib tukā apoitāt=O Peter, the master calls you"; "Heleni māmie, Igārjent yetāigī?=O Helena, do you come to the church?"; "age Mārie, kossi assāi", *or* "Mārie, kossi assāige?=O Mary, how are you?" "Mārie bāye, makā apoitāigī?=Mary, do you call me?" *or* "age Mārie bāye, makā apoitāgī?" *or* "Mārie bāye, makā apoitāige?" "ye Forsa babā, makā yēk Rupoi dī=O Mr. Francis, give me one Rupee"; "Sāibā, hukum diā=O lord, give order"; "Silā-re=Oh Silvester (boy)", "are Silā, yē=come, O Silvester", *or* "Silā, yē-re"; "votz-re, lutzā=go, O rascal"; "Māriā-go, lānkuḍ āḍ=O Mary (girl), bring firewood", *or* "ago Māria"; "Mojea burgeā, yē amā=O my dear child, come"; "moja burgeā, khā baḷā=O dear child, eat"; "Amā" and "baḷā" must be separated from the affected Noun.

From these examples we may form a rudimental rule about the use of these particles.

a) Re and go are placed after the affected word; if this is alone, immediately after it; if there is a sentence, joined, often at least, to the Verb. "Emmānueli-re=O Emmanuel",

"Emmānueli, yē-re = come O Emmanuel"; Māria-go = O Mary", "Māriā, yē-go = come O Mary".

b) **Are** and **ago** are immediately prefixed to the affected Noun; this may be alone or in a sentence; "are Emmānueli = O Emmanuel", "are Emmanueli, vāur kār = O Emmanuel work".

c) **Mā, māmie, babā, bāye** are put after the affected Noun.

d) **Agā** and **age** are put either immediately before the affected Noun, or afterwards, but joined to the Verb and losing the initial **a**.

e) **Sāiba, Suāmiā,**", addressing a person, are generally used without the proper Noun.

f) **Amā** and **baḷā** are separated, usually, from the affected Noun; but "burgiñ baḷañ" is used.

As to speaking not to, but about superior persons, the corresponding titles "mām (shortened 'ām'), māmi, bāb, bāy, sāib, suāmi, sāibiṇ" are put after the affected Noun; ("agā *and* age", "ago *and* are", "re, go" have no Nominative). Examples: "Anton mām Bombai gelo = Antony went to Bombay"; "Serpin māmi gārā nāñ = Seraphina is not at home"; "Nern bāb piḍent poḍlo = Mr. Nern fell sick"; "Reicklin bāy vilāyet geli = Mrs. Reichlin went to Europe"; "Hohenlohe sāib mantri zālo = Lord Hohenlohe became minister" *etc.* As for girls and boys, no title is given when speaking about them, as also to others, when no honour is intended. Remark that the Plural is used very seldom to show respect; generally they use the Plural speaking to Priests, or to very high persons; out of these cases, very seldom, except some customary cases, *e.g.* a daughter-in-law uses the Plural to the mother-in-law; the son-in-law to the father-in-law, the father-in-law to the son-in-law; the "yei" and "yeñ" (father or mother of bride and of wife's bridegroom) and the "sāḍu" (husbands of two sisters) among themselves. Remark moreover that "bāy" may mean also older sister and child; in both these cases "bāy" is neuter, although declined according to the first declension. "Bāb" may mean also elder brother.

CHAPTER II.

Suffixes modifying the meaning of Words

1. Emphatic **ta** or **ta**: (see page 81.) It is used moreover for many other purposes, *e. g.* to make a Verb frequentative. (See Syntax.)

2. Quasi diminutive **so**. This termination gives such a meaning to the affected word that now I do not find a more suitable word for it than "quasi diminutive". Some examples will show what I mean to say thereby. "Boro = good", "boroso = apparently good, or which seems to be good"; "piso = foolish", "pisoso = giving some signs, although not certain of foolishness"; "kărtā = he does", "kărtāso = he seems to do"; "găr = house", "gărseñ = a thing which seems to be a house"; "bukaso = some papers which seem to be a book".

Yet sometimes this termination has a really diminutive meaning; *e.g.* "boroso" may mean also "a little good", not perfectly good; "tarnoso = a little green", not perfectly green; "tāp = fever", "tāpasaso = feverish"; "lonkaḍ = iron", "lonkḍāso = of iron", "lonkḍāsaso = ferruginous, containing particles of iron", and so in many other cases.

There is a common sentence which shows clearly the meaning of this **so**, (**si**, **señ**). If a person complains to me against another, and I do not like to offend neither this second nor the first, I say to this second: "āuñ mārleñseñ kărtāñ, tūñ răḍleñseñ kăr = I will do as if I had beaten, you do as if you weep", viz. by saying something, not serious, but having the appearance of a serious reproach against the accused person. Hence it appears that this **-so** is just the contrary of the emphatic **-ta**. (See p. 82.)

Which is the use of this **-so**? *a*) First it is joined as one word to the affected word. In order to make it known to the readers, I will separate it at least sometimes by a hyphen.

b) It is joined to any part of the speech, as I said of the emphatic **-ta**, except perhaps Interjections.

c) It is changed into **-si** for the Feminine and **-señ** for the Neuter; *Plur.* **-se, -seo, -siñ** *etc.*, just as the Adjectives of three terminations; so if added to a Neuter Noun, it is **-señ**; if to a Feminine Noun, **-si** *etc.*

d) The word to which it is joined does not undergo any change; *e.g.* "kăr = do", becomes

Pres. Sing. 1. kărtāñ-so, kărtāñ-si, kărtā-señ;
2. kărtai-so, kărtai-si, kărtai-señ;
3. kărtā-so, kartā-si, kartā-señ.
Plur. 1. kărtāoñ-se, kărtāoñ-seo, kărtāoñ-siñ;
2. kărtāt-se, kărtāt-seo, kărtāt-siñ;
3. kărtāt-se, kărtāt-seo, kărtāt-siñ.
Past. āuveñ keleñ-señ *etc.*

Although this **-so** can be used without adding any other word, yet the Verb "distā = appears" is very often added; and the word to which **-so** is added, is considered as an Adjective; *e.g.* "kunkaḍ ubtaseñ = the hen flickers", *or* "kunkaḍ ubtaseñ distā".

This **-so** is a beauty of Konkani. Other such niceties doubtless are to be found which would show that Konkani, if cultivated, may surpass even some European languages.

3. The terminations of the diminutive may be also reckoned here (see Chapter II. Art. III. § iv.); yet those terminations are not common to many parts of speech; hence they are better put in the 2nd Part.

4. The words **ago, are, -ge, -re,** *etc.* in addressing may be also considered as changing the meaning a little; but they may be written in two words, whereas I speak of joined particles; secondly, they are not peculiar to Konkani and present no difficulty.

5. **ī** or **ai.** I spoke of this **i**, in Part II. Ch. II. § 6. p. 79; but it is added also to other words; hence we must speak of it again here; **i**, added to Pronouns or Adjectives, gives to them an indefinite or general meaning, as the Latin *libet*, in Italian *siasi; e.g.* "kăssoloi = any", "kòṇākai = to any one." The

particle "-kăi" has also a similar meaning. (See *l.c.*) I said i *or* ai; yet this second is seldom used.

This i is added also to Verbs and Nouns, and gives them a permissive meaning ("although" *etc.*). This particle is put at the end of the Verb ("keleări = though you did"), but with Pronouns, Adjectives and Conjunctions, it may be put also in the middle of them; *e. g.* "zărtăr = if", "zărităr = although (if also)"; "kòṇiyěk = any". Instead of i, sometimes "ui = also" is used, almost in the same sense as i; *e. g.* "teñui = that also" (*or* "teñi"), a compound of "teñ = that", and "ui"; so "zărităr Deu amkăñ šikšă ditā, amso mōgui kărtā = though God punishes us, yet He loves us". The same i is used in the very common phrase "zăleări = yet", compounded with "zăleăr = if it happened", and "i = though".

This i sometimes added to a word, has only the meaning of *also*, chiefly if added to Nouns. The context must decide which meaning must be preferred; perhaps the permissive meaning is not different from the meaning of *also;* this particle in certain context naturally takes a permissive meaning.

CHAPTER III.

Interrogative Particle

1. To ask, "gī" is used, joined to the word which it affects in one word; *e. g.* "did you perform your duty?" Here the word affected by the interrogation is "perform"; hence this must have the interrogative particle. "Tuzo kăido kelăingī?" Remark that this "-gī" can be used not only in direct, I may say, interrogative sentences, but also in sentences which expressed directly would be interrogative, *e. g.* "kedea santošăn ăuñ ăilogī moṇ tumiñ saumzayet = you may understand with what pleasure I came". Here a direct interrogation may be supposed "Did you come with great pleasure?" and in a similar way this "-gī" can be used whenever a similar *oratio obliqua* occurs. Some use "-gai" instead of "-gī".

2. This particle is commonly used only in asking; yet sometimes I have heard it also in non-interrogative sentences; *e. g.* "tukā kitleñ assāgī, makā titleñ assā = as much is to you, so much is to me".

3. This particle is not used with words, which of themselves, I may say, are interrogative; *e. g.* "kōn = who?" "kiteñ = what?" in a similar way as in Latin, though in Latin we may say sometimes *quidnam?* This particle "-gī" is exactly the Latin *nam* or *num*. So we cannot say "kiteñgī? *or* kòṇgī?" only "kiteñ *or* kòṇ" *etc.* is used. But if these words ("kiteñ *etc.*) are used as Indefinite Pronouns, then they can take "-gī." This "-gī" is used in the common and vulgar sentence "assāgī nāñ = is it (or) not?" used as intercalar at every step. Besides in interrogations this "gī" is used in the sentence: "kăsseñgi moḷḷeār" as if you say = "*e. g*". Finally, distinguish this "-gī" from "-ge" shortened from "age". (See Ch. I.)

CHAPTER IV. NEGATIVE FORM

Art. I. Substantives

Substantives are formed negative by prefixing ă, (like the Greek *alpha privativus*), if the Noun begins with a consonant, or an, if the word begins with a vowel, "ăpă (*vulg.* ak-), nis-, nir-" *etc.* But these prefixes cannot be used promiscuously, nay, use does not allow us to make certain Nouns negative by any particle. Examples: "măriād = honesty" "ăñmăriād = dishonesty, impoliteness"; "upkār = benefit", "ănupkār" *or better* "ănupkārpoṇ = ingratitude"; "kăpăṭ = simulation", "niškăpăṭ = sincerity"; "băruăso = hope", "ăpăbăruăso = despair"; "dhăir = courage", "ăpădhăir = fear, despair"; "mān = honour", "ăpămān (*vulg.* ăkmān) = offence"; "bāg = happiness", "nirbāg" *or better* "nirbāgipoṇ = unhappiness". Sometimes, as in English so in Konkani some Nouns can be made negative, by changing the sentence into the negative; *e.g.* "this has not been done nicely = yeñ sarkeñ kärunknäñ". Finally some Nouns are made negative by prefixing "näñ"; *e.g.* "päsänd = approval", "näñpäsänd = disapproval"; "bolaiki = health", näñbolaiki = unhealthiness".

If we have an English or Latin Negative Noun, which cannot be rendered by any of the above prefixes, then let us see whether there be some other word, although not in the Negative form, which corresponds to that word; if no word exists, then we must resolve it, chiefly by the Gerund Negative in "tanañ" or by the Negative Participles; *e.g.* "pik = ripeness" cannot be made Negative; but the non-negative "tarnepoṇ" exists, which has the same meaning. We might also resolve it thus: "unripeness causes harm = piknatạlleo västu lukšän kärtät = unripe things cause harm".

Art. II. Adjectives

These are made Negative *a*) by affixing "natullo", Negative Participle of "assä" to the Positive Adjective; *e.g.* "sarko = exact", sarkonatullo". By this termination we can not only change some Adjectives into the Negative, but we can also form new Negative Adjectives, *i.e.* by adding this "natullo" to Nouns; *e.g.* "morn-natullo = immortal"; "jiv-natullo = lifeless".

b) Negative Adjectives are formed by adding "vin = without" to a Noun; *e.g.* "mornä-vin = immortal".

c) Adjectives are made Negative by prefixing "näiñ" or "niñ"; *e.g.* "näiñzallo = not becoming".

d) By affixing "näiñ assolo", another Negative Participle of "assä", we may change the Adjective from Affirmative into Negative; *e.g.* "fävo-näiñ assolo = not being worthy, unworthy".

e) The above prefixes of the Nouns (an-, nir- *etc.*) may be used also for Adjectives; *e.g.* "nirbägi = unhappy", "anupkäri = ungrateful"; "niškäpṭi = sincere".

Usage does not allow us to use all these particles p cuously or in any case; then the above indicated plan fo. Nouns must be employed also for the Adjectives.

Art. III. Pronouns

(See page 80.)

These have no proper Negative form, but the Affirmative Pronoun is used with the Negative Particle joined to the Verb; *e.g.* "I know nothing = makā kāiñ kā̆ḷnāñ"; "I know nothing at all = makā kāintz kā̆ḷnāñ". "Nobody came = kòṇ yeunknāñ". Sometimes it seems that the Negative Particle is joined to the Pronoun itself and thus an apparent Negative Pronoun is formed; *e.g.* "Who is there? = thā̆iñ kòṇ assā?" "Nobody = kòṇnāñ"; "What have you = tukā kiteñ assā?" "Nothing = kāiñāñ". But this is only an appearance; because if no Verb is there, the Negative Particle must, of course, be joined to some word; hence it happens that sometimes the Negative Particle must be joined to the Pronoun. Or we may say, that in the sentence "khā̆iñnāñ" (see above), that "nāñ" is itself the Verb, *i. e.* the negative form of "assā" (see p. 104). And so also for the, I may call, Emphatic Negative Pronouns; *e.g.* "none"; the particle "i (*or* ui) = also" affixed to the primitive Pronoun and the Negative Particle are used; *e.g.* "no impure soul can enter into heaven "yēkui nitā̆ḷnatullo ā̆tmo sā̆rgār riganāñ".

Art. IV. Verbs

The negative form of the Verbs has been given in Part II., as it is an important and a great part of the conjugation. Yet remark that the given negative form is not the only one used even in Mangalore, as I hinted (p. 99). So, *e.g.* some say "keleñ-nāñ" instead of "kā̆runknāñ", "kā̆rtāt-nānt" instead of "kā̆rïnānt", although this second example is not so common.

Art. V. Adverbs

The Adverbs usually follow the rules of the Adjectives, as we have seen when speaking of their Comparative and Superlative (p. 67). Yet we must distinguish the true Adverbs, I mean, true in form and meaning, from the apparent Adverbs, which are really Substantives. (See below Chapter on Derivation). The true Adverbs may be either original (see Part II. Ch. V.) or derived; the original Adverbs have no proper form, just as in English; the common way of using them is to use a negative sentence; *e. g.* "āz = to-day", "āz niñ = not to-day". The same can be said of the Adverbs which are only the Instrumental of the Substantive; *e. g.* "săsărāyen = easily", "not easily = săsărāyen niñ". The derived Adverbs follow mostly the rules of the Adjectives.

Yet, as to Adverbs, we must consider which form they take in each case; because often the negative form is suggested naturally by the Adverb itself, considered *in concreto;* whereas a general rule might seem obscuring rather than clearing up this point.

Art. VI. Conjunctions

What has been said of Pronouns, can more or less be said of Conjunctions, *i. e.* the Affirmative Conjunction is used with the Negative Particle joined to the Verb, if there be any; and so the Conjunctions formed by adding "ī = also" (Indefinite or Emphatic Conjunctions) are made negative in the same way; *e. g.* "he is neither in the town nor in the village = to šerāntināñ nāḍāntināñ = *lit.* he in the town also not, in the village also not"; "he is neither good nor bad, he is a middle thing = to boroi niñ, pāḍi niñ, sumārso zāun vortavatā".

CHAPTER V. DERIVATION OF WORDS

Art. I. Nouns

Nouns are derived by adding chiefly the following terminations, **-poṇ, -ai, -kai, -ap, -gär** or **-kär, -där, -an, -sän, -neñ, -ni, -sarkeñ, -i, -ist** or **-st.**

To what are these terminations to be added? They are often added to the stem of the original word, which frequently is found in the concrete Noun or simple Adjective; *e.g.* "mög = love", "boro = good"; *stem* "moga, borea"; but euphony requires us very often to add these terminations not to the stem, but to the root or to the pure form of the primitive word, as the examples will show.

Now to explain each terminations. With **-poṇ** many Neuter Abstract Nouns are formed; *e.g.* "koṭṭo = wicked", "koṭṭepoṇ = wickedness"; "boro = good", "borepoṇ = prosperity"; "nitäl = pure", "nitalpoṇ = purity"; "kuḍḍo = blind", "kuḍḍepoṇ = blindness". It seems that **-poṇ** is more commonly added to Adjectives, which themselves may be derived; *e.g.* from "mög" you get "mogāḷ = dear", from it "mogāḷpoṇ = amiability"; yet we find **-poṇ** added also to Nouns; *e.g.* "monis = man", "monšapoṇ = humanity", "Deu = God", "Deupoṇ = Deity".

By **-kai** and **-ai** are also usually formed Abstract Nouns; *e.g.* "niškal = chaste", "niškalai = chastity"; "neṇto = humble, innocent", "neṇtuai = humility"; "äskät = weak", "äskätkai = weakness".

These derived Nouns in **-ai** and **-kai** are for the most part, if not always, Feminine. I say "derived", because non-derived Nouns in **-ai** may be of another Gender; *e.g.* "upāi = means".

By **-ap**, not to be confounded with **-äp** or **-óp**, are formed many Nouns which mostly express either action as in Latin *-io* or *-tio* or something abstract; *e.g.* "bärei = write", "bärap = writing"; "sīk = learn", "sikap = instruction". These derived

Nouns in -ap are mostly Neuter; but Nouns in -ăp or -op, or -ab may be often of another gender.

By -găr or -kăr are formed concrete Masculine Nouns, as in Latin by *-tor; e.g.* "găr = house", "gărkăr = householder"; "motzo = shoe", "motčegār = shoemaker"; "gāḍi = carriage", "gāḍiegār = bandyman".

By -dăr are formed concrete Nouns about in the same way as by -găr and -kăr; *e. g.* "nīt, -i = justice", "nītidār = judge"; "monsub = judgment", "monsubdār = judge".

The terminations -găr or -kăr are often used to indicate origin from a place; *e. g.* "Goiñkār = a Goanese"; "Tčinkār = a Chinese". Yet some Nouns of this kind are formed differently *e.g.* "Roman = Romanso".

Yet this -kăr cannot be used so often as the Latin *tor;* use does not allow us to form such Nouns except in certain cases. Then we may use the Participle in -tolo, although this termination seems to express in a transitory way what is expressed by -kăr; *e. g.* "buyer, Lat. *emptor* = molăk kaṇeitolo"; "seller, Lat. *venditor*, or better *vendens* = iktolo". This termination can generally be used.

By -sāṇ are formed some Nouns (usually Feminine) chiefly from qualificative Adjectives; *e. g.* "koḍu = bitter", "koḍsāṇ = bitterness"; "gòḍu = sweet"; "gòḍsāṇ = sweetness".

By -neñ are derived many Abstract Nouns which correspond to our Verbal Nouns; *e. g.* băir-găl = put out", "băirgălneñ = expulsion"; răḍ = weep", răḍneñ = weeping". Remark that the Verbal Nouns can be expressed not only by -neñ, but also by -ap, (see above) and -čeñ (which last is the termination of the Absolute Infinitive), or, seldom, by -ni or -an; *e. g.* "sōḍ = leave", "soḍni = abandonment"; mór = die", "moraṇ = death"; "kăr = do", "kāraṇ = cause". By the above terminations can be formed not only Verbal Nouns, but others too; *e.g.* "jie = live", "jiṇi = life", "kăr = do", "kărṇi = action" (although these two Nouns might be considered in some way as Verbal Nouns).

Sărkeñ corresponds to the English *-ility* or Latin *-bilitas; i. e.* it expresses suitableness etc. for any thing; *e.g.* "docility = sika-sărkeñ"; "vanti-sărkeñ = divisibility".

By i many Nouns are derived which have about the same meaning as the word from which they are derived, except that they are concrete; *e. g.* "šăstrə = religion", "šăstri = religious man, or doctor, chiefly of a sacred science (D. D.)"; yet it seems that such Nouns can be used, often at least, also as Adjectives; *e. g.* "bezări = tired", as also sometimes by i Abstract Nouns are formed from Concrete Nouns; *e. g.* "dōst = favourite", "dōsti = favour, grace".

-ist or -st is employed to form Concrete Nouns almost in the same way as -kăr or -tolo; *e. g.* "sərmauñ = preaching", "sermavist = preacher"; "mukhia = principal", "mukhiest = head"; "buiñ-măp = geometry", "buiñ-măpist = geometor" *etc.*

To this point of derivation we may reduce the derivation of the Feminine from the Masculine. The Feminine is derived from the Masculine very often by adding n or in; *e. g.* "gărkăr = householder", "gărkărn = house-wife"; săib = lord", "săibin = lady"; "Goiñkăr = Goanese (man)", "Goiñkărn = Goanese (woman)"; sometimes by changing o of the Masculine into i; *e. g.* "pădko = small bullock", "pădki = small cow"; "bogdo = mutton", "bogdi = sheep". Yet many are formed irregularly; *e. g.* "dădlo = man", "băil, *or* ăstri = woman"; "bău = brother", "boin = sister"; "burgo = boy", "čoduñ = girl"; "peto = dog", "kolgeñ = bitch"; "pădo = steer", "pădi = cow" *etc.*

Corollary: If we compare the above terminations with the Latin terminations, -pon and -ai or -kai correspond to *-tas* or *-us* of the Abstract Nouns; *e. g. sanctitas, servitus*, -ap, -ni, -neñ, -čeñ correspond mostly to *-tio* or *-ctio*; *e. g. scriptio, clatio, actio, ambulatio;* -găr, -kăr, -dăr, -ist, -i correspond very often to *-tor* or similar termination of the Concrete Nouns; *e. g. scriptor, emptor, Mangalorensis, Goanus, Bombayensis;* -san corresponds to *-do* or *-udo* of qualificative Nouns; *e. g.*

dulcedo, amaritudo; sărkcă corresponds to *-bilitas* or *-ilitas*; *e. g. divisibilitas, docilitas;* -an seems to correspond to *-ctio* or *-tio;* sometimes it expresses something permanent.

Art. II. Adjectives

1. The most common form of derivation is by adding -so, -ċi, -ċeñ or sometimes -lo, -li, -leñ. The first termination is usually added to the stem of the corresponding Noun; the second termination is added more frequently to the 1st Locative of the Noun; consequently these Adjectives in -lo seem to imply some locative meaning; *e.g.* "sauñsărāntlo monis = man (living) in the world". The Adjectives in -ntlo (-lo added to the 1st Locative) are used moreover to indicate coming out of ...; *e.g.* "mătientlo = coming out of the earth"; sometimes the termination -lo is the termination of the Past Participle; *e.g.* "koṇḍ-lo = fossil", from "koṇḍ = dig"; then it is not added to the 1st Locative. The Adjectives in -so usually mean quality, taking the word "quality" not in a rigorous sense.

Some Adjectives are formed irregularly, *e.g.* from "sărg = heaven", "sărgiñso" instead of "sărgāso"; from "găr = house", "gărso" instead of "gărāso" or better, "gărso" means "domestic, a member of, or living in, the family"; "gărāso" means "of the house", *e.g.* "the roof of the house".

1. As regards the above terminations "-so, -ċi, -ċeñ" of derived Adjectives, we must now expressly observe, what has been already cursorily remarked in Part II. Chapter IV. page 122, viz. that the exact spelling (*i. e.* according to the pronunciation of high castes) of these terminations would be "-tso, -tċi, -tċeñ". Up to this I wrote "-so, -ċi, -ċeñ"; for this spelling is more simple and more usual, yet it is not so exact. But if an Adjective in "-so" is not derived, it may have "-so" not "-tso"; *e. g.* "piso". Moreover the quasi-diminutive "-so" is exactly "-so", not "tso".

2. All Adjectives in "o, i, eñ", if used for the 1st Person Singular, according to the best pronunciation have a nasal termination; *e. g.* "āuñ boreñ nīñ = I am not good".

2. Another rather bold manner of forming Adjectives is to add the terminations -lo, -li, -leñ to the 2nd Locative in

-ger (see p. 14), omitting **r** of **-ger** on account of euphony; so we get "gelo, geli, geleñ" instead of "gerlo, gerli, gerleñ"; *e.g.* here in Mangalore the Adjective "Mādringelo" is common; it is derived from "Mādringer", 2nd Locative Plural of "Mādri = nun", meaning "at the nuns or being at the nuns"; hence "Mādringelo" has the meaning as "at the Nuns"; *e.g.* "Mādringeli rivāz = custom as the nuns, or coming from the house of the nuns". So they form from "Deu = God", the Adjective "Devāgelo", which exactly means "as at the house of God or devout"; *e.g.* "Devāgelo monis = devout man"; from "to = that", they form "teāgelo = he who, or that which, is there, or at that place"; from "mārañ = Parias", the Adjective "mārañgelo" is formed. We might say also that these Adjectives are formed by adding **-gelo** to the original; yet I prefer to say that they are formed by adding **-lo** to the 2nd Locative in **-ger**, because this seems to be the origin of that **-gelo**; moreover the meaning of these Adjectives suggests this explanation; consequently it is easier to be retained and more reasonable. In a similar way many other Adjectives might be formed, for which we have no corresponding Adjectives of one word in our European languages, Italian, English, German *etc.*

3. Some Adjectives are derived from Nouns by adding to the root of the Noun the termination **-ést**; *e.g.* "piḍa = sickness", "piḍést = sick"; "čintna = thought" has "čintést = gloomy".

4. Another rather difficult way of deriving Adjectives is to add "-šilo *or* -velo". The meaning which the Adjective receives thereby is strange; I explain it by examples; "lāgiñ = near", "lāgšilo = he who is near *or* that which is near"; "pois = far", "poišilo = he who is far *or* that which is far"; "mukār = before", "mukāvelo = he who is before *or* that which is before"; "pāus = rain", "pāušilo = rainy". Now some sentences:—Seeing two boys, one far, the other near, I say: "lāgšilo yeundi = he who is near shall come", "poišilo yeundi = he who is far, shall come near (*or* come near)"; "moja

lāgšilo votz = go far", *or literally:* "you who are near, go from me (far), *or* go from being near to me"; "poišilo yē = come near, *or* come from being far (to me), *or* come thou being far (to me)". We may explain the use of these Adjectives with philosophical terms, thus: In Konkani the *terminus ad quem* is omitted and only the *terminus a quo* is expressed; in our languages the *terminus ad quem* is expressed, and the *terminus a quo* is omitted. This is an easy way, I think, to explain these Adjectives which seem to imply a contradiction. The Adjectives in "-šilo" and "-velo" which have no relation to place, *e.g.* "pāušilo" do not present such a difficulty.

5. Some Adjectives are derived, or rather formed, as in Kanarese and Tulu, viz. by adding to the Nominative of the Noun the Past Participle of "assā = is", which almost corresponds to the Latin *habens; e.g.* "podvi assollo = being powerful (having power)". But this kind of Adjectives is more frequently used joined immediately to a Substantive or at least not used as predicate; *e. g.* "podvi assollo monis = a powerful man". We could not say: "to monis podvi assollo zāun assā = this man is powerful".

6. Some Adjectives are formed by adding to the stem of Noun "dig"; *e.g.* "mānadig = glorious"; "foḷ-a-dig = fruitful". Sometimes only -ig is added; *e.g.* "amolig = of infinite price", or some other letter is put before "-dig".

7. Many Adjectives are derived from Postpositions and Adverbs, chiefly by adding -so or -lo, *i.e.* as Adjectives are derived from Nouns (see above 1.); so from "hangā = here", comes "hangāso = of here"; "bităr = within", "bitărlo = interior"; "voir = above", "voilo = of above"; "lāgiñ = near", "lāgso", and "lāgšilo (see above 4.); "ādiñ = before", "ādlo"; "māgir = after", "māgirlo"; "modeñ = in the middle", "modlo" *etc.* (See Part II. Chapter V.)

8. The Adjectives which in Latin end in *-bilis* are formed by adding to the Nominative of the Substantive "fāvozallo = due"; *e.g.* "nămăskār fāvozallo = *adorabilis*". Sometimes instead

of "făvozallo", the termination -so added to the stem may suffice; *e. g.* "kaṇṭālo făvozallo, *or* "kaṇṭālaso = abominable"; this 2nd termination is more vulgar. In the above case the termination *-bilis* means "due". If it means possibility of doing something, then the Adjective is formed by adding the Participle "assollo" to the Potential Mood in -yet; *e. g.* "accessible place = votsayet assollo zāgo"; "accessible mountain = čăḍāyet assollo porvot". In the negative form the Participle is added to the Necessary Mood of negative form; *e. g* "votsun nozo assollo zāgo = inaccessible place" [1].

9. By -sărko some Adjectives are formed, which mean "fit to do.. "; *e. g.* "saumzăisărko = fit to persuade"; "movāḷaisărko = fit to move"; sometimes before adding "-sărko" another intermedial word is inserted; *e. g.* "făr = explosion", "fărazăi sărko = explosive".

10. Some Adjectives are derived by adding to the stem of the Noun the particle -vănt, which seems to denote possession; *e. g.* "bud = wisdom", "bud-i-vănt = wise"; "nīt = justice", nītivănt = just".

11. Some others are derived by adding i; *e. g.* "mosor = envy", "mosri = envious"; "souṅsār = world", "souṅsāri = wordly, laic". See on page 169 the meaning of this i.

12. The Participles derived from the Verbs and the quasi-diminutive so and the emphatic -ts (see Ch. I.) may also be reckoned here.

Chiefly pay attention to the Participles of the Potential and Necessary Mood explained in § 5. If a Past Participle is used as an Adjective, then it doubles the l, as it contains some emphasis.

There are some other difficult Adjectives; of these we will speak when treating of Participles, in the Syntax.

---

[1] This is a Negative Participle of the Necessary Mood not given in the Part II.; it is formed by adding the Past Participle of "assā" to the Present Negative of the Necessary Mood; or we may say that it is the same as the Past Tense (see page 114).

Corollary: The termination -tso shows quality or also what is due, -lo place, the Participle "assollo" possession (of quality), -dig also quality, (sometimes it has a causative meaning, *e.g.* "mānadig = causing honour, or glorious"); "fāvozallo" means something due, "assollo" with the Potential means possibility, with "nozo" impossibility, "vānt" possession, "sărko" fit to; -se (quasi-diminutive) corresponds to the termination *-neous* (*ferrugineous*); -ts has an emphatic or also exclusive meaning.

Art. III. Verbs

If we distinguish Derivation from Composition, as we really do, it seems that a very few Verbs can be called derived; because the derived word of course must be not so simple as the word from which it is derived; but many Verbs not compounded seem to be themselves the primitive and most simple form of the word, from which other forms are derived; or at least often the root of the Verb (2nd Person Singular Imperative) is as simple as the corresponding Noun or as other corresponding part of speech; *e.g.* "măr = beat", Substantive and Verb. Notwithstanding there are some Verbs not compounded which seem to be really derived from a more simple form. Of these I intend to speak.

1. The most simple mode of derivation is to add some vowel to the primitive or at least approaching to the primitive form, *e.g.* "kărtz = expense", "kărtči = expend"; about the change of -tz into -tč (see below Chapter VIII.); "gām = perspiration", "gāme = perspire". Thereby it seems that the Verb expresses the act of that thing which is expressed by the original word, so that if the original word implies a Neuter meaning, the derived Verb is Neuter; *e.g.* "gām, gāme"; if the original word implies a transitive meaning, the derived Verb is transitive; *e.g.* "kărtz, kărtči".

Yet sometimes by the addition of i we have a Causative Verb, and by the addition of a we have a Neuter Verb. (See here below, and Part II. Chapter IV. Art. II. § 1. 3.)

2. Another mode of derivation is to add to the simple or approximately simple form ăi (sometimes ai, ei, oi or only i), if it ends in a consonant; or only i or uoi or some other irregular termination, if it ends in a vowel; or dai or voi (with some little change in spelling), if it ends in â. Thereby we have Causative Verbs (see *l. c.* and p. 145, 2nd footnote).

3. A third mode of derivation is to cut off from the Causative Verb the termination by which they become Causative. Thereby we have the original non-causative Verb, Neuter or Transitive as it was before being made Causative; *e.g.* "kărăi = cause to do", "kăr = do"; khăuoi = cause to eat", "khā = eat"; "mānuăi = cause to please", "mānuă = please". Yet we must remark that many Verbs by losing only the Vowel i of the Causative termination, become Neuter; this is the case not with all but with some Verbs, having the root ending in a vowel; provided the meaning allows it, and provided they have not become doubly transitive by the causative termination; *e.g.* "khā = eat", "khăuoi = cause to eat". So from "paloăi = extinguish" we get "paloă = get extinguished, be extinguished by itself". Of the Transitive Verbs ending in a consonant, now I recollect only one "kātŭr = cut", "kātărăi *or* kātrăi = cause to cut", which becomes Neuter or in some way passive by taking away -ai and making the a of the root long, "kātŭr = cut"; as in Sanskrit "nāhyăte = he binds", "nahyăte = he is bound". (See Max Müller's Sanskrit Grammar Chapter xv. § 398.) There may be some other Transitive Causative Verb which becomes Neuter by taking away only i, or by producing the vowel of the root. See another mode *l. c.* § 3 *n.* 4, and some explanation of this 3rd way *l. c.* § 1 and *alibi.* Art. II.

This 3rd mode, as the reader sees, is not properly a derivation; because the non-causative Verbs are not derived from the Causative, but rather the Causative are derived from the non-causative Verbs; yet I put them here for the sake of convenience.

Art. IV. Adverbs[1]

1. Very often the Instrumental of the Substantive is used as an Adverb; this happens chiefly in Adverbs of manner, because the Instrumental has also this meaning; *e.g.* "kăšṭăn = with difficulty".

2. Sometimes the Neuter of the Adjective is used as an Adverb; *e.g.* "boreñ = good or well". This happens with Adjectives of three terminations.

3. Many Adverbs are formed by using the Gerund in -un of the required Verb added to the Substantive; *e.g.* "attentively = čit diun = giving attention"; "boreñ kărn kărunknāñ = (he) did not perform it well". In this example we have, I may say, a double Adverb; for, "boreñ" is one Adverb, to it the Gerund in -un (contracted into -n) is added; or perhaps we may say, that "kărn" is added to "boreñ" considered as a Substantive. This way is rather a composition.

4. From Pronouns (Relative and Demonstrative) Adverbs of manner are derived by adding to the stem "-sseñ"; *e.g.* "tăsseñ = in that manner", "asseñ = in this way", "kăsseñ *or* zăsseñ = in that way in which (= as)"; though, properly speaking, these are Adjectives in the Neuter Gender used as Adverbs.

5. From the same Pronouns are derived Adverbs of place by adding -ṇeñ; *e.g.* "teṇeñ = through that way, in that side"; "yeṇeñ = in this side"; or also by adding "-ssiñ", *e.g.* "issiñ, tissiñ = here and there". This "yeṇeñ" and "teṇeñ" are the Instrumental of -o and -to of Feminine Gender, and "issiñ, tissiñ" are shortened from "yeā kusin, teā kusin".

6. If the Adjectives have only one termination, Adverbs of manner are formed from them by adding "zāun" or some other Gerund; "khăṇḍitzāun = positively" from "khăṇḍit = positive", "mukhiăzāun = chiefly" from "mukhiă = principal". This last method, *i. e.* by adding "zāun" is very often used,

---

[1] What I say here, cannot always be called properly Derivation; for the sake of convenience I put things together which should be separated.

and whenever we cannot use another way, let us try this last form; this "zāun" can be added not only to Adjectives but also to Nouns. Sometimes the Instrumental of the corresponding Substantive may be used as an Adverb; *e. g.* "sobitāyen = nicely", from "sobitāi = nicety" and this from "sobit = nice".

7. Finally the negative form, the emphatic **-ts** and the quasi-diminutive **-so** are other modes of derivation belonging not only to the Adverbs but also to the other parts of speech. (See above Chapters II. & IV.)

CHAPTER VI. COMPOSITION OF WORDS

Following the order observed in the former chapters of this Third Part, I should speak first of all about the composition of Nouns; but as this is not completely settled as yet, let us speak first of the more common composition, I mean the composition of Verbs.

I must remark from the very beginning that under the name of composition I include not only those words which must be written as one word, originating from two or more words, but also those words which are written or at least might be written separately and those words, about which there is some doubt whether they are better written as one or more words. About this see below.

Art. I. Verbs

1. As the first mode of composition of Verbs, let us put the mode in which foreign Verbs are Konkanized.

Many foreign Verbs are Konkanized by affixing to their foreign Infinitive the Verb "kăr = do", if transitive, or "zā" if intransitive; *e. g.* "kanonizār kăr = canonize", "kanonizār zā = get canonized". But this should be, as far as possible, carefully avoided, as there is such an inclination to Konkanize foreign words in this way, that Konkani would become very soon half Konkani, half English or Latin. Although it is difficult to translate literally many foreign words, yet accommodating ourselves to the nature of Konkani, we can find the Konkani corresponding word.

2. Another mode of composition is to join a Substantive or an Adjective to a Verb. The Substantive may be of any kind, but the Verbs more commonly used in this composition are "kăr = do", by which perhaps half the Konkani Verbs are formed; then "gāl = put"; "dī = give"; "ghē = receive"; "zā = become"; *e. g.* "mōg kăr = love, *lit.* make love"; "bautism dī = baptize, *lit.* give baptism"; "badlām gāl = calumniate, *lit.* put calumniation"; "jīvănt zā = rise from death, *lit.* get alive *etc.*"

3. Another thoroughly Konkani mode of composition is to join the Gerund in -un of the principal Verb to another Verb in a finite Mood, *i. e.* in the Mood and Tense required by the meaning. Remark that this other Verb is not an Auxiliary Verb; both Verbs might be called principal, although that -un seems to prevail, *e. g.* "abolish = kāḍn *or* kāḍun gāl, *lit.* having taken away, put *or* put down". This way of composition is common to Kanarese and Tulu, and, as I have heard, also to the Malayālam language. I will speak more distinctly in the Syntax about it, as this point is not so easy.

4. A fourth form of composition is to prefix some Adverb to a Verb; but this perhaps is not exactly a composition, because the Adverb does not make one word with the Verb; *e. g.* "approach = lāgiñ pāu, *lit.* reach near". Postpositions are not prefixed, as in Latin *perficio*, *conficio etc.*, because all Postpositions are joined with Substantives (at least understood, if not expressed), Pronouns and Participles. (See page 154 *n.* 9.)

Art. II. Nouns and other Parts

As to the composition of Substantives, if we do not consider the matter thoroughly, we might think that there are no Compound Substantives, and I myself was of this opinion some time ago. Yet I hold now as certain that there are many

Compound Nouns. But here we must distinguish; for, there are two modes of composition: the first is to change the governed Noun into an Adjective and then there is no composition, but a mere apposition; *e.g.* "clergyman", we may express it by "Igărjeso muniări = minister of the church"; another way is to join immediately the two Nouns into one word. In this case there is a true composition. How is this composition to be made? I do not know a perfectly fixed rule, as I have no example to go by. I propose the way which is certain as to the pronunciation; but as to writing, it should be introduced now. The most common way therefore to make this composition is to put first the governed Noun in the Original case, Singular or Plural according to the meaning, and then to join to it the governing Noun in one word and give to the compounded Noun the Gender of the second or governing Noun as in German. But how to join the two Nouns, by hyphens or without hyphens? Following the analogy of other languages I would suggest a hyphen between the 1st and 2nd word, to show more distinctly the composition. Yet, if we write Konkani with Kanarese or Mahrătti letters, we should omit the hyphens. You find many compound words in the Dictionary, some of which are used, some are not commonly used, because in many cases the idea itself does not commonly exist in this country; yet they are Konkani words, formed according to the nature of Konkani language. Examples: for "convent" here many say "koñvent", and in familiar conversation we may use it; but if we want to speak correctly and a pure language, we might say "săngăt-văsiñ-măṭ (*n.*)" from "săngăt-văsi = cenobite", and "măṭ = convent", or shorter, only "măṭ"; this word is not used at all; yet all elementary words are used, except "măṭ" which is used only for pagan convents; why could we not use also the compounded word? Either we must follow this way or use foreign words; which is better? As we see from this example, there may be a composition even of more than two words. "Chapter (of Canons) = koṇikañ-mĕḷ (*m.*) *lit.* = reunion of canons", from "koṇik = canon" and "mēḷ = reunion". In both cases the governed Noun has been put in the Original Plural, because the meaning required it; in the following the Singular is used: "Igărje-muniări, *lit.* minister of the church".

As to the Verbs, we might write them with a hyphen, if they are joined to an Adverb, though not true compounds. But if they are joined to a Noun, *e.g.* "mōg kăr = love", it seems better not to join them at all, and really sometimes the Noun is separated from its Verb; *e.g.* "Deu amso mōg tzăḍ kărtā = God loves us much". So also the other compositions considered above (Art. I. *nn.* 1, 3.) are not true compositions; consequently the two words are written separately. As to the composition, chiefly of Nouns, we must remark that the above rule of joining the governing Noun to the Original of the governed Noun, cannot be used in every case; the prevailing custom is to be observed, which in some cases requires a true composition, sometimes only an apposition of a Noun and an Adjective.

Besides the composition of two or more Nouns, there may be a composition of other parts of speech, *e.g.* of a Noun and an Adjective, as "sǎma-poḍneñ = harmony"; "sărvụ-podvi = almight"; of a Noun and a Postposition, *e.g.* "săkăl-poḍneñ = downfall"; of two Adjectives, *e.g.* "sărvụ-boro = infinitely good"; of a Pronoun and an Adjective or of two Pronouns, *e.g.* "kòṇ-yēk = some", "kòṇ-yēklo = somebody" (see pp. 79-80); of a Conjunction and another part of speech, *e.g.* "sāngleăr-i = although you said"; "amkăñ-i = to us too"; "kòṇăk-i = to any one"; "ăuveñ kărunk-nāñ = I have not done" *etc.* To this point we cannot reduce, it seems, the emphatic -ts and the quasi-diminutive -so (see above Ch. II.); because -ts and -so are not words used also separately, but only suffixes.

As to the way of joining; if Nouns are joined, the second is joined more commonly to the Original of the preceding Nouns, as I said; yet in some cases this rule is not observed;

because the Nominative instead of the Original is used, or some change is made; *e. g.* "aple ičhādhipāti = despot", shortened from "aple iče-adhipāti"; if not two Nouns, but a Noun and an Adjective or some other parts are joined, either they are simply joined in their primitive form, or the changes indicated throughout the Grammar are made, or some other way is followed which can be fixed later; for, these rules about composition are very rudimental, and consequently must be completed and perfected after having carefully considered this branch of the Grammar. Even in the composition of this second kind I would, for the sake of distinction, suggest a hyphen, unless there be evidently a mere apposition.

As to the declension of these compound words, if one Noun is joined to the Original Case of another Noun, the first part is not declined at all; the declension takes place only in the governing or second Noun. I say "if...joined to the Original", because I remember now one word apparently compounded, "bāuṭo-kāṭṭo = lighthouse", which is declined in both parts.

CHAPTER VII. NASAL SOUND

This and the following Chapters may be considered as a πάρεργον to the Part I., as the preceding Chapters are like a πάρεργον to the Part II. Yet the things treated of in these Chapters are in some way also etymological; and as they are common to all or at least to many parts of speech, we can consider these points as belonging to the Synetymology.

My readers might have been surprised in seeing the nasal sound ā̃ so often used; but they must know that Konkani is a nasal language κατ'ἐξοχήν. For this reason it is required to form some rudimental rules about this ā̃.

1. First of all, in the beginning I thought it unnecessary to use ā̃ also in the middle of the word; yet afterwards I was aware that sometimes we cannot avoid it without losing much

exactness; hence you find ñ also in the middle, contrary to what I said in Part I. Chapter I.

2. When is it used? A complete rule cannot be given; we can give some cases in which it is used. It is used:

a) In all oblique cases of the Plural of all declensions, and in the Nominative Plural of Neuter Nouns;

b) In the Nominative Singular of the Neuter Nouns ending in e and, very often, in i and u;

c) In all cases of some Feminine Nouns ending in i of the 4th Declension (see pp. 32, 34); some Nouns in uñ seem also to keep this ñ in all cases of the Singular;

d) In the Neuter Nominative Singular of the Adjectives and Participles of three terminations; and also in the Masculine and Feminine Nominative Singular of all Adjectives and Participles of three terminations, if used for the 1st Person, *e.g.* "āuñ boroñ niñ = I am not good";

e) In the Nouns ending in au; *e.g.* "Juāuñ = John"; "guniāuñ = fault".

f) As to Verbs, in all Neuter Persons of declinable tenses, and also the 1st Person Singular and Plural of any Gender, if ending in a vowel, (except -ungi of the Imperative); the forms in u (Subjunctive, Imperative *etc.*); the Gerunds in -tana and true Participles in -tā and -to (nidtāñ nidtoñ). As it is too difficult to remember all forms with ñ, let us proceed *per exclusionem:* In the Verbs this ñ is not used, of course, if the form ends in a consonant. Then, generally a form of the Verb ending in a vowel has ñ, but with these limitations: 1) the 2nd and 3rd Person Singular and Plural Masculine and Feminine of declinable tenses, 2) 2nd and 3rd Person in indeclinable tenses are not nasal; the forms neither conjugable nor declinable (not modifying terminations in any person) ending in a vowel (as the Subjunctive and Optative), follow the general rule, *i.e.* take ñ. The Participles in o, i, eñ follow the rules of the Adjectives (see above). A few exceptions to this rule can be found out by the reader himself.

The above rules about Nouns and Adjectives can be applied to Pronouns. As to the other parts of speech, I cannot for the present frame a certain particular rule. Generally I can say, that if a word ends in a vowel, it ends more frequently in ñ; chiefly all words compounded with the final negative particle nãñ or niñ are nasal; for nãñ or niñ are nasal.

3. What change does this ñ undergo? The following rule, if not general, contains at least many cases.

a) If to a word ending in ñ some consonant is added, *e.g.* the emphatic tz, it becomes more similar to n, but not always in the same way; euphony is the rule; so if a guttural consonant is added, it becomes similar to the Canarese letter ಙ, or as -ñg in singing (see p. 18, *Note* 2); if it is followed by a palatal, it seems to become a little palatal like ṇ, and so on. I do not always mark these differences in the Grammar, as they are too subtle.

c) If it is followed by a vowel, frequently it seems to become a pure n. I have a faint remembrance of words in which this ñ is found also before vowels.

d) The ñ of the Nominative is usually left out in the oblique cases, chiefly if the termination to be added begins with a consonant; in some rare cases it is kept (see p. 34).

e) About other changes of ñ see pp. 41, 116 and Art II. of Chapter IV. Part II. and *alibi*.

Some might think it unnecessary to pay attention to these niceties. I answer: In some cases it may be true; for this "ñ" has many degrees, in some cases it is difficult even to native learned men to ascertain whether there is "ñ" or not; yet in some cases it is so clear that by omitting it, the meaning would be changed; chiefly if another consonant, *e.g.* "tz," is added, if you do not take into consideration this ñ, you would get a wrong composition, *e.g.* "âuñ = I", "âuntz = myself". If you do not pay attention to that ñ, you would get "âutz" which is not understood at all, and so in many other cases. (See also pp. 6, 7.)

CHAPTER VIII. CHANGES OF LETTERS

Although something has been said about this in Part I., yet only now are we enabled to understand these things better.

The letters which not exclusively, but chiefly undergo some changes, are s, z, o, ñ, é, i, u, a, u, d, t; about ñ a peculiar chapter has been put. As regards s, z, as a general rule we may say that whenever a declinable part of speech ends in the Nominative Singular in s, z, or so, zo, this s is changed into č and z, into j in the cases in which the termination of the Nominative Masculine is changed; *e. g.* in the Neuter Nominative and in the oblique cases; so "rus" or more exactly "ruts = taste", *Orig.* "ručik *or* rutčik"; "dobazo = pomp", "dobajea"; "rāz = kingdom", "rāja"; "mozo = mine", "mojeñ, moja". Consequently the words ending in -tso following the third declension change this s into č. Many Adjectives and Participles are formed with the termination -tso; hence "kărtso, kărtčeñ"; moreover the English Genitive is usually changed into the Adjective in -tso. Yet this change does not always take place in the Nouns; *e.g.* "kuris = cross", "kursa", because it is "kris" not "krits". Chiefly as to the termination -so of the Adjectives, we must distinguish the true termination -so from -tso or -tzo; we have seen that the true terminations of the Adjectives in -so corresponding to the Genitive would be -tso; whereas -so is the termination of the quasi-diminutive and of some other Adjectives. The first mostly undergoes the above change, not the second; because (as I think) this -ts in Kanarese and in Maharātti is written with a letter which in Kanarese usually, in Maharātti often sounds like č; consequently if this letter -ts before some letters does not sound so euphonical, it is changed into its cognate č; so this -ts does not sound so well before ea, a, e, as before o; therefore before a, ea, e is changed into č. The same is to be said of z and j. This z is written with a letter, which in Kanarese usually, in Mahārātti often, sounds like j. If this last reason of harmony does not satisfy, as it does not fully satisfy me, let us keep the rule without the given reason.

Now I am aware that the above rule is not very suitable, if we do not distinguish the **s** which sounds **ts** or **tz** from the **s** which sounds simply **s**. Up to this I have very seldom made this distinction in writing, and this for the sake of simplicity; but simplicity must not prevail over exactness or be a source of confusion. Consequently in the Dictionary I will try to distinguish these two letters; moreover, as not all words can be put in the Dictionary, chiefly derived words, this rule may throw some light. The following words must be written with **ts** instead of **s**: 1) The derived Adjectives in **-so** (**-tso**). 2) All Adjectives corresponding to the Genitive (see Part II. Ch. II. Art. I. § 2, p. 51)[1]. 3) All forms of the Verbs ending with a sharp **so**; these are the Participles in **-tso** of the affirmative form, *e. g.* "nid-tso", the Gerundive, the Future of the Negative form, the Infinitive, the Negative Participle in "-tsonāñ" and so on; but the Negative Participle formed by adding **so** to the Negative root, of which I will speak in the Syntax, *e. g.* "nidanāñ-so", and the Imperfect Subjunctive are written with a pure **s**. Generally speaking, the sharp **s** is equal to **ts**, a simple, not sharp, **s** is written **s**. Paying attention to the pronunciation, we can distinguish these two **s** very easily. Examples of 1. "kaṇṭālatso,"; of 2. "Devātso"; of 3. "kărtso".

As to Nouns, not so many are written with **ts**.

Therefore we have to distinguish these similar sounds: simple **s** as in "piso", sharp **s** or **ts** (**tz**) as in "Devātso", **č** as in "čar", **tč** as in "kărtči"; and so also **z**, as in "mozo", **j** as in "moji". **Ts**, **tz** and **tč** are written in Kanarese and Mahrātti with one letter; yet **tč** is somewhat different from **ts** or **tz**. After these distinctions we may lay down the above

[1] The Adjectives of this second kind are not entirely distinct from the Adjectives under *n.* 1.

rule more clearly, thus: The words ending in ts or z, so, zo in the Nominative Singular, or in the first Person Singular Masculine, change ts into tč, and z into j, in the cases in which the termination of the Nominative or of the first Person Singular Masculine is changed. Examples: "motso = shoe", Plural: "motčo"; "mār = beat", Future Participle and Gerundive: "mār-tso, mār-tči, mār-tčeñ"; Future Negative: "mār-tsoñ-nāñ, mār-tčiñ-nāñ", *etc.* Future Negative Participle and Negative Gerundive: "mār-tso-nāñ, mār-tči-nāñ" *etc.*, but "mārināñ-so, mārināñ-si *etc.* = which cannot be beaten"; and so also "mārisoñ, mārisiñ"; (Imperfect Subjunctive): "khărts = expense"; "khărtči-tāñ = I expend"; "khărtsountso = expending"; (here ts is not changed into tč, because o follows). "Bātso = nephew", "bātčeāk = to the nephew".

From these examples it appears that if the termination of the Nominative is changed, and an o follows, ts or z may remain.

If some words have ts or z followed, not by o, but by another vowel in their original form, more frequently they do not change ts or z. Yet there may be some exceptions against this point, as also there may be some words not changing ts or z, according to the above rule.

Words ending in a simple s, or in a simple so, usually do not undergo such a change; now I recollect only "mănis = man", which changes s into ṣ̌, *i.e.* into a cerebral š. But the reason of this change seems to be quite peculiar to this word; in Kanarese it is written in the Nominative ಮನುಷ್ಯ, viz. with a cerebral š [1]. Very probably there may be some other words changing a simple s into č or into a cerebral ṣ̌, or into a simple š. I have a faint remembrance of such words. Remark that tč seems to sound very often like a simple č on account of euphony.

[1] This "š" is used by the Authors of some books printed at the Basel Mission Press, as the sign of a cerebral "ṣ", for which I have no sign pp. 5, 6. (See Chapter IX.)

When a word has the root ending in **s**, then the following **ts** cannot sound distinctly **ts**; and when this **ts** is changed into **č**, the first sibilant **s** cannot remain sibilant according to the rules of euphony; but it is changed into a somewhat thick **s**, similar to the Latin *s* in *assis* (see p. 105. *n.* 1); *e.g.* "hās= laugh", "hās-tso (hāsso), hās-tči (hās-či). For this thick **s** I did not put any sign in the Alphabet; this can be done in future time; for the present we may use š, because this š is the nearest letter to the thick **s**. Moreover a sibilant **s** becomes thick almost naturally before **č**; consequently there is not an urgent necessity to find out a sign for it. Perhaps the above change of **s** into a thick **s̬** may take place in some other cases. I have indicated the most common case.

As to **o**, we have hinted in the Paradigm that **o** is changed into **e** in the Future and Past Perfect **-lolo** (see p. 88, *n.* 2) viz. when **o** of the penultimate syllable is not followed by another **o** in the last syllable. The same change takes place in other words of a similar form. In some other words **o** of the penultimate seems to be changed into **ạ**; *e.g.* "assolo, assạlli" *etc.* I say "seems", because it is not so easy to distinguish what kind of vowel is such substituted vowel. Further some change this **o** not in **ạ** but into another letter; *e.g.* some say "assollo, assilli, assilleñ", and "kăssolo, kăsseli, kăsseleñ". The forms laid down in Part II. seem to be more common and more correct; therefore they should be used in order to have some uniformity and to elevate the language.

As regards **u**, we may say almost the same as of **o**; namely it is changed in some tenses into **ạ**, chiefly in the Feminine and Neuter (see Part II. Ch. IV. §§ 2, 3, 4, 5). Moreover it is changed often into **v**, *e.g.* in many Nouns ending in "āuñ", in Verbs ending in **au** etc. (See Part II. Ch. IV. Art. I. § 5, Art. II. § 1 *etc.*)

About **e** I have only to remark the change of this **é** into **è** (see p. 24, *n.* 4). About this point perhaps some rule may be found later.

About i only one change is here to be remarked. As I write Konkani with Roman characters following the Latin pronunciation, consequently I write, *e.g.* "sobitāi" not "sobitāy = beauty"; but in the oblique cases this last i sounds like y, consequently it should be written also y, although I have not always done it, because by writing, *e.g.* "sobitāi-en", according to the Latin pronunciation we get nearly the same sound as by writing "sobitāyen" (see page 18, *n.* 1). The best way of getting rid of many niceties would be to write Konkani with Kanarese characters.

A̤, corresponding to the Kanarese ˂, as has been observed in P. I., should be written at the end of all words which do not end in a vowel, if we write according to the Kanarese. But this would not be the case, if we had an Alphabet in which we could have words ending in a pure consonant; because this kind of ˂ is so small in many words that it is not different from the half vowel which is naturally pronounced at the end of a word ending in a consonant, in all languages, which consequently can be omitted; and as I write in the Roman Alphabet, which has no ˂, hence I do not write it. Yet it is true that in some words this ˂ is somewhat more distinct; in those cases I write, though not always, a̤. If some consonant is added, to such a word, *e. g.* ts, then this a̤, written or understood, appears and seems to be changed almost into an ă; *e.g.* "āpuṇāts" from "āpuṇ" or more exactly "āpuṇa̤". Yet in this point we must make a very fine distinction. I say that if some consonant is added, the ˂ is very often changed into ă, or at least, ˂ is pronounced much more distinctly; sometimes it becomes not ă but ŭ or perhaps i. Of the change of ˂ into i I do not now recollect any example; but this is a fact that, *e.g.* "livr = book", which is pronounced with a kind of half vowel at the end, becomes "livrütz", and "gurt" also pronounced with ˂ becomes "gurtütz" by adding ts, and so in some other cases. When is the final ˂ changed into ă by the addition of a consonant, and when into u or perhaps i? I have no general rule; yet it seems that those Nouns which are written by me with a final ụ, more often change ‹ (or ụ) into ŭ, and those written by me with ḁ, change it more often into ă. Whether this be quite certain or not, the fact is that the Kanarese ‹ is pronounced in Konkani words not always in the same way; *e.g.* more commonly ‹ of "văst", is pronounced differently from the ‹ of "īṭ = fertility"; the ‹ of the first is nearly u; the other is scarcely heard, or approaches a.

The change or resolution of ‹ sometimes into a, sometimes into u, was one of the reasons why I put down in the Alphabet two signs for the Kanarese ‹; because although I was not well aware of this change, yet I had some suspicion, and I was well aware of the two different sounds of this ‹ if used in Konkani. Yet I acknowledge that we could express these two Konkani sounds ḁ and ụ only by one letter, as in the Italian words *oro* and *molto* the o has two different sounds, viz. ò, ó; moreover the difference between ḁ and ụ sometimes cannot be exactly perceived.

Somebody might write my ụ by u; this perhaps could be done; but then the simple rule about accent (P. I. Ch. II.) should be changed and another, if there be any, more complicated should be laid down; because if you write "văstu", then the accent is upon the penultimate, and you should establish a rule to know which words have the accent upon the penultimate.

Ḁ, ụ and u of the Nominative of some Nouns disappear in the Plural (see p. 24), ḁ and ụ mostly also in the Singular; *e.g.* "dūd-ụ, dūd-an = milk, by milk".

Finally ụ in the Nouns of the 5th Declension is changed into u in the Plural. (See p. 37, *note.*)

To this point we may reduce also the omission of some vowels (see page 13.), and the change of ă into ā (see p. 175).

The cerebral letters ḍ, ḍh, ṭ, ṭh, if a vowel follows, are pronounced cerebral, yet keeping the nature of d and t; but if another dental letter follows, they seem to sound like r, not fully but nearly. Although ḍ, ḍh *etc.* be before dental letters, or be final, some pronounce them almost r; and I hear that in Goa usually this ḍ is pronounced like r.

Finally the rule of assimilation seems to hold good, *i. e.* that for the sake of euphony, if a letter comes together with another of a different kind with which it does not perfectly agree, the first letter changes the following letter into another cognate letter with which it can better agree. But what is this other letter? We might say that cerebral agrees with cerebral, palatal with palatal *etc.* Consequently if two letters of different kind do not agree, the above principle is applied. I say if they do not agree, because in some cases different letters agree very well; practice is required; *e.g.* l which is the initial letter of the termination of some tenses, becomes ḷ, if preceded by ḷ.

Here we may remark also, that the aspirated letters commonly cannot be used, if another consonant, at least of the same kind, follows; the reason is, because the aspiration supposes a kind of half a vowel after the aspirated letter; else it is not possible to pronounce it, but such half vowel is not there, if an aspirated letter is followed by another aspirated, at least of the same kind.

About double letters remark that in some cases it is altogether required to pronounce them; and then I write them; in some cases it is doubtful; then I omit them, because this point requires a long practice. I omit chiefly the double consonant when it would cause some obscurity; *e.g.* "dīs = day" can be written, nay must be written, according to the Latin, with one s; but if you write in the oblique cases "dissā" *etc.* what reason can you give of one s added? Especially as people seem to pronounce one s and according to the Alphabet laid down in Part I., it renders also one s satisfactory enough. Many other things should be said about this point, which for the present must be omitted.

CHAPTER IX. ON CERTAIN LETTERS

At the end of this Part III., for the sake of convenience, let us make some remarks which properly do not belong to this part. I said in Part I. that I omit some signs which exactness would require. I say a few things here about them.

First, I think that in Konkani there are three or four a, or better, that a has at least three sounds; the first is ȧ, pronounced approximately as *u* in the English *but*, or as *a* in the Italian word *farò*, passing over *a* very quickly and approaching somewhat to ó. The second is ă which is about equal to aa. The third is a (see Part I. Alphabet) which is pronounced as a common Latin *a*, not too long nor too short. Examples: "kăḍ" is nearly "kaaḍ", "mar" is as in Latin the *a* of *aro*; "kȧr" is like the a substituted in some dialects, to the e of "legno (lȧgn)". Moreover I remember to have found some words in which ȧ is pronounced slowly, almost ăă; consequently if we had to express the sounds with as many signs, we should say that there are two ȧ and two ă, *i.e.* one ȧ pronounced quickly, one ȧ pronounced slowly, one ă pronounced not very slowly, one ă pronounced very slowly; ȧ might be called *closed* a, ă might be called *open* a, just as I said of ó and ò which can be moreover ǒ and ō. Yet for the sake of simplicity, let us keep only two a (ȧ, ă) as in Kanarese, Mahrătti and Sanskrit; moreover a common a for the common cases; nevertheless *haec meminisse juvabit.*

I have put only one š, yet there are some words which have a cerebral š *e.g.* "šeḷ = cold"; this š corresponds to the Kanarese ಷ, whereas the simple š corresponds to ಶ. We could express such a sound by ṣ̌, as we use the dot underneath also for the other cerebral letters; so we simplify these things. Max Müller expresses it with sh; in the Tuḷu Grammar and in the Polyglot Vocabulary printed at the Basel Mission Press, I find š; in the Mahrătti Grammar sh, in the Kanarese

Grammar by Hodson **ṣh**, as he uses **sh** instead of **ś**. Yet I must acknowledge that the cerebral sound of this **ṣ** is somewhat different from the cerebral sound of the other cerebral letters.

I remember moreover to have heard some words with a kind of very guttural sound expressed by the Kanarese ಙ, which sound can be explained only orally; it is pronounced almost entirely with the throat. It is expressed by Max Müller in his "Sanskrit Grammar", by the Author of the "Student's Manual of the Mahrātti Grammar", by the Author of the "Tuḷu Grammar" and by the Author of the "Polyglot Vocabulary" printed at the Basel Mission Press in Mangalore, by **ṅ**; in the Kanarese Grammar by **gn**; yet I must acknowledge that I have heard some words pronounced so guttural that their **ṅ** seems to be remarkably different from **ṅ** of "sing" which is the example given in the Mahrātti Grammar for this **ṅ**. (See p. 18, *n.* 2.)

Finally another sound is ಋ and ೠ, represented in the above mentioned books by **ṛi**, **ṛî** (but in the Polyglot Vocabulary **ṛ**, **ṝ**, in the Tuḷu Grammar by **ṛi**, **ṛī**); this sound is approximately represented by **rĭ** and **rī**, or better by **r** with a kind of vowel, which seems to be nearly ' or half vowel (see p. 20, *n.* 2.)

What I write **gn** (not **g-n**) is in Kanarese represented by ಞ, and in the above quoted Vocabulary by **ń**, in the Grammar of Max Müller and in the Mahrātti Grammar by **ñ**; as for me, I prefer **gn**, because the Latin **gn** is pronounced nearly in the same way; because I was compelled to choose **ñ** as the sign of the nasal **n**, and because it is, perhaps far easier to distinguish so many different **n**, if we write **gn**. (See p. 5.) What I write **g-n** would be expressed in Kanarese by joining the two consonants ಗ and ನ or ಣ. Also by writing **jn** we would get almost the same sound, as the Konkani **j** is thinner than the English **j**.

The reader might have observed that very seldom or never are **ĭ**, **ŏ**, **ŭ** used, although put in the Alphabet. The reason is, because, as I said in Part I., I use these signs only when there is any necessity; but for ă very often there is a necessity, not so for ĭ, ŏ, ŭ.

Those who know Kanarese and Mahrātti might have remarked that for the Kanarese ಜ and Mahrātti ज, I put two letters (j, z); the reason is because this letter ಜ has two sounds in Konkani; and as I do not know a rule to distinguish the two sounds, so I write two letters. The same must be said of ಚ, Mahrātti च, for which I put c̆, tc̆, ts, tz; ts and tz may be considered as equal; c̆ is not so sharp as tc̆, yet sometimes it does not differ much from tc̆; moreover euphony does not allow us to write tc̆ in all cases in which tc̆ should be written; hence you find sometimes c̆ instead of tc̆; but ts or tz differ somewhat more from tc̆ and still more from s. The same must be said of ts, *i.e.* if euphony requires us to write s instead of ts contrary to the above rules, I write henceforth s not ts. Perhaps if we write Konkani with Kanarese letters, we could put some sign, *e.g.* a dot above ಜ and ಚ to distinguish these sounds; as we could put the Sanskrit and Mahrātti "virāma" to express the absence of any vowel or half-vowel at the end of a word, the "virāma" is marked by an oblique line placed at the foot of a consonant (्).

About f. Properly speaking, no f should occur in Konkani, but only aspirated p (ph), and really in the villages this f does not usually occur; *e.g.* they say "phoṭ", "phālea", *not* "foṭ" "fālea"; yet in the town this f is used, so let it pass.

About v. This letter is very often indistinct, so that it is not easily perceived whether it is u or v. One of the reasons may be, because the Konkani words beginning with o take a kind of v or u before them, as the words beginning with e take y. We have a proof of this in the way in which some Natives pronounce Latin: some say, *e.g.* *yeleison*, *yergo* instead of *eleison* and *ergo*, nay some seem to add this *y* even in the middle; *e.g.* *meyam* instead of *meam;* and some seem to say *vordo* or *uordo* instead of *ordo*. This depends, I think, on the Kanarese pronunciation.

About aspirated letters. Besides the aspirated letters given in the Alphabet some others may occur; *e.g.* m of "mèḷo" is pronounced somewhat aspirated. What to do in such cases? If we write Konkani with Roman characters, the easiest and most simple plan is to write h after that letter, just as with the other aspirated letters; if we write with Kanarese characters, we can use the Kanarese letter ಹ joined to the letter which is to be pronounced aspirated. This must be understood if the aspiration belongs to the consonant, *i.e.* if the aspiration must sound between the consonant and the following vowel; if the aspiration must sound after the vowel of the consonant, then in Roman characters we may use h as above, in Kanarese characters we should use the medial ಃ; here we could not use the above ಹ, because ಹ is a consonant, whereas that aspiration after a vowel is a vocalized h. We have a proof of this in the union of all vowels with ಹ, so as to become ha, hi, hu, he, hei, ho, hou, which union does not take place with ಃ. So, *e.g.* "dūkụ = pain, sorrow", exactly should be written "dukhụ".

There are some Nouns which end in a kind of half-vowel, *e.g.* "jin = life"; this half vowel seems to be changed into i in the stem, "jinie"; consequently this would be an example of a new letter different from ạ and ụ, namely it would be i̥; yet it is better and more simple to explain this change by saying that in some Nouns the stem is formed from the Nominative by adding not only one vowel as usually, but two vowels (see p. 16, *n.* 8). The stem, however, is not always formed from the Nominative (see p. 30, *n.* 3).

Here let us remark that by writing y instead of i, *e. g.* ya instead of ea or ia, we would simplify very much the rules about accentuation of diphthongs. I said (page 7) that many diphthongs have the accent upon the second vowel, many upon the first, or, shorter, no suitable rule has been given. By writing y instead of i, whenever it is possible, many apparent diphthongs would disappear; consequently their accent would become known at once. The final diphthongs which usually have the accent upon the first vowel are chiefly au or ao, ou, eu, ei, ou or oi. Ai commonly has the accent upon a, if this is long; *e.g.* "khāiñ = something"; upon the 2nd vowel, if a is short; *e.g.* "khăiñ = where", "kăiñ = when". On the contrary eo, ie, ui, io, ea, ia etc. which in Kanarese would not be diphthongs, have the accent upon the last vowel. The terminations aie, ua, ie and the like which occur in some Declensions, have the accent upon the last vowel; *i.e.* the termination has the accent.

Finally we must pay attention not to confound ä with o; in many words they seem to be very similar; yet exactness does not allow us to change these two similar sounds. In pronouncing ä the mouth is more opened and the voice deeper than in pronouncing ó. The difference between ó and ä appears especially when ä has the accent; in other cases we would not lose much exactness by pronouncing ó instead of ä. Europeans must pay attention not to pronounce this ä, especially accented ä, like the German ö or French eu; this pronunciation is entirely wrong.

About this ä remark further that in the same word it may become ā, modifying thereby the meaning; *e.g.* "isär *or* visär = forgetfulness", "isār *or* visār = forget"; "kätär = cut", "kātär = be cut" (see p. 175); the same may happen with other vowels.

These things may be settled in future times, as in this first attempt many niceties were to be omitted. If we write Konkani with Kanarese or Mahrātti letters, many things will be settled by themselves, *i. e.* only by writing in a more suitable Alphabet, especially if we prefer the Mahrātti or Sanskrit; because with Kanarese something would remain still doubtful, *e.g.* the final ‘ which cannot be omitted in Kanarese, if no vowel is there, and which must be often omitted in Konkani, unless we introduce some new signs to modify the Kanarese letters and make them suitable to Konkani.

PART IV. SYNTAX

CHAPTER I. AGREEMENT OR CONCORD

For the reader, for whom I write, many particular rules are not required, for they are the same as in our languages. Between the different parts of speech there must be concord in Gender, Number and Case.

This rule contains a great many particular cases. But the following restrictions are to be made:

1. If a word is to agree with many others of different Genders, that word is put in the Neuter Gender; yet sometimes it might agree with the nearest one, at least in Gender, and often also in Number. So if an Adjective has reference to men and women, it is put in the Neuter Gender. Nay, this happens not only with Adjectives, but sometimes also with Substantives; *e.g.* "mănis = man". If it is used for a man and a woman, as in the example: "the first men were Adam and Eve", "monis" becomes Neuter and is declined according to the Neuter of the 2nd Declension; whereas absolutely it is Masculine and follows the Masculine form of the 2nd Declension; so also "gărtso = domestic" *etc.* The same rule holds for the Verbs; *e.g.* "tiñ geliñ = they went", speaking of a man and of a woman.

2. The Participle and some tenses of Transitive Verbs have quite a peculiar concord, which will be explained later on. For the present read page 118, *n.* 6, and consider that if a Verb has no subject or the subject is a sentence, the Neuter Gender of the Verb is used.

3. It has been mentioned already that speaking (*a*) to or (*b*) about a respectable person, chiefly Priests, the Plural is

used, viz. the Verb is put in the Plural, in the 2nd Person in the (*a*) case, in the 3rd in the (*b*) case; in the Masculine Gender, if the person is a man; in the Neuter, if a woman. Yet this rule is not always observed, so that the rule expresses rather what is allowed to do (to use the Plural) than what is commanded to do. Especially the part of the rule about women is not certain; doubtless I heard some examples according to the above rule; for this reason I have put the observation 4th (page 72); yet I heard also many examples contrary to it. Consequently the part of the rule to use the Plural when we speak *to* a woman of high rank, is certain; the part of the rule to use the Plural when we speak *about* a respectable woman and even in the Neuter Gender, is uncertain; and, *omnibus consideratis*, it seems safer to use the Singular. Not only the Verb, but also the Adjective and the Pronoun which have reference to a respectable person seem to be put in the Plural

4. The Nouns of the 1st Declension ending in a, not used in the Plural, require the Verb in the Plural, if the meaning is Plural (at least I have found some examples according to this rule; I cannot ascertain whether this is the common case).[1] But the Adjective in such a case may remain in the Singular; *e. g.* "souñsārāči čintna yetāt".

5. A Noun in apposition agrees with its name; *e. g.* "the town of Mangalore = koḍyāl šār". Here read the note page 39, to which we may add that if a Substantive (especially or only Proper Noun) is followed by a title or by a similar word, the first Substantive either is not declined or put only in the Original; *e. g.* "Dāvid-rāyān = by king David". (See also page 16, *n.* 9.)

---

[1] I heard sometimes Feminine Nouns of the 1st Declension having the Verb in the Neuter Plural, *e. g.* "monšānīñ vāiţ čintna čintleānt = bad thoughts have been thought by men". I cannot tell whether it was a mistake or not.

6. If an Adjective of three terminations is a predicate, as in the example "God makes us good", or if an Adjective takes the place of the Genitive in the Compound Verbs, it is left in the Nominative, Singular or Plural, according to the Number of its Substantive; *e.g.* "Deu amkāñ pātkāntle soḍeitā= God delivers us from sins"; "Deu amkāñ bore kārtā = God makes us good"; "peleāso mōg kār = love thy neighbour". The same happens sometimes with Substantives, viz. if they are used as predicate or as indirect object of a Transitive Verb, they are placed in the Nominative: "tūñ tukā kōṇ moṇtai = thou whom doest say?" Moreover, if an Adjective in Nominative Case, corresponding to the Genitive (see Part II. Chap. II. Art. 2), has another Adjective before itself, this preceding Adjective is put in the oblique case Masculine or Feminine or Neuter, Singular or Plural, according to the Gender and Number which the Genitive converted into Adjective had before being changed into an Adjective; *e. g.* "boreañ monšānči sóvói = the custom of good men"; yēka borea monšāči sóvói = the custom of a good man;" "yēka tarāči nessoṇ = dress of one kind". The same rule is observed, if two Genitives are changed into Adjectives; the subordinate Genitive is not put in the Nominative; *e. g.* "the name of this boy's father = yea burgāčeā bāpāčeñ nāuñ". This rule seems to hold good for all kinds of declinable Adjectives.

7. The Adjectives or Pronouns "kāsso, tāsso *etc.* must also agree with their Substantive; although in English we have an Adverb, *e.g.* "how do you do = kāsso assāi?" But what is this Substantive with which they must agree? Sometimes it is difficult to know it. This rule may make easier this point; translate the English sentence into Latin using *qualis* for "how" and see which word is qualified by this *qualis;* that is the word with which "kāsso" must agree; *e.g.* "how did you succeed in that affair? = tukā teñ kām kāsseñ zāleñ, *lit.* what did that affair turn out?" "How did God create the world? = Devān kāsso souñsār rātzlo?"

8. The Adjectives in -ntlo (see p. 84) agree regularly with their Substantive, if they are used as attribute; *e.g.* "the men of the world = saunsārāntle monis"; "by the men of the world = saunsārāntlean monšāniñ"; but if they are used in some other way, it does not appear with which word they should agree; then they are put in the Instrumental of the Singular; *e.g.* "who among you has ever suffered such a pain as our Lord Jesus Christ? = tumčer bitārleān kōṇeā Sōmia Jozu Kristā bārits tassālo kāšṭ soslā?" The same may happen with other Adjectives, chiefly with Adjectives derived from Postpositions or Adverbs. Generally speaking it seems that such Adjectives, if their agreement is not evident, are put in the Instrumental Singular; *e. g.* "mukhāveleān votz = go before".; yet here too, cases occur in which these Adjectives agree with a Noun with which, it seems, they should not agree; *e.g.* "God separated the waters above the sky from the waters under the sky = Dēvān moḷabā voir assāliñ udkañ moḷabā khāl assāliñ udkāntliñ vingāḍ keleānt". Here we could use also the Instrumental.

9. If an Adjective is used as a Predicate in a Participial sentence contracted from a Relative sentence in which it was used as a Predicate in the Nominative or Accusative, this case is kept also in the contracted sentence although, perhaps the Noun with which it should agree be not in the Nominative; *e. g.* "honour Our Lord, exposed on the Altar = Altārir ukto kārn dovorleleā Somiāk mān diā". We might perhaps generalize the rule by saying that in such sentences the Adjective is left in the case in which it was in the full sentence.

I explain by two examples, in order to be shorter and clearer what I mean to say by Predicate and Attribute. "God is good; God makes us happy in heaven" *etc.*; here the Adjective is Predicate; "the good God" "the happy man"; here the Adjective is Attribute.

10. Sometimes the Adjective agrees with its Noun not grammatically, but according to the meaning; *e. g.* "innovator" can be translated by "nove māriādegār"; here we should

say grammatically "novo mǎriādegār"; but this Noun "mǎriādegār", derived from "mariād = habit, custom", means a man making customs; in order to get the meaning of "innovator", we must add "of new things"; hence, omitting thing, we get "nove" in the oblique case; exactly we should say "noveañ". In the same we may explain "dispoḍte vordi = journalist". If we say "dispoḍto vordī", the meaning would be "daily man of news", whereas the meaning requires "man of daily news". Not all speak so; yet this mode seems to be more correct and used by more learned men.

11. The Adverbs formed with an Adverbial Declinable Adjective joined to the Gerund in -un (see p. 176), either may be declined and follow the general rule of concord (as far as regards the Adjective united with the Gerund), or may be not declined, *ad libitum; e. g.* "behave yourself well = borǫ kǎrn tsǎl, *or* boreñ kǎrn tsǎl".

The Adverbs in -eñ (Neuter of the Adjective) may be declined, or not declined *ad libitum; e. g.* "to boro vātstā, *or* to boreñ vātstā = he reads well".

12. If the subject of the sentence is 3rd Person Plural of Neuter Gender, the Verb may be put in the Singular; *e. g.* "tāṇeñ apliñ pātkañ sānglañ = he has confessed his sins". Nay, sometimes the Singular of the Verb is used, although the subject (real, though perhaps not grammatical subject) is Masculine; *e. g.* "āuveñ poise kaneilāñ = I have taken money". Very probably this second manner is a mistake: the first manner is not certain.

13. We must ṛemark that in Konkani some words are considered as connected which in Latin and English would not agree (see below about Adjectives); consequently those words must follow the rule of concord; *e. g.* "dusreāntso rāg = anger of others"; whereas we would say "anger against others". This point cannot be taught by rules: practice is required. Further some words may have a double relation, *i. e.* to two or more words of different Genders *etc.;* then often it is

allowed to choose among those words as terms of agreement, that which we like whether it be the nearest one or not. So also the Absolute Infinitive in some cases may agree either with the word governing it or with its object; *e.g.* "ničeu dosmānkai dorči saitānātso"; *or* some say also: "ničeu dosmānkai dortso saitānātso". The first expression is better.

14. Finally we must pay attention to those Adjectives which correspond to the Latin indeclinable *quantum*, *minus*, and the like, as "uṇo, titlo, kedo, tedo"; but in Konkani are declinable, and if joined to another Adjective, they agree with it; *e.g.* "kedi voḍli = how big?" (Feminine), in Latin *quam magna*, "uṇi ajapāči = less admirable"; "tedo boro = so good" *etc.*

Many other things should be said about this point; but, in order not to overwhelm the mind and not to make this chapter too difficult, I will speak of them in other places, as they occur.

Exercises

Bāpai, āuoi, boiṇi, bāu, sākāṭ bāir-geleānt. Kòṇ gāra rāunk-nāñ. Mozo mām ani moji māvoḷṇ bhou boriñ: tīñ makā sārginči vāṭ sikoitāt. Poiliñ monšañ Ādāuñ ani Yēv, tīñ sāmestañ monšāñtso ārāmb[1] (*origin*). Sāibānu, moja gārā yeun, takā bessāoñ diā. Pādri khāiñ" geleāt? Takā āpoun āḍ (*call him*). Sāibiṇ Agatha durbāḷeānk tovoḷ tovoḷ (*from time to time*) ismāl ditā[2]. Sāibiṇ Rejin gārā āiligī? Yedoḷ pāriānt yeunknāñ, atāñ yeteli. Amiñ rāsārkārčea veḷār, sābār pāuṭi sāuñsārāči čintnā yetāt; amiñ teo bāir-gālizāi. Ritan pāṭān Kadra pāṭnā prās voḍleñ. Thāiñ kitlo lók astit? Āuñ sārkeñ neṇāñ: moje ālōčeni pārmāṇe tsāḍ-uṇeñ ponās hazār lók assāt (*may be*). Āuoi bāpānu, tumčea burgeānk

---

[1] In Kanarese they say ಆರಂಭ viz. "ārāmbha", yet the Konkani Christians seem to pronounce "ărămb"; this remark holds good for some other words.

[2] "Agatha" in Konkani should be "Agdu"; but as "sāibiṇ" is not commonly used for Native ladies, it is better to keep the Latin word *Agatha*.

bore kārā; kiteāk moḷeār tumiñ tanče višiānt lek dīzāi. Burgeā, boro tzāl ani āuoi bāpāk mān dī; yea vorviñ tukā kurpā ani suk meḷteleñ. Yea gārāčea dhāniātso išṭ kāl melo: teā pasun dhāni āz gārā nāñ; to mornāk gelo.

CHAPTER II. USE OF EACH PART OF SPEECH

Art. I. Nouns

A. General Observations

The Nouns, except the names of common things, are rather seldom used in Konkani, particularly Abstract Nouns. Though there are some Abstract Nouns, and Verbal Nouns also, yet, except in a few cases, it is better to avoid those Nouns and change the sentence so as to get a finite Mood of the Verb. I say "finite Mood", because Verbal Nouns are the same as the Infinitive of the Verb in the Neuter Gender. The Tense of finite Mood, which may be substituted, is, very often, the Conditional in -leār (see Conjugation); *e.g.* "learning is useful": though we might say: "sikčeñ upkārāk poḍṭā", yet it is better to say: "sikleār = if you learn". The Conditional is, we may say, the favourite Tense in Konkani; for, it is like a panacea to supply the pretended poverty of this language. For this reason too, I do not put down in the Dictionary all Verbal Nouns. What I say must be understood of the common and vulgar language, not of the high and cultivated language or rather of the language to be cultivated; because there is no cultivated language.

After these general considerations let us say something in particular about the more difficult Nouns.

The fundamental difficulty regarding the use of the Nouns, may be this, viz. many Nouns do not exist in Konkani. How to express, *e.g. hypostasis, hyphen, hydrostatics, hypothesis, abstraction*?

To this difficulty I answer: look in the Dictionary and you will find the translation, without circumlocution, of the above and other similar words, although such words cannot be popular, as they are not popular even in our cultivated languages.

The second difficulty is about the use of Abstract Nouns. We have already seen (Part III. Chapter V.) that Abstract Nouns are formed chiefly by the terminations **-poṇ** and **-kai** or **-ai**. This kind of Abstract Nouns is usually rightly employed, and the greatest part of them are of this kind; yet there are also some primitive Abstract Nouns; *e. g.* "**kărt** = improvement, especially material"; "guṇ = improvement, especially immaterial."

The third difficulty is about Verbal Nouns corresponding to the Latin Nouns ending in *-ctio* or in a similar termination. The easiest way of getting rid of this difficulty would be to use the Infinitive of the Verb which is at the same time a Verbal Noun; yet this is not elegant and according to the nature of Konkani. Another way would be to change the Verbal Noun into a Verb; and though this is not against the nature of Konkani, it is too low, at least often. Yet sometimes this way may be well employed. The third and best way is to use the termination given in Part III. Chapter V. The more common termination is **-neñ**; yet the termination **-ap** is not so rare, the other terminations given *l. c.* are rather rare, at least for real Verbal Nouns.

The fourth difficulty is found in the Nouns which end in *-ility* or in a similar termination. The way of translating these Nouns is to add "**-sărkeñ**" (*v. l. c.*). This "**sărkeñ**" means *equality*, hence, *e. g.* "**vāṇṭi-sărkeñ**" means "a thing which is equal to parts *or* a thing which *in potentia* is equal to its parts". This is the only or, at least, the chief termination, as far as I remember, by which we can form this kind of Nouns. This mode although very philosophical, more perhaps than the Latin, English, German, French, Italian modes, is not popular. The negative form of this kind of Nouns is somewhat difficult; I speak of it here below.

The fifth, quite a peculiar difficulty, is about some Negative Nouns. You find many of these Nouns in the Dictionary under In-. First remark that common people often change the sentence into the Negative, *i. e.* instead of making the Noun Negative they make the Verb Negative; *e. g.* instead of saying "ămorăṇ = immortality", they say "ătmo moṛănāñ". This popular mode may be employed with advantage in some cases in which the Negative Noun would not sound well; yet generally speaking the best mode is to use the Negative form of the Noun, as has been explained in Part III. Chapt. IV. Among those terminations, the most common is "-nāñ" prefixed to the Noun. The termination -ăñ, or sometimes only ă, occurs also. But the other terminations are not frequent. Besides the terminations given *l. c.* there are some others, such as "be-"; *e.g.* "ābru = character", "beābru = want of character"; "āḍ- = against", *e. g.* "ālōčen = judgment", "āḍālōčen = a judgment against . . ."; "čintna = thought", "āḍčintna = against thought (distraction)"; "-nāstanāñ = *lit.* not being", *e. g.* "kāraṇ-nāstanāñ = no cause (unreasonably)"; as the reader sees, some of these modes are not simply negative, but rather contrary. Compare this with the *Propositiones contradictoriae* and *contrariae* of the philosophers.

The Nouns in -sărkeñ may be made Negative in many forms; the first is to prefix -nāñ, *e. g.* "nāñ-vāṇṭi-sărkeñ". The second is to insert -nāñ in the middle before "sărkeñ"; *e. g.* "sika-sărkeñ = docility"; "sikanāñ-sărkeñ" *or* "nāñ-sikā-sărkeñ = in-docility". Not only the Nouns in "-sărkeñ" but also some other words may be made negative in many ways, as some Nouns are derived from the primitive form in many ways.

In Konkani we must remark the use of Nouns compounded with two or more Nouns, one of which is accompanied by some Postpositions, or at least not put in the Original Case, as it should be, according to the general rule; *e.g.* "angār-poḍneñ

= inroad, assault". The reason is, because the Verbal sentence is "angār poḍ = *lit.* fall on body"; hence the Noun is used keeping the original form; else the meaning would not be the same.

In Latin and in some other languages different words must be used for the fruit and for the tree bearing the fruit; so *malum*, *malus*, *pirum*, *pirus* In Konkani usually the same word may express both fruit and tree, *e.g.* "limbo, nāring", although we may add the word "rūk = tree" to express more distinctly the tree, *e.g.* "limbeātso rūk", if from the context the meaning is not clear. Yet there are some Nouns which are used only for fruits, and some only for trees; *e.g.* "nārl = cocoanut", "māḍ = cocoanut-tree (palm-tree)"; "keḷeñ = plantain; "keḷambo = plantain-tree" *etc.*

B. Cases.

§ 1. Nominative.

Omitting things well known to those who have some knowledge of Grammar, as I always suppose those to be for whom I write, I make these few remarks about the Nominative.

1. The Nominative is used when a Noun is used as an explanation of another word; *e.g.* "he has been appointed Governor *or* as Governor = takā ădhipăti nemsilā"; "Jacob took Rebecca as his wife = Jākobān Rebekāk āpli ăstri moṇ kāṇeileā". In these examples the first direct object is put in the Accusative, the 2nd object, indirect and explanatory, is put in the Nominative with "moṇ", which "moṇ" will be explained later on.

2. The Nominative is used, instead of the Accusative *a*) with inanimate objects (see pp. 12. 19); *b*) sometimes also with animate objects, chiefly if they are Proper Nouns. This second case is rather an exception than a rule, whereas the first is ordinary. "Deu = God" is often put in the Nominative,

when it should be put in the Accusative; *e.g.* "Deu kāṇeitāñ = I receive God (H. Communion)".

3. In Verbs having in some Tenses passive meaning, the word which in Latin would be put (in Passive Verbs) in the Nominitive, is put sometimes in the Accusative, as I explain later on.

Exercise

Rāṇien N. Sāibāk mēlnītidār nemsilā. Somia Jezu Kristān Sant Pedruk Apostolānčeñ mostāk kārn dovorlā. Burgeānu, vāiṭ burgeānk išṭ vintzun kāḍnakāt; kiteāk moḷeār tanče vorviñ tumiñ pāḍ zāšāt. Deu āple kurpen amkāñ aple išṭ kārtā ani sārginče dāiji. Frask yea dākṭea burgeāk aplo posko pūt kārtā. Sāmestañ monšānk tuzo sezāri moṇ čint (*consider all men as your neighbour*), ani sāmestānk kumok dī; tukā sārgār tzāḍ inām meḷteleñ.

§ 2. Dative

About this Case as also about other Cases there may be different opinions; for somebody might perhaps say that what I call Nominative is not Nominative, but Accusative, as in Latin *bellum;* or again that in the example: "bāpāk āpoi = call the father", the Dative "bāpāk" is used instead of the Accusative; but all these are questions *de verbis.*

Now I see that the Author of the Mahrātti Grammar really calls Dative what I call Accusative. I have said that the Accusative is equal to the Nominative in inanimate objects, equal to the Dative in animate objects. He says on the contrary that animate objects are put in the Dative. The final conclusion is the same in both ways; yet I prefer the first manner; because thereby the things seem to be more simple, and because the first manner seems to be more satisfactory to the mind; at all events *in dubiis libertas.*

The Dative is used 1) to show purpose or aim; *e.g.* "kiteāk āiloi? = to what (why) did you come?" "javaṇāk āiloñ = I came for dinner". The second form of the Infinitive in -unčeāk is just this Dative, formed from the Nominative -untso; *e.g.* "to boreunčeāk āilo = he came to write". Instead of it we might use also the Original with "pasun"; *e.g.* "fārikpoṇāk, *or* fārikpoṇa pasun = for reparation".

2. It is used with many Verbs, with which the use of the Dative is quite natural; yet in our languages we have a different construction. So, as there is no word meaning exactly "have" in Konkani, the Dative is used as in Latin *mihi liber est* = makā yēk pustak assā". About this Dative it must be observed that, if the thing possessed, is such a thing of which instead of "I have...." we could not say: *apud me est*, then the Dative is used; if we could say *apud me est*, then very often the Original with "kāḍe *or* lagiñ" is used. Hence we can say: "makā yēk gār assā = *mihi est domus*"; on the contrary "moje kāḍe yēk pustak assā = *apud me* (*mihi*) *est liber*", *or* "moje lagiñ yēk pustak assā".

3. In some Konkani phrases; *e. g.* "dotorn makā yetā = I know the Catechism, *lit.* to me the Catechism comes"; "makā ugḍās yēnāñ = I cannot remember, *lit.* remembrance does not come to me" *etc.*

4. To show motion to a place, the Dative may be used, though the 1st Locative is also used; *e. g.* "Igārjek vetāñ = I go to the Church" *or* "Igārjent vetāñ". In the meaning there may be a little difference between Dative and Locative. Some Proper Names are used without any change, to show motion; *e. g.* "āuñ Jeppu vetāñ" = I go to Jeppoo (see above Declension of Proper Nouns.)

5. To show advantage or disadvantage two Datives are used, as in Latin "*hoc tibi commodo est* = yeñ tukā upkārāk poḍtā," *lit.* it falls to thee to benefit".

6. To show for whom a thing is done, and the like, the Dative is used; *e. g.* "this has been done for me = yeñ makā zāleñ", *etc.* This case might be reduced to the preceding.

7. To show time in answering the question: "how many times a day, a week, a year?" the words day, week *etc.* are put in the Dative; *e. g.* "voršāk yēk pāuṭi puṇ Bombai vetāñ = at least once a year I go to Bombay"; in these cases it might be used also in the Original with "modeñ = in the middle, during"; but this is not so exact.

8. To say: "I give something to .." the Dative may be used; yet very often the Original with "kāḍé *or* lagiñ" is used just as I said in the second case.

9. The Dative seems to be used also with the Verb "moṇ = say", if it has the meaning of "call", namely "call by name". The thing which is called by name is put in the Dative, the name itself in the Accusative; *e.g.* "tumiñ yea fatrāk kiteñ mhoṇṭāt? = how do you call this stone?" and the same in similar sentences.

10. Price is frequently expressed by the Dative, provided the Verb allows it; *e.g.* "vo sāmān kitleañ Rupoiānk kāṇgelai = for how many Rupees did you take (*or* buy) this article?" But if you use "poḍtā = falls", *or* "lāgtā = is applied", you must use not the Dative, but the Nominative, because the meaning of the Verb does not allow the use of the Dative. So, "takā dhā Rupoi lāgle = it cost ten Rupees", *or* "takā dhā Rupoi poḍle". With these two last Verbs, the thing itself should be put in the Dative; for, translating literally, in our languages too, the Dative of the thing and the Nominative of the price would be used, "to it ten Rupees fell *or* have been applied".

11. The Verbs meaning "to speak, to say" and the like, may be used with the Dative of the person to whom we speak; yet very often the Original is also used with "lagiñ" *or* "kāḍe"; *e.g.* "āuñ tumče lāgiñ ulcitāñ = I speak to you", "mestri burgeāñ kāḍe vitzārtā = the master questions the boys".

12. Sometimes Dative is used to show place as in the sentence: "tīn disāče vāṭek gelo = *lit.* he went to a way of three days, he walked three days".

13. Finally, we may perhaps call Dative that which (p. 19) has been called Accusative, *e.g.* "rukāk mār = beat to the tree", and similar examples; yet this may be explained also in some other way. (See *ibid.*)

Exercise

Devān amkāñ kiteāk rätzleāt? Takā voḷkunčeāk (*or* voḷkunk) ani meleā uprānt särginčeñ suk bogunčeāk (*or* bogunk). Somia Jezu Kristāčea kälzāk äkmān kelleā pasun fārikpoṇ diunčeāk amiñ kiteñ kärizāi? Amiñ disā modeñ sābār pāuṭi tačentz käliz ani tačea kälzāče seguṇ takā beṭāizāi, särvụ vāstu thāiñ tače kušie pärmāṇe tzālāzā: ani amčeñ kirkoḷi kaliz takā dīzāi: tovoḷ amkāñ tačeñ äširvād meḷteleñ ani bhou vegiñ amiñ seguṇā thāiñ (*in virtue*) sompūrṇ zateleāuñ; mukhiāzāun tači tzāḍ äjāpāči sālgi meḷteli (*familiaritas stupenda nimis invenietur*). Kälikuṭāk votzunk kitliñ uorañ lagtit? Pāivāṭen tzālleār, sābār dīs zāi; āgbōṭin sumār dón dīs zāi. Ani Bombāi votzunk kitleñ zāi? Sumār čār dīs. Kōṇāk yēñ vāstur kelāiñ? Makātz. Pātak ätmeāk ani kuḍik lukšānāk poḍtā. Koṭepoṇāče mānis, sāngtā povitrụ pustāk, ārdejiṇient mortele. Disāk kitle pāuṭi ami Dēvātso āṭou kärizāi? Tanktā titleñ (*as much as you can*). Dēvāk meḷon ätme gāḍie gāḍien apleñ käliz Dēvāk beṭaitāt, ani yea sauñsārānt astānañi, sārgār tančeñ mon assā. Burgeā, moje kāḍe (*or* makā) tujeñ käliz dī: asseñ uleitā Somi Jezu Krist. Pedru mamā, yea rukāk tumče bašen kiteñ moṇtāt? Akāgī? Amiñ voḍātso ruk moṇtāuñ. Ani teā rukāk kiteñ moṇtāt? Sāibānu, makā gottunāñ (*I do not know*). Yeñ bhou sobit pustak: takā kitle Rupoi lagleāt? Yeñ bhou mārāg pustak; sumār pānz Rupoi poḍleāt takā. Tasseñ asleār, makā kuši nāñ yeñ pustak molāk kāṇeunk.

§ 3. Accusative

First of all, as the Accusative is very often (especially in animate objects) equal to the Dative, sometimes (especially in inanimate objects) to the Nominative, we require some rule to know when the same form is a sign of one case and when of another. This principle may be laid down: According to the philosophy of the grammar, Accusative indicates the direct object of the action expressed by the Verb (from *accu-*

sare); the Dative denotes the indirect object of the action of the Verb, or the object *cui accidit*, or to whom really or metaphorically the action of the Verb (which directly aims at the word put in the Accusative) is indirectly given (from *dare*); *e.g.* "God has given His Son to the world"; *Son* denotes the direct object of *has given*; *to the world* denotes the thing *cui accidit* or *cui datur*, to which is given the direct object of *has given*. Of course I do not speak of any kind of Accusative and Dative, but of that Accusative and of that Dative which are *simpliciter* and, I may say κατ'-ἐξοχήν, Accusative and Dative. Hence I do not consider here the Accusative and Dative governed by Postpositions *etc.* Moreover this fundamental principle may be somewhat modified according to the nature of the different languages, *e.g.* in English we say "I study the Latin Grammar", whereas in Latin they say "*Studeo Grammaticae Latinae.*"

Hence we may draw a corollary, *i.e.* that it is more agreeing to the above principle to say, "Accusative of animate objects has a termination equal to the termination of the Dative," than to say "animate objects are put in the Dative, although they are the direct object of the Verb". For this reason I said (p. 206) that the first manner is more satisfactory to the mind.

After these preliminary remarks, let us see when the Accusative is used. This case is used

1. In all cases in which the direct object of the action of the Verb is denoted, unless there be some peculiar exception. This first point is the same as in other languages; consequently it does not require further explanation. This first point includes, we may say, all ordinary cases in which the Accusative is to be used.

2. According to the above principle we should also consider as Accusative the two first cases considered on p. 205 as Nominative; because although their form is equal to the Nominative, yet the meaning does not allow us to call them Nominative.

3. To express time in answering the question how long; *e.g.* "the war lasted three years = zuz tīn vorsañ urleñ".

4. To express space or measure to the question "how high", "how broad"; *e.g.* "this field is twenty feet long = vo gādo vīs fuṭi lāmb".

Exercise

Burgeā, kiteāk āz titlo toḍou kārn aịlāi? Bāpā, āz iskul[1] saḍe tīn uorañ urlāñ. Phoṭ mārtai; keḷḷuloi. Nīñ, bābā: āuñ phoṭ mārināñ, mēstri kāḍe vitzārā. Vāgo rāu, nakāzālle sāngnakā: phoṭ tuja tonḍār distā. Antoni, makā yēk pēṭ zāi. Sāibānu, kedi vōḍ lāmbāi, ani rūndai? Tīn vāri lāmb ani dēḍ vār rūnd. Kāḷḷeñ, Sāibānu; poise diā, foḷiñ, kiḷe ani yer sāmān āḍunk. Fāḍpoši vāur kārnakā; sārkeñ kārināñzaleār, āuñ tukā sambaḷ kāiñ disonāñ. Zāit, Sāibānu; Anton kedintz fāḍpoši vāur kārināñ. Foḷiñ aḍleānt, puṇ tanči lāmbai pāvānāñ; ani sā Rupoi diā, kuši asleār. Ah, lutčeā, tūñ naḍi kārtai, dillo duḍu tzāḍ zatā.

§ 4. Instrumental[2]

This case is used:

1. To show the *agent* in the tenses of passive meaning (or of passive construction) of the Transitive Verbs (see below those tenses); *e.g.* "Devān amkāñ rātzleāt = God has created us"; "Burgeān tanṭe keleāt = the boy has done mischief".

2. In some tenses of the Neuter Verbs (see those tenses below); *e.g.* "āuveñ votzazāi = I must go", "āuveñ votzunk gārz assā, = *lit.* by me to go is required; in Latin = *a me iri necessitas est*"; "tāṇeñ votzayet = he may go".

[1] The Konkani word would be "vidyā-sāl" or "vidyā-šāl", used also in Mahratti; "iskul" is entirely foreign and not a good word. I use for the present this and also some other foreign words only because they are often used; but they are a corruption of the language.

[2] For the sake of convenience, I speak in this paragraph not exclusively of Nouns, but also of other parts of speech. This remark must be applied to other paragraphs too.

3. To express cause or instrument; *e.g.* "to takā tālvārin mārta = he kills him with the sword", "to monis ariče piḍen melo = that man died of palsy".

4. To express the material out of which a thing is made, although in this case the Adjective may also be used; *e.g.* "Dēvān amči kuḍ mātien keleā = God made our body out of earth".

5. To express manner; *e.g.* "mānān ulei = speak reverently", "mānān kāṇge = receive with honour".

6. To express direction; *e.g.* "to tēṇeñ gelo = he went in that direction", "to yeṇeñ gelo = he went in this direction"; (these two words "teṇeñ, yeṇeñ" are irregular Instrumentals); "tea margān gelo = he went through that way". In this case sometimes the 2nd Locative or the Dative are used; *e.g.* "Bāḍgāk = at the North", we may say also "Bāḍgān".

7. To express the relation through a place; *e.g.* "go through the town". Yet here we must use the Instrumental, not of the Substantive, but of the derived Adjective in -lo or in -tso. With the Substantives usually the Adjective in -ntlo is employed, with the Adverbs sometimes the derived Adjective in -lo is used, sometimes the derived Adjective in -tso. The Pronouns of the 3rd Person (to, o) have an irregular Instrumental to express going through a place (see above para. 6). Examples for all these cases: "to šerāntleān gelo = he passed through the town"; "rāy angāčeān vetā = the king goes through here"; "to mukhāveleān vetā = he goes before (*i. e.* through a place which is before)"; "poisleān vetā = goes through a distant place"; "tāntleān votz = go through that place", "āntleān votz = go through here" *etc.*; "ṭeṇeñ, yeṇeñ votz = go through that, this (place)". See about the Adjective in -ntlo, p. 54.

As regards Adverbs, when is the derived Adjective in -lo to be used, when the derived Adjective in -tso? Some Adverbs have the corresponding Adjective in -tso, some in -lo; hence if the Adverb has the Adjective in -tso, this Adjective is to be used; if the Adverb has the Adjective in -lo, this second

Adjective is to be used. Very seldom or never an Adverb has two different corresponding Adjectives, *i. e.* in -tso and -lo. In the Chapter V. Part II. the derived Adjectives are given; the Adjectives in -lo are more frequent: I mean to say Adjectives derived from Adverbs of place.

With the Substantives, we might use, I think, also the pure Instrumental; *e. g.* "šerān" instead of "šerāntleāñ", although perhaps not so correctly. I think also that as to Adverbs, the rule given here should be observed also to express direction put under para. 6; *e. g.* "paṭleān votz = go behind."

8. The Instrumental is used also to express how much one thing is superior to another; *e. g.* "yeñ lugaṭ tea lugṭā prās tīn vāriniñ lāmb = this cloth is three yards longer than that cloth." In this case we might use also the Dative or, still better, the Accusative.

9. If a Verb is in the Negative Necessary Mood with "nozo", then the *agent* or the person to whom something is impossible, must be put not in the pure Instrumental, but in the Instrumental of the derived Adjective in -tso; *e. g.* "bāvāčān nozo = it is impossible to the brother"; "mojeān (*or* mojāñ) nozo = it is impossible to me".

This and the form under para. 7 are the forms of which I spoke in Part II.. Ch. III. § 1. Observations 8, 9.

There are some Adverbs which express direction by themselves; *e. g.* "thāiñ = thither". These Adverbs may be used without any change, although we might also say "tāntleāñ" instead of "thāiñ"

Exercise

Moja Dēvā, āuveñ sārgāčer ani tuje mukār pātak kelāñ, bógós, Somia; tuzo pūt moṇunk makā fāvo niñ. Pāṭie, Devān tujeñ pātak bogšilāñ; yea mukār pātak sukoi. Monšān kiteñ kārizāi sompūrṇ zāunk? Sāmest vāstu ikun, Jezu Kristātso paṭlāu kārizāi. Tumiñ sāngā-nakāt; amčeān nozo; kiteāgai moḷeār, Devān amkañ ādhār dileār, sākāṭ vāstu tanktāt. Sākrān rāvāzāigī? Tāṇeñ votzayet, tačeñ kām zāleñ. Naiñt[1] sisār assā; ani lokāk vāiṭ kārtā; kiteāk tumiñ tikā bănduken mārināṅt? Bietātgī? Phālea aitārā amčeñ mostak yetolo,[2] amiñ takā mānān kāṇeizāi. Sipoiān Somia Jezu Kristāči kăḍvāl tālvārin papsilā, tantleñ rāgat ani udāk bāir sārlāñ. Burgo kăinče piḍen melo? Tāpān. Khăinče dikān Goyiñ assā? Goyiñ Koḍiālā băḍgān assā. Koḍiālboilāk votzunk yeā mārgān (*or* mārgār) votzāyetgī? Teṇeñ votzāyet, yeṇeñ votzāyet; dōni Koḍiālboilāk vortāt. Bombăi votzunk Goyāntleānt votzazāigī? Nīñ, āgboṭin nīṭ Bombāi pāvayēt. Ratnāčea Tāsildārātso sambaḷ kitleañ Rupoiāniñ Kadrāčea Tāsildārāčea sambaḷā vorn tsăḍ assā moṇ āuñ sārkeñ nēṇañ.

§ 5. First Locative

Usually the Grammarians of Indian languages do not distinguish between 1st and 2nd Locative; yet I was obliged, for the sake of distinction, to distinguish them, 1) because the termination is different, as every one knows, 2) because the meaning is different. As to the 2nd point, we may say that the fundamental meaning of the 1st Locative is *in* (not considering whether this *in* means on the surface) and *inside;* whereas the fundamental meaning of the 2nd Locative is *upon*. Yet it is true that in some cases, as to the meaning both cases can be used indifferently, because *extrema se tangunt*, or also sometimes the fundamental meaning does not appear clearly, as it happens also with some other cases.

The first Locative is used:

1. To show that a thing is in a place, as I said above; *e.g.* "to kuḍānt assā = he is in the room". Yet, this is not always expressed by the Locative; for this may be also expressed by "thāiñ" and "bitār". Though I cannot yet explain the exact difference between these three particles, I think we

---

1) Strictly speaking, we should write "naiñat". *Cf.* p. 82. para. 8.

2) Although "mostak" grammatically is Neuter, the Verb is put in the Masculine Gender, because the meaning is Masculine.

might say perhaps thus: The first Locative means to be really in a true physical place, not considering expressly that the place is surrounded; it expresses also *inside;* "thăiñ" means more commonly a metaphorical place; *e. g.* "Dēvā thăiñ kitle zôṇ assāt? = in God how many persons are there?" "ātmeā thăiñ = in the soul" *etc.* "Bităr" is as the Latin *intra*; *e. g.* within two years the building will be finished = don vorsañ bităr bāndăp tirsat"; "gărā bităr sămādān assāgī? = at home is there peace?" Yet in many cases "bităr" and the 1st Locative can be used indifferently; hence it is impossible to establish a complete difference between these three manners. As already mentioned, -nt becomes -niā in the Plural (see Part II. Ch. I.). I think, this -nt is just as in Kanarese ಅಲ್ಲಿ which is not a word having a certain meaning by itself, but a pure termination to show place; this is one of the reasons, why I made of it a peculiar case.

2. The 1st Locative is used to show motion to a place; *e.g.* "to nāḍānt vetā = he goes to the village". Better, use the Dative.

3. It is used to show cause; *e. g.* "to monis tea piḍent mêlo = that man died of that illness". The Instrumental is better.

4. It shows time; *e. g.* "tea disānt = on that day".

Exercise

Sāib gărā assāgī? Vôi, to kuḍānt assā. Tāntu kiteñ kărtā? Yēk kāgad boreitā. Tūñ šerūnt[1] vetāigī? Āuñ atāñ votzānāñ. Votānt takā ulăp ailo. Kăiñčea disānt Somi Jesu Krist yeā souñsārānt yetolo? Nimāṇea disā. Yēk pātkiān prăčit kelleānt, boḍve săntos pāutāt.

§ 6. Second Locative

The 2nd Locative seems to be the abbreviation of a longer expression, viz. of "voir = upon". If this "voir" is shortened into r, this r is joined in one word with the Noun. Though

---

[1] Some say "šăr" or "šyăr" instead of "šer".

"voir" means chiefly upon, yet it is used in many cases in which the Original meaning disappears. This 2nd Locative is used:

1. To show relation of place (upon); *e.g.* "gāḍiāl mezār assā = the watch is on the table".

2. To show time in answer to the question "when"; *e.g.* "sānjer = in the evening (Ital. *sulla sera*)".

3. To show place, as in English *to* or *at*, the 2nd form of this Locative given in the Declension, is used; *e. g.* "mādringer vots = go to the nuns"; "dhu āvoiger assā = the daughter is in the house of the mother"; "amger = in our house"; "Tolager = in the house of Tola"; "kòṇāger assā to? = in whose house is he?"

4. With the Verbs "believe, trust, hope" and similar others, the person in whom you believe etc. is put in the 2nd Locative; *e.g.* "Dēvāčer patie = trust in God"; "Dēvāčer sātmānd = believe in God".

5. To show place, when we should use *in*, if a high place is meant, or the surface of a thing; *e.g.* "sūriār = in the sun" (Latin *in sole*); yet in this case, sometimes the 1st Locative may be also used; *e.g.* "souñsārānt = in the world".

6. To show manner; *e.g.* "tea tārār kār = do it in that way" *or* "tea jinsār kār".

7. In many Konkani expressions; *e.g.* "porječer rasvotkāi kār = reign over the people".

8. To express "to be present at...or during..."; *e.g.* "misār aščeñ = to be at mass", "misār = during mass"; "kāmār assā = he is on duty".

9. This case seems to be used sometimes also in the meaning of "*against*"; *e. g.* "to mojer uleitā = he speaks against, me"; yet more frequently it is joined with "āḍ = against"; *e.g.* "to mojer āḍ-uleitā".

This 2nd Locative is used, I said, under 2, to show time; yet this is not the general way of expressing time, because the general rule is this: to the question "when", time is expressed *a*) by the pure stem, *e. g.* "aitārā = on Sunday";

b) by the Accusative, *e.g.* "aităr"; *c*) by the stem of the Feminine Adjective Singular derived from the Noun, *e.g.* "aitărăĉe"; *d*) by the 1st Locative. To the question "during what time", we use *a*) the stem with the Postposition "modoñ = in the middle", *e.g.* "disă modeñ = during the day"; *b*) the Adverbial phrase compounded of the Adjective and the Substantive "vóḷ = time" in the 2nd Locative; *e.g.* "rātĉe vēḷăr = during night". To the question "within what time", *a*) the stem with the Postposition "bităr" is used, *e.g.* "tīn vorsañ bităr = within three years"; *b*) or the 1st Locative.

Sometimes the time is expressed by the Adjective, which agrees with a Substantive with which it seems not to have a strict relation of agreement; *e.g.* "tāṇeñ aitărātso vāur kelă = he worked on Sunday, *lit.* he made work of Sunday".

Exercise

Mezār lugaṭ gallăiñgī? Galtăñ. Suriăr kiteñ assā moṇ, amkăñ sărkeñ kăḷnăñ: zikpi mănis moṇtăt, suriăr săbăr kŭtañ assăt. Kitleañ uorănĉer amiñ yēzăi? Dăñparā yā sānjer. Amiñ Devā kurpā sāmbaḷtāuñ moṇasăr, Deu amger rāutā. Pătkiănger Deu rāutăgī? Rāutā, puṇ ișṭa bări niñ. Tuzo pūtụ khăiñ assā? To seireănger assā. Tūñ khăiṇĉea gărānt assăi? Āuñ Porbuger assăñ, mozo bāu Kāmtiger, moji boiṇ Năikăger, moji māusi Šēṭiger, mozo sentur Šeṇăiñger[1]. Somi Jezu Krist vāur kărtālo, teătz jinsăr tūñ vāur kăr ani asseñ sompūrṇ zatoloi. Zōkōṇ Jezu Kristăĉer sătmăndinăñ, pătienăñ ani tătso mōg kărinăñ, takā zărti zāun zăli.

§ 7. Original

This, as I said on p. 11, is a new Case *quoad vocem*, not entirely *quoad rem;* because it is what is called in Kanarese *crude state*, although the Konkani Original seems to be more extended and used much more than the Kanarese crude state (which is not a peculiar case); hence we can make of it a particular case. I see now that in the Mahrătti Grammar

[1] These five names: "Porbụ (*or* Probụ), Kāmot, Šeṭ, Năik, Šeṇai" are the names of five classes of persons; their original meaning seems to have been "lord, cultivator, merchant, warrior, writer". Even now the families are often called by these names.

the Original or crude state is included in the Vocative. As for me, I prefer to make a peculiar case; because the meaning is quite different from the meaning of the Vocative. If the same termination were a sufficient reason for making of two different cases only one case, then in Latin too we should make, *e.g.* of the Dative and Ablative Plural one case, because in all Latin Declensions the Dative and Ablative Plural have the same termination.

This case is used:

1. We may say with nearly all Postpositions, because, a few excepted, these are added to the stem, *i.e.* to the Original.

2. With the Comparatives, *i. e.* the Noun preceded by "prăs, vorn" *etc.* is put in the Original; *e.g.* "mŏnšāñ prăs Dēvātso mōg kărizāi = we must love God more than men".

3. Instead of the Genitive when this is not converted into an Adjective; *e.g.* "Dēvā kurpā = divine grace".

4. With compound words, *i.e.* if two Nouns are joined as one word, the governed Noun is usually put in the Original. See Part III. Chapter VI.

5. If many Nouns, which should be put in a certain case, come together, only the last is put in that case, the preceding Nouns are put or may be put in the Original (see p. 16, para. 9).

6. If a Proper Noun in an oblique case has an apposition, the first Noun is put in the Original (sometimes in the Nominative); *e.g.* "Loreñsa (*or* Loreñs) Sāibāk", or, seldom, "Sāibā (*or* Sāib) Loreñsāk"; "Ankuāri (*or* Ankuār) Măriek"; "Koḍiāla (*or* Koḍiāl) šerānt"; but in the Nominative only "Loreñs Sāib Koḍiāl šer" *etc.* (see p. 39, *note*).

7. In some Konkani expressions, *e.g.* "gără votz = go home", "gără assā = (he) is at home" *etc.*

8. With the Nouns which imply a repetitive notion, *e.g.* "every month = moineā moineāk", "every year = vorsā vorsāk". In such cases the Noun is repeated just as with repetitive numerals, except that here the whole Noun is repeated and

the first time it is put in the Original, the second time in the Dative. If from these Nouns Adjectives are derived, the first Noun remains in the Original *e.g.* "moineā moineātso = monthly, of every month".

Exercise

Romā šerānt adiñ purviñ Čičero ani Čezār nāvāḍle zālo. Dōvātso mōg sămestañ văstu prăs moläḍig: duḍuā prăs, grestkāye prăs, bolāike prăs, santōsā prăs, nāzuk khāṇā prăs (*above delicate food*) boro. Dēvā kurpā sămestānk zāi. Añkuār Māri sărgā ani sauñsārāči rāṇi zāun vortautā. Kōṇ gărā assāgī? Kōṇ nāñ. Dēvā Putrāk sămestāniñ dimbio gālizāi, sărgān, souñsārān, yemkăṇḍān. Ankuāri Māriek Gabrielā boḍveān kăbar āḍlyā, tiče kusin Dēvā Putrụ sămbāutolo moṇ. Arkanj[1] St. Mingelik Saitānā kăḍe yek zūz assalleñ, povitrụ pustăkānt sangleā părmāṇe.

§ 8. **Original Case**, with "lagiñ *or* kăḍeñ"

This is called in Tulu, *Communicative* Case; because it is chiefly used when we communicate with others. In Tulu it has a peculiar termination, joined in one word with the Noun. Hence in that language it may be called a peculiar case, but in Konkani it is not so. It is formed like the other kinds of Original (with Postpositions), of which I will speak hereafter, namely, by adding (not in one word) to the stem the above named Postpositions. Yet as it is very frequently used, I will say a few words about it separately. This Original followed by lagiñ or kăḍe, which, for the sake of brevity, we may call Communicative, is used with Verbs meaning 1) to talk or to speak, 2) to ask, 3) to beseech, 4) to inquire, 5) to show relation to another, *e.g.* "my heart is not good with him", 6) to show possession of a thing, where we could substitute in Latin *apud* (see above). In all these

[1] The pure Konkani word would be "mel-boḍvo" or "šresṭ-boḍvo".

cases the person, whom you ask etc. is put in the Communicative Case; yet sometimes the Dative might also be used. Examples "Dēvā lagiñ māg = pray God"; "moje kāḍeñ duḍu nāñ = I have no money"; "Mojeñ mon tāče thāiñ boreñ nāiñ = my heart is not good towards him".

Exercise

Dēvā lagiñ māg, ani to tukā tujā monāčeo kušeo dādos kārtolo. Khāiñ khārentz suk meḷta moṇ souñsārūčeañ monšāñ kāḍe itzār nakā, tankañ kāḷnāñ dekun. Sāng nakā "mojeñ mon tea monšā kāḍe vāiṭ niñ; mātrụ āuñ tače kāḍe uleināñ; tujeñ mon tukā phoṭāitā; motint āḍ kiteñ Somi Jezu Krist amče lagiñ moṇtā moṇun: "tuje thāiñ tuja bāvā kāḍe kāiñ asleār, tuji kāṇik altārir soḍn, votzun bāvā kāḍe samādhān kār; māgir pāṭi yeun, tuji kāṇik Dēvāk beṭāitoloi". Amiñ Pādri lagiñ sākṭañ amčiñ pātkañ sāngleār, amkāñ Dēvā thāun tančeñ bogsaṇeñ meḷteleñ; ače šivāi, pātkānčeñ bogsaṇeñ meḷnāñ.

§ 9. Original Case followed by other Postpositions

This is just as the Communicative Case, namely, it is formed by adding, in a separate word, to the stem of the Noun, the Postposition required by the meaning; *e.g.* "Pātkiāñ pasun māg = pray for sinners"; "Dēvā višiānt ulei = speak about God" *etc.*

Here a large field would be open to explain the use of the Original followed by the different Postpositions; but this cannot be done for the present. Only I shall say in general, that the use of the different Originals with Postpositions is suggested, *quoad substantiam*, by the chief meaning of the Konkani Postpositions, although sometimes the knowledge of this chief meaning is not sufficient to know all the uses of the Postpositions; among these Postpositions, "thāiñ" is one of the most difficult; hence I shall say a few words about the Original followed by "thāiñ.

The chief meanings of "thăin" are *there* and *in*, as explained above (§ 5). Hence the Original with "thăiñ" is used

1. Chiefly to show the relation of one thing to another. But the Postpositions "kăḍe" and "lagiñ" are also used in this meaning; how can we then distinguish which Postposition is to be used? Perhaps in this way: When we could express in English that relation also by *in* or a similar word, then more frequently "thăiñ" is used; when we could express that relation more properly with the Dative or with the Latin *apud*, then more frequently "kăḍe *or* lagiñ" is used. Yet these three words are used sometimes promiscuously. Examples: "we have many duties towards God = Dēvā thăin amkăñ săbār kāide assāt"; "the children must show to their parents love, reverence, obedience = burgeăniñ apleañ āuvoi băpăñ thăiñ mōg, mān ani khaltepoṇ dākeizāi".

2. It is used to show place, not material in the common meaning; *e. g.* "Dēvā thăiñ guṇănči sompūrṇăi assă = in God there is fulness of perfections".

Now I should speak of the Vocative and Genitive: As to the Vocative, it does not present any serious difficulty; about the Genitive I speak in the article on Adjectives, for the reason explained more than once.

Somebody might think it not well done to have eliminated the Genitive, which exists also in Mahrāṭṭi and in Kanarese.

But what use is there in keeping this case, if we can eliminate it? Perhaps the reasons which we have for Konkani do not hold good for Mahrāṭṭi and Kanarese. Are perhaps the cases which remain too few? That we can eliminate the Genitive, nobody who considers the matter, will deny (see p. 11). Moreover I had a peculiar reason to eliminate, *i. e.* the great number of the other cases.

Again, somebody might think that one case which exists also in Kanarese and in Mahrāṭṭi has been omitted, *i. e.* the Ablative, which should express the source whence any thing proceeds, and would correspond to the Kanarese termination ದೆಸೆಯಿಂದ (deseyinda) and to the Mahrāṭṭi ऊन, हून.

I answer that we have no necessity to introduce this case in Konkani; because the Kanarese and Mahrāṭṭi Ablative can be expressed either by some case of the derived Adjective in "-ntlo *or* -lo" (see pp. 54, 199 *etc.*), or by the Original followed by "thăun = from", or by a similar Postposition.

But somebody might insist by saying: Just what you have put as Instrumental of the Adjective in "-ntlo" should be considered as Ablative.

I answer: If you wish to have it as Ablative, you may keep it; as for me, I see three good reasons for not considering "-ntlo" as a peculiar case: first, it follows the rules of the Adjectives, mostly at least; moreover considering that "-ntlo" as an Adjective, its construction is not so difficult; whereas in the other case it is almost inexplicable; finally, also without this Ablative, we have cases more than enough, if not to overwhelm the mind, at least to make the Konkani Declensions somewhat difficult; so let us avoid at least the cases which are not absolutely necessary.

Exercise

Nimāṇo dīs pāunčea adiñ sàbār khuṇa zāteleo moḷabār ani buiñčer. Dēvā hujir amiñ kiteñ? Kāiñ nāñ. Atāñ tukā boroñ zāleñ; yeā fuḍe pātak kärnakā, tukā kāiñ tzāḍ vāiṭ zāinasseñ. Yeā fuḍe to kiteñ kartolo? To vetolo. Säkāṭ karčeo văstu kelcā uprānt, amiñ sāngiāñ: upkārāk păḍānātulle săkor amiñ. Votzun lesāuñ bāipāṭ kăr (*learn by heart*); tače māgir inām tukā diviet. Gāḍiegārā, atāñ gāḍie paṭleān rāu. Rūkāñ voir săbār sukniñ gāyan kārtāt (*sing*), ani Dēvāk argāñ ditāt. St. Pedruče Igārječe dărṇi ponda ani yek buiñtli Igārz assā; thāiñ săbār navāḍleañ monšānčeo kuḍi isou kāṇeitāt. Vāḍilānu, tumče khāl asleānči zātan kāṇeyā; kiteāk moḷeār, tumiñ Dēvāk tančeñ lōk dīzāi. Somi Jezu Krist kursa taḷa tīn pāuṭi poḍlo. Pātak sorpa bări tuje pōis" kăr, ani tukā Dēvāčeñ āšīrvād pāuteleñ. Dēvā thāiñ tèg zoṇ assāt. Bāvānu, ătmea pasun kiteñ kārtāt? Kuḍiči lakšā kāṇeitāt, tītz puṇ ătmeāči kāṇeitātgī? Kurpe bitār mortāt, te săргār vetāt; mahā pātkānt mortāt, te yemkanḍānt vetāt. Igārje bāir votzun, Dēvāče aikālleñ utar visārnakāt; puṇ tače pārmāṇe tzālā. Zo-kōṇ Jezu Kristā sangatā luanāñ to simpḍaitā. Zo-kōṇ Dēvā sārsilo vingāḍ zatā, to apleāñ dusmānānčea gulāmpoṇānt poḍtā. Sāmestañ pasun rāzār kāriāñ. Mogalā Jezuts, Dēvā Bāpā lagiñ māg. Ankuāri Mārie, amāñ pāpiā kātir vinoti kăr atañ, ani amčeā morṇāče kāḷiñ. Moje pasun yea vadālak ārāmb zālo: makā dāriānt uḍeyā. Jeruzaleñ moḷḷeñ šer kainčeā dikān assā? Koḍiāla baḍgā asṭamti (*north-west*) dikān assā. Bombāi thāun Europ pāriant kitle kōs (*miles*) assāt? Mojān sārkeñ sāngunk nozo: āgbōṭin poināk sumār vīs dīs lagtāt; puṇ poināčeā veḷār sābār pāuṭi tāru ā rāutā, drāšṭāntāk (*e. g.*): Aden ani Portesaid moḷḷeañ bāndrañ kāḍe (*maritime towns*). Pātkāñ vorviñ Dēvāk ākmān zatā, ātmeāk sārg antartā; ani sābār yēr dāgḍ yetāt. Pātak ādarn soukāsai meḷčea bādlāk (*or* suāter) tzurtzure ani kāšṭ ani khānt meḷtā. Gārje šivāi aitārā vāur kārunk nozo. Amčer āḍ yeunčea kārit (*or* šivāi) Somiā Jezu Kristātso paṭlāu kārunk nozo.

(*Here I add a few examples of Postpositions which govern the Nominative or Dative. See Chapter on Postpositions.*) Kārt (*master*) gārā assāgī? Yedoḷ moṇāsār yeunk-nāñ. Tuzo khāvānd (*lord, master*) dhā uorañ thāun tīn vorañ pāriānt kiteñ kārtā? Makā gottunāñ. Ani tīn uorañ dārn pānz pāriānt kiteñ kārtā moṇ tukā kaḷtāgī? Āuñ kāiñ neṇañ. Hangā thāun gār pāriyant ani kitleñ zāit? Yēk ulo, Sāibānu (*a call, i. e. as far as the voice reaches*). Sūraṭān (*by carriage*) Igārz moṇasār votzayetgī? Nāiñ, bābā: pāivāṭen tzālazāi. Bāpai putrāk virōdh assolo, putrụ bāpāk porto. Zo-kōṇ apleā bāvāk porto tzaltā, to Dēvātso sārkeñ mōg kārināñ. Saštrāč āḍ ulcinakā: ani apleā peleāk virōdh tzāl nakā.

Art. II. Adjectives

§ 1. Adjectives in General

Generally speaking we may say that the Adjective is very frequently used, though there are not many original Adjectives. A general rule might be perhaps as follows:

Whenever a word does not express a substance, but affirms or denies only a quality or a similar thing of another, the Konkani language prefers to use the Adjective in **-tso, -tāi, -tōeñ,** or -lo, -li, -leñ, though in our European languages another part of speech is used. Hence the Adjective is used.

1. To express the Genitive; for, the Genitive expresses something of the governing Noun; *e. g.* "bāpāčeñ gār = the house of the father", the words "of the father" answer to the question "what father?"

2. To show origin; hence usually the Adverbs of place or time are converted into Adjectives, if they are used to explain in some way the Nouns; *e.g.* "this man is of here"; in this example the Adverb "of here" is like an Adjective of "this man" hence the Adverb is changed into Adjective "vo monis hangātso"; or, to speak more simply, if we have in English the Adverb preceded by "of", in Konkani we make an Adjective of it, adding **-tso, -či, -čeñ**, or **-lo, -li, -leñ**, which, of course, must agree with its Noun, according to the general rule. There may be some exceptions to this rule.

3. Some other Adverbs or adverbial phrases, or a Noun with a Preposition are often translated in Konkani by an Adjective, if they are an explanation of some Nouns. Thus "aitārātso vāur = work on Sunday, servile work"; "dusreāntso rāg = anger against others". In both examples the Nouns with the Preposition are like Adjectives, though not grammatically. Yet we could say also: "aitārā vāur kăr = work on Sunday".

4. Adjectives are used in many elliptical sentences; for, they qualify a Noun not expressed. Thus "rātče = during night", here "veḷār = in time" is understood; "sonoārāče = on Saturday", here too "veḷār *or* dīs = day" is understood.

5. The Adjectives in **-tso, -tči, -tčeñ**, (usually the Neuter Singular) are used in sentences corresponding to the Latin *consulis est providere reipublicae*, *hominis est errare*; *e.g.* "tzukčeñ monšāčeñ, puṇ pātkānt rāunčeñ koṭeponāčeñ = to fail is human, to persevere in sin is wicked".

6. The Adjective (or Genitive) is used also often to show the material out of which a thing is made; *e.g.* "mātietso = of earth, earthen".

7. The Genitive or Adjective is used when in Konkani the Verb is compounded of a Verb and a Substantive and, translating it literally, we should put the Substantive, which is the direct object of the Verb, in the Genitive; *e.g.* "I explain the doctrine", "explain = vivor sāng, *lit.* say explanation";

hence we should say: "I say the explanation of the doctrine = dotornitso vivor sangtāñ"; yet this rule is often not observed by common people.

8. The Adjective is used when some Pronoun or Adverb is followed by the Particle "bări = as", Latin *instar;* as this Konkani Particle usually is not joined to Adverbs or Pronouns, the Adverb and Pronoun are changed into an Adjective; *e. g.* "ădlea bări = as before"; "amče bări = as to us".

9. Instead of the corresponding Noun, see p. 15, para. 3.

10. With the Adjective "sărko" and the like; *e. g.* "tače sărko = similar to that". Yet we may also say "takā sărko", especially if it means "similar to him"; but "Dēvā-sărko" is more common than "Dēvāče sărko".

In all these cases more commonly the Adjective in -tso is used, seldom the Adjective in -lo. Yet properly speaking, there is some difference between these two Adjectives. The 1st has the meaning of the above explained cases, the 2nd in -lo seems to express, we may say, a local quality or, more clearly, the Adjective in -lo seems to be a contraction of a whole sentence which shows the place of a thing; *e. g.* "the men who are in the world"; the whole sentence "who are in the world" is like an Adjective of "men", showing the place in which they are. Hence the whole phrase may be expressed with one Adjective in -lo added to the 1st Locative. Thus we get "sauñsārāntlo mănis." Yet sometimes this could also be expressed, although seldom, by the Adjective in -tso or by translating literally the whole phrase. Nay, sometimes we meet still bolder contractions; as we have seen two Postpositions joined together (see p. 153, *n.* 6), so we might form similar Adjectives; but they are not in common use.

Remarks: *a*) We have seen that often our Adverbs are expressed in Konkani by Adjectives. Sometimes just the contrary happens, viz. our Adjectives are expressed by Adverbs. This is the case, when our Adjective is a predicate as in "*homo est mortalis*" and we might change it into an Adverb without any detriment to the meaning, then, I say, in Konkani the Adverb with the Gerund in un may be used; *e.g.* "be firm = tirzäun rāu = *lit.* remain constantly".

b) The Genitive follows the rules of the Adjectives, keeping, however, some signs of a Noun especially in some points of the concord. The first sign is this: a Pronoun which refers to a preceding Noun converted into the Adjective, follows the Gender of that Noun, although regularly it should follow the Gender of the Noun with which that Adjectival Genitive agrees; *e.g.* "...*et memorari Testamenti sui Sancti quod juravit* (Luc. I. 73) = ani părmāṇāṭso ugḍās kărunk jeñ tāṇeñ ....keleñ". The 2nd sign can be found on pago 52, para. 1. The 3rd sign is to be found in the construction or *collocatio verborum;* because the Genitive converted into an Adjective is indeed placed before its Noun, at least usually and in the common cases; yet if there are other Adjectives belonging to the same Noun, more frequently it is put before them, as if it were a Noun; *e.g.* "a sign of charity = mogātso yēk gurtụ, *lit.* charitable a sign"; whereas we would say "a charitable sign". So also "Dēvāčiñ bhou vortiñ dēṇiñ = the very sublime gifts of God, *lit.* the Divine very sublime gifts". I need not say that although the Konkani Genitive grammatically can be considered for the sake of facilitating its construction as an Adjective, as to the meaning it may differ from common Adjectives, as in the above first example, there is some difference in English between "a charitable sign" and "a sign of charity"; yet in Konkani the same word and the same construction can be used in both cases. This little difference as to the meaning may be a reason for distinguishing the Genitive-Adjectives or Adjectival Genitives from the other Adjectives, but cannot be a reason for making of it a peculiar case with the only advantage of making, I may say, an inexplicable and imaginary case.

§ 2. Adjectives in Particular

In the first place we should speak of the Genitive-Adjectives; but as they have nearly the same construction as the common Adjectives and are in some way general, so we have put them in the preceding paragraph. Those which I am going to speak of in para. 1, are also in some way general, yet they present some peculiar difficulty; hence we can speak of them here.

1. *Adjectives derived from Postposition*

This point which has been touched upon (pp. 54, 153, *n.* 5) must be now particularly explained, although it is contained in the above general rule. An easy, although not very scientific, rule may be this: A Postposition is changed into the corresponding Adjective wherever the Adjective can be substituted without detriment to the meaning; *e.g.* "who among you has stolen my watch?" Here we may change, not in English but in our mind, that *among* into an Adjective of *who*; hence we say "tumče bitărleān kōṇeñ moji gădiāl tzorlyā?" See their construction on page 199, para. 8.

More scientifically we may express the same thing as follows: When a Postposition with its governed word explains like an Adjective, some Noun etc., this Postposition with the governed word is converted into an Adjective.

When is the Postposition with its governed Noun to be considered as such an Adjective? This is the difficult and practical point. From many examples which I considered, I think we can draw this rule, which alone is sufficient for the right use of this kind of Adjectives in the common cases: the Postposition can be changed into the corresponding Adjective, whenever this Adjective could be resolved into a relative sentence. This relative sentence would consist usually as follows: the Relative Pronoun which refers to the Noun affected by that Postposition-Adjective, the Verb "to be" in the tense required by the meaning, the Noun governed by the

Postposition, finally the Postposition itself. Examples will explain what I now said. There are some cases which seem not to be explained enough by this rule; yet I think it holds good for all cases, although not always very clearly. Examples: "go before me"; here we must say "mukăr", not "mukăvelo", because we cannot resolve "mukăvelo" into a relative sentence. If we said "mukăvelo votz" the meaning would be: "you who are before me (lo the relative sentence!) go"; "who among you can suffer everlasting pains?" Here we can use "bitărlo", because we can resolve that "bitărlo" into a relative sentence, *i.e.* "which man, who is among you, can" *etc.* = kōṇ tumče bitărlo sasnăče kašṭ sosit?" Now I put some other examples to show the application of the rule; the reader himself will make the application. "The birds are singing upon the trees = sukniñ rukăñ voir găyăn kărtăt"; "let the man come down from the tree = to mănis rukă voilo deundi"; "the men in this place are frugal = yeă găvăntle mănis hăḷtăn khătăt"; "in this place there are many learned men = yeă găvănt săbăr sikpi mănis assăt"; "put a hurdle before the window = zanelă mukăr yĕk izăi găl"; "that hurdle before the window prevents light = zanelă mukăveli izăi uzuăḍ kăḍtă"; "come after me = moje păṭi ye"; "he who comes after me shall come before = moje păṭlo mukăr yeundi"; "he came down from the mountain = porvotă voilo deuñlo (he who was upon the mountain)"; "go away, O devil, from that man = teă monšă voilo votz, bŭtă".

When the Adjective in -ntlo, instead of the Adjective in -lo or -tso, must be used, can be known from § III. p. 54 *etc.* Again, when the form -ntleăn (Instrumental) must be used, can be known from § 4, para. 7, p. 212 *etc.* By the above explanation also the construction of these Adjectives has been facilitated.

For further understanding of this rule see page 171, para. 4. Something more about this point will be said perhaps in Art. VI.

Remark that not all Postpositions, *e.g.* "thãun", have a corresponding Adjective commonly used; then necessarily the pure Postpositions must be used. A similar thing happens with the Adverb. See derived Adjectives in Part II. Chapter V.

Remark finally that the use of the pure Postposition instead of the Adjective seems also allowed, although perhaps not so correctly and so elegantly.

2. *Adjectives corresponding to the Latin Adjectives in*..bilis

The touchstone, we may say, of a Konkani scholar is the right use of the Adjectives corresponding to the English *divisible*, *impermeable*, *inflammatory* and the like, and to the Latin Adjectives in...*bilis*. In Part III. Ch. V. their derivation has been explained, *i.e.* by "sărko". Yet sometimes this "sărko" does not suit, or we get too long words especially in the negative form. Then we may use other forms, *i. e.* the Participial Adjectives in -so; *e.g.* instead of "riganāñ-sărko = impenetrable", we may say "riganāñ-so". This Participle has not been given in Part II.; yet it is also used, and has nearly the same meaning as "riganāñ-sărko". We must not confound this -so with the quasi-diminutive -so, although the spelling is the same. Moreover we may use the Gerundive in -tso (affirmative) and "-tsonāñ" (negative); but the meaning is not entirely the same; the meaning of these Adjectives is best rendered by the Latin Gerundives; *e.g. amandus, non amandus* = to be loved, not to be loved". Another way, which, although very elegant, is rather long and not so easy, is to use the Participial Adjectives of the Potential or Necessary Mood. They are formed as I have indicated on pp. 127, 173, *note*. Their meaning corresponds to the tense to which they belong; *e.g.* "kăriyet assolo = which might be done"; "kărizăi assolo = which is to be done"; "sătmandunk nozo assolo = incredible" *etc.* Yet sometimes it is better to resolve such long Adjectives into Verbs in a finite mood as common people usually do.

3. *Quasi-diminutive Adjectives*

Another kind of difficult Adjectives are the dubitative, the diminutive and the like. These have sometimes a proper word; yet mostly the quasi-diminutive -so must be added to them (see Part III. Ch. II.); *e.g.* "improbable" may be expressed in many cases by "sätmandunk nozoso": "sätmand = believe", "sätmandunk nozo = is incredible", "sätmandunk nozo-so = approaching to be incredible"; "dovo = white", "dovoso = appearing to be white (gray)" *etc.;* "boro = good", "boroso = somewhat good, or apparently good".

4. *Adjectives corresponding to the Latin* instar.

Another kind of Adjectives difficult to translate are those which correspond to the English *as* or to the Latin *instar; e.g.* "he is as a lion". The best way is to use the Particle "bări = *instar*", preceded by the governed word; yet I have heard also Adjectives formed from "bări", *i. e.* "băriso". So they say "sivā băriso mănis = a man like a lion". I need not say that such Adjectives are not popular. Distinguish this "băriso" from "bărit" which is used to form some other Adjectives of different meaning; *e.g.* "fălabărit = fertile", from "făl = fruit" and "bărit": "băriso" comes from "bări" and the *quasi-diminutive* "so". We may remark here what has been omitted in Chapter V. that some Adjectives are formed also by adding -al; *e.g.* "īṭ = fertility", "īṭāl = fertile"; and not only by -est (see p. 171, *n.* 3) but also by -ist or only -st, and by some other termination.

5. *Verbal Adjectives*

Rather strange Adjectives are those which etymologically are Verbs, but are used as Adjectives. I mention here these two Adjectives: "yĕnăñ zalo = he refused (to come), *lit.* he became 'I do not come'." Here "yenañ" is used according to the meaning as an Adjective. So also: "Taṇiñ käiñ zăp diunk-nozo zali = they could not answer any thing, *lit.* they became incapable of giving any answer". Both Adjectives seem to be indeclinable.

6. *Complex Adjectives*

Sometimes a whole sentence takes the place of an Adjective; this happens chiefly with the Participial sentences. About this later on.

7. *Participial Adjectives*

Here the Participial Adjectives can be mentioned; but we must be very careful in the use of them, because out of the Participial sentences, they can be seldom used properly.

8. *Numeral Adjectives*

Although about the Numeral Adjectives many things should be said, I must limit myself to say these few things.

a) As to the declension, it is true that all may take "añ" in the oblique cases, if joined to a Noun (see p. 61, para. 3); yet they can take sometimes also "i". So we find "dōniñ, tīniñ, cāriñ" *etc.*; *e.g.* "cāriñ vāreāntleān = from the four winds" *etc.* Sometimes they seem to prefer i instead of a in the oblique cases; this happens especially if they are not joined to Nouns.

b) The number "dhā = ten" is often taken in an indefinite meaning; hence "dhā-zoṇ = committee, *lit.* ten persons".

c) Distinguish between "sāt" and "sāṭ", the first is not cerebral; moreover it seems to be pronounced not so slowly as "sāṭ".

d) The vowel ă of să (6) is short, but pronounced slowly. This and the preceding example show that there are really two ă and two ā, as stated on page 191. If perhaps these two examples are not sufficient to persuade my reader, he must know that there are many other examples, clearer than these two.

e) Some pronounce the vowel eñ after uṇ for 29, 39, *etc.* The full form would be really "yēkuṇeñ tīs" *etc.*, and seems also to be better, as hinted on page 60, although in the list of the numerals that eñ by chance has been omitted in 29.

9. *Comparative and Superlative*

Here I will put some difficult cases. If two Adjectives are compared, the common rule is not suitable; *e.g.* "he is more holy than learned", we should say according to the common rule: "zanteā prăs bhāgivont", *or* "zanteāčeāki prăs bhāgivont"; but this is not used; we must change the sentence in some way: I say "some" because there are many ways; so the above example may be rendered thus: "kitlo zantogī, tačeāki bhāgivont = *lit.* how much he is learned, above that holy"; or "to zantoi, pun tsăḍ bhāgivont = *lit.* he is learned indeed, but more holy". In a similar way, if we have the comparative of inferiority of Adjectives, we may translate it, changing the sentence somewhat. The comparative of equality is best rendered by "kitlo—titlo = as much—as much"; *e.g.* "he is as much learned as holy = kitlo zanto titlo bhāgivont".

The English "too much" is expressed with "tzăḍ" (pronounce nearly "tzăăăḍ"); *e.g.* "that is too much = yeñ tzăḍ". This word is used especially with the comparatives of a form somewhat different from the ordinary one, when, namely the thing in which one term is compared with the other is not expressed but understood; *e.g.* "A. is more than B. = A. B. vorn tzăḍ". I heard, as far as I remember, this "tzăḍ" used, although the comparative has a common form, just as we would use "more", and as "ădik" is sometimes used (see p. 65, *b*). The same word "tzăḍ" is used to express the English "too long, too short, too bad *etc.* = tzăḍ lămb, tzăḍ moṭvo, tzăḍ văiṭ".

Another not easy mode of forming the comparative is to use "ani". The first meaning of "ani" is "and"; yet in some sentences it seems to mean "more"; or we may suppose its meaning to be this; because its construction is as if its meaning were "more". It is used especially when the terms of comparison are not distinctly expressed; *e. g.* "there is something more (than you believe) *etc.* = "ani kăi assā, *lit.* = there is also something". It corresponds to the Latin *et* which in some cases means *etiam* or *adhuc* and may be used in a similar way to the Konkani "ani". In one word, the construction of "ani" is similar to the Latin construction of *et* when it has the above meaning.

Another form of the comparative compounded of this "ani" is "aniki". Etymologically it seems to be derived from "ani" and "-ki" used sometimes instead of "vorn" or "prăs" (see p. 65). Its meaning seems to be that of an Adjective, which in itself is comparative and corresponds to the English "some more"; *e.g.* "aniki utraĩ moṇ = say some words more". We might render it in Latin thus: *adhuc supra (ea quae dixisti) verba dic.* It is indeclinable.

As to the Superlative I mention here the mode of expressing such a degree by repeating the same Adjective; *e.g.* "boro boro = very good", (the first Adjective is pronounced with pathos), which mode is used also with Nouns, as in Hebrew.

Among the modes of strengthening the superlative and comparative, I mention here only *a*) "sărivin = without comparison", *e.g.* "sărivin boro = incomparably good"; *b*) "voir = above", *e.g.* "deki voir = *lit.* above example", or "so high that he cannot be imitated, *or* inimitable"; *c*) "tzăḍ = much", *e.g.* "tačo prăs tzăḍ budhivănt = he is much wiser than he"; and *d*) "jīv soḍn = *lit.* giving up life", *e.g.* "jīv soḍn khăuñtso = eating very much". This last mode is often used, but rather with Verbs and Verbal Adjectives, for animate objects, and in certain sentences only.

Exercise

O mănis hangātsogī părki? O mănis hangătso nīñ; zalcāri, hangāči bhāš tzălti uleitā. To mănis khăiñ thāun ăilo? To Ritan šerāntlo ăilo. Ritan šer khăinčea gāvănt assă? Kălpăṇa moḷḷea jilleānt. Pāusăče veḷār (*or* pāusānt) lok kostăt, gimāčeā veḷār pik luntăt. Tujeñ kām kiteñ, burgoā? Mojeñ kām siunčeñ. Disātso sămbaḷ kitlo? Čār aṇe kūl, Săibānu; kăšṭān yeã vorviñ mojeañ burgeãnk postãñ. Hålt nastanãñ khãunčeñ monzãtičeñ; mitmerin khãunčeñ monšãčeñ. Yeñ aidãn kăssaleñ? Yeñ aidãn mãtiečeñ; teñ bangãrãčeñ. Tumče bitorlo kõṇ yemkaṇḍãntso uzo sosit? Somi Jezu Krist sărgã voilo deuñlo. Bãpui apleãn burgeãñ lagšilo pois sărlo. Kumsãrã vorviñ Deu yeke jinsiñ ătmeã voilo Saitãnãk sõḍaitã. Sămestãñtso[1] mõg kărizãi, sămest mănis amče bãu dekun. Dusreãntso rãg aileãr, Somia Jezu Kristãče kăšţ niãḷ ani tači dék kaṇe.

Art. III. Pronouns

§ 1. Pronouns in General

1. All Personal and Relative Pronouns add one a to the k by which the Dative and Accusative of Nouns are formed.

2. In the Pronouns the Accusative is more frequently equal to the Dative, although used sometimes for inanimate things. (*Cf.* pp. 12, 17, *etc.*)

3. The Original does not exist pure; what has been put in Part II, Ch. III. as Original followed by Postpositions, is not the pure but the derived Original, *i. e.* of the corresponding Adjectives. Yet in the Pronouns of the 3rd Person and in the Relative Pronouns and in some others too a kind of pure Original occurs; but it is not commonly used except when followed by some Postpositions; hence we can say that the pure Original does not exist; the Original followed by Postpositions exists in some Pronouns; in some others the derived Original is used.

§ 2. Pronouns in Particular

1. *Personal Pronouns*

a) The Personal Pronouns usually are not omitted, if they

---

[1] If the Adjective or Participle is used as a Pronoun, it takes the termination "-tso" of the Genitive or Adjective as a Noun; this takes place although the Adjective itself be derived by the addition of "-tso", then it takes this termination twice; *e.g.* "kăróeãtso vivor = programme".

are the subject of a sentence, except in some peculiar cases, *e.g.* in some interrogative sentences, *etc.*

b) Among the Pronouns only "āuñ" seems to have two roots, one in the Nominative, Instrumental and perhaps Vocative, the other in the other cases. Compare its declension.

c) The Personal Pronouns are used when in English the derived Adjectives would be used as in this and similar sentences: "my head is turning = makā mātēñ guvntā = to me head is turning". Yet we may use also the Adjective.

d) The Pronoun o of the third person, or Demonstrative Pronoun, if you like to call it so, must be used besides, to fix the attention chiefly when it is joined to the Relative Pronoun, as in this and similar sentences: this is the man whose house is burnt = to mănis zāčeñ găr lāsleñó, *lit.* that man whose house burnt, is this". Here that "to" seems to be only a kind of article; hence we could translate also thus "the man whose house burnt, is this". About this "to" remark that it seems to be used sometimes really as determinate article; *e.g.* "āuñ vortautāñ to khăro gouḷi = I am the good shepherd".

The Adjectives derived from the Personal Pronouns, chiefly those of the 3rd Person, have been explained in Part II. Ch. III. Here only remark that the table on p. 74 gives the combinations only of one or mostly of two (as Masculine and Neuter are equal), derived Possessive Adjectives, and even these are incomplete, because by chance the Singular "tantso, tanči, tančeñ" have been omitted, as you may see from p. 73 in which "tantso" is given. Besides those combinations of the Masculine (and Neuter, equal to the Masculine) Gender there are as many combinations of the Feminine "titso" which is put on the same page 73. Further from the Proximate Pronoun o, i, yeñ, are derived "atso, ači, ačeñ" (from o, yeñ) and "itso, iči, ičeñ" (from i); each of these two derived Adjectives has the same combinations as "tatso"; consequently altogether we have 48 (if not 60) combinations, and these are not only theoretical but also practical. Yet if we keep in our mind the rule given on p. 74, the great number of combinations will not overwhelm our mind, but only show the fulness of the Konkani language, called by some, poor and good for nothing.

Now I give some examples to show the application of this rule: "This is my mother; her love towards me is very great = ī moji māi, itso mōg bhou vōḍ"; "this is my father, his name is Peter = uo mozo bāpui, ačeñ nāuñ Pedru"; "this is my brother, his age is 20 years = uo mozo bāu, ači pirāi vīs vorsañ"; "those men are my friends, their house is far = te moje išṭ, tančeñ gār pois" *etc*.

2. *Relative Pronouns*

A peculiar and distinct explanation would be required for the Relative Pronouns; yet the most difficult things about them are connected with the Participles; hence for the sake of brevity we will speak of them more distinctly later on. For the present let us say only a few words. First, instead of the Relative Pronoun 1) the corresponding Participle, as in Latin, or 2) the Demonstrative "tātso" is used, or 3) the Relative Pronoun is simply omitted; this last case takes place especially in correlative sentences. Examples: "he who commits evil, hates his own soul = vāiṭ kārtso mānis aplo ātmo kaṇṭaltā" = in Latin "*Faciens malum odit animam suam*"; or according to the third way we may say: "vāiṭ kārtā, to aplo ātmo kaṇṭaltā = *lit.* (he who) commits evil, that (man) hates his own soul". This "kārtā to" is that Participle of which I said (Part II., Ch. III., Art I. § 2.) that it is not a true Participle. The second manner cannot be used in the above example, but only in this and similar sentences: "the tree, the roots of which are long, is very large = ruk tačiñ pāḷañ lāmb, bhou vōḍ". In the 3rd case, the construction is as if the Relative Pronoun had not been omitted: this is the most simple and exact rule for using the 3rd mode.

As for me I think that this substitution of the Demonstrative to the Relative is only a popular way in order to avoid a less obvious construction, as

happens in our languages, when common people speak. Hence it seems more correct to avoid this mode of substitution.

In order to explain more distinctly this difficult point, let us add a few observations.

a) If in sentences in which Demonstrative and Relative Pronouns occur connected, we use the true Participle, then, in the second part it is not required to use "to"; *e.g.* "pātăk kărtolo apṇāk kanṭaltā = he who commits sin hates himself"; yet, I think, we might also use it. With "zo-kōṇ = whosoever", we must use the corresponding "to"; *e.g.* "zo-kōṇ pātăk kărtā, to apṇāk kanṭaltā".

b) Though it is quite according to the nature of the Konkani language to omit the Relative Pronoun, yet the sentences are sometimes so complicated that we do not know how to change them into participial expressions; then it is better to keep the Relative Pronoun. Oñ the contrary, sometimes the Demonstrative Pronoun is omitted and not the Relative Pronoun, as in this and similar sentences: "That which you say is true = jeñ moṇtai, khăreñ", as in Latin "*quod dicis* (*id*) *verum est*". Again, we may use the Relative Pronoun, but then in the correlative sentences, the Latin construction is preferred (*qui-is*), viz. put first the Relative, then the Demonstrative Pronoun. But here too, sometimes the sentences are so complicated or so arranged, that it is difficult to put the Relative Pronoun first. In such a case, keep that construction which is more natural and clearer; *e.g.* "tūñ to zo yeuñtso assā, zāun vortautāigī? = *an es tu is qui venturus est?* are you he who is to come?" Remark also that the Demonstrative Pronoun can be put at the end, although its Verb be put in the beginning and separated from it; *e.g.* "jeñ tuveñ deveñ assā, teñ dī"; or "dī tuveñ deveñ assā teñ = give what you owe".

c) In such connected sentences the two connected Pronouns may be in different cases, *i.e.* the Relative may be in one case, and the Demonstrative Pronoun in another case; and even in this case the Relative Pronoun may be omitted, though it be accompanied by a Preposition; *e.g.* "to gelo mārog boro = the road on which he went, is good". "Buddhi prăkāšāk pāule gāḍie apṇāk Dōvāk beṭailo = the moment in which he came to the use of reason, he offered himself to God".

About these Relative Pronouns remark that they are to be found in many other forms, although somewhat modified; but the fundamental form and meaning always remain; *e.g.* from zo the Adverb "zăin" is formed, which means "where, in the place in which"; "zăiñ ăuñ vetāñ, thăiñ tumiñ yeunk nozo = *non potestis venire quo ego vado* = you cannot come where I am going". This "zăiñ" may be used also instead of the 1st Locative "zantu"; *e.g.* "poḷeyā to zāgo zăiñ takā gāllo = see the place in which they have put him". Again from zo is formed "zosso", Correlative Pronoun, meaning "as", Lat. *qualis*, which Pronoun has a suspensive meaning, *i. e.* it requires a Correlative Pronoun. Hence it appears that the sentence in which the Relative Pronoun in its original or derived form occurs, must be a secondary or dependent one; this is the principle which may guide us in the use of this Relative Pronoun.

What has been said about the Adjectives derived from the Personal Pronouns, must be applied, *servata proportione*, to the Adjective derived from zo; here we have at least 24 combinations.

3. *Correlative Pronouns*

As some of these Pronouns are intimately connected with the Relative Pronouns, a few things about them necessarily have been said in the preceding para.; here they must be explained more distinctly.

First of all let us explain the distinction of these Pronouns into Proximate and Remote Pronouns, which distinction is to be applied also to some other Pronouns. This distinction springs from the difference between o and to hinted at on p. 74, *n.;* "o" means "this, close by"; "to" means "that, far", absolutely or relatively; so also the derived Pronouns or Adjectives. An application of this rule is to be found on page 82; "itlo = as much", *i. e.* when the term of comparison is close by, hence "as much (as this)", "titlo = as much"; *i. e.* when the term of comparison is far, hence "as much (as that)"; of course, the term of comparison is not always expressed, then we must consider the meaning; *e. g.* keeping in my hand some coins, if I say of another, that he has as many coins, I must say: "takā itliñ nāṇiñ assāt"; if another has the coins, with which I compare those of a third person, I should say: "takā titliñ nāṇiñ assāt". This distinction is well-grounded and certain; yet common people often do not observe it, and we hear "titlots ugḍās assā = that is all what I remember". The same thing must be said of "asso—tasso, yedo—tedo" *etc.*

As the word itself shows, these Pronouns are connected each other, so that where one is, the other too must be. But this must be understood thus, *i. e.* when they are used as Correlative, because some at least of these Pronouns can be used also absolutely (see p. 83, *n.* 2). Moreover one of the Pronouns can be understood, *e. g.* "to sangtā tāssentz zāleñ = it happened just as he says"; the full sentence would be: "kāsseñ to sangtā tāsseñtz zāleñ". Nay sometimes both Pronouns are omitted; *e.g.* "āuñ zaṇañ sangleñ = I have said what I know". Generally, only the first of the Correlative Pronouns can be omitted, or both are used; the omission of both Pronouns is wrong.

a) "Kosson—tasso"[1] correspond to the Latin *talis qualis*, or *quemadmodum ita*, or *sicut...ita*; *e.g.* "as he came so he went = kosso ailo, tasso gelo". If "kosso—tasso" refer to a Noun,

[1] According to the Kanarese we should write "koso, taso". Further, some people pronounce "kaši, kašeñ" in the Feminine and Neuter. This pronunciation is not common even among educated people; moreover according to the general rule (see Part III. Ch. VIII.) it seems better "kăsi, kăseñ". Finally "o" is changed int "ă"; "kăsi, kăseñ", *etc.* (See Part III. Ch. VIII.)

showing some quality etc., they are often changed into "kăssolo—tăssolo, *i. e.* into the derived Adjective, but used in the same way; *e.g.* "as life so death = kăssăli jiṇi tăssăleñ mòrn".

Both "kosso" and "tasso" can be used also absolutely; then "kosso" corresponds often to "how", (see its concord above in Ch. I.) and "tasso" means "such *or* in that way". They can be used in the Neuter Gender too and then they are a kind of Adverbs; so "tasseñ = in that way". The Proximate Pronoun of "tasso", is "asso"; and the Proximate Adverb is "ăsseñ".

b) "Zosso (zăssi, zăsseñ)—tasso". The 2nd is the same as the Correlative of "kosso" (*v. supra*); the first is derived from "zo"; consequently the meaning is: "in which way... in that way". Here properly we should say: "in that way...in which"; but in Konkani the Latin construction is preferred, viz. to put first the Relative Pronoun *qui—is*, *qualis—talis*. This "zosso" can be replaced by "kosso" with nearly the same meaning, except that "kosso" seems to indicate more expressly some quality or a similar thing, whereas "zosso" expresses directly the connexion between two things; *e. g.* "zosso ailoi, tasso vōtz = *lit.* in which way you came on that go"; "kosso ailoi, tasso vōtz = as you came in the very state go". Moreover "zosso" cannot be used absolutely (see above).

As to the construction of "zosso—tasso", the same things said about the construction of "kosso—tasso", p. 198, must be applied to these Pronouns too. This construction cannot be fully understood before explaining the construction of the Verbs. Here let us put only some examples "zăsseñ bāpān makā dhaḍlā, tăsseñ āuñ tumkāñ dhaḍtāñ = as the Father sent me, so I send you"; "zăsseñ zăglaṇeñ bāir sărtā udienti thāun ani dișți poḍtā ăstamti păriant, tăssents zateleñ yeṇeñ mănšăčeă putrăčeñ = as lightning cometh out of the east, and appeareth even into the west, so shall also the coming of the Son of Man be.

c) "Kitlo—itlo" (*proximate*), *or* "kitlo—titlo" (*remote*) correspond to "how much...how many", not in quantity but in number, as in Latin *quot tot;* but it differs from the Latin, because it can be used also in the Singular. Yet some use this "kitlo" also in the meaning of "how much", of quantity, in Latin *quantum*. Both "kitlo" and "itlo" *or* "titlo" can be used also absolutely; *e.g.* "kitleñ = how much?" Further they may be joined to a Noun; *e.g.* "kitli pirāi = how great age?"

d) The Pronouns which express the Latin *quantus tantus* are "kedo..yedo", (*proximate*), and "kedo...tedo" (*remote*) = "as great...as great". Yet some express the same meaning also by adding "vōḍ = great", or some other Adjective, declining this "kedo" according to the Gender; so they say: "kedo vōḍ, kedi vōḍ, kedeñ vōḍ = *quantus*, *quanta*, *quantum*; "kedo sobit = how nice". This manner is similar to the Latin *quam magnus*. From "kedo" the Adverbs "kedoḷ = how long time (perhaps shortened from "kedo vēḷ), "keda veḷa, *or* kedaḷa = when"; from "tedo" the Adverb "teda vēḷa" or shortened "tedaḷa = then, at that time" are derived. To all these Adverbs the Indefinite i can be added (*or* ai); *e.g.* "keda vēḷai = at any time", *etc.*

e) "Zo...to" has been already explained.

In the first member or πρότασις of correlative sentences the Particle "gi" can be used. (See p. 163, para. 2.)

4. *Pronoun* "Apuṇ"

This Pronoun refers to the person who speaks *etc.* Properly it is a Pronoun of the 3rd Person, although sometimes used also for the 2nd and 1st Person. The derived Adjective "aplo" should be used as in Latin *suus*, in English "own"; yet not seldom "tasso" is used instead of "aplo". I think that this is not quite correct; at least I do not see any reason to justify this use.

Among the forms hinted at, but not given, on p. 77, here I mention "āpāpint" or emphatic "āpāpints"; *e.g.* "Dēu āpāpints assolo = God was in Himself", as we see in the common catechism.

5. *Interrogative Pronouns*

a) "Kiteñ". This Pronoun besides the meanings given in Part II. has also the meaning "that which", as in Latin *quod; e.g.* "kiteñ monṭai, khăreñ niñ = what you say is not true". It is used in the same way as the Latin *quod*; the demonstrative Pronoun -teñ correlative to "kiteñ", is not absolutely required, but it is better to use it (see p. 239); *e. g.* "kiteñ monṭăi teñ (*or* yeñ) khăreñ niñ". This "kiteñ" is used sometimes instead of "kaintso = which"; *e. g.* "tujeñ nāuñ kiteñ = what is your name?" "akā kiteñ monṭăt = how do you call this?" But *vice versa* the Adjectives are used instead of Interrogative Pronouns sometimes; *e. g.* "kăssăleñ = how, *lit.* which?"

b) There are two or three Interrogative Pronouns or Adjectives which are very similar; these are "khăiñtso, kontso, kōṇto": "khăiñtso" may mean either "of what quality" (from 'khaiñ = what') *or* "of what origin" (from 'khăiñ" = where'), the context must decide; "kontso" is derived from "kòṇ"; hence it means *which* almost in the same meaning as "kòṇ". More frequently this "kontso" is used when the question is about few things, *e.g.* "in which hand do you feel pain? = kontso hăt duktā?" If the question is about many, "kōṇto" could be used; yet this difference is not strictly observed. This "kōṇto" literally means "who that?"

Examples to show the difference between these Adjectives: "What kind of bread do you like? that coming from A or that coming from B? = khaiñtso uṇḍo tukā rutztā?" "what kind of man is he (good or bad)? = khaiñtso mănis to?" "which person of the most Holy Trinity became man = kontso zoṇ mănis zālo?" "which man (who) is he who came? = āilo mănis kōṇto?"

6. *Indefinite Pronouns*

First, there seems to be some difference between the Indefinite Nouns formed by doubling the first syllable and those formed by i. The first are rather distributive, the others are indeterminate; *e.g.* "yeyēk mănis yēundi = let each man come"; "kossoloi mănis yēundi = let any man come". Again, both seem to differ from "kaiñ"; "kaiñ" means "something"; this fundamental meaning is kept also when it is used as an indeterminate Pronoun; *e. g.* "Dēvāk kaiñ pātak lagātgī? = may perhaps something of sin be attached to God?" "Dēvāk kaiñ pātak laganāñ = to God no sin is attached". Perhaps the Particle "kaiñ" might be called dubitative in questioning, emphatic in answering. It corresponds to the Latin *num* or *an* and to *prorsus*; to the English "any" and "at all" ("not, nothing"), to the German "*irgend*" and "*gar*". If we keep in view the derivation and original meaning of these Pronouns and Adjectives, we may succeed in using them correctly.

From the examples given, it appears that these Pronouns can be joined also to Nouns, and thus be used as Adjectives. Strictly speaking, some Pronouns, if used as Adjectives, should change their form somewhat; *e. g.* "yēklo" Pronoun; "yēk" Adjectives; yet I have heard "yēklo" used as Adjective also.

Exercise

Kurpek ăḍ vetā, to soukāsāi bogināñ. Mănis začeñ kaliz sadeñ năiñ, Devāk mānuonāñ. Yeuñtso assā, to āilogī? To mănis kōṇākui soukāsāyen rāvonk soḍināñ: to săkṭānk dostā. Šastrāk săma kāiñ moṇ Sabathā-dis yekā piḍevontāk boreñ kărčeñ (Luk. xiv, 3.)? Pharisevāñ bităr yeklcān, šastrāzāṇāran, vitzārleñ Jezu lāgiñ: Mēstri, sămărtitso voḍlo upades kōṇ to? Ruk khăiñ[1] poḍtāgī, thăiñ rāutā. Kōṇānki tankleñnāñ Somia Jezu Kristāk utrānt sāmpaḍăunk. Rāyān lek geunk suru kărtăts, hāḍlo tače lagiñ yekleāk, zaṇeñ takā deve zatale dhā hazār talent. Jezun poḷeun gouji ji kărtāle vhaspi mănis ani yer lōk, sangleñ: Vāṭ soḍā; čeḍuñ morunk-nāñ:

[1] "Khăiñ *and* thăiñ" are two Correlative Adverbs which follow the rules of the Correlative Pronouns.

ani te takā bepārveān hasle. Vāurādi zo piuṇeāk lāglo zāun assā, grestātso zāināñ. Yēk pāuli Rupoiātso kedo vāṇṭo? Yēk pāuli Rupoiātso āṭvo vāṇṭo[1]. Māi sōṇeānt,[2] vis[3] tarker Koḍiāl aili; mojea bāvān tikā pāuoili.

Art. IV. Verbs

A. Verbs in General

§ 1. Tenses and Moods

I. Indicative Mood

It is in most frequent use, even in many cases in which in Latin the Subjunctive is used, as we shall see in the explanation of the tenses.

1. *Present.* It is used and has the same meaning as in our languages, except that it is very often used for the Future *a*) to show a very near future thing, *b*) to show the certainty of a future action, *c*) to show a future thing connected with our present resolution, *e.g.* instead of saying "I am resolved to do so", they say, "I do..."; again, to the question "will he come?" they answer "yetā = he comes"; to the question: "will you do it?" they answer "kărtāñ = I do". Moreover it is used in the *oratio obliqua* instead of the Imperfect or other tense; *e.g.* "yetāñ moṇ taṇeñ sāngleñ = he said that he would come". This point will be explained more distinctly later on. Other cases in which the Present may be used for the Future, *e.g.* the historical present are as in Latin.

2. *Imperfect.* This tense is used generally as the Latin *amabam* or as the English "I was loving", yet not so often, as

---

1) This is the easiest way of expressing the fractions, *i. e.* to join the required Numeral Adjective to "vāṇṭo = portion"; so we get "āṭvo vāṇṭo = $\frac{1}{8}$", "dhāvo vāṇṭo = $\frac{1}{10}$", "sōḷāvo vāṇṭo = $\frac{1}{16}$" *etc.*

2) A month corresponding nearly to our September. See Appendix to the Dictionary.

3) To express the date the cardinal numbers are used.

in Latin; for, sometimes, the Past is substituted. Besides, while we use in Latin very often the Imperfect to show time, *e.g.* *cum regnaret Servius Tullius...quando ipse ambulabat...*; in these and similar examples, the Konkani language prefers to use the Participle with "veḷār=in time", or the Gerund in "-anañ", although it can be used also in the Imperfect with "kăiñ=when"; *e.g.* "when Tippu-Sultan was reigning = Tīpu-Sultān rāsvot kărtanañ", *or* "Tīpu-Sultān rāsvot kărčeā veḷār", *or* "kăiñ Tīpu-Sultān rāsvot kărtālo".

3. *Past.* This tense is used like the Latin *amavi*, as this "*amavi*" is translated by the English Past (for, *amavi* is expressed by: "I loved, *and* I have loved"); moreover it is used in some cases in which we should use the Imperfect; *e.g.* "to ghăṭ zāuñ assolo=he was (*erat*) strong".

4. *Perfect.* It is expressed by the Latin "*amavi*", as this is expressed by the English "I have loved". It seems to be used, especially when it expresses a time entirely passed; *e.g.* "last year I went to Bombay=gelea vorsānt āuñ Bombāi gelāñ".

5. *Past Perfect.* In Latin *amaveram.* This tense properly expresses a time past, compared to another past time. As such it is rare; because *a*) when this tense is governed by a Conjunction (when, after...), it is translated by the Participle; *b*) sometimes the simple Perfect is used; but, on the other hand, sometimes this tense, perhaps not quite correctly, seems to be used instead of the Perfect; *e.g.* "taṇeñ apleñ kām kărunk natụlleñ=he has not performed his work". Again, sometimes it is used for the Imperfect, "to nidụllo=he was sleeping". As emphatic, viz. as an Emphatic Perfect, it is often used; and this seems the most common meaning of this tense.

Let us try to give a better explanation of the three last tenses. Although Past, Perfect and Past Perfect are very near as to their meaning, for which reason sometimes they are used promiscuously, yet in some cases we must distinguish them, and use them not promiscuously. As far as I could learn from many examples considered in this minute and difficult point, this difference is made in Konkani: Past is used to show a past thing which does not any more continue; Perfect shows a past thing which in some way still continues, or at least, it is unknown whether it ended; if two past things are considered, expressly or implicitly, of which one is anterior to the other, the Past Perfect is used, although in English the Perfect or Past perhaps would be used. Examples: "Yesterday I wrote a letter = kāl āuveñ kāgad boreileñ". If we say: "boreilāñ", it would implicitly show something which still continues; *e.g.* "up to this I did not get any answer". "Where is your brother? = tuzo bāu khāiñ assā?" "he is gone to Bombay (and is still there) = to Bombāi gelā"; "Antony died three years ago = Anton tīn vorsañ adiñ melā"; "yesterday I walked three hours, to-day two hours = āuñ kāl tīn uorañ tsalṇlloñ, āz dōn uorañ tsalloñ".

Although this seems to be the difference between these tenses, we cannot pretend to explain all cases according to this rule or to have it observed by all.

6. *1st Future Absolute.* It is used *a*) to show a future thing, without any doubt; *b*) yet sometimes it seems to be used also for an uncertain future event, chiefly if it was considered at a particular past time about to happen; *e.g.* "hariyekā kšaṇa amkāñ bēñ distaleñ to moṛuñ moṇ *or* mortolo moṇ = we were every moment afraid that he would die". Yet to show a doubtful future the Contingent or the Potential Future (see below) is commonly used, viz. the Future in añ or iñ. *c*) It is used also in this and similar sentences: "Why should he run? = kiteāk dāuntolo?" although such sentences might be expressed also by the Necessary Mood; *e.g.* "kiteāk dāvazāi?" or also by the Infinitive as in Italian "*perche correre?* = kiteāk dāunčeñ?" *d*) It may be used also to show not a future thing, but a potentiality; *e.g.* "he has no teeth, how can he bite? = takā dānt nānt, kosso sābtolo?" yet, here, it would be better

to use the Potential Mood. *e*) Finally it is used to express aim or purpose instead of the Supine; *e.g.* "zărtăr ăuñ favote jinsiñ săngtoloñ ani tumiñ băktien aikateleăt, devăči kurpa amkăñ zăi = for me to speak properly and for you to hear with devotion, is required the grace of God". This last mode is not very common, although it seems to be elegant.

7. 2nd Future or Past Future: in Latin, *e.g. vocavero*. This tense is seldom used; for, if the Latin 2nd Future is preceded by some particle, the Participle is used; moreover the 1st Future is often used instead of the 2nd. If, however, it is required, the Potential Future (in -ăn or -in) is used by many; yet see p. 119, para. 9, from which we can understand that "nidtoñ assoloñ" can be considered as the 2nd Absolute Future, "nidlo astolo *or* nidun astolo" as the 2nd Contingent Future; whereas "nidăn" seems to be an incorrect form of the 2nd Future. Moreover a periphrastic 2nd Future often occurs, corresponding to the Latin; *e.g. si fecerit omnia quae praecepta, sunt vitam vivet* = to upadēs sambaḷăt zaḷeăr, jiṇ jietolo": *i. e.* the Future Potential joined to the Conditional of "zată", *lit.* "if it happens (that) he will keep the commandments" *etc.* Hereby its construction is also known. It seems chiefly used with a Future preceded by "*if;*" about this later on.

II. Imperative Mood

This Mood is used not only to command, but also 1) to inquire, to consult, *e.g.* "amiñ kiteñ kăriăñ? = what can we do?" 2) to exhort, *e.g.* "răzăr kăriăñ = let us pray".

Pay attention to the difference between the 1st and 2nd Person Plural, *h.e.* the 1st Person is "nasal", as usual, the 2nd is not "nasal". The 2nd form of the 2nd Person Plural is used only in some cases. The form in a may be always used.

Many forms of Imperative have been given in Part II. The first form is more common in the really imperative meaning, except the 1st Person "-ungi" which does not often occur.

The 2nd form in "-uñ" is rather permissive, optative and benedictive, or rather it expresses also Imperative, but mixed with the Benedictive, Permissive and Optative Mood (the Benedictive which is put by Max Müller in Sanskrit, may be considered as contained in the Optative); if nothing of Imperative is expressed by the Verb, then it is only Optative or Subjunctive which has the same form. The 3rd form, periphrastic, cannot be used promiscuously, because it seems to express some permanent thing; we may see whether in English or Latin we could use that periphrastic form; then we may, usually, employ it also in Konkani; so we cannot say: "*fias transiens* = become crossing (*e.g.* the river)". The last form expresses not only command but necessity: therefore it cannot used indifferently, we may employ the plan just now suggested.

III. Optative Mood

As hinted above, the meaning of this mood implies not only desire, but also blessing etc. Consequently in Konkani there is no necessity to distinguish Optative from Benedictive with Max Müller. By this we do not mean that whenever desire or blessing is expressed, the Optative Mood must always be used; often the Indicative or some other Mood may used; *e.g.* "makā nidunk khuši assā = I am willing to sleep".

Only three tenses have been given, because usually those tenses are sufficient. If some other tense be required, it will be not difficult to find out from the given forms of the paradigm, a suitable one to express this other tense. The Future Optative may be expressed by the Imperfect; yet in our European languages also a pure Future Optative is not commonly found. That "boreñ" or "puro" put in the paradigm, is not necessarily to be used, but can be used in the Imperfect and Past, as strengthening the meaning; or rather, it expresses explicitly what by omitting those words, would be implicit; "assāllen" can be omitted as usually.

IV. Subjunctive Mood

As in this Mood many tenses are contained, which differ considerably one from the other, and on the other hand I do not wish to introduce new moods, without necessity, so it is somewhat difficult to speak of this Mood generally. Hence I will speak of each tense in particular.

1. *Present.* It is very seldom used as a pure Subjunctive (often as Optative), yet sometimes it occurs *a*) like a permissive Verb; *e.g.* "buk mezār gāluñ = he may put the book on the table"; *b*) to consult or to ask "ãuñ kiteñ kăruñ? = what can I do? = *quid faciam?*" It coincides almost with the Imperative, or we may say that what has been given as Imperative is, strictly speaking, rather Subjunctive. The Latin Subjunctive, as in the sentence "*qui possum scire* = how can I know it", may be expressed by the Absolute Infinitive, sometimes, "ãuveñ kăseñ zāṇa zãuučoñ?"

2. *Pure Imperfect*, as in Latin *indigebamus gratia Dei ut faceremus bonum.* First remark that on p. 109 the 3rd Person Plural has been omitted which however has been put at p. 90. Remark moreover that the s of the termination, is to be pronounced not as ts, but as a pure s. It occurs very seldom, and only in this meaning, as in the above example, viz. to show aim. In reading, I remember to have found it about three times. It seems to have only two persons in the Singular and one in the Plural, but three terminations for the three genders. What is to be done, if another Person occurs? Another Person can very seldom occur, because this tense, in Transitive Verbs, has a passive meaning. Yet, if it occurs at least in Neuter Verbs, I heard the given terminations of the 3rd Person are suitable also for the 2nd Person; at all events we can use another tense, *e. g.* the Supine. I have not heard the other persons used, *i. e.* 2nd Singular and 1st and 2nd Plural; hence I could not put them down, in order not to invent a language; by seeking more exactly, we may perhaps find them. I must, however, add that I

tried, by asking, to find whether the other Persons in oi etc. could be used; but from the answers which I received, it seems that they are not used. Common people do not use this form; books do not exist, at least in such quantity as to throw sufficient light; hence it is not so easy to determine this point. If we find a difficulty in this tense, we may use some other tense for it, *e.g.* the Supine.

Besides the given form of this tense, another occurs sometimes; *i.e.* instead of adding "-soñ" *etc.* "-sărkoñ" is added, modifying this "-sărkoñ" in the same way as "-soñ".

Let us now give some examples to explain this tense: "Jesus Christ sent the Holy Ghost in order to enable the Apostles to preach the Gospel all over the world = Jezu Kristān Spirita Săntāk daḍlā Apostolānk Evanjel săgḷea souñsărānt părgăṭ karisso"; "I give you a prize in order to encourage you to learn = āuñ tukā yēk inām ditāñ, sikunk tukā dhăirivont kărisso"; "the father gives a punishment to the daughter in order that she may become good = bāpui duvek šikšā ditā, tikā bori kărissi".

Though I have used this tense also in the negative form, yet, I think, this is not so often used, and instead of it, the Supine Negative might be used; *e.g.* "āuñ tukā šikšā ditāñ pātkānt portun poḍanāñ zāunk = I give you punishment in order that you may not fall again".

3. *Past*, *Perfect*, *Past Perfect*. A special form for them does not exist. I will show in the Appendix how they can be expressed. For the present it is enough to know, that very often the Indicative or the Participle or the Gerund are used in their place.

4. *1st Conditional.* Latin *si facerem*. In general, the Conditional form is most largely used; because it is used not only when we should use the conditional, but in many other cases too, provided the meaning does not forbid it. This tense does not only express the Latin *si facerem*, *si fecisset*, but also any tense preceded by "si = *si vis*" *etc.*, though on the

other hand not always is a tense preceded by *si* to be translated by the Conditional in "-leär." Hence as many English tenses have not their corresponding tenses in Konkani, the Conditional is one means of supplying the apparent deficiency in some way; *e.g.* "you should go to the church every day"; this "should go" has no exactly corresponding tense in Konkani; hence we may express it by the Conditional thus: "tuveñ häriyëk dïs Igärjent geleär bhou boreñ = *lit.* if you were to go every day to the Church, this would be very good". Yet there are other modes of translating such sentences. This 1st Conditional therefore is used, *a*) as I have just now said; *b*) sometimes to show time (though perhaps not quite correctly), instead of the Gerund in "-anañ"; *c*) sometimes it expresses desire, but then it is Optative; *d*) common people use sometimes the 1st Conditional instead of the 2nd Conditional; but this is wrong.

Remarks. *a*) There are at least three forms for expressing this Conditional, viz. 1) the termination "-leär"; 2) "zärtär = if", with the Contingent Future, *e.g.* "zärtär to sikat = if he learnt" (see the distinct explanation of "zärtär" in Art. VII.); 3) "pokšek = in case that..."; it is used like a Postposition, *i.e.* joined to the Participle; *e.g.* "pätak aḍarlelea pokšek = in case that sin should be committed". "Pokšek" is the Dative of "pokša = side".

b) Sometimes the termination "-leär" takes an i at the end: then the meaning is "*although*". Instead of this i, "zäritär" may be used with the Contingent Future.

c) The first part of the Negative form should be conjugated as the Negative Present Indicative: "nidanäñ zaleär, nidanäiñ zaleär" *etc.*, although common people do not conjugate it. See below § 2.

5. *2nd Conditional.* Many things said about the 1st Conditional can be applied to the 2nd Conditional. Instead of it we may use "zärtär" with the Past Perfect; to express "*although*", i is added to the 2nd part, or "zäritär" (zäritäri) is used with the Past Perfect; *e.g.* "širäp tukä, Korozäim, ši-

rāp tukā, Bethsaida; kiteāk zărtăr tumče thăiñ zallyo-tăssălyo podvedig kărnyo Tyrus ani Sidon muḷḷea šerānt zallyo, te bhou témpa adiñ prăčitačeñ văstur ani gobor găln prăčit aḍarunk pāute assalle = woe to thee, Chorazim, woe to thee, Bethsaida, for if in Tyre and Sidon had been wrought the miracles that have been wrought in you, they had long ago done penance in sackcloth and ashes". (Matthew xi. 21.)

6. *1st Conditionatum*, in Latin the 2nd part of this sentence, *si diligeres Deum, servares ejus mandata.* In Greek it is called ἀπόδοσις. I call it *Conditionatum*, because it expresses what would happen, if a condition be fulfilled (as in Theology *Conditionata*). See page 120, para. 11, about the exact form of the 1st Conditionatum, and its meaning.

Though the regular and usual Conditionatum is as given in the paradigm, yet sometimes it is allowed by the meaning, to use also the Present or the Future in its place; in such a case it seems that in the πρότασις the form in "-leār" is not properly used; the Present or some other tense, as the meaning requires, should be used instead of "-leār"; *e.g.* "zărtăr tuñ Dēvāče kušie pārmāṇe tzăltai, tukā santōs meḷtā = if you walk according to the will of God, you will find joy".

7. *Past or 2nd Conditionatum.* First observe that by accident the more common form of it in "-tolo" given in § 2, has been omitted in § 4. Then see page 120 for the exact form and different meanings.

The tenses of the Conditional and Conditionatum, strictly speaking, should form a peculiar Mood.

V. Potential Mood

This Mood, as distinct from other Moods, does not exist in many languages; its meaning is expressed by some other Mood or with circumlocutions. In Konkani we must distinguish this Mood, because it has peculiar terminations, at least in the principal form ("-iyet"). I find this Mood also in the Kanarese Grammar by Hodson, although this author comprehends under such a name also what I call Necessary Mood. I do not see this Mood in the Tuḷu Grammar or in the Grammar of the Mahrätti language which should have, as some think, great similarity with Konkani. The fact is that Mahrätti might have had great similarity in former times; now many things are different, and we cannot make objections against some rules of this Grammar by saying that in Mahrätti the things are not so. I must however add that in Mahrätti there are Potential Verbs, derived from a simple Verb by the addition of व to denote possibility.

After these introductory remarks, consider, that although in the paradigm (p. 110 etc.) in some forms the neuter of "assā" has been given, sometimes the context may require another Gender; *e.g.* "assolo" instead of "assḷeñ". Remark further, that this Mood is varied in many different ways, which can be hardly reduced to rules. The given forms are only the most common and even these are formed by some in a different way.

1. This Mood is used to indicate *a*) whether a thing is allowed, *b*) whether there is probability that a thing will be done, *c*) whether there is power (*potentia physica*) to do something. To indicate the first meaning, more commonly the first form in "-iyet" is used; to indicate the second meaning, the same first form in "-iyet" is used, or often also the third form; to indicate the third meaning, more commonly the second form with "tanktā *or* tank assā" is used. This must be understood of the affirmative form. For the negative, in the first meaning, "-naye" is used, or often also "nozo"; in the second "nozo", in the third "tankanāñ". As regards the Future Potential a distinct explanation is required; for it is of very frequent use. This Future in an (or in) is used *a*) to show a future thing, but with some doubt, *e. g.* if I ask, "is such a thing found in the bazār"? If there is some probability of finding it, they answer: "meḷat = it will be probably found". On the contrary, if they are certain to find such a thing, they

answer: "meḷtā" or "meḷteleñ". So, if seeing a sick man we say: "to mortolo" we mean to say: all signs of approaching death are there. If we say: "morat", we mean to say: "I do not see certain signs of approaching death, yet he may die". *b*) This future is used also to express these and similar English phrases: "I should like to ask you = āuñ tujeñ lagiñ itsāran", you might perhaps say: "tumiñ sangšāt".

2. With the Potential Mood a kind of periphrastic conjugation takes place by adding the Verb "assā" in the required tenses to the form in "-iyet"; *e. g.* "poḷeiyet assalleñ = it was to be seen". And again the same form of Potential prefixed to some Participles, becomes an Adjective corresponding to the Latin Adjectives in *-bilis; e. g.* "poḷeyet assạlleo văstu = *res visibiles*", *h. e.* exposed to the sight of all, or which are worthy to be seen. About this see below.

VI. Necessary Mood

This Mood is not put in the Kanarese, Tuḷu and Mahrātti Grammars, which I have seen; yet its meaning occurs in all languages; why, therefore, introduce this new Mood? I answer: because it seemed to be as necessary, as I thought the Original and the 2nd Locative are, which are not to be found in Kanarese and Mahrātti. I must, however, acknowledge that, strictly speaking, we might perhaps have avoided this new Mood by saying that its meaning is expressed by adding "zāi" to some other tense of the Verb, or by using the periphrastic conjugation, as in Latin *necesse est ut faciam, faciendum est etc.* I preferred to make a special tense; because *a*) the union of "zāi" with the Verb seems to be not only an apposition, but a real composition. It is true that the termination "zāi" does not change, and another peculiar termination does not occur; yet the first reason *probat nimis*, because it would prove also that the Potential Mood is not a peculiar Mood, which nobody will grant; the second reason proves only that not all tenses or forms of this Mood are peculiar to this Mood; and I grant that if no peculiar termination would occur, I would not have introduced this new Mood.

b) The Necessary Mood renders this part of Grammar much easier and clearer. This reason must be joined to the first reason in order to have its strength. You will perhaps say: *non sunt multiplicanda entia sine necessitate.* In this matter a great utility can be considered as *quaedam necessitas;* moreover, although this could not be called *necessitas*, why must be prohibited *multiplicare modos cum magna utilitate?* All philosophers say that *ex duobus bonis melius est eligendum vel eligi potest.* At all events, *in dubiis libertas*, you are allowed, as for you, to eliminate this Mood, which is not absolutely required.

After these introductory remarks, a few words about its use.

1. The necessity expressed by this Mood may be of any kind, *i. e.* moral (obligation), or physical, or of every day life, not regarding obligation; consequently it can be used whenever some kind of necessity is to be expressed, although such a necessity be concealed by different expressions of other languages; it corresponds to the Latin *debeo*, *necesse est*, *convenit*, *expedit*, and to many other similar expressions. It is used moreover, joined to the Conditional of "zatā", to express sentences like this: "if you wish to go to heaven, keep the commandments = sārgār votsazāi zaleār, sambaḷ upadēs". Here two notions are expressed at the same time: first, the conditional notion, then the necessity of doing this and that, in order to obtain what is expressed by the Conditional.

2. The use of the different forms of Necessary Mood is understood by the translation of each form given in the paradigm. Only you must remark that this Mood is managed in so many various and elegant ways as to render it impossible to give all the different combinations or to reduce them to certain rules; practice will teach you; yet something will be said hereafter. The given forms are the fundamental forms only.

3. "Zāi", which expresses necessity in general, has no conjugation not only when it is used alone, but also when it is joined to another Verb. If this "zāi" is used to express necessity in general, the other tenses may be formed by adding the corresponding tenses of "zatā" to "zāi"; *e.g.* "makā zāi zatoleñ = I shall be in need of..." (see p. 136, § 7, para. 4). Its construction is regular, viz. the thing which is necessary is put in the Nominative, the person to whom it is necessary in the Dative, just as if the literal meaning were: "it is necessary". In the Negative form the root is different, for the reason shown in the conjugation. This "zāi" is often pronounced "jāi"; some say also "jè"; but this pronunciation seems to be vulgar.

4. Not all tenses of this Mood are used. Hence what is to be done if we require such tenses? I think, that the periphrastic conjugation may help us to supply those deficient tenses.

VII. *Infinitive Mood*

This Mood, along with the Gerunds and Participles, presents many difficulties.

1. *Absolute.* This mood has two forms, viz. either "-tso, (-či, -čeñ)" *or* "-untso, -unči, -unčeñ" (see pp. 92, 121, para. 14). It is used *a*) absolutely to express the meaning of the Verb: we would say in Latin τὸ *legere*, τὸ *scribere; b*) like the Gerund in di of the Latin: *voluntas discendi*; *c*) for the Future (see p. 246, para. 6); *d*) for the Subjunctive (see p. 249, para. 1). In the *a*) case it agrees with its object; *e.g.* "to read a book = yēk pustak vātčeñ"; "to beat a beast = yēk monzāt mārči"; "to do a work = yēk kām kārčeñ". In the *b*) case it agrees with the Noun governing this Genitive. If this Infinitive has moreover an object, the Infinitive may agree with the object or with the Noun governing the Genitive, *e.g.* "sārgār vetči khuši = the desire of going to heaven"; "yeñ kām kārčeñ khuši = the wish of doing this work", or "yeñ kām kārči khuši". Yet see p. 201, para. 13. The four pre-

ceding cases are easy and more or less used also by common people. The two following cases are somewhat high and elegant. *e*) The Absolute Infinitive is used for the Present in descriptions, as in Latin the Historical Infinitive; *e.g.* "taṇeñ sakālinčeñ ani sānječeñ rāzār kărčeñ bhou aprup; taṇeñ sakrament kāṇgeunčoñ bhou uṇeñ=he recites (recite) his morning and evening prayers very seldom; he receives (receive) the sacraments very little (seldom)". Yet we could explain this example literally also in this way: his reciting prayers (is) very rare" *etc.;* then this Infinitive would not be used for the Present: the former explanation however is more natural; *f*) it is used, as in Latin the Accusative with Infinitive, *e.g.* "khăinčea-i mănšān tuje lagiñ māgči tukā gărz nāñ móṇ, yea vorviñ amiñ sătmandtāuñ tuñ āilāi móṇ Dēvā lagtso= thou needest not that any man should ask thee, by this we believe that thou camest forth from God". Remark that "māgči" agrees with "gărz", although it is in a different sentence. In these cases, the subject of the Infinitive is more frequently put in the Instrumental, although the Verb be Neuter. In the cases *e*) and *f*) it seems to be not only more frequent, but also usual to put the subject in the Instrumental; this point will be explained more distinctly below. As regards the construction of the Instrumental with the Infinitive, the rule is the same as in Latin, *i.e.* the subject is put in the Instrumental, the Verb in the Absolute Infinitive; if there be some Noun by which this Infinitive is governed, as in the above example, it agrees with that Noun; else it is put in the Neuter. No Past Infinitive is in use, as we shall see below. *g*) It is used in the Dative instead of the Supine; because the Dative is used also to express purpose; but then as to the meaning it is rather the Supine: "Dēvān amkāñ rătsleăt āmtso ătmo bačău kărunčeāk=God has created us to save our soul". Yet in similar sentences, generally speaking, it is better to use the Supine, or the Participle with "pāsvot".

Remark *a*) that the Absolute Infinitive having a declinable form can be not only conjugated but also declined; *i. e.* put *e.g.* in the Dative just as Nouns, if according to the general rules one or the other case is required (see p. 123, para. 10 and *alibi*); *e.g.* "boreunčeāk lāi = *lit.* apply to write (cause to write). Remark *b*) that in some cases it may used promiscuously with the Supine, even in some of the cases stated above; *e.g.* "morunk makā khuši assā, *or* morči makā khuši assā = I wish to die". Remark finally *c*) that the *a*) case comprehends also the Verbal Nouns as stated at page 168, *l.* 8, *a fine.*

The Absolute Infinitive, as regards the form, is the same as the Participle Future, the Gerundive etc.; hence the context must decide. Somebody might perhaps reduce all forms in "-tso" to one; for the sake of distinction we are allowed to keep them separate.

2. *Supine.* *a*) The chief meaning of the Supine is to show purpose or aim and corresponds to the Latin Supine in *um* and to the forms with "*ut* = in order that". *b*) Yet sometimes it is used also to show an implicit aim, *i. e.* when in Latin we should use neither the Supine nor *ut*, there being however the notion of some aim implied in the sentence; *e.g.* "do you like to go? = votzunk tukā khušigī?" *c*) Finally it may be used sometimes for the Absolute Infinitive, although no aim seems to be expressed; *e.g.* "peleātso mosor kārunk pātakgī? = is it sin to hate the neighbour?"

Remark that to express aim very often instead of the Supine we may use the Participle, especially that in -tso with some Postposition having a meaning agreeing with the fundamental meaning of the Supine; *e.g.* "pāsvot = for"; "khātir = for"; so we may say: "sākaṭ vāstu moje motin poḷeileāt bud sikunk = I have considered all things with my mind in order to learn wisdom", *or* ". . . bud sikčea pāsvot"; "magā ani tumkāñ meḷteleñ, tumtso santos bhorpur zāunčea pāsvot = ask and you shall receive: that your joy may be full". The use of "pāsvot. . ." with the Participle is perhaps more common than the Supine, especially when the Verb has an object. The Future can also be used for the Supine (see p. 247, *c*).

In some Verbs the termination -onk seems to be used instead of -unk.

VIII. *Participles*

1. *Present.* There are many forms; almost all may be used as Adjectives or as Pronouns; *e.g.* "vätstolo mänis = a reading man", or only "vätstolo = he who reads".

The form in -tso is the same as the Future Participle. It seems that, strictly speaking, the Participle in -tso cannot be used also as a Pronoun, whereas the Participle in -tolo can be so used; *e.g.* "väiṭ kärtolo sikšä bogtolo = evil-doer will suffer pain"; we could not say correctly: "väiṭ kärtso....."; we should say: "väiṭ kärtso mänis.."

The form in -tä to is not a true Participle, and does not follow the rules of the Participle, but the rules of the correlative sentences (see *passim* Part II. Chapter III. and Part IV. Chapter III.); *e.g.* "God will give a reward to those who walk uprightly = (je) säma tsältät, tankäñ Dou inäm ditolo". The most simple rule for the right use of such a Participle in -tä to is not to consider it at all as a Participle, but to consider to as a Correlative Pronoun of zo understood. This kind of Participle is, however, often used even in cases in which we should not use a correlative sentence; *e.g.* "the man, who is coming, is my brother = yetä to mänis mozo bäu". It seems that it is used instead of the forms in -tolo or -tso, when we want to give some emphasis or to point out some thing.

As regards the Participle in -tolo, -teli, -teleñ, although I have heard it also used as a Future Participle, yet as it cannot be used promiscuously, it will be safer, especially for beginners, to use for the Future Participle only the form in -tso, and to use the form in -tolo only as a Present Participle. The rule, however, seems to be this: the form in -tolo, -teli, -teleñ (see p. 119, para. 10) is used as a Future Participle, but following the rules of the Correlative Pronouns, as we have said of the Participle in -tä to; the form in -tolo,

-tāli, -tālsā" (*s. l. c.*) is often used as a Future Participle, but following the rules of the common Participles.

The Participle in -tāñ is used in composition, chiefly *a*) with "astanañ" in the Present Gerund "kărtastanañ", or shortened, "kartanañ = doing, or been doing, or while doing"; *b*) with "zāuñ" in the compound form of the Imperative "nidtañ zāuñ = let him be sleeping"; *c*) in the periphrastic conjugation: "āuñ kărtāñ thāiñ assāñ". Now I remember only "mortāñ mănis = decrepit man", in which sentence "mortāñ" is used out of composition, (if it is really a Participle, from "mor = die" and not another original word). The chief meaning of all these forms of the Present Participle, except that in -tā to, and perhaps the Participle in -tāñ, is, mostly, like the meaning of the Latin Present Participle in -ns, *i. e.* the contraction of a relative sentence; *e. g.* "nidtolo *or* nidtso mănis = the man who sleeps" *etc.*

The Participle in -un, or shortened, -n, is, I may say, every thing, viz. Participle Present and Past Gerund etc.; for this reason you find this form among Participles and Gerunds. As a Participle it is used but seldom in the periphrastic conjugation, *e. g.* "nidun assā = he is sleeping"; it has some times also a passive meaning, *e.g.* "boreun assā = it is written".

Besides the given forms, another occurs compounded of "tăssolo = such", added to the Participle in -tolo *etc.*; this "tăssolo" is added also to the other Participles; *e. g.* "kărtalo tăssolo, kello tăssolo" *etc.* What is the construction of this Participle? If we consider it as a real Participle, its construction cannot be satisfactorily explained; just as I said of the Genitive, which is almost inexplicable, if it is considered as a Noun. If we consider that "tăssolo" as the Pronoun which means "*such*," added as a Konkanism to the Participle, its construction is easy; because it is the same as the construction of such a Pronoun if it were used to strengthen the Participle; *i. e.* as we have seen, "tăssolo" is correlative of "kăssolo"; the first correlative is often omitted; hence it remains only "tăssolo".

In the common cases it has no peculiar difficulty, yet there are some sentences in which it cannot be easily explained otherwise than by making the supposition stated above; *e.g.* "ătmo ăskăt zatā, yā pātkā vorviñ mortā, dekun takā portun ghăṭ kărunk, vo mahā pātkānčea gratèarān jīv kāḍlolo tăssā-leāk portun jivont kărunk thoḍeañ voktānči gărz assā = the soul becomes weak or dies by sin; therefore in order to give her new strength or to give her a new life, if she unfortunately should have been deprived of her life, some medicines are required". Here the Participle "kāḍlolo tăssolo" is divided into two parts, one of which agrees with "jīv (kāḍlolo)", the other agrees with "takā"; why such a division? No reason can be given if this Participle is like the others; on the contrary if we consider "tăssolo" as I said, then it is very easy, because we can translate so: "...or to strengthen such (a soul) deprived of her life..." *etc.;* or, more literally: "...she (who has been) deprived of her life by mortal sin, to such to give ...". This literal translation explains in the most simple and natural way the construction of "tăssolo".

I said that "-un" is sometimes contracted into "n"; this contraction cannot always be made; euphony and use must be consulted; *e.g.* "kāpeun" cannot be contracted. It seems that the Verbs having the root ending in a consonant take only "n" whenever it is not too hard to pronounce it. The Verbs having the root ending in a vowel, more frequently, if not always, take "nn". Moreover I have often heard "on" instead of "un"; this may be a variety; yet it seems rather convenient to use "on", if "v" precedes, as is the case with the Verbs in "au" which change "u" into "v" when the termination to be added begins with a vowel. (See p. 143, para. 2.)

2. *Imperfect.* This is the contraction of the Relative Pronoun with the Imperfect Tense "*qui faciebat* = kărtalo". It may be used also in the correlative sentences; *e.g.* "the man who was yesterday laughing, died to-day = kāl hastālo mānis āz melo". This Participle is better used, adding to, *i.e.* as the Participle in -tā to (see above). It may be used also as a Pronoun.

Though really this Participle seems to differ from the Present Participle, yet common people are not aware, I think, of such a difference.

3. *Future.* This is, as the Latin *venturus*, a short expression of the Relative Pronoun with the Verb in a Future Tense "*ille qui venturus est* = youñtso". Besides the form in -tso we may use also the form in -tolo (see above, Present Participle).

This Participle is used *a*) to contract sentences with the Verb in a Future Tense; *b*) in the periphrastic conjugation with future meaning "youñtso assā = *is venturus est*."

4. *Past.* This is the contraction of a relative sentence with the Verb in a Past Tense: *qui venit*. In Latin we have no Past Participle corresponding to this *qui venit*, except the deponent and a few other Verbs; in Konkani, we have it, if the Verb is Neuter; "āilo mānis = *homo qui venit*".

But in the Transitive Verbs, the Participle has a passive meaning, because the Participle has the same nature as the tense, of which it is a contraction; hence, as the Past of the Transitive Verbs has a passive meaning, the Participle too has a passive meaning; yet sometimes I have found it used in an active meaning; *e.g.* "kākult kelcānk kākult meḷteli = *lit.* those who have done mercy will find mercy". Yet there is a way of explaining this example without saying that the Participle has an active meaning.

Although this Participle exists, yet it is very seldom used; generally they use the Past Perfect Participle; so "āz tukā meḷḷo mānis mozo bāu = the man whom you met to-day (is) my brother." This Past Perfect Participle is used especially in contracted relative sentences.

5. *Perfect.* This should be "kelā"; but it is not used, except by a few, it seems. Yet the form "kelā to" might be used in the same way in which "kartā to" is used; *e.g.* "to those who have performed their duty I give a price = aplo kāido kelā, tankañ yêk inām ditāñ".

6. *Past Perfect.* It differs from the preceding Participle, only because the l is doubled, or, if this is not allowed by

the nature of the consonant, o or u is inserted[1] (see Part II. Ch. IV.); *e.g.* "kelo" is Past Participle, "kello" Past Perfect. The chief meaning of this Participle is the same as the meaning of the Past, as I said just now; moreover it is emphatic. Hence in the formation of the Adjectives called Participial Adjectives, as there is a certain emphasis, this Participle is used; *e.g.* "adorable = nămăskăr făvozallo" *etc.*

1. What I said about the Past Participle, viz. of its passive meaning, must be said, of this Participle too and of the Perfect Past.

2. The Participles in "lo" are declined as Adjectives of three terminations if they are used as Adjectives, as Nouns of the 3rd Declension if they are used as Pronouns; *e.g.* "yŏk pătki prăčit keleănt Anjea thăiñ santos assă = *lit.* in having a sinner done penance, angels rejoice". Here "keleănt" is 1st Locative from "keleñ".

3. Here the Participle in "to" must be also mentioned. This, as I said on p. 119, para. 10, occurs only or chiefly in composition with a Verb. I have found it also joined to a Noun, just as the other Participles, but very seldom, and used only by some, as in the sentence "kăḍto voḍto tăp = intermittent fever."

IX. Gerunds

1. *Present.* As appears from the paradigm, it has two forms, or rather only one form written in two ways, long or short. The 2nd form is a compound of the Present Gerund of "assă", and of the Participle in "-tăñ". Hence "tsăltastana" means "be walking".

This Gerund is used chiefly to show time, as in this and similar sentences: "When God invites you, follow him = Deu tumkăñ apoitanañ, tačeñ utar aikă". It is used by preference by these people, even in cases in which it seems out of place. This Gerund with the Conditional is a makeshift to supply the deficiency of some tenses. This Gerund is Present, yet used sometimes for the Imperfect, Past, and Future; *e.g.* "*Cetera autem, cum venero, disponam* = ăuñ yetanañ, dusreo văstu săma kărtoloñ". By this Gerund we may translate many cases of the Latin *Absolute Ablative*, with this difference that in Konkani the subject is not to be put in the Ablative,

[1] At Goa, so I have heard, they always put this "o" between the two "l".

as in Latin, although the subject of the principal sentence were not the same as the subject of the secondary sentence; *e.g.* "*Regnante Servio Tullio, Roma munita est*=Servius Tullius rasvot kărtanañ, Rom moḷḷeñ šăr ghăṭ zaleñ".

Instead of using this Gerund, the Participle with "vēḷ= time", put in the 2nd Locative can be used; *e.g.* in the above example "Servius Tullius rasvot kărčea veḷār=*lit.* at the time (in which) Servius Tullius reigned...". This second way of expressing time is also very frequent (later on I put its construction). Yet this 2nd form can be properly used when, translating literally the Konkani into English, as in the above example, the meaning is not altered.

2. *Imperfect.* In form it is the same as the Participle Imperfect given above; but that Participle has also the meaning of a Gerund. It is used *a*) as in Latin the Gerund in *do*, meaning manner and cause; *e.g.* "by doing evil you cause loss to your soul=văiṭ kărn, aplea ătmeăk lukšăn kărtai=*malum agendo, damnum infers animae tuae*"; "to bób mārn gelo=he went away crying". Probably in the 2nd example it is not a Gerund, but the Participle Present; in Latin we could translate it thus: *ipse clamans abiit;* in Italian we should use the Gerund: *se ne andò gridando. b*) It is chiefly used when the Conjunction "*and*" between two Verbs is omitted as in this and similar examples: "go and ask"; omitting "*and*" we get "going ask=votsun itsār". This way of speaking is almost universal; it is a true Konkanism; if we put "*and*", they would understand it; but it would not be, often, according to the character of Konkani. *c*) It is used to form many compound Verbs (see hereafter these Verbs); *e.g.* "ukoḷn-dor= keep raised"; "Jezun sămzon te čiṇtăt móṇ apṇă lāgiñ vitsărunk sāngleñ=Jesus having known that they intended to ask him, he said"; this 3rd case, *quoad substantiam*, is not different from the second. *d*) It is used also to denote time in cases in which we should use in Latin *postquam etc.*; strictly speaking, in this case it is Past Gerund, *h. e.* it has the meaning

of the Past Gerund, although materially it is the same; *e.g.* "kumzăr zăun kitlo témp zălo? = after you have confessed, how much time passed?" "gară votzun kiteñ kăruñ? = after having gone home, what can I do?" In some of the examples given above it appears rather as a Present Gerund.

Instead of the Gerund in -un to express manner, cause *etc.* we may use also the Past Participle with "-pasun *or* -nimtiñ = on account of", or "vorviñ = by"; *e.g.* "to burgo sikleă vorviñ ušăr zălo = that boy having studied became clever".

3. *Past.* There are two Past Gerunds very different in their use.

a) The first in "tăts" is used like an Ablative Absolute of the Past Tense. Generally it could be translated by *cum* and the Past Perfect of the Subjunctive; yet the subject is not to be put in the Ablative, as in Latin. An example will make it clear: "Somi Jezu Krist iñ utrañ sangtăts gelo = after Jesus Christ spoke these words went away = *cum Jesus Christus haec dixisset, abiit*, or *his dictis abiit*". In some cases the subject is put in the Instrumental, as I say later on. Instead of this Gerund we might use the Past Participle with "uprănt"; *e.g.* "iñ utrañ sangleă uprănt gelo = *lit.* these words said after, went".

As appears from the given examples, this Gerund is not declined; because, generally speaking of Gerunds and Participles, only the forms ending in o are declined.

b) The 2nd Gerund (in -un) is the same, materially, as we have seen, as the Participle and as the Imperfect Gerund. Sometimes its meaning is of a Past Gerund as in the above examples: "kumzăr zăun kitlo témp zălo? = after you confessed, how long time is it?" It is somewhat similar, *e.g.* to the Latin sentence: *eo profecto multa mala nobis acciderunt.*

This Gerund is used 1) if '*and*' is omitted, viz. the preceding Verb is put in this Gerund, it may be in a Present or in a Past Tense. Although the Verb preceding '*and*' were in a Present Tense, yet the resulting Gerund is Past; because if we translate it literally, we get in English also a Past Gerund; *e.g.* "votsun itsăr=go and ask, *or* after having gone ask". 2) It is used to show time, elapsed, as in this and similar examples: "after he died, three years elapsed=to morn pāvon tīn vorsañ zāliñ". 3) It is used sometimes instead of the Conditional, as in Latin *quum* or *postquam* are used sometimes, although perhaps not quite correctly, instead of *si*. The 2nd case may be reduced to the first; in the second case too, we might use the Participle Past with "uprānt"; *e.g.* "to morn pāulea uprānt tīn vorsañ zāliñ".

4. *Future Gerund.* Properly speaking, this is not a Gerund, but the Future Passive Participle; in Latin it is called *Gerundivus*; *e.g.* "*faciendus*, *amandus*." It has the same use as the Latin *Gerundivus*, and it includes the meaning of necessity; hence it may be used instead of the Necessary Mood, chiefly in the periphrastic conjugation. Thereby we may express many English tenses which seem not to exist in Konkani; *e.g.* "you should have done it=yeñ tuveñ kărčeñ assḁleñ= *hoc a te faciendum erat or fuisset.*" Although properly speaking, it can be used only with Transitive Verbs, as it is passive, yet, as in Latin, so in Konkani, even Neuter Verbs may take this form; *e.g.* "*veniendum est*=yeuñčeñ assā". Sometimes it seems to have the meaning also of possibility; *e.g.* "kărtso= which must be done, *or* which can be done"; it can be used sometimes instead of the Adjectives in "sărko". I would almost say that this Gerund expresses also the effect of.., as in the example "poḍaso kărtā=causes to fall"; yet it is more natural to say that here "poḍaso" is Imperfect Subjunctive (which can have also this meaning), as its termination shows.

Materially it has the same form as the Participle Future Active; hence the context must decide whether it is Active, Passive or Neuter.

What has been said in this paragraph about the use of tenses must be understood only of the obvious cases and of the more common and more correct way of speaking; it is therefore neither exclusive, nor applicable to less obvious cases.

§ 2. Some other forms of Tenses

1. First I will mention some other forms of Verbs not expressly noted in Part II. §§ 2, 4; some of these have been hinted at in several places. I will put them here together.

Imperfect Indicative. Although commonly the vowel a is not changed into e in the Plural, yet sometimes I found this change. It does not seem to be very exact; hence, to have uniformity, we should not use the form in e.

Past Perfect Indicative. Some seem to use a full u, instead of ụ; *e.g.* "nidullo" instead of "nidụllo".

Past Conditionatum. The form "nidtoloñ assoloñ" is as common as "nidtoñ assoloñ".

Participles. The Participle in "-to", *i. e.* formed by adding only "-to" (-to, -teñ) to the root, seems to be used very seldom; yet I think that this form, if really used, has been used to avoid a more difficult pronunciation; *e.g.* "voḍ-to" and "dis-to" instead of "voḍ-tso" and "diš-tso". Hence this form does not seem to be correct and common. The Participle, or whatever the form in "-toñ" may be, which seems to be shortened from "-toloñ", is the same as the above Participle, but used, only joined to the Verb, not as a true Participle.

Among the Negative forms, remark the form, *e.g.* "dīna-tullo" instead of "diunatullo", the Participle of the Potential; *e.g.* "kărunk-nozo assollo"; and the Conditional "nida-nāñtcleār" instead of "nidanāñ zaleār". Recollect moreover the Imperfect in "sărko", the Participle in "tăssolo", the Negative Participle in -so meaning possibility and some other forms, if there be any more omitted in Part II. but explained in Part IV.

For the sake of convenience, I add a few words about "assā".

First instead of "assāñ" etc. some say "astāñ, astai" *etc.;* then the Verb would be regular. Some say that there is a small difference between the two forms: "astāñ" should mean

"I am and shall still be" *etc.* Moreover in the Past Tenses many say "ăssulo, ăssullo" *etc.* instead of "assolo", and change u into i, or e, instead of changing into o; *e.g.* "ăssilli, ăssellen". This form seems to be not very rare. Further some say "natulleār" instead of "nāñ asleār".

Some other forms both of "assā" and "zatāñ", as also of the Regular Verbs, may occur, which cannot be explained, else there will be no end; practice will teach you.

2. Besides these easy forms, there are some others more difficult, which depend on the modified meaning; *e. g.* we meet also the form "dusro apoilo assayet = it may be that another be called". This form seems to be Past Potential, which according to the paradigm, should be "apoyet assollo". Yet this would not render the meaning of the above English sentence, because the Konkani means "it was possible to call another, *or* it may be that another has been invited". Hence according to the English meaning we must invert the order, and instead of saying "apoyet assolo" we must say: "apoilo assayet". Perhaps we might explain this example more satisfactorily, by saying that this "apoilo assayet" is Present Passive of the Potential, as I explain below.

Some other forms similar to this may occur.

3. The most difficult and important forms are those which result from the different combinations of the simple, or also of the compound tenses in a finite mood. Hence it is rather a difficult task to enumerate all of them, on account of the different combinations. Therefore I will limit myself to laying down the fundamental principle, with some deductions or examples.

This principle may be expressed, in the most general form, thus: The forms given in the 2nd and 4th Part, are joined together according to the meaning; *e. g.* in some cases the meaning of a Future Tense is joined to the meaning of the Conditional Tense; then we must use the Contingent Future joined to the Conditional; *e. g.* "when thou shalt sit to eat with a prince, consider diligently what is set before thy face = kuvorāger seuši zaleār, tuje mukār gāleleā višyānt tsātrai kāṇge" (Prov. xxiii, 1). The Holy Bible expresses here not only, what would happen, if a certain condition is verified, but also that you may perhaps find yourself invited to take dinner with a prince.

At other times the meaning of a Conditional is joined to the Present; *e.g.* "if there is a man swift in his work, he shall stand before kings = yēk tzurk mānis assā zaleār, to rāyā dōstint rigtolo" (Prov. xxii, 29). A similar explanation is to be given here as above. And so many other similar combinations many occur, the knowledge of which can show a good Konkani scholar. As the reader sees, here we have a kind of periphrastic conjugation, but different from the Latin and English, because in Konkani both tenses are put, or may be put in a Finite Mood, whereas in Latin we have the Auxiliary Verb "*esse* = to be", joined to some Participle of the principal Verb. We may better understand this kind of conjugation, if we remember that in Latin we have also a similar construction, except that in Latin the Conjunction should be expressed; *e.g.* the last sentence could be translated into Latin thus: *si fiat* (*ut*) *adsit vir velox in opere suo, is coram regibus stabit.* Sometimes we meet very complicated forms of this kind, which, however, can be easily explained by supplying in our mind the Conjunction "móṇ = that"; *e.g.* "ani te dīs moṭve zāinān̄ zatit zaleār, kossolo jīv vānčasonān̄ = and unless those days had been shortened, no flesh should be saved" (Matt. xxiv, 22); consequently the construction of such Verbs is as if "móṇ" had been put. The Conditional Negative (nidanān̄ zaleār) seems to be of this kind; for this reason I said in § 1, that it should be conjugated in the first part; so "nidanai zaleār = if you do not sleep", or better "if it happens (that) you do not sleep". See another example p. 255, para. 1.

Remark that in this way we can not only translate sentences of the above kind, but also more simple sentences, and use it also for expressing the passive meaning; *e.g.* "he is bound"; no passive occurs in the Present; hence we can do so by employing the above plan; "bound = bāndlo", "is = assā"; hence "bāndlo assā" or perhaps also "bāndun assā". Of course such a proceeding is not indifferently allowed in all cases, we must consult also the use, for this is the key.

§ 3. Deficient and corresponding Tenses

In English and much more in Latin there are certain forms, besides the given regular ones, which you could hardly translate into Konkani, looking only to the paradigm. Therefore I will give here some general principles, reserving a more distinct explanation of each difficult form in particular, to the Appendix; you will find a great help for this purpose in the preceding paragraph, if you know it thoroughly; besides that, we may lay down these rules:

1. If you find in Latin or in English some form, for which you cannot find the corresponding one in Konkani, look whether that form is preceded and governed by some particle. If so, use the Participle Present or Future or Past, as the meaning requires, followed by the Postposition which corresponds to the Latin or English particle; *e. g.* "*Cum Marcus Antonium aggressus sit, ab Antonio occisus est*". Here we have the Perfect Subjunctive, which in Konkani does not exist. This *aggressus sit* is governed by *cum* = because", in Konkani "pāsun = on account of". Hence we may translate it with the Past Participle followed by the Postposition "pāsun". Thus we get "Mārk Antoničea angār poḍlea pāsun, Antonin takā jivsi mārlo = *lit.* Marcus on account of having assaulted Antony, has been killed by Antony".

This way is nearly always possible, if the Verb is governed by some Preposition or other Particle. I say "Preposition or other Particle", because although it is not a Preposition in English, we can employ usually the Postposition in Ḳonkani, provided the meaning does not reject it altogether. Moreover, although the Verb is not expressly preceded by a Particle, yet we should try, if possible, to translate it by a Konkani Postposition, because this form is more according to Konkani; *e. g.* "having heard his words, he went away = hīñ utrañ aikaleāñ uprānt gelo *or* hīñ utrañ aikun gelo".

2. Another way of translating the above given and similar examples is, to look whether there is a Particle or Conjunction corresponding to the English or Latin Particle. In the above example "*cum* = because" can be translated by "kiteāk moḷeār" *or* "dekun"; we can therefore use this Particle and employ the Indicative Past, instead of the Perfect Subjunctive. This is therefore the second way, useful in some cases only, to employ the corresponding tense of the Indicative, if we have not the tense of the Subjunctive exactly corresponding: "kiteāk moḷeār Mārk Antoničeā angār poḍlā" *etc.*

3. The third way is to see, whether the Conditional might be used instead of the defective tense, because this is another of the favourite tenses of Konkani; *e. g.* "themselves should do this work = taṅiñtz teñ keleār boreñ". Yet to express this "should do" and the like which imply the notion of a duty, but not rigorously, we could well employ "distā = appears"; *e. g.* "I should visit my friend = mojeā išṭāk bēṭ kārunk distā". We could use also the quasi-diminutive -so (see below).

4. A fourth way is to employ the periphrastic conjugation, joining the Participle required by the meaning to that tense of "assā *or* zatā", which is required by the context. This periphrastic conjugation in some cases is very easy; yet sometimes it is made in such a way, that it presupposes a certain knowledgo of the language. This more difficult kind of periphrastic conjugation is formed, as I said in § 2, not only by joining the Participle to "assā *or* zatā", but also by joining two tenses of finite mood; *e. g. si hoc fecerit, punietur.* Although this "*fecerit*" could be translated by the Conditional "keleār", yet it is much better to use this periphrastic conjugation "yeñ kārit zaleār, sikšā bogtolo = *lit. si fiat (ut) hoc faciat*".

5. If you cannot find at all, by the above rules, a tense corresponding to our tense, then, keeping in your mind the meaning, see whether one of the given tenses might in some way render the meaning of the English or Latin Verb; if not, we must change the sentence, keeping however the substance of the meaning.

This change is often to be made, because the nature of Konkani is very different from that of our languages; hence by not changing the sentence, we could not get an expression agreeing with Konkani. This is the way of translating into Konkani, English or Latin sentences, viz. to accommodate ourselves to the nature of the language, not to accommodate the language to our European grammars. This is the key to the Konkani language. If this is not taken into consideration, Konkani may seem very poor and deficient, whereas the poverty is only about English-Konkani sentences, not about true Konkani ones.

As I see that these observations are rather general, I will show in a table the correspondence of Latin and Konkani *difficult* tenses; "vātz = read, *lege*".

1. Vāts-unk (Supine) = 1) *ad legendum*, 2) *ut legam*,
3) *ut legerem*, 4) *lectum* (Supine) = in order to read;
5) *legendi* (e. g. *voluntas*) = of reading;
6) *legendo* (e. g. *paratus*) = to read.

The first four meanings are about the same. The two last are very nearly the same.

2. Vāts-so (Infinitive Absolute).
1) τὸ *legere* (*Neut.* "vāts-čeñ") = reading;
2) *legendi* (*voluntas*) = of reading;
3) *legens* = reading;
4) *lecturus* = (he) who will read;
5) *legendus* = to be read.

3. Vāts-tolo = *legens* (*qui legit*) = he who reads,—is reading.

4. Vāts-tā to (*qui*) *legit*, *is* (e.g. "vāts-tā to ušār burgo = *qui legit*, *is laudabilis puer est*) = (he who) reads, that...

5. Vāts-talo = *legens* (*qui legebat*); or, better, "vātstalo to = he who was reading".

6. Vāts-lo = *lectus* (= seldom *qui legit*, he who read) = read (not often used).

7. Vāts-lā to = *lectus*, which has been read, that...... (*qui*) *lectus*, *is*....

8. Vāts-lolo *or* vāts-ɥllo = *lectus* (*qui fuit or fuerat lectus*) = read. It means also "it had been read, *or* it has been read, *or* it has been truly read".

9. Vāts-tanañ = 1) *cum legeret*, 2) *cum legebat*, 3) *inter legendum* = while reading.

10. Vāts-un 1) *legens* (not meaning "*qui legit*" but "*legens est*") = reading;
2) *lectus* (as "vātsun assā = it is read");
3) *legendo* (manner and cause) = in or by reading;
4) *cum legisset* = having read.

11. Vāts-tāts 1) *cum legisset* or *lectus esset*, 2) *lecto* (*libro*), 3) *postquam legerat* = having read.

12. Vāts-an 1) *potest esse quod legam* = I may read;
2) *vellem legere* = I would like to read;
3) *legero* = (whatever) I shall have read.[1]

13. Vāts-iyet 1) *licet legere*, 2) *nihil obstat quominus legatur*, 3) *possum legere* (*physice*) = I may or can read.

14. Vāts-unk tanktā 1) *possum legere* (*physice*), 2) *licet* (*mihi*) *legere*, 3) *nihil obstat quominus legam* = I can read.

15. Vāts-an zaleār 1) *si fiat* (*ut*) *legam* = if I should read;
2) *si legero* = if I should (have) read.

---

[1] In this and similar sentences it seems that the Future in "-an" can be used correctly as 2nd Future.

Now let us give some examples of the tenses with Postpositions. The Principal Postpositions are "pāsun *or* pāsvot = on account of *or* for", nimtiñ = on account (not often used; "pāsun" is used instead of it), "vorviñ = by, through", "uprānt = after", "adiñ = before", "veḷār = in time, while, during" (this "veḷār" is the 2nd Locative of "véḷ = time"). Among these Postpositions "uprānt" usually governs the Past Participle[1], "Adiñ" is not joined, usually, to the Past Participle, but to the Participle in -tso; the others govern the Participle in -tso or the Past Perfect Participle, as the meaning requires. It is not quite correct, it seems, to use the Past Participle with the above mentioned Postpositions. "Uprānt" might be used with the Past Perfect Participle, when the meaning of the Past Perfect Tense occurs, although also in such a meaning the Past Participle is more common. Therefore

16. Vāts-čeā adiñ 1) *lectum ante*, or *antequam legam*,
2) *antequam legerem*,
3) „ *legerim*,
4) „ *legissem* = before I read, before I had read.

17. Vāts-leā uprānt = *lectum post*, or
1) *postquam legerim*,
2) „ *legissem* = after having read.

18. Vāts-čea veḷār = *dum lego* = while reading.

19. Vāts-ųlleā veḷār = *dum legerem* = while reading.

20. Vāts-čeā pāsvot 1) *ut legam*, 2) *ut legerem*,
3) *ad legendum*, 4) *lectum* (Supine)
5) *quia lego* = in order to read, on account of reading.

---

[1] What has been said above that the Past Participle is not commonly used, must be understood with some limitations; we might perhaps say that, if the Past Participle is used as an Adjective or in a similar way, in such a case, more frequently, it is changed into the Past Perfect Participle; so in the compound tenses formed with the Past Participle, the Past Perfect Participle is used; *e.g.* "āuñ gelloñ asleār = if I had gone". Yet euphony may require sometimes the Past instead of the Past Perfect Participle; *e.g.* "apoḷḷo".

21. Vāts-ụlleā pāsvot = *quia legi* = on account of having read.
22. Vāts-čeā vorviñ = *per lectionem*, 2) *legendo* = by reading.
23. Vāts-ụlleā vorviñ = by having read *etc.*

I said, there is no Past Infinitive as in Latin "*amavisse*". But this Infinitive is resolved by "ṃóṇ = *quod*, that", or by some other particle into a finite mood. The construction of "móṇ" will be explained below. The Future Infinitive, as in Latin *amaturum esse*, is resolved in a similar way into a finite mood by "móṇ" or some other particle. Yet sometimes there occurs a kind of construction similar to the Latin construction of the Accusative with the Infinitive, except that in Konkani the Instrumental is used instead of the Accusative, as the Infinitive has often a passive meaning; such Future Infinitive is the Absolute Infinitive, the termination of which is the same as the termination of the Future Participle. So we can say: "taṇeñ večeñ āuveñ čintāñ = I think that he will go, *puto eum iturum essē*". (*Cf.* p. 257, para. *f.*)

1. As in English, there are some tenses which seem not to exist in Konkani, on the other hand in Konkani there are some forms which are not used in English. One of these is the Past Participle, chiefly of the Verb "zatā = I become", which is inserted after Nouns followed by a Postposition, when we do not use it; *e. g.* "after mass = mis zaleā uprānt, *lit.* after mass done".

2. About the Participle governed by other Postpositions see Art. VI.

§ 4. Passive Voice

There is no regular passive form, how then can we express passive meaning?

First of all, let us distinguish passive meaning from passive construction; the second may be used, although there be no passive meaning; and again, passive meaning may occur without a passive construction. In this paragraph I speak especially of passive meaning; passive construction will be taken into consideration as far it is required for the explanation of the passive meaning, or, sometimes, although not absolutely required here, it will be touched upon only; the passive construction will be fully explained in Chapter III.

Now in order to answer this question, I say that there are many modes to express the passive meaning; the following modes are more in use.

1. There are some tenses which in Transitive Verbs have only or chiefly passive meaning. Those tenses are *Past*, *Perfect*, *Past Perfect*, *both Conditionals*, the pure *Imperfect Subjunctive*, the tenses with the form -iyet of the *Potential*, and with the form zāi of the *Necessary Mood*, the Participles derived from the *Past*, *Perfect*, *Past Perfect*, *Gerundive*. Moreover sometimes the following tenses: *Supine* and *Absolute Infinitive*, the Participle in -n or -un, and the Gerund in -täts, and, seldom, also that in -tanañ. The Intransitive Verbs also take a kind of passive form (as in Latin *ventum est*, *veniendum est*) in the Gerundive and also in the Infinitive and in the Gerund in -täts; *e. g.* "yeuñčeñ assā = *veniendum est*"; and always in the Necessary Mood with "zāi" and in the Negative form with "nozo". About this see Chapter III. In order to help our memory to retain all these tenses, we may say: *a*) the Past and the tenses derived from it (Perfect, Past Perfect, Conditional, Participles in -lo); *b*) Potential (-iyet) and Necessary Mood (-zāi, -tso); *c*) sometimes the forms in -täts, -un and -tso (či, čeñ) have passive meaning in the Transitive Verbs.

a) If the passive meaning occurs in the above tenses which usually are passive, nothing is to be done; for they are already passive. Their construction consequently is as if they were passive, although not entirely. Thus "mārlo" from "mār = beat", does not mean "I beat", but "I was beaten". Hence it appears that the different persons of Transitive Verbs in the Past Tenses, have not the same meaning as in Latin or English. For this reason, I did not put a Transitive Verb as an example of a conjugation. Yet the passive meaning is not so attached to those tenses as to exclude entirely the active meaning. Though seldom, yet sometimes active meaning occurs in those tenses.

If somebody thinks this is not a passive meaning, I say that we may at least suppose it as passive; because thus their construction is more easily understood; moreover these Verbs in their concord follow mostly such rules as if they were passive.

Consequently if we have to translate English sentences in which those tenses occur in active meaning, we have to do with them, what we should do in Latin with sentences of active meaning in which the Verbs "*vapulo* = I am beaten" or "*veneo* = I am exposed to be sold", should be used in Past Tenses, namely change the sentence into passive and then translate it into Konkani.

b) The tenses of which I said that they often have a passive meaning, are employed as passive, if the context requires it; and then it is clear, the Nominative is put in the Instrumental, although the Verbs were Intransitive which, as I said, sometimes, are used as passive; *e.g.* "tuveñ yeuñčeñ assā = *tibi veniendum est* (lit. *a te...*)".

Remark, however, that we might perhaps exclude from those tenses the Gerund in -tänañ. I certainly found it used also in passive meaning or form; yet this is not quite correct, at least I am inclined to think so. Moreover it seems that the Gerunds in -un and -täts can be considered as passive or active indifferently, at least often. The same seems to hold good for the other tenses of this *b*) class. In one word, if we have in English passive sentence in the tenses of this *b*) class, these tenses can be considered as passive, although we might consider them also as actiye. Such is not the case with the tenses of the *a*) class.

c) For the tenses which have no passive meaning, the easiest way is to change our passive voice into active and then translate it into Konkani, as we do in Latin, when we have to translate a passive sentence with a deponent Verb.

2. Another way, not always possiblo, is to use the Verb "zatā". A great many Konkani Verbs are compound with "kăr = do" and a Substantive, or some other part of speech as in Latin "*commonefacio* = *lit.* I make admonition, *admoni*-

tionem facio". As in Latin the Verbs in *facio* are made passive by substituting *fio* for *facio*, so in Konkani Verbs compounded with "kăr", are made passive by substituting "za-tā" = *fio* for "kăr-tāñ". This way of making the passive voice can be used not only in the tenses which have no passive meaning, but also in tenses which have a passive meaning. Hence it appears that in Verbs compounded with "kăr", the passive meaning in the above mentioned tenses can be expressed in two ways, viz. *a*) by employing "kăr" put in one of those tenses, *b*) by employing "zatā"; *e.g.* "suru kăr = begin, *lit.* make beginning"; "I begin my work = mojea kāmāči suru kărtāñ"; Passive: "mojea kāmāči suru zatā"; in the Past: "mōjea kāmāči suru zali *or* mojea kāmāči suru keli".

Somebody might say: this is not a true passive form, but a neuter Verb. I answer: grammatically speaking, this is true; yet it expresses in some way the passive meaning; and if we have no better forms, we must be satisfied with what we have.

3. Another way, suitable for some Causative Verbs, is this: Take away from the Causative Verb the causative sign (ăi, or ei, or oi, or i), or sometimes only i, the remainder will be the passive voice; *e.g.* "tsăḍai = increase", taking away ăi it remains "tsăḍ = it is increased" (*superabundat*); "paloăi = quench", "paloa = get quenched". The Verbs made causative by adding only i, very often (if not always) are made passive or Neuter, substituting a for i; *e.g.* "porti = turn", "portă = be turned". It is true this is rather a Neuter Verb; yet this too expresses in some way the passive meaning.

I said above "some Causative Verbs", because only the Intransitive Verbs made causative by adding "ăi *or* ei", can usually be made passive in such a way. And even the Intransitive Verbs are not always made passive by taking away the causative sign; *e.g.* "tsălai = cause to walk", taking away ai, you get "tsăl = walk". It depends, therefore, on the nature of the Verb. The Transitive Causative Verbs, by taking away the causative sign, become simply Transitive, whereas with the causative sign, they were double Transitive, *e.g.* "kăr = do", "kărăi = cause to do" (by another); "āḍ = bring", "āḍăi = cause to bring". About this point see Neuter Verbs, below, B., § 6.

4. The preceding ways might be called rather a supplement of the passive voice than the passive voice. The following can be called passive, although not general, viz. *a*) add the participle in -un to the Verb "zatā *or* assā"; *e.g.* "boroun assā = it is written"; "born zatā = it is filled, *impletur*"; or *b*) add the Past Participle in -lo of the principal Verb to "zatā *or* assā"; *e.g.* "*omnis collis humiliabitur* = sărvụ guḍo khālto astolo = every hill shall be brought low". Yet, in the 1st example there is not a pure passive meaning; "boroun assā" is corresponding to the Latin *scriptum est; e. g. in libro Moysis*, to the Italian *sta scritto*. Moreover such a mode is not in common use.

5. Another mode is to substitute for the Active Verb some Verb which in itself implies a passive meaning, although it has no passive form. This mode is used especially with Verbs compounded with "dī, gāl, kăr" *etc.*; *e.g.* "bāptizăr kăr = baptize", "bāptism gē = receive baptism"; "badlām gāl = put calumnies", "badlām gē = receive calumnies *or* be calumniated".

6. This, which I am going to speak of, is the most perfect mode of expressing the passive meaning, although this too is not general. On page 175, *l.* 26, I expressed the suspicion that there may be other Verbs besides "kātăr", which become passive by producing the vowel of the last syllable of the root. That suspicion has been changed into certainty, and although I have not as yet examples enough to establish a general rule, I can however say that there are many Transitive Verbs, which can express the passive meaning by producing or making the vowel of the last syllable of the root open, and this in all tenses; *e.g.* "tóp = prick", "tòp = be pricked"; "badăl =

change", "badāl = be changed"; "bór = fill", "bòr = be filled"; "gắḍ = found", "gāḍ = be found" (*or* happen); "móḍ = break", "mòḍ = be broken"; "vóḍ = pull", "vòḍ = be pulled" *etc.*

This rule supposes that that syllable has a closed vowel; what is to be done, if the syllable has a long or open vowel?[1] Then the rule does not hold good. There are, however, some Verbs ending in a long or open vowel, which can have both meanings, *i.e.* active and passive; *e.g.* "tās = ḥew" and "be hewn"; "pind = tear" and "be torn". Later, perhaps it may be found that there are many such Verbs; for the present this rule must be left incomplete, because longer consideration is required. Remark that by the above mentioned change of vowel, those Verbs can become either neuter or passive as the meaning requires; *e.g.* "suri katārtā = the knife cuts", "ruk katārtā = the tree is cut". This rule is in conformity with Sanskrit (see Max Müller, *l.c.* on p. 175).

7. Finally there is one way, yet doubtful, hinted at in Part II, page 134, § 4; *i.e.* some Verbs express the passive meaning by changing the o of the last syllable of the root into u; *e.g.* "fóḍ = break", "fuṭ = be broken"; "sóḍ = leave", "tuṭ = be left, get rid". But as these Verbs change also the consonant (ḍ into ṭ), somebody might think that "fóḍ" and "fuṭ" *etc.* are two different original Verbs. See another mode B., § 6.

B. Verbs in particular

§ 1. Zatā and assā

In many cases, especially in the conjugation, we must use sometimes "zatā", sometimes "assā", even in the same tense. When is the former to be used, and when the latter? This depends on their fundamental meaning. "Zatā" originally means "become", in Latin *fio;* it expresses therefore some act, some passage, real and metaphorical, from one state to another:

---

[1] About the difference between long and open, short and closed vowels, see page 2, *l.* 13.

"assā" means "to be", not any being, but existence either absolute, *i. e.* opposition to nothing, or relative, *e. g.* existence of prudence in a man; moreover it means to be in a place. Consequently "zatā" and "assā" correspond partially to the philosophical expressions *in fieri* and *in facto esse*. If the English "to be" is used to say, *e.g.* that "a man is good, bad...", then the Verb "zāun assā *or* zāun vortautā *or* vortautā" must be used. Yet if some, I may say, exterior quality is denoted, "assā" is used; *e.g.* "bāgil uktēn assā = the door is open". Nay, we find some examples in which "assā" is used also for true qualities: whether this be wrong or not, I cannot tell with certainty; doubtless such is not the general rule. It seems that "assā" used as Auxiliary Verb, can express also some quality. The Verb "to be" in Konkani is usually omitted in the Present, if it expresses quality; *e.g.* "Deu bhou boro = God (is) very good."

Therefore in the conjugation we must keep in view this fundamental meaning of the two Verbs, in order to know which Verb must be preferred; yet much practice is required for it. Nevertheless in some cases "assā" or "zatā" can be used indifferently.

The fundamental meaning of "zatā" can explain many cases in which this Verb is used when we should omit it altogether; *e.g.* "he came as governor = ădhipăti zāun ailo"; "obediently = khalto zāun"; "after mass = mīs zalea uprānt". The Konkani language loves to express by "zatā" the different stages through which a thing must pass, which in other languages are either understood or expressed simply by particles, affixes etc. The Verb "zāun assā" will be better understood by comparing the compound Verbs in -un (see below).

§ 2. Causative Verbs

We must carefully remark that the Causative Verbs are used not only when the causative meaning occurs in the usual form, *e.g.* do, cause to do; laugh, cause to laugh;

but also in many other cases in which the causative meaning is concealed by different expressions; *e. g.* "excite" may be considered as causative of "rise", hence we may express it by the causative form of "uṭ = rise". And so almost innumerable other English expressions, which cannot be rendered literally, can be expressed in a truly Konkani mode by some causative form, concealed in the English expression. You find many examples in the Dictionary. This is the proper way of getting at the nature of Konkani; some might try to translate English into Konkani, keeping the same form; and as this very form often does not exist, he will say that Konkani has no expressions for many English sentences. But first I could say the same of the English, *h. e.* that English has no expression for many Konkani expressions; because trying to translate literally Konkani into English, certainly often you will not find the corresponding English sentence. Secondly, I say that in Konkani very beautiful expressions are to be found, but unknown to those who complain about the poverty of Konkani.

Yet, as I remarked in Part II., not all Verbs have a causative form, especially those which have in their original non-causative form a causative termination; *e. g.* "borăi = write", "lăi = apply", "ulăi = speăk" *etc.* How can we distinguish those which can be made causative? Mostly the more commonly used causative forms are given in the Dictionary; but I could not put them all. Moreover some causative forms might be used, though they are not popular, (provided they be not *against* the nature of Konkani) because in this uncultivated language we cannot limit ourselves to the popular forms and words; of many things the common people everywhere have not even the idea. What is to be done with those Verbs which have not the causative form we are in need of? We must betake ourselves to some circumlocution. The most common Verb used for it is "lăi = apply" (see p. 145, *note* 3) which expresses a really causative meaning as the form in -ăi. Sometimes "dī = give" is also used; *e.g.* "sămzăun dī = give to understand, *or* cause to understand".

As regards the rule given in Part II. for making Causative Verbs, I need not say that there may be some other rare forms. The same rule could be laid down more clearly, distinguishing Verbs having the root ending in a pure consonant, Verbs ending in a vowel, and Verbs ending in ă. The Verbs ending in a vowel may again be subdivided into Verbs ending in a diphthong (au...) and Verbs ending in a pure vowel. For each case the rules are somewhat different; you may find them by comparing with § 1, p. 145, *notes* 2, 3 and *alibi*.

§ 3. Frequentative Verbs

They correspond to the Latin *dormito*, *cursito* etc. Sometimes the frequentative meaning can be expressed by the emphatic ts (see Part III., Ch. II.); *e.g.* "he goes often to that house = to tea gărăk vetats". Sometimes although seldom, the repetition of the same Verb expresses in some way the same idea, or "portun portun" is added to the principal Verb, yet, strictly speaking, this mode is emphatic rather than frequentative, or frequentative and emphatic mixed. Both ways cannot be used in every case; use is the master. The third way is to use some circumlocution; *e.g.* "tovoḷ tovoḷ = from time to time"; "săbăr păuṭi = many times"; "sovoi assă = custom is".

§ 4. Emphatic and exclusive Verbs

These are formed by -ts, as stated on p. 82. As to the exclusive meaning, I must say that -ts is not used commonly with the exclusive meaning with Verbs, but with Nouns etc. (see p. 82, *note*). Yet it sounds Konkani also with Verbs; hence if there be necessity, we might use it; *e.g.* "ăuñ poḷeitats = I only look". These Verbs differ from Solitary Verbs.

§ 5. Inceptive Verbs

They correspond to the Latin *splendescere*, *lucescere* etc. and to the English: "begin to say, to speak" etc. This meaning may be expressed in many ways, yet a thoroughly Konkani mode is to use the Verb "-lāg = *lit.* be attached"; *e. g.* "moṇunk lāglo = he began to speak"; "uzuāḍ zāunk lagtā = it begins to get light"; "porzālik zāun lagtā = it begins to become shining". We might use, although not always so elegantly, "suru zatā = *lit.* beginning becomes".

For the sake of convenience, I mention here another mode somewhat similar to the preceding one; our English: "come so far as, to...", and the Latin *eo pervenit ut* can be rendered with the very form, *i. e.* "pāu = reach"; *e. g.* "by not avoiding idleness, he came so far as to commit a great sin = ālsai kārn vóḍ pātak aḍarunk pāulo." This Verb "pāu" is used in some other elegant expressions, as practice will teach you.

§ 6. Neuter Verbs

There are many original Neuter Verbs; *e.g.* "rāu = remain", "tzāl = walk" *etc.* I do not mean to speak about these, as they have no peculiar difficulty, but about those which are connected with the Causative Verbs, as hinted at on p. 134, para. 3, and touched upon again in A., § 4; here they must be explained more distinctly. These Verbs are sometimes a mean, both as to meaning and form, between active and passive form; *e. g.* "kātār = cut", "kātār = get cut", "kātrailo = has been cut". They can indeed, as I said above, be used also to express the passive voice; yet strictly speaking, their first meaning is Neuter, partaking somewhat of the passive meaning too. At any rate their construction is not the construction of Passive Verbs, *i. e.* requiring the agent (if this is an animate subsistent agent) in the Instrumental, in the same way as the really Transitive Verbs, of which I spoke above. So we may say: "divo pāloatā = the light gets extinguished"; we may even say "funkin dīvo pāloatā = the light is extinguished by a blow"; but it does not seem the general use to say, *e.g.*, "teā mānāān dīvo pāloatā *or* pāloalā = the light is or has been extinguished by that man".

In order to simplify matters about Neuter Verbs connected with Causative Verbs, keep this simple rule: "by taking away from the Causative Verb those letters by which it became Causative, the Verb becomes what it was originally, *i.e.* Neuter or Transitive. Hence, as the Verbs ending in a pure consonant more frequently become Causative by adding ăi, by taking away ăi you get the original; and as the Verbs ending in a vowel, more frequently become Causative by adding only i, by taking away i you get the original Verb; and if the original Verb, in both cases, was a Neuter Verb, that is the Neuter Verb which we aim at". We might express this rule more simply thus: Many Verbs can be made neuter by adding one a to the root or by producing the vowel of the last syllable of the root. These two modes cannot be used indifferently; the first mode especially cannot be used if the Verb ends already in a or e. To this simple rule we must add these remarks or limitations.

1. Some Verbs seem to have a middle form between the causative and the original active form, *i. e.* a neuter form. This 3rd middle form is obtained, either by producing the last short vowel of the root of the original, or by adding to that root one a; *e. g.* "kātăr = cut", "kātrăi = cause to cut", "kātār = cut", *e.g.* the knife cuts; "tās = hew", "tāsăi = cause to hew", "tāsā = be hewn". Sometimes, instead of adding anything, the original form itself is used both in active and neuter meaning: "tās = hew, get hewn".

2. Some Verbs are used only or chiefly in the causative form; *e. g.* "goḷăi = chew"; some others are used only or chiefly in a neuter form and meaning.

3. We cannot from all Causative Verbs form a derived Neuter Verb, although in itself it would seem possible; use must be also considered.

4. The same Verb may sometimes have a merely neuter meaning, sometimes it may almost coincide with a Passive Verb; the context and the different combinations must decide;

e.g. "dīvo pāloalo = the lamp ceased to burn"; "dīvo funkin pāloalo = the lamp has been extinguished by a blow".

5. Consequently these Verbs too, sometimes, can be made passive in certain tenses in two ways, *i. e.* by using either the Neuter Passive Verb, or the Causative Verb in a tense of passive meaning; the first mode is not thoroughly passive and cannot be used when the agent is animate and subsistent; *e.g.* "dīvo funkin pāloala *or* mānšān divo pāloailā".

6. More frequently Verbs ending in a are neuter connected with a Causative Verb.

§ 7. Reciprocal Verbs

About this point I only remark, that the reciprocal form and meaning can be concealed, by some different expressions and way of thinking; then also we can use the reciprocal form, after having tried to give to the foreign expression a Konkani dress; *e.g.* "the father will betray the son, the son will betray the father"; although we can translate this as in English, yet we can use this shorter form: "bāpui ani pūt yekāmekā kuṭ kārtele".

§ 8. Reflective Verbs

The form "-itleāk" can be used not only in the meaning explained in Part II., but if it is applied to mental operations, can express a really logical reflexion; *e.g.* "āikalleñ tumče itleāk čintā = think over, ruminate what you have heard". Yet this meaning could be expressed also in some other way; *e.g.* by "portun = again", which is derived from "porti = turn" (transitive) *or* "portā = turn" (intransitive), corresponding exactly to the Latin *reflecto*.

§ 9. Dubitative and Quasi-diminutive Verbs

By the often mentioned -so we can express very elegantly and shortly these dubitative and quasi-diminutive Verbs. Some examples have been given in Part III., some in the Dictionary. Here only I remark that this -so cannot be used indifferently; *e. g.* it would not sound well "āuñ čiṇtāñ-so = it seems that I think"; because it would almost show that I do not know certainly whether I think or not. But of another I can say "to čintā-so = he seems to think".

As stated above, the affix -so gives not only a dubitative meaning, but also a diminutive one and the like; thus "to apleñ kām kărtāso distā" means not only "he seems to do his business", but also "he performs it perfunctorily"; "to čintā-so" means not only "he seems to think", but also "he shows inclination to think so and so" *etc.* Yet the original meaning from which the others are derived is dubitative. Further, remark that use sometimes does not allow us to employ this -so, although in itself it would seem right. Finally, many English sentences which cannot be rendered literally, can be rendered by this -so, which is a nice Konkanism; this happens especially in some dubitative or diminutive sentences; so, *e. g.*, we might express the English sentence: "I should do this and that" by this -so, "yeñ, teñ kărizāi-señ distā". In this last quasi-diminutive meaning it is not commonly used with Verbs; yet it does not seem to be against the nature of Konkani; consequently we might use it, if there be any urgent necessity.

As to its construction, it must be joined to the word which is affected by the dubitative or quasi-diminutive meaning; as above, the affected word is "kărizāi". It does not change the construction, just as if there were no -so; hence in the above example we must say -señ not -so; because the subject of that "kărizāi" is "yeñ teñ"; hence it must be put in the Neuter.

§ 10. Compound Verbs

1. *Compound Verbs in* -un

This kind of Verbs is compounded of the form -un or -n of one Verb and of another Verb in a finite mood; *e. g.* "pull down = kāḍn gāl = *lit.* drawing put". Here really there are two

Verbs, which, however, express one idea which in Latin and in some other languages, may be expressed by one Verb.

The way of understanding these Verbs is this: as this language sometimes has no Verbs in sufficient number to express a certaïn notion, what means does it employ? It divides, I may say, the idea into two parts, one of which is as *genus*, *determinabile*, *materia*, *i. e.* element to be determined, the other is like *differentia*, *determinans*, *forma*, *i. e.* determining element; both together give the whole notion; *e. g.* "choose = vintsun kāḍ = *lit.* seeking take out". The idea of choosing is divided into the first part, which is required in order to choose viz. to seek; and into the second part which follows the act of seeking, viz. to take out or to take up. Consequently the Verb in -un expresses the *genus*, the *materia*, the *determinabile*, and the means by which something is obtained; the other Verb expresses the *differentia*, the *forma*, the *determinans* and that which is obtained. This manner, although it seems to be a sign of poverty, is, however, a great nicety and elegance of Konkani, and far superior to our European manner of expressing the same thing. Many of our simple Verbs must be translated in this way. This is another means of getting at the nature of Konkani. Which are those Verbs? You find many in the Dictionary; here I can only say that such Verbs are especially those, which explicitly or implicitly involve the above mentioned compound notion of means and end, determining element and element to be determined; yet the right use of them is not so easy. Moreover there are some consecrated by universal usage, others which, although right in themselves, are not in use. Many Verbs compounded with an Adverb or with a Preposition, are also translated often by this kind of Verbs. The English Preposition sometimes can be omitted; *e. g.* "go away = votz"; sometimes it can be rendered by a Konkani Postposition or Adverb, *e.g.* "go before = mukār votz"; sometimes it can be translated by this kind of Verbs, *e. g.* "pull down". "Pull" could be rendered by "kāḍ", but the Preposition "down" changes somewhat the meaning, *i. e.* "by pulling, put it down"; hence we may translate "kāḍn gāl". This kind of Verbs is so peculiar to Konkani, that it is used also when there is no strict necessity; *e.g.* "show" could be translated by "dākei"; yet Konkani prefers to say "dākon dī = by showing give *or* having shown give, *or* give shown"; so also "offer" is translated by "beṭoun dī" instead of the simple "beṭei"; "dison yetā" instead of "distā = appears". This shows that this kind of Verbs is not used only on account of poverty, but as an elegance of Konkani. Here let us put down only a few ex amples: "apoun āḍ = call, *lit.* having called bring"; "kāṇeun ye (or shortened 'kāṇ ye') = having taken come"; "dāṇ dī (exactly 'dāḍn dī') = send, *lit.* having sent give"; "ukoln dór = raising keep, *lit.* keep raised"; "āḍn dī (vulgar 'āṇ dī')= purchase"; "rāun ulei = stammer, *lit.* speak stopping". Many such Verbs are used also by common people very elegantly. Such Verbs are used also in cases in which they seem out of place, yet well considered they add much beauty. So, to say "receive the Blessed Virgin as a Mother" can be translated "Ankuāri Māriek āuoi kārn kāṇge = *lit.* having made the Virgin Mary (as) your mother, take her". And so in many other similar examples which cannot be taught but by practice. We shall see below that many of our Adverbs are expressed in this way.

2. *Other Compound Verbs*

In Latin, in English and in German especially, the Verbs compounded with Postpositions are often difficult; not so in Konkani. I have already said elsewhere that the composition of Postpositions (or Adverbs) with Verbs, seems to be a mere apposition, viz. so many Latin and English Verbs compounded with Prepositions (or Adverbs) are translated, if the Adverb or Postposition is to be expressed, by simply joining the Adverb to the Verb; more frequently the Latin Prepositions in compound Verbs must be translated by an Adverb; *e. g.* "proceed = mukār vots"; sometimes the compound Verbs in -un must be used. Moreover there are other kinds of compound Verbs (see p. 177).

What case do they govern? This depends on the word which is united to the simple Verb. Generally speaking to know what case is to be used, try to make a literal translation of the Konkani word into English or Latin, and the case which would be required in using this literal regular translation, is the case which is to be used in Konkani. There are some exceptions, but very few; *e.g.* "saitānāk pāṭi-kār = send back Satan", although the simple Postposition "pāṭi" seems to govern the Original (or better "pāṭleān", because "pāṭi" seems not to be used as Postposition). Probably "saitānāk" is here governed by "kār", not by "pāṭi".

Art V. Adverbs

§ 1. Adverbs in General

If we consider as Adverbs only those parts of speech, which have a form grammatically distinct from the form of the other parts, then we could almost eliminate the Adverb from the Konkani Grammar, because except the original Adverbs given almost all in Part II., the others usually called Adverbs, have either the form of a Noun in the Instrumental Case, or of an Adjective, or of a Gerund *etc.* Further the original Adverbs themselves are changed into Adjectives, we may say for the slightest reason. Nevertheless, if we consider this question from a higher point, *i. e.* from the regions of philosophy, we are not allowed to eliminate so many Adverbs. I explain my meaning. Adverb in its essential notion expresses some determination of the Verb, whereas the Adjective expresses something of the Noun *cui adjicitur.* Hence it follows that those parts of speech which determine the Verb are to be considered as Adverbs, although they may have a form of

Adjective or Gerund etc. After this fundamental observation, let us go to say something about their use.

1. There are not many original Adverbs, *i. e.* parts which determine the Verb, grammatically distinct from the other parts of speech, as stated above. How does Konkani express so many other Adverbs? It uses other parts of speech, especially Adjectives, Gerunds, Nouns.

a) As to Nouns, this happens also in our European languages; *e. g.* the Ablative of the Noun is used to express manner just as the Instrumental in Konkani; *e. g.* "with difficulty = kăšṭān"; hence there is no need of further explanation.

b) As to Adjectives, Konkani not only uses them for Adverbs, but, which is peculiar to Konkani, also lets them agree with a word, with which they have no strictly logical connexion of agreement; *e. g.* "to boro vhaztā = he plays well." Here the word "boro" determines "vhaztā"; yet it agrees with "to", with which it has some remote relation. Yet we might use also the Neuter: "to boreñ vhaztā". The first mode, although perhaps apparently not so logical, seems to agree better with Konkani.

c) As to Gerunds, Konkani is particularly fond of expressing Adverbs, chiefly of manner, in a way similar to the compound Verbs in -un (see above § 10), because the Gerund in -un expresses also manner; so instead of using, *e. g.* "čitin = attentively", the Noun with the Gerund in -un of the required Verb is used. This required Verb is often "zatā"; hence we find so many Gerunds with "zāun". The meaning of such Adverbs is similar to the meaning of the compound Verbs in -un, nay we might perhaps consider this kind of Adverbs not different from that kind of Verbs in -un. Such a mode of using the Adverbs is similar to the Kanarese mode in ಆಗಿ (āgi), Participial Gerund of "ಆಗು (āgu) = become", and to the Tuḷu mode in ಆದ್ (ādụ), Participial Gerund of "ಆಪಿನಿ (āpini) = to become"; "zāun" is exactly the Participial Gerund of "zatāñ = I become". The construction of such a kind of Gerundial

Adverbs is not different from the construction of Gerunds (see above).

2. Many of our Adverbs are translated by Adjectives; namely, if the Adverbs are in a sentence which is explicitly or implicitly a relative sentence, then the relative sentence is changed into a participial sentence: but such a sentence is somewhat different from the common participial sentences; because here instead of changing the Verb into a Participle, the Adverb (or Postposition) is changed into an Adjective; *e.g.* "you, who are far come near = tuñ poislo lagiñ ye". In such a case sometimes a strange thing happens, viz. the English Adverb is translated by a Konkani Adverb which seems to have the contrary meaning; *e.g.* "go far = lagšilo votz"; "come near = poislo ye". The reason of this paradox has been given at p. 172, para. 4. Some derived Adjectives have not been given on pp. 147-150; *e.g.* "purto" from "puro", *etc.*

3. Finally remark that the same words may be used either as Adverbs or as Postpositions according to the different combinations to which they are liable; *e.g.* "adiñ, mukār, uprānt".

§ 2. Adverbs in Particular

Now each Adverb given in Part II. Ch. V. should be carefully explained, and this would be, no doubt, worth while; but as this would require too long a time, I shall limit myself to the most necessary observations, leaving some more peculiar ones to the Dictionary. Some Adverbs, however, will be explained in Art. VI., because many Adverbs are also Postpositions.

1. *Correlative Adverbs.* As we have found Correlative Pronouns, so we find also Correlative Adverbs; *e.g.* "zăiñ—thăiñ = where—there, *or* whither—thither"; and as the first of the Correlative Pronouns can be omitted, so also the first of the Correlative Adverbs can be omitted; *e.g.* "whither I go, thither you cannot come = āuñ vetāñ thăiñ tumiñ yeunk nozo". In English too, one of the Correlative Adverbs could be omit-

ted, but, usually, the second of them, or better (as there is no fixed place for them) the "ἀπόδοσις"; whereas in Konkani the "πρότασις" is omitted. This is the best way, it seems to me, to understand some elliptical sentences, which are very different from the English or Latin forms of speech. Interrogative, Relative etc. Adverbs need no explanation, or will be learnt by practice.

2. *Adverbs of place.* If used absolutely, they are as given in Part II. Ch. V.; if the notion "through...." is expressed, then they are changed into an Adjective and put in the Instrumental according to the rule (see pp. 212, 213, para. 7). If the notion "from..." is expressed, they can be used followed by "thāun" or some other word without making any change; this must be understood also of other Adverbs. Sometimes the original Adverb is used also in this meaning. So we say "haṅgāčeān=through here"; "tāntleān=through there"; "poisileān=through a distant place"; "haṅgā thāun=from here"; "āz legun=from to-day". About this point we must remark, that not only can the same word be used both as an Adverb and as a Postposition as stated above, but also the Instrumental of the derived Adjective can be used as Postposition. So we can say: "to moje mukāveleān vetā", instead of "to moje mukār vetā=he goes before me".

According to the above explanation we could not use the form in -eān, if the Adverb is used absolutely; yet sometimes we meet such a form: I doubt about its correctness. Consequently we say "to mukār assā, to pāṭi assā" (some also say "mukāveleān, paṭleān assā)"; "to mukāveleān vetā *or* mukār vetā"; "to moje mukār vetā" (*Postp.*); "to moje paṭleān vetā". In the last example we cannot use "pāṭi"; then the meaning would be "he comes back, returns". This "pāṭi" therefore seems to be used only as Adverb.

3. Some of the given derived Adjectives are seldom used; *e.g.* "vegiñtso".

4. To some Adverbs the Particle -gi gives an indefinite

meaning; *e. g.* "khăiṅgi gelo = (he) has gone somewhere, (he) has gone I do not know where"; "kosseṅgī kelāñ = in some way or other has been done (somehow or other)". To express such a meaning it seems to be necessary to add this -gi. Moreover it can be added as a pleonasm to the Correlative Adverbs. (As to the correlative pronominal sentences see p. 241.)

Art. VI. Postpositions

§ 1. Postpositions in General

These are just the opposite of the Adverbs, because the Konkani Postpositions are as frequent as the Adverbs are rare, I mean grammatically. Many English or Latin tenses are expressed by Postpositions (see above); some Conjunctions too can be rendered by a Postposition; *e.g.* "because = pāsun", Latin *propter*. The Postpositions are, I may say, the favourite part of speech of Konkani. But on the other hand they are not so frequent as in English; because so many Verbs compounded with Prepositions can be rendered by a simple Verb. Moreover we have seen (see pp. 5, 227) that sometimes they are changed into Adjectives. This use of Postpositions renders the sentences more simple; because out of two or more sentences only one sentence is formed, which, however, is so long and complicated that we do not gain much perspicuity.

1. About the case governed by Postpositions you have the list in Part II. Ch. VI. If some other Postposition should occur, what case does it govern? As far as my knowledge goes, the Original: I do not remember now to have ever found (except "pois" which can be joined to the Dative, *e.g.* "santipoṇāk pois = far from sanctity") any Postposition, which governs the Dative or Nominative besides the given ones. Yet remark that it is not prohibited to join them, if the meaning requires it, also to the 2nd Locative as hinted at on p. 153, para. 6; *e.g.* "from the carriage = gāḍier thāun", here we want to

express descending from a high place. Perhaps some Postpositions might be joined also to some other case.

2. The Postpositions can be joined to Nouns, Pronouns (sometimes to Adjectives too), Verbs, *i. e.* Participles, Adverbs.

3. As regards the union of two Postpositions (see p. 153, para. 6) this must be understood not only of the 2nd Locative, (for I said that the termination r of the Locative can be considered as a contraction of "voir"), *i. e.* not only can a Postposition follow the 2nd Locative, but also two real Postpositions can be joined. This takes place when two notions, as stated at p. 153, are to be expressed, which are not sufficiently expressed by one Postposition. The Postposition which more frequently is joined to other preceding real Postpositions or Postposition-Adjectives is "thāun"; *e. g.* "moje lagiñ thāun pois votsā = *lit.* go from near to me far"; if we consider that "pois" as a Postposition, we would have three Postpositions together. Yet here "pois" seems to be rather an Adverb. "Dēvā kāḍe thāun sărvụ ailāñ = *lit.* everything came from near to God". As to the example given *l. c.* "sărgarānt", in which not two pure Postpositions, but two cases are confounded, *i. e.* the terminations of the 1st and 2nd Locative together are added, this, I say, is not in common use. I have put it down, because I have heard or read it somewhere, but this must be considered as an incorrect form. To express such an idea this expression is more common "ūnts sărgār = aloft in heaven", "ūnts mezār = aloft on the table"; or the 1st Locative only will suffice.

4. About the change of Postpositions into Adjectives see p. 227. Further what is said in Art. V. about the change of Adverbs into Adjectives *servata proportione* holds good also for Postpositions.

About the construction of Postpositions, chiefly about the long sentences which they govern, see Ch. III., below.

§ 2. Postpositions in Particular

Here too, it would be worth while to explain each Postposition; I must limit myself to these few points.

1. First, there are some Adjectives derived from Postpositions not laid down in pp. 147-150; *e. g.* "phuḍlo" from "phuḍe"; "uprāntlo" from "uprānt" *etc.* Moreover some other Postposition not given there may occur; *e.g.* "višyāñt = about", Latin *de;* "bări = Latin *instar*"; this last, "bări", although perhaps strictly not a Postposition, has, however, nearly the same construction: (see also p. 225 para. 8). About this "bări" remark further, that some use "porri" instead of "bări", chiefly in religious matters.

2. "Moṇasăr, păriant = until". "Moṇasăr", if used with Verbs, is often shortened into "săr" (see Appendix to the Grammar). Both "păriant" and "moṇasăr" seem to be used indifferently. Both can be used also with Verbs, although with Verbs more frequently "moṇsăr" is used.

3. "Porteñ" is derived from "porti = turn"; hence it means "turning" and is like a Participle, which must be declined as I said of "kosso" *etc.*; as to the meaning, it is a Postposition, yet grammatically it is an Adjective; *e. g.* "the father will be against the son, and the son against the father = pūtu̧ bāpāk porto astolo, ani bāpai putāk". If we say "porteān" or "portun", the meaning is "again".

4. "Āḍ" and "virōdh" are, very often, used indifferently with "porteñ".

5. "Phuḍeñ" is a strange Postposition, because it seems to have two contrary meanings, *i. e. after* and *before.* Yet this is only in appearance; its original meaning is *close to*, but still in future; hence according to the way of conceiving such a meaning, it can be expressed either by "before" (close to, in future) or "after" (after this time, in future). So we can say: "yea phuḍeñ pātak kărnakā = in the time which is be-

fore thee *or* before thy face (in future) do not commit sin". "Phuḍeñ" seems to come from "phuḍa = future time".

From it the Adjective "phuḍlo = future", or that which is immediately after the present, or before another thing, *e. g.* "Paskā phuḍlo upās = Lent, or fasting which is before Easter".

6. "Uprānt, magir". Both have the same meaning "after" as in Latin *post*; "uprānt" seems to be more used as Postposition, and joined as far as possible with the Participles of Verbs; "magir" is more common as Adverb; *e.g.* "kām kelcā uprānt = after having performed the business"; "āuñ magir yetāñ = I come afterwards". Yet sometimes they can be used indifferently. "Uprānt" and "magir" are usually joined to the Pure Past Participle.

7. "Paṭleān" is the Instrumental of "paṭlo" derived from "pāṭi = back". It may be used also as Adverb, *e.g.* "to paṭleān yetā = he comes behind". Yet, although it be used as Adverb, as to the meaning it may differ from "pāṭi"; so "to pāṭi yetā = he comes back"; "to paṭleān yetā = he comes behind (after us)". The reason of such difference may be this: "pāṭi = back", "paṭleān = through that way which is measured in going back, or behind" (see above).

8. "Voir" properly means "upon"; yet figuratively it can be used also to express "in", but with a certain emphasis; *e.g.* "saitān teā mānsā voir assā = the devil is in that man". Instead of "voir" we may use the 2nd Locative, but not in every case; use must be consulted.

9. "Săkăl, khāl, tala, ponda = under". Sometimes they can be used indifferently; in many cases however they must be distinguished: "săkăl" seems to be used rather of material things and of a non-contiguous inferiority, and, more frequently as Adverb, *e. g.* "săkăl poḍlāñ = it fell down; "khāl" more commonly is used in figurative meaning, *e.g.* "to mojea khāl assā = he is under my jurisdiction". The Goanese use "khāl" also for material things. "Tala" and "ponda" are used more

frequently for contiguous inferiority; "ponda" is the most common Postposition to express "under" and "below".

From these Postpositions we have the derived Adjectives: "săkăilo, khălto, pondlo".

10. "Kăḍe" has been explained elsewhere. About it remark only the Adjective "kăḍtso" which is used in a strange manner, to express "from" instead of "thāun"; the reason has been given elsewhere, *i. e.* "kăḍtso = that which is *or* was near"; "Somi Jezu Krist Bāpā kăḍtso āilo = our Lord Jesus Christ came from the Father, *lit.* came being near to the Father". Some say "găḍe" instead of "kăḍe".

11. "Bhāir = out" is used not only to express place, but also figuratively; *e. g* "gărje bhāir = without necessity"; "more than I am obliged = kăideā bhāir"; "beyond your power = podvie bhāir" *etc.*

12. "Vin, *or* viṇe" is not often used, because the English "without" is better expressed by the Negative Gerund in "-tanañ" or by the Conditional Negative, or by "šivāi". Nevertheless it occurs in this and similar meanings: "without necessity = gărje viṇe", "without comparison = sări vin" *etc.* If "without" occurs with a Verb, it is expressed by the Negative Gerund, as I said; if it occurs with a Noun, then it is translated sometimes by the negative form of the Verb, if such a Verb is understood; *e. g.* "without communion man cannot live a supernatural life = kumgăr kāṇeināstanañ săimba-vorto jīv jieunk nozo." We have seen already that "bhāir" can be used also in the meaning of "without".

The derived Adjective "bhāilo" means "exterior", *e. g.* "bhāileo mādri = exterior Nuns" (Tertiaries), as they say here in Mangalore.

13. "Sañgata = with" properly means "society"; and even in this meaning of "society", it is replaced sometimes by "kăḍe", if our "with" expresses directly the term of an action; *e. g.* "to have to do something with"; consequently "sañgata" seems to express directly "company". Notwithstanding in

some cases "sañgata" and "kăḍe" *or* "lagiñ" might be used indifferently; *e.g.* "Dēvā kăḍe" *or* "Dēvā sañgata meḷon mănis ajapañ kărtā = man united with God makes wonders". In this example however "sañgata" is better used.

14. "Viñgăḍ", strictly speaking, seems to be an Adjective, meaning "separated"; yet its use corresponds to the English "apart, aside"; *e.g.* "Somi Jezu Kristān apostolānk viñgăḍ dovorleāt = Our Lord Jesus Christ took apart the Apostles." Instead of "viñgăḍ" we can use "veg!o = separated". Some say that "veg!o" is used for persons, "viñgăḍ" for things, yet such difference is somewhat doubtful.

15. "Pasun, pasvot". Commonly these two Postpositions can be used indifferently in the meaning of "on account of" and "in order to" or also "for", Latin *pro*. Yet if I were to judge from the use made by some of these Postpositions, I would say that "pasun" means "on account of", "pasvot = in order to *or* for". Future considerations may determine this point.

16. "Khātir" seems to be more commonly used in the meaning of "for", *e. g.* "moje khātir māg = pray for me."

17. "Nimtiñ" can be used in the same meaning of "pasun", *i. e.* "on account of"; it is rather rare.

18. "Părmāṇe" seems to be an old Original, from "părmāṇ = manner", not used except in the Original. We have a sign of its origin from a Substantive in the sentence; "făvoteā părmāṇe = in a proper way". Notwithstanding it follows the rules of the Postpositions; so we say "kăideā părmāṇe = lawfully"; "šastrā părmāṇe = according to or in conformity with religion"; "povitrạ pustakānt sănglea părmāṇe khăiñ mhĕḷeñ sărgăr rigănāñ = as it is said (according to the said) in the Holy Bible, no unclean thing enters into heaven". This Postposition can be joined also to the Past Participle.

19. "Bhountaṇiñ" (not "băuntaṇeñ", as on p. 152). It is derived from "bhouñ = go round"; it seems to be the Instrumental (see p. 24, para. 5) of some old Substantive, no more in use. It is used in this and similar sentences; "Roman

pārzā yeun Jerūzaleā bhountaṇiñ veḍo mārteli = the Roman people will come and put a siege around Jerusalem."

20. "Veslean" seems to be the Instrumental of the obsolete Substantive "veslo"; yet it is more natural to say that it comes from "issiñ = in this way"; "issilo = which is in this side", "issileān = through this side"; the initial v is prefixed as this is often the case with words beginning with i.

21. "Dikān" is the Instrumental of "dik = side, direction": hence it may require sometimes the Original of the Adjective instead of the Original of the Noun. From the explanation given of "vesleān" we can learn that "dikān" and "issileān" are synonyms indeed, yet not to be used always in the same way. In order to know which must be used, recollect that "dikān" means "in the direction of", "issileān" means "in this side *or* through this side"; in a particular case consider which of these two literal translations is more suitable. Examples: "In what direction is Europe? = Vilāyet khāinčea dikān assā?" Here we could not use so properly "issileān". "Europe is in this side = Vilāyet issileān assā"; "the country called Gnosis is in the direction of the place called Energeia = Gnosis moḷḷo gāuñ Energeyā moḷḷea gāuñčeā dikān assā."

22. "Thāun", as hinted at, means "from", as in the sentences which express distance, real or metaphorical; *e. g.* "from good resolutions to execution there is a great distance; therefore the Holy Bible says: desires kill the lazy man = boreā ničevā thāun sovoi pāriant bhou pois assā; teā pasun povitrą pustak moṇṭā ki khušeo aḷsi mānšāk jivsi mārtāt móṇ". This Postposition has been explained elsewhere also.

23. "Poltoḍi" originally means "on that side"; *e.g.* "of the river *or* beyond"; in the metaphorical meaning of "beyond" it seems not to be often used; "bhāir" is rather employed in such a meaning.

From "Poltoḍi the Adjective "pelo = ulterior" is derived; it means exactly "that which is beyond...."; *e.g.* "pelo burgo yeundi = let the boy come who is beyond the....".

24. "Altāḍi" is the opposite of "poltoḍi": the derived Adjective is "āilo".

25. "Vorviñ" means "through", in German "*durch*" as in the sentence: "through continual prayer we shall save our soul, and obtain from God every thing = khālinastanañ magčeā vorviñ amiñ amtso ātmo bačāu kārteleāuñ ani Dēvā thāun sārvụ kurpā zoḍteleāuñ". It means therefore "means, instrument, cause".

26. "Šivāi *and* karit" correspond to *practer; e.g.* "tače šivāi = beside this". They are used also to express the English "except"; *e.g.* "except sin nothing is a true evil = pātkā šivāi vāiṭ kāiñ nāñ". By this Postposition we can also translate elegantly many negative conditional sentences; *e.g.* "if we do not suffer now with Jesus Christ, we shall not enjoy with him everlasting joy = Jezu Kristā sañgatā amiñ atāñ sosanāñ zaleār, tačeā sañgatā sasnāčeñ sukh bhogunk nozo". The meaning itself of "šivāi" seems to exact, if joined to a Verb, the Participle in -tso; yet there may be some rare case in which some Past Participle might perhaps be used.

27. "Badlāk" comes from "badāl = to exchange" hence literally it means "at or in the substitution of"; thereby its meaning and use are already known.

28. "Suāter" is the 2nd Locative of "suāt = place"; yet its construction is as if it were a Postposition. I must however acknowledge that its use is rather complicated, and connected with the construction of Participial sentences; *e.g.* "by unworthy communions, instead of receiving God's grace, you drink your own judgment = uo uṇḍo fāvonāiñ astanañ seutā to, ani Somia kals pietā to kurpā zoḍče suāter apṇākạts zāḍti seutā ani pietā móṇ Sāñ Paul sangtā".

29. "Višyānt" is like the Latin *de* or the English "about", *e. g.* "if we love God, we shall speak of Him willingly = amiñ Dēvātso mōg keleār, tačeā višyānt kušālāyen uleizāi".

From "višyānt" I found somewhere derived the Adjective "višyātso = which is about, relative", *e.g.* "Dēvā višyātso niāl =

meditation about God"; many do not acknowledge it as a Konkani word; yet it seems to sound well.

Art. VII. Conjunctions

§ 1. Conjunctions in General

We can say of the Conjunctions what we said of the Adverbs, viz. that if we understand by this name any word which performs the office of the English or Latin Conjunctions, there may be many Conjunctions; if we understand words which *formaliter* and grammatically also may be Conjunctions, distinct from all other parts of speech, we must say that there are few; because *a*) many of our Conjunctions are expressed by Postpositions, as Konkani is very fond of them, *e. g.* "because" is often expressed by "pasun" with the Participle: "you commit sin, because you do not pray = māgṇeñ kārnatullea pasun pātkānt poḍtai". We could use also the true Conjunction "kiteāk moḷḷeār"; *b*) sometimes the Pronouns are used instead of Conjunctions, *e. g.* "as—as = kosso—tasso, *or* zosso—tosso; *c*) sometimes the English Conjunction is omitted in Konkani, *e. g.* "in one or in the other way = kossogi"; "is it right or wrong? = tsuk sāmagī?" *d*) The Negative Conjunctions are expressed by the Affirmative Conjunctions, with the Negative Particle joined to the Verb, *e. g.* "a proud man does not please either God or man = gārvi mānis Dēvāki mānšānki mānuānāñ = *lit.* to God also to men also does not please".

§ 2. Conjunctions in Particular

A few words about the most common Conjunctions:

1. "Kiteāk" means "why? *lit.* to what?" Dative of "kiteñ". Instead of "kiteāk" we may use "kitea pasun? = for what?" as in Latin *propter quid*, instead of "*cur*". Its construction is regular, *e. g.* "kiteāk poḷetai tuñ teñ kuskuṭ tujea bāvāčea doḷeānt ani čintinai to tóḷ zo assā tujea doḷeānt? = and why

seest thou the mote in thy brother's eye; but the beam that is in thy own eye thou considerest not?" (Luk. vi. 41.)

2. "Kiteăk moḷeăr = *lit.* to what if you say", used for "because". The construction is regular. Both are put in the beginning of the sentence, as in English. Sometimes only "kiteăk" is used. Instead of it very often a corresponding Postposition (pasun....) with the Participle, is used, or

3. "Dekun". If this is used as a Postposition, it is put at the end of the sentence, *e. g.* "Dēu lekăvorto boro dekun amiñ tatso mōg kărizăi = we must love God, because he is infinitely good." Sometimes "dekun" and "kiteăk" are joined together thus: "....kiteăk Dēu boro dekun". The first mode seems to be better. "Dekun" can be used also as an illative particle; then it is put in the beginning; *e.g.* "Dēu amtso rătsnăr, dekun amiñ tači sevā săkri kărizăi = God is our Creator, therefore we must serve Him". "Dekun" is used also as Postposition, instead of "pasun", but seldom; *e.g.* "mănis bhou ăskăt, tea dekun takā Dēvăči kumok zăi = man is very weak, on this account he is in need of God's help".

4. "Thăr" is commonly used as an illative particle in the beginning of a sentence: "souñsăr amkăñ phoṭaitā, thăr amiñ kiteñ kărizăi? = the world deceives us, then what to do?" It is joined to "zăr" and "zări" (see below).

5. "Puṇ=but", Latin *sed*, German *aber*. If "but" corresponds to the German *sondern*, *i. e.* in oppositions, more frequently "bogăr" is used. When this *but* is in connexion with "not only" and the like, the preceding "not only..." is translated by the Negative particle and the emphatic -ts; *e.g.* "God is not only good but also just = Dēu năints boro, bogăr nītivănt".

It seems that the English "but" is very often omitted in Konkani, unless there be a peculiar emphasis upon "but".

6. "Thări" is compounded of "thăr" and "i = also, although". It may be used absolutely as in this sentence: "forty years long I was near to this generation, yet it did not know my

way = āuñ čāḷis vorsāñ ye kulie lagiñ assullo, thări tiṇeñ moji vāṭ voḷkunk-nāñ (Ps. xcvi. 10, 11). It can be used also joined to "zari" (see below).

7. "Zaleāri" is compounded of "zaleār" and "i", hence the literal meaning is "although it happened". It can be used however also absolutely, *i.e.* as the English "yet *or* notwithstanding"; *e.g.* "yeñ vojeñ bhāradik khărentz; zaleāri sosazāi = this burden is heavy indeed, nevertheless (we) must suffer it".

8. "Zărtăr, zărităr" (see p. 155). Here only about its construction. The first can be used to express the conditional (*if*) and the second for the permissive (*although*). If the meaning is merely conditional or permissive, then they govern more frequently, the tenses indicated at p. 251. Yet sometimes the conditional or permissive notion is mixed with some other notion (see p. 268, para. 3); then we might use that tense which comes nearer to the notion which is to be expressed. I cannot say more here in general; for the particular cases may be very many and different. Remark however that common people may use some forms which do not agree with the philosophy of grammar, considered together with the use of more learned people; hence those forms can be eliminated as wrong. Among these wrong forms we might perhaps reckon the compound form of "zărtăr *or* zărităr *and* -leār"; *e.g.* "zărtăr tuveñ yeñ keleār, tukā yēk inām meḷat = if you did this, you would receive a prize". This form is not acknowledged as right by some natives themselves. "Zărităr *and* zăritări" can be used indifferently; the only difference is that "zăritări" has twice the permissive particle i.

9. "Ki, móṇ". Many things should be said about these; but as they are intimately connected with the construction, I shall speak of them in Ch. III. More exactly we should write "mhóṇ".

10. "Vo, uo, yā". Such Conjunctions are not often used, they are not seldom omitted especially in interrogative sentences (see § 1). All three mean "or".

11. "Muṇčeñ" is the Infinitive Absolute of "muṇ = say"; it corresponds exactly to the English, except that Konkani leaves out "that is".

12. "Nāñ, nāiñ, niñ = no". The English *no* is translated by "niñ *or* nāiñ", if some quality is denied and the Verb "to be" is understood; in other cases "nāñ" is used. Very often the whole sentence is repeated, in the negative form, as in Latin; *e.g.* "āilogī to? = did he come?" "yeunk-nāñ = no, he did not come" see p. 104. "Niñ" probably is "nāiñ", but pronounced quickly.

13. "Sāit" means "also, together"; its construction is thus: either it is placed after the affected word without modifying its case, or it may govern the Original of the affected word; *e.g.* "soul and body together will go to heaven = ātmo ani kuḍ sāit sārgār vetāt, *or* ātmeā ani kuḍi sāit sārgār vetāt". I cannot ascertain whether this 2nd form is quite correct, although it occurs.

Some other Conjunctions and Particles can be found, with their use in the Dictionary.

CHAPTER III. CONSTRUCTION

Art I. Partial Construction

§ 1. Verbs of Finite Mood

The Mahrātti Grammarians distinguish in this point three "Prayōgas" or Constructions, *i. e.* "Kartari" or Subjective, "Karmaṇi" or Objective, "Bhāvi" or Neuter construction. As the "Kartari Prayōga" does not differ from our construction, and the "Bhāvi Prayōga" is seldom used, so I do not follow this rather difficult mode of explanation, but I explain this point according to the rules of Passive Voice especially, which exists in our languages; so it will be easier, for there is a transition *a noto ad ignotum*. This point proves once more that Konkani has not always the same rules as Mahrātti, as some think.

The "Kartari" Construction is the same as the construction in Latin or English in similar sentences, therefore it can be omitted; generally, in the points which are not indicated as irregular, we may follow nearly the same construction as in English or Latin. For the other points we must distinguish Transitive and Intransitive Verbs.

1. *Transitive Verbs.* The Transitive Verbs in the tenses of passive meaning (see page 276) have a construction, as if they were passive. Hence the subject is put in the Instrumental, the Accusative in the Nominative, and the Verb agrees with this new Nominative; *e.g.* "āuveñ mojeñ kām keleñ = I performed my business, or by me was performed..." To this general rule we must add these limitations:

a) If the direct object of the Transitive Verb is an animate subsistent object, it remains in the Accusative also in the tenses of passive meaning, although the Verb agrees with this Accusative in gender, number and person (Karmaṇi Prayōga).

b) If the direct object of the Transitive Verb is a person, and sometimes also if the subject is not a person, it seems allowed (although not often used) to put the Verb, if it is in the above named tenses, in the neuter; so "taṇeñ bāpāk āpoileñ= he called the father", instead of "taṇeñ bāpāk āpoilo". (Bhāvi Prayōga).

c) In the Potential Mood, the Noun which should be put in the Instrumental, can be put in the Dative, or if it is a Pronoun, in the Instrumental of the derived Adjective. So: "he may eat = taṇeñ khāviet", *or* "takā khāviet", *or* "taceān khāviet", from "khā = eat".

d) As to the Potential and Necessary Mood, the Transitive Verbs have the above construction only, if the forms in "-iyet", or in "-zāi" occurs; as to the Negative Necessary, the agent is put in the Instrumental in "-čeān" *or* "jeān" (see p. 213, para. 9).

e) If the agent is the 2nd Person Singular, in the Past, Perfect, Past Perfect, the Verb remains in the 2nd Person

Singular Neuter; *e.g.* "did you hear my words?=tuveñ mojiñ utrañ aikälāiñgī?" (some seem to use the Masculine "aikäloigī"). In non-interrogative sentences it seems allowed to have the Verb agreeing with its object; *e.g.* "tuveñ mojiñ utrañ aikäleānt, *or* aikalāiñ = you have heard my words". So in confessions, when asking we must use the 2nd Person Singular Neuter. Instead of the Neuter 2nd Person Singular, some use the Feminine; *e.g.* "tuveñ mojeñ utrañ aikäleāigī?"

f) There are a few Transitive Verbs which have the same construction as the Intransitive Verbs. These are the following: "sik = learn", "visär = forget", "jeu = eat" (rice), "pie = drink", "nes = dress", "pāñgurụ *or* pāñgru = cover oneself", "tsuk = be missing *or* mistake", "hās = laugh", "bhēṭ = visit", "voḷkā = know", "ulei = speak", "somza = understand" and a few others which use will teach you; *e.g.* "to uloilo iñ utrañ = he spoke these words".

2. *Neuter Verbs.* These, as also those few Transitive Verbs now excepted, have the above construction, *i. e.* the Nominative goes in the Instrumental in the following cases:

a) If they are joined to "zāi", *e.g.* "āveñ votsazāi = I must go"; and also more commonly in the Potential Mood in "-yet", *e.g.* taṇeñ votsayet = he may go".

b) In the Past Gerund in "-täts", *e.g.* "mänšāniñ tsāḍ pietäts säma uleinänt = if men have drunk much, (they) do not speak rightly". Yet with this Past Gerund the Neuter (as also the Transitive) Verbs may follow the common construction; *e.g.* "mänis pietäts....."

c) In the Infinitive corresponding to the Latin Accusatives with Infinitive; *e.g.* "tumkañ gärz assā āveñ večeñ = *expedit vobis me ire*". Yet here too we may follow the "Kartari Prayōga": "āuñ vetsó tuṃkañ gärz assā".

d) With "nozo" the Instrumental in "-čeān *or* -jeān" is used. (See p. 213, para. 9.)

In other cases the Intransitive Verbs have a regular construction.

§ 2. Participles

Though the Participles follow the general rule, yet they require a particular explanation, because the application of the general rule is difficult. First, about their construction in relative sentences.

1. *Omission of the Relative Pronoun.* If we have a sentence governed by the Relative Pronoun, this is omitted and the Verb is changed into its corresponding Participle; *e.g.* "the man who was working died = vāur kărtālo mănis melo". The omission can take place, although the Relative Pronoun is accompanied by some Postposition; *e.g.* "the road on which you walked yesterday, has been spoiled = tūñ kāl tsăllo mārog, pāḍ zālo".

The omission of the Relative Pronoun, which naturally precedes its Noun and can have, as we shall see, before itself some other word either as Subject or as Object, gives rise to very long and rather difficult sentences, which will be more conveniently explained below. (Art. II. § 1.)

2. *Concord.* With which Noun must this Participle agree? The following is the answer and general rule:

The Participle agrees in Gender, Number and Case, not with any word which may be a part of the relative sentence, but with that word, of which the relative sentence is like an explanation or like an Adjective.

In the example, given above, the words "on which you walked" are an explanation and used as an Adjective of "road"; therefore the Participle agrees with *road.* "Tūñ" before "tzallo" is the Nominative of the relative sentence; hence it must not be taken into consideration in this point.

If we had had above a Transitive Verb in a Past Tense, then we should have said "tuveñ"; because the Participle has the same construction as the Original Verb; *e.g.* "the road, which you have seen, has been spoiled = tuveñ poḷeilo mārog pāḍ zalā".

Corollary 1. In order to change a relative sentence into a participial sentence *a*) omit the Relative Pronoun, *b*) change the Verb into the corresponding Participle, *c*) let this Participle agree in Gender, Number and Case with the word, of which the relative sentence is an explanation, *d*) leave the words of the relative sentences in the same order, *e*) place the participial sentence before the affected Noun, (see an example here below).

Corollary 2. In a participial sentence there may be a Nominative or other Case before the Participle; *e.g.* "to boro zalleã pasun sărgăr gelã = he went to heaven, because he had become good". "Zallea" is Original, "boro" Nominative, because we should say: "to boro zallo"; hence the Participle, although in the Original keeps the same construction. Moreover there may be an object governed by the Participle, *e.g.* "the tooth with which the tiger bit the ox, is this". First literally: "dăntu̧ zaņeñ văgăn băilăk săbu̧llo uo"; now a participial sentence according to the first corollary: "văgăn băilăk săbu̧llo dăntu̧ uo". There are numberless examples like this. This last corollary must be well remembered in order to understand some long participial sentences, in which the Participle is accompanied by many Nouns.

The above rule is not to be applied to the so-called Participle in "-tă to". (See pp. 236, 259.)

Although this participial construction is very frequent, the use of the Relative Pronoun is not prohibited. (See its construction, p. 236).

3. *Case governed by Participle.* From the given examples we learn that the Participles of Neuter Verbs have no Accusative, except in a few cases similar to the Latin *vitam vivere etc.* Participles of Transitive Verbs govern the same case as the Verbs from which they are derived and have the same construction and meaning. Hence if we have a compound Noun of a Transitive Participle, and of another Noun governed by this, the first Noun is not put in the Original (see p. 179); *e.g.*

"lugaṭ siuñtolo = he who stitches a cloth"; but "lugṭa siuñkār". Consequently no change of case takes place by changing the Verb into the corresponding Participle; *e.g.* "he went home = to garā gelo"; "to the house to which he went = to geleā garāk"; "he cut a tree = taṇeñ yēk ruk kātărlo"; "the tree which he cut is very large = taṇeñ kātărlo ruk bhou vōḍ".

Art. II. Complexive Construction

§ 1. Collocation of words

The following principle may throw some light: "The less important words precede the more important ones"; hence *a*) the secondary sentence precedes the principal; *b*) in each sentence the Adjective, if taken as an attribute (see p. 199, *note*) precedes the Noun; *c*) a whole sentence which takes the place of an Adjective precedes the affected Noun; *d*) the Verb is put at the end; *e*) if many subordinate Nouns occur, the governed Noun precedes the governing one; *e.g.* "I gave my book to the son of the brother of my friend = āuveñ mojeñ pustak mojeā išṭāčeā bāvāčeā putāk dileñ"; *f*) if there be two words or cases independent of each other, there is no fixed rule; yet here too the above mentioned principle might be applied.

We may say also thus: the various parts of a sentence are very often so connected that some are like *genus, materia, determinabile;* some are like *differentia*, *forma*, *determinans: genus* etc. precedes *differentia* etc. Yet we cannot explain all examples by these two ways; use is the master. Hence *a*) in preaching and religious matters a somewhat different construction is used, as *b*) often also in familiar conversation; *c*) in some cases the complication of words requires some other arrangement.

This most general rule will be explained for the sake of brevity, with some examples. "The man who has been created by God to His own image with great love, becomes dear to God by Divine love = Dēvān apleā sărkeatso tsăḍ mōgān rătsụllo mānis mōga vorviñ Dēvāk mōgāḷ zatā". The sentence beginning with "who" is like an Adjective of "man"; hence omitting the Relative Pronoun, "mānis" is put after it. Further in the same relative sentence the Participle is put at the end, immediately before "mānis", as Verb; "by God" precedes "to his...", as the second part has more emphasis; and again, "aplea sărkeātso" precedes 'tzăḍ mōgān", because this second part determines "rătsụllo". The following words need no explanation.

"The brother of the father of my friend, has to suffer 1) on account of the war, 2) which took place 3) between the King of Arsuzia and the Emperor of Kadimeri 4) in the 2nd year 5) after his arrival 6) in this country = moje iśṭāčea băpaitso bāu yeā gāvānt ailleā dusreā vorsā Arsučitsca rāyā ani Kadimeričea mahā-rāyā bitār zallcā zuzā vorviñ sostā". At the end the Verb, in the beginning the subject preceded by the governed Nouns; and among these, that which is governed and governs, precedes; of the remaining words this is the order of determination: "1) on account of the war, 2) which took place, 3) between ..., 4) in the 2nd ..., 5) after his arrival, 6) in this country". The 2nd determines the 1st, the 3rd determines the 2nd and so on; consequently we must put them in this order: 6), then 5), then 4), then 3), then 2), then 1). In this example you see also how the Participial sentences must be constructed.

Although this is the nature of Konkani as to construction, yet if such long sentences occur, it will be better to resolve them into smaller sentences. Yet even in smaller sentences the same rules which have been laid down above, and shown in the above two examples must be observed. Many other things about this important point should be said, which however for extrinsical reasons must be omitted. At any rate the gist of them has been touched upon.

Remark further 1) that titles are usually put after the affected word, seldom before; *e. g.* "pādri sāib". 2) The interrogative words are put as close as possible to the Verb; if this is not expressed, at the end; *e.g.* "why does your hand tremble? = tuzo hāt kiteāk kamptā?" "who is that man? = to mănis kōṇ?" If we say "kōṇ to mănis:" it means "what kind of man is that?" 3) The article "yēk" prefers to be joined immediately to its Noun, if there are other Adjectival Genitives; *e. g.* "a man of this country = yeā gāuñtso yēk mănis"; if we say "yēk gāuñtso mănis", some understand "a man of a country". Some more examples about construction will be given perhaps in the I. Appendix.

§ 2. Connexion of Sentences

There are co-ordinate and subordinate sentences; each kind can be subdivided: here I speak only of some subordinate sentences; the others are either easy or are explained in the Dictionary. Secondary sentences are connected with principal ones by Postpositions and Participles (see p. 274 *et alibi*), very often by "móṇ *and* ki = that". Their construction is this:

1. Put first the secondary sentence, then "móṇ", then the principal one; *e.g.* "to phaleā yetolo móṇ āuñ čintāñ = I think that he will come to-morrow". Yet if the Verb is not put at the end as often happens, "móṇ" also is not put at the end; *e.g.* "to assā móṇ apleā gărānt āuñ čintāñ = I think that he is in his house". Yet it is better to put the Verb at the end.

2. Put first the principal sentence, then "ki", then the secondary sentence; *e.g.* "āuñ čintāñ ki to yetolo = I think that he will come".

3. Put first the principal sentence, then "ki", then the secondary sentence, then "móṇ"; *e.g.* "āuñ čintāñ ki to yetolo móṇ".

4. Omit altogether the Conjunction; "āuñ čintāñ to yetolo". Among these modes, the first seems to be more correct. In such sentences the Verb is put in the mood required by

the meaning; if the meaning is imperative, exhorting and the like, then the Imperative is used; *e. g.* "request God to forgive you = Dēvā lagiñ māg bogos móṇ". Therefore if in Latin or English we have an *oratio indirecta* governed by "móṇ", in Konkani the *oratio directa* is often used, retaining, however "móṇ" as in Hebrew; *e. g.* "he requested him to lend him a book = tače lagiñ māglāñ yēk pustak dī móṇ"; "*cum responsum accepissent ne redirent* = having received the answer not to go back = zāb meḷtāts, portun votsanaye móṇ". Gi or gai seems also to be used to connect sentences both co-ordinate and subordinate; it may be joined also to "móṇ"; *e. g.* "kāiñ, khāiñ ani kòṇā pasun mag-ṇeñ mòṇazāigai móṇ poḷeyā = let us see when, where, for whom we have to pray".

Remarks. 1. Using "móṇ" is the easiest way of expressing in Konkani the Latin Past or Future Infinitive. I say "the easiest way", not the "only way", because the construction of Instrumental with Infinitive, can also be used (see p. 257). Even the above examples might be expressed in some other way; *e. g.* "to fāleā yēuñk puro = he might come to-morrow", which has nearly the same meaning as "to fāleā yetolo móṇ āuñ čintā"; the exact meaning of the 1st sentence is: "it may be that he comes to-morrow".

2. Instead of "móṇ", we can use also "moṇun", namely if an *oratio indirecta* is reported. It is just like the Hebrew *dicendo dicit* and the Tulu ಅಂದ್ = andụ or ಅಂದ್ದ್ = ăndụdụ.

3. "Móṇ" is sometimes changed into "moḷḷeñ = said", nay sometimes it is declined like an Adjective; *e. g.* "by thinking that I have offended God, I am very much displeased = āuveñ Dēvāk akmān kelā moḷḷi čintnā makā zāḷaitā". When is this "moḷḷeñ" to be used? when we could substitute in a literal translation "said" for "saying".

4. "Móṇ" is used also in the *oratio directa*, as in the Holy Bible: *dixit quod ego veniam*; so also: "tikeñ rāu, āuñ yetāñ móṇ = wait (that) I come" (see above *l.* 3). It is used, although another word of a similar meaning is there;

e. g. "to somzunknāñ kāseñ gaḍleñ mόṇ = he did not understand how it happened". To use the *oratio directa* with "moṇ" is usual. Nay it seems that this "mόṇ" is used as a general means of connexion, although there is no "that" or similar particle in English: to learn such a use great practice is required. Here I can only say in general that Konkani prefers to join secondary sentences with principal ones expressly; hence if no other joining particle is there, "mόṇ" is used.

5. Some English secondary sentences do not require a peculiar connexion in Konkani, because they are embodied in the principal sentence so as to form one sentence. This is the case especially with the participial sentences governed by Postpositions (see above).

CHAPTER IV. CONSIDERATIONS ABOUT KONKANI

Art I. Origin of Konkani

Konkani is derived from Konkan, a province along the Western Coast of India, approximately between 16° and 20° of latitude. Hence Konkani language etymologically should mean the language originally spoken in Konkan. Yet now Konkani is spoken in provinces far away from Konkan, *i. e.* in South Kanara by almost all Christians, by many thousand pagans, and also somewhat in Malabar and, so they say, still more South. We must however distinguish two branches of Konkani: the Goanese branch spoken in Goa and, as I heard, elsewhere also, and the Konkani of South Kanara; of this only I speak both in the Grammar and the Dictionary.

This language, formerly called Kanarine language, is so called, because the Konkani speaking people are said to have come from Konkan in ancient times.

The language of Konkan was and is, mostly at least, Mahrātti; this shows that most probably Konkani is derived from Mahrātti, as French, Spanish, Portuguese etc. are said to be derived from the Latin. Indeed many Konkani words and some rules too agree with the Mahrātti, yet not to such an extent as to enable us to make much use of Mahrātti. Those who know Mahrātti are well aware of this; for those who do not know Mahrātti, out of many proofs I choose these few:

1. For the Mahrātti termination ऊन, which has no genders, Konkani has -ntlo (-i, -eñ).

2. The multiplicative numbers in Mahrātti are formed by पट, in Konkani by "doḍo".

3. Adverbial numbers of frequency are formed in Mahrātti by दां; this mode is no longer common in Konkani.

4. आपण is used for "your honour" *etc.*; not so in Konkani.

5. The Causal Verbs are formed by वि, in Konkani by ai,

6. There are moreover the terminations of the cases and of the conjugation, which, although sometimes similar, are however often quite different.

Although Mahrātti seems to be the chief stock, Kanarese, Tulu, Malayālam etc. seem to have also contributed to form Konkani. The fact is that there are in Konkani many words which occur also in Tulu, Kanarese etc. I cannot ascertain whether these have been adopted into Konkani on account of their vicinity, or were common to Konkani and those languages; the first supposition is more probable, because there occur in Konkani some words used also in some of the abovementioned languages, and as far as I could learn, not used in Mahrātti. The most probable reason of it seems to be this: as Konkani for a long time has been neglected, especially or also on account of its having abandoned the seat of the mother-tongue, many Mahrātti words have been abandoned, and on the other hand it has taken up some words from its new neighbours. Consequently, although Konkani in the main seems to be a Gaurian languages (for it seems to be the niece of Sanskrit), yet it partakes of some of the qualities of Dravidian languages, as Kanarese, Tulu, Malayālam *etc.* are reckoned by Caldwell (Comparative Grammar, page 9) as Dravidian languages.

Art II. Present state of Konkani

Konkani is a rich and beautiful language, although at present in an ignoble state, because it is far more perfect than many European languages; yet it is altogether uncultivated and appears to be the most imperfect. But as to this point the Konkani spoken by Hindus, as far as I can gather, is in a somewhat different condition from the Konkani spoken by Christians. The Hindus, besides some little varieties in pronunciation and also in some words, have not adopted into their language so many Portuguese words as the Christians.

What are the reasons for saying that Konkani is in an ignoble state? The reasons are: *a*) the total neglect of this language; hence no common written language, no uniformity, and therefore, what is worse, many Natives themselves despise it as a good-for-nothing language; *b*) it is corrupted, particularly in the town of Mangalore, by very many foreign words, especially Portuguese and, latterly, also English. We might say that certainly a great part of religious words, especially the more elevated, are foreign. The reason of so many foreign words in religious matters is to be found, most probably, in the history of the conversion of their ancestors. *c*) Above the varieties of Konkani according to the castes, which thing cannot be avoided in familiar conversation, there is no really cultivated language common to all castes, as there is in our European languages, which have a form above all the dialects of the same language.

Notwithstanding the present miserable state of Konkani, I will never call Konkani a corruption of Mahrātti, in its derivation; for, if the derivation, under any form, of one language from another is to be called corruption, then many

European languages should be called a corruption of another language. If people mean to say that Konkani is a corruption of Mahrātti, because it is a dialect of Mahrātti, without proper forms or rules, I certainly deny it. For *a*) the similarity of forms of one language with the forms of the mother-tongue cannot be called corruption; *b*) there is no want of ruling principles and of common forms at least on the way of perfection; because notwithstanding some varieties, common forms and ruling principles exist, as the whole Grammar shows. Corruption of a language is the introduction of extraneous elements which are a beginning of resolution into elements (see S. Thomas, III. *q.* 50, *a.* 5, *c.*). Consequently a dialect, without common forms and rules can be called a corruption of the stock-tongue. But this is by no means the case with the language of which we speak, as we have already said in this article, and study will show, although we can say that it has, as it is spoken by many, some elements of corruption, which in the long run would bring on a true corruption or rather destruction. The reason of the first part of my assertion, *i. e.* that Konkani is a rich and beautiful language, is partly given in this Grammar, partly in the Dictionary, but cannot be fully understood but by careful study and future cultivation of this language.

Art. III. What Konkani can become

As Konkani in itself is a beautiful language, but is reduced to servitude, it can become, or rather can be shown to be a beautiful language, if taking pity on it, we deliver it from slavery. To such a work first of all the natives themselves should contribute; for after religion, one of the most important elements of civilization in a nation is its language. It is truly a pity to see a people endowed by God with so many gifts, without a language. To gain this end what should be done?

Some might think we should borrow from Mahrātti or Sanskrit, both words and rules, or at least words.

This would not perfect but destroy Konkani, or make of it either a phantom of Sanskrit and Mahrātti or an aerial language. Whatsoever may be the origin of Konkani, we must now take it as it is and try to elevate it. I grant, however, that we may borrow from the Mahrātti or rather resuscitate some Konkani words which, as all probability shows, must have been used in former times and even now are more or less understood by more learned people, and I have done so in the Dictionary. But whenever we do not find a Konkani word for some idea, to take it from the Mahrātti, would be wrong: this could be done perhaps if Konkani were a dialect of Mahrātti. *A fortiori* I would call it wrong to borrow in such cases, the words from Dravidian languages, although some words can be borrowed also from them, as is the case with all languages What is therefore to be done? Out of many things which I could propose, I choose only the following ones which, I hope, will meet the common approbation.

1. We must avoid so many foreign words and expressions. Foreign words are well employed, if there are no proper words; but using foreign words when there are proper words, and even without a grave reason, is against Philology. I make one exception for religious words. A great part of them are Portuguese, yet Konkanized, as they have been used since centuries; moreover it would not be without some risk to use the true Konkani words, used only by Konkani-Hindus. Perhaps we might use the Konkani word for secondary religious matters. I said "Portuguese", because the English words used also by some are not lawfully Konkanized as yet.

2. But on the other hand we must avoid eliminating those words, which although Kanarese or Tulu originally, are in common use. Let us hear what a great master says on this point.

Ut silvae foliis pronos mutantur in annos
Prima cadunt; ita verborum vetus interit aetas;
Et juvenum ritu florent modo nata vigentque.
. . . .
Multa renascentur quae jam cecidere, cadentque
Quae nunc sunt in honore, vocabula, si volet usus,
Quem penes arbitrium est et jus et norma loquendi.
(*Horace*, *De Arte poetica*, *v.* 60-73.)

If there be any extravagant Purists, let them well meditate these verses of one of the greatest Latin Poets; especially the last verse is always to be kept in view in order not to go astray both in rules and words. Consider however that one thing is *usus*, another *abusus;* Horace speaks of *usus*; *e.g.* employing so many foreign words, although in use, must be called *abusus.*

3. You will say: For many things there are no Konkani words.

I answer: There are many Konkani words, not in common use, yet good; moreover many words are said not to exist, because Konkani is not studied, or because some try to find a literally corresponding word or expression, which way is often wrong. Moreover (and this is the third thing which we should do) we must employ new words, not in common use. How? Especially by way of composition (see P. III., Ch. V.). This way cannot be used indifferently or by every one; the rules laid down *l. c.* and especially harmony and usage must be taken into consideration. By "usage" I mean to say whether a word, though new in form, sounds as Konkani to Konkani people. You find very many such words in the Dictionary marked also as new words, which, however, have been tried to a Konkani ear. This way is necessarily to be followed, else two other ways only or chiefly would remain, *i. e.* either to use foreign words or to use circumlocutions. But although foreign Mahrătti or Kanarese words are not entirely in discord with Konkani, yet this way is against the philosophy of languages; words of Latin origin, *e. g.* English or Portuguese, or also of Greek origin, except a few, are thoroughly foreign to Konkani and require translation; the 2nd way, viz. to use some circumlocution or some words which approximately express a certain notion; but this evidently is childish and a sign of ignorance.

But on this point of the composition of words I am in a somewhat difficult position. I will explain my position candidly to the reasonable and interested reader. In other formed languages the words have already a fixed meaning: but before reaching that fixed meaning, many years have elapsed; many events have sometimes contributed to the meaning of a word; sometimes a chance was the origin of some words, which events and chance however through many years have been forgotten and the meaning of the word became, we might say, independent of the first etymological meaning; *e.g.* philosopher = φιλόσοφος, originally means "friend of wisdom", which meaning afterwards became a less obvious meaning. Hence although the etymology of many words can lead us to find the corresponding Konkani compound words, yet in many cases especially with words of the above mentioned kind as "philosophy", the etymology cannot be kept in view. Then what remains? There remains to be considered the essential notion of the thing to be termed, and to find a fit expression. But without speaking of the long time which would be required, it is almost impossible to find a new expression which now may have the same much extended and commonly accepted meaning as the similar Latin or Greek word; for the Latin word itself underwent many vicissitudes before receiving such a fixed meaning. Consequently there remains only to try now to choose the most suitable word, as far as this can be done within the short limit of time, which is at my disposal, leaving the perfection and settlement of the things to Divine providence which *ludit in orbe terrarum.* I do not give any examples, for the Dictionary is almost a continued example. Here only

I mention the words *harmonium*, *organ*, *diameter etc.*, the general etymological meaning of which has been restricted by long usage to the present meaning. So "diameter" etymologically means "measure through", but now it means "a line passing through the centre...". If we translate "diameter" literally, *e.g.* "āḍ-mezap", such a word would not be taken in the same limited meaning, as "diameter", except after a long use. In the beginning, it would be taken in its general etymological meaning. Such words are many: hence the difficulty. I remark finally that this mode of composition is not entirely new; for many compound words in common use exist already; moreover this is used also in other Indian languages, *e.g.* in Kanarese, much more is this used in many European languages, especially in German and English. It is however true that Konkani is perhaps not in need of so many compound words as some other languages are; for, one simple Konkani word is used to express many other connected meanings, for which other languages have different words; and what seems to be a sign of poverty, is a sign of perfection; for the fewer the means required to obtain an effect, the more perfect, *ceteris paribus*, is the cause; in a similar way to God, who in His infinite simplicity obtains the most varied effects. Many proofs of this assertion are to be found in the Dictionary; some have been given throughout Grammar.

Art. IV. Some rules for beginners

in speaking Konkani, especially with common people

1. Avoid carefully abstract terms, because such terms are few in common use; there are many others, but their use requires some practice and often are not understood. If therefore you have to translate into Konkani abstract terms, resolve them.

2. Express metaphysical and abstract notions by words taken from material things, which have some similarity with

that notion. Although this is the case in all languages, particular attention is to be paid to it; because in other languages the material origin of many words has almost disappeared; hence in our languages we do not think about the first material origin, whereas if we hear the Konkani word, the first notion which we get usually is the first original meaning, *e. g.* hearing "to retract" (one's word), we do not think of its origin from *trahere;* and when we hear the Konkani "kāḍ" we do not think of the meaning "retract", but only "draw" (*trahere*) *etc.;* hence without considering this rule, we might perhaps go far to seek a corresponding word for "retract", and as perhaps we could not find it, we would say there is no Konkani expression for "retract", and we would use a circumlocution, whereas we may use the same "pāṭi kāḍ" which in the main is the same as "retract". From this example judge of many others.

3. If there are many synonyms which slightly differ, do not seek as many Konkani corresponding words; be satisfied with one or few; so, *e. g.*, "*think*" and "*imagine*" differ, no doubt, yet be satisfied with "čint". So generally the most common term is used for the various English synonyms, and the general term is used also for the particular one.

4. The numerous compound Verbs of European languages are either translated by the simple Verb or by the Verb and the required Adverb. Yet sometimes a different Verb is required.

5. Often, in order to be understood, the English word must be expressed by a circumlocution; and the English sentence must be expressed by a different Konkani sentence, keeping however the meaning. This is the case especially with figurative sentences; because many figures of European languages differ from Konkani figures. If you do not know whether an European figure can be used in Konkani, substitute for the figurative expression the proper one and then translate.

6. Resolve complex sentences into simple sentences; else you would not be understood, or you would not be able to finish the sentence.

7. Peculiar attention must be paid to the construction, (see Ch. III.) even when speaking with common people who use also Participles; yet if the beginner finds any difficulty, he may use the full relative sentence.

8. Not only Abstract but also some Concrete Nouns are not used by vulgar people; *e.g.* not many Nouns in "-găr *or* kăr" are used.

9. The parts of speech more to be used are Verbs, original Nouns, concrete original Adjectives, original Adverbs and Postpositions.

Yet if we write, then we should use Abstract Nouns, derived words etc."

Art. V. Peculiarities of Konkani

In this Article I explain some general peculiarities, if I may be allowed to say so, which may show in some way the different manner of conceiving many things. A more distinct knowledge of this point, as far as I could learn, (because a full knowledge requires many years' practice) can be got by a collection of Konkani phrases and sentences which will form one of the Appendixes to the Dictionary. Some of the following remarks have been touched upon throughout the Grammar. I thought it useful to collect the principal of them.

1. Konkani makes a great use of Postpositions, and, when possible, prefers to substitute them for Conjunctions and sometimes for Adverbs too (see p. 294). These are at the same time the most common connexions of sentences, changing thereby two or more sentences (English) into one (Konkani) without changing however the cases; this is done by joining certain Postpositions to Participles (see p. 274).

2. The Participles are also frequently used, especially by omitting the Relative Pronoun; this may be united to a Pre-

position (in English). The Participles are inserted also without any real necessity (see p. 308).

3. The Compound Verbs in -un are very often used; by them many Latin Compound Verbs are expressed. The same form in -un, sometimes accompanied by a Noun, is also often used instead of our Adverbs (see p. 291).

4. The Conjunctions are often omitted or replaced by Postpositions (see p. 302).

5. The Present is often used for the Future, and even rather long time is expressed by words meaning short time.

6. A great number of notions for which English or Latin has different expressions, are expressed by -ts and -so (see *passim*).

7. Negative notions very often are expressed by the Affirmative form and by the Negative joined to the Verb: (Compare Part III. Ch. IV.) Among common people the Negative form is expressed by "-rān" and the Negative Gerund in "-tanañ" (see p. 114).

8. The more important or emphatic words are very often put quite at the end (tuñ kōṇ?).

9. A large use is made of Causative Verbs (see p. 281).

10. Konkani loves to express the different stages through which something must pass (see *l. c.*).

11. Even long sentences, explanatory of some word, are considered as Adjectives; hence so many long sentences sometimes precede the Noun, in which sentences many cases may occur.

12. A use almost continual, of "mōṇ" is made not only to express our "that", but also, I might say, like a comma, or to breathe a little: the nearest word to it, besides "that", is perhaps "as", although in many cases we cannot translate it at all. It is used also as a particle connecting sentences. Nevertheless I do not see a great nicety in its too frequent use, at least I doubt of its correctness. Our common people

in Europe also use some particles out of place (see pp. 312, 313, 314).

13. Konkani prefers to conceive things, very often, in a way similar to *genus* and *differentia* or to *materia* and *forma* (p. 288).

14. Konkani often expresses the comparative degree without a proper form (p. 65, *c.*).

15. Konkani is bold in concord (Part IV. Ch. I.).

16. Konkani likes harmony; hence so many euphonic vowels (p. 116).

17. Konkani is a nasal language (p. 181).

18. The ruling principles in arranging sentences are chiefly 1) importance of words (p. 310), 2) order of dependance (p. 311), 3) strict connexion (p. 314), 4) unity (p. 323).

After these general considerations or recapitulations, let us consider the use of some Verbs peculiar to Konkani.

1. "Mār = beat", yet on account of analogy it is used in innumerable other cases; *e. g.* to express beating with sound, to apply pressure, to ring, to sew a piece to a cloth, to pitch a tent *etc.*

2. "Meḷ = be found, *or perhaps* be attached"; but it is still more used than "mār", to express that some thing reaches in possession of, or is received from; so it is used for "to meet, to receive, to be united, to find" and the like.

3. "Pōḍ = fall", but it is used also very often when some sudden thing appears, in any way, *e.g.* the rainbow, folds, *etc.*

4. "Kāḍ = pull", but it is used to express the notion of drawing, or taking out, or of doing something with some application, *e. g.* to make the sign of the holy cross, to put liniment *etc.*

5. "Lāg = to be attached", is used in many cases in which the original meaning seems almost to disappear; yet if we consider well, still remains figuratively; *e. g.* make impression as a sermon, begin to.... *etc.*

6. "Lāi" perhaps is the Causative Verb of "lāg"; it is used especially to express the action by which some thing becomes attached, really or figuratively; hence it means "apply, plant, induce, ascribe, give (food)".

7. "Zatā" is used not only for "become", but also for many other connected meanings; *e.g.* happen, be fit, agree *etc.*

The original meaning of the above-mentioned Verbs does not render the notion which we, Europeans, have in mind, when we wish to express the other connected meanings, that is to say, the way of conceiving itself is different, and the figures are different.

These are some of the most used peculiar Konkani Verbs; a great part of the Konkani sentences or figures are expressed by these Verbs; but only few hints have been given, more will be said in the Dictionary, and still more you will learn by practice. Let us conclude with an example in which we show the different way of Konkani construction.

"If also men of such a sublime holiness fell into temptation and went so far as to commit such faults, then we who are men very far from their holiness and who are weak, how much have we to fear?"

First let us translate into Konkaṇi literally: "zărtăr yēk mănis săit tedea vortea santipoṇăče talnient poḍle ani tedeo vóḍ tsuki adarunk păule, dekun amiñ je zăun vortautăuñ mănis bhou pois tančea santipoṇăk ani bhou askat, kitleṇ biyeunk făvonăiñ?"

Now let us translate with the Konkani idiom: "zărtăr tedea vortea santipoṇăčea mănis legun talnient poḍon tedeo voḍlyo tsuki adarunk păule, tăr tančea santipoṇăk bhou pois ani ăskăt zăun assaḷleañ vorviñ amiñ kitleñ biyeunk făvonăiñ?" The reader himself may consider the difference, especially the use of Participles.

Another example: "There is no other means so strong to resist the violence of anger, of envy, of luxury as to receive often holy communion". Literally: "dusro upăi itlo ghăţ rāgāčeñ, niskusarāčeñ ani mostičeñ boḷ moḍunk zosso kumgār nāñ". The same in a manner more according to Konkani: "krodhāčeñ, niskusarāčeñ ani mostičeñ boḷ moḍunk kumgār kāṇeunčea bāri tzāḍ boro upāi yekui nāñ".

From all these observations we may perceive a little the nature of Konkani, very different from the nature of European languages; hence we cannot, usually, translate literally English into Konkani or *vice versa:* to this point especially we must pay attention. In order to know a little more of the nature of Konkani, the reader should go through the whole Grammar, from which here only a few points have been collected; Chapter III. of Part IV. especially contains many peculiarities of Konkani.

APPENDIX I.

Explanation of some difficult modes of speaking

A. Some Particles and Tenses connected with them

Ut = in order that

1. *Ut* meaning "aim" is expressed *a*) by the Supine, *e.g.* "*veni ut te viderem* = I came to see you = tukā poḷeunk āiloñ"; *or b*) by the Participle followed by "pasun (*or* pasvot) *or* nimtiñ = *propter*, on account of", as: "āuñ tukā poḷeunčeā pasun āiloñ".

In some cases it may be expressed by the pure Imperfect Subjunctive.

2. *Ut*, called "consecutive", is expressed by "ki", Indicative Mood preceded by "itlo *or* aseñ jinsiñ = so", *e.g.* "God is so good as to forgive also great sinners = *Deus est tam bonus ut parcat etiam magnis peccatoribus* = Dēu itlo boro (*or* aseñ jinsiñ boro) zāun assā ki voḍā pātkiānk legun bogšitā".

This "*tam*" is expressed in Konkani by an Adjective which must agree with the affected word, as appears from the given example.

3. *Ut*, meaning "although", is expressed *a*) by the Conditional in -leār, followed by i; *e.g. ut desint vires, tamen est laudanda voluntas* = tankanāñ zaleāri, bore khušiek mān dīzāi = although strength be wanting, yet the good will is to be praised"; *b*) by "zāritār *or* zāritāri = although", *e.g.* "zāritār tankanāñ, bore khušiek mān dīzāi".

4. *Ut*, meaning "time", is expressed by the Gerund in "-tāts", *or* in "-tanāñ", *or* in "-un", *or* by the Participle followed by "uprānt = after", *e.g.* "*ut S. Franciscus X. venit in Indias, apostolicos labores exantlavit* = Sāñ Frančis Zaver Indient aileā uprānt bhou tsāḍ vāur kelo, *or* S. Frančis Zaver Indient yetāts, *etc. or* S. Frančis Zaver Indient yeun....".

Ne = that not

1. *Ne*, meaning "aim", is expressed *a*) by the Negative Supine, *or b*) by the Participle Negative followed by the Postposition "pasun"; *c*) by the Negative Imperfect Subjunctive; *e.g.* "in order that we may not fall into sin, we must pray = *Ne incidamus in peccatum, orandum est* = pātkānt poḍanāñ zāunk māg-ṇeñ kārizāi *or* pātkānt poḍanatulleā pasun *etc.*"

2. *Ne*, after the Verbs of "fearing" is expressed *a*) by "móṇ" with the Future Potential; *e.g.* "I fear that he may fall sick = *timeo ne..* = āuñ beatā to piḍent poḍat móṇ"; *b*) by the Future Indicative "poḍtolo móṇ"; *c*) by the Negative Supine; *e.g.* "*ne... offendas ad lapidem pedem tuum* = lest thou dash thy foot against a stone = yēk fātor tujea pāyāk laganāñ zāunk".

Quominus = that not

This may be expressed by the Supine or by some circumlocution; *e.g.* "*Religio non impedit quominus officia urbanitatis impendamus* = religion does not prevent us from observing politeness = monšāñ thāiñ māriādin tsālunk šastir aḍvarināñ".

Quin = that not, *or* without

Quin, after the Verbs of doubt, may be expressed *a*) by the simple "ki *or* móṇ = that": "*Non dubito quin veniat* = I do not doubt that he will come = to yetolo móṇ āuñ dubāvanāñ"; *or b*) by some change of the sentence: "dubāunastanañ to yetolo = no doubt he will come"; *c*) if it corresponds to the English "without", followed by the Gerund, it may be expressed also by the Negative Gerund in "-tanañ", *e.g.* "*Si abierit quin faciat hoc...* = if he will start without doing this = yeñ kārinastanañ to geleār"; or by "šivāi" with the Participle: "*Non intras in coelum quin tibi vim inferas* = you do not enter into heaven without doing violence to yourself = tukā bòḷ karinastanañ sārgār riganāi"; *or d*) by the Conditional.

Quia = because

Quia may be expressed *a*) either by "kiteāk *or* kiteāk moḷeār = because", with the Verb in the required tense of the Indicative, *or b*) by "pasun = on account of", *or c*) by "vorviñ = through", preceded by the Participle; *e. g.* "*Quia credidit sanatus est* = because he believed he has been cured = kiteāk moḷeār pātielā to boro zālo, *or* pātieleā pasun to boro zālo"; "*quia studuisti, doctus factus est* = because you studied you became learned = sikųlleā vorviñ sikpi zāloi *or* kiteāk moḷeār sikpāk lagloi, sikpi zāloi".

Quippe qui = since

"*Animus fortuna non eget, quippe quae probitatem.... neque dare neque eripere potest* = the soul needs no fortune, since goodness she can neither give nor take away (*Sall.*) = atmeāk gratsārāči gārz nāñ, akā segun diunki kāḍunki tanknaṭalleā pasun".

Ac si = as if

"*Lacrimatur ac si vapulasset* = he weeps as if he had been beaten = to rāḍtā mārn paulleā bari".

Remark: a) "bāri" in Lat. *instar*, joined to the Participle.

b) An elegant use of "pāu" to express the passive voice, *lit.* "as one who reached beaten."

Quum, or *cum* = when, as

a) If it means "*quia* = because" (see above *b*): "*Cum J. C. sit exemplar nostrum eum imitari debemus* = as J. C. is our exemplar, we must imitate Him = Somi J. K. āmtso nāmuno assąlleā pasun amiñ tači dék kāņeizāi".

• *b*) If it means "when", it may be translated as *ut*, meaning "time" (see above) or also literally by "kāiñ *or* yedvān = "when", followed by the required tense; *e.g.* "kāiñ ruk fôḷ ditā, tumkāñ kāḷtā gim lāgiñ pāulo móņ = when you see that the tree gives fruit, you know that the dry season has approached"; "kāiñ koṭepoņ ṭemplānt poḷeišāt = *cum videritis abominationem* = when you will see the abomination in the temple";

"*cum venerit filius hominis, putas quia fidem inveniet?* = when the Son of Man will come, will he find faithful? = mānšātso putrų yetanañ, bāvāḍti meḷtitgī?"

Postquam = after

It is expressed *a*) by the Gerund in -tāts, *b*) by the Gerund in -un, *c*) by the Participle followed by "uprānt"; *e.g.* "*Postquam autem abiero mittam vobis Spiritum veritatis* = āuñ sārlea uprānt, tumkāñ sātāčea Spiritāk daḍtoloñ = after I shall have gone, I will send you the Spirit of truth"; "*postquam adimpleveritis omnia praecepta, dicite: servi inutiles sumus* = after having fulfilled all commandments, say: we are useless servants = sākāṭ upades sambāḷn, sangā: upkārāk poḍanātulle sākār[1] amiñ". Yet the Gerund in -tāts seems to be better in this meaning.

Antequam, Priusquam = before

It is expressed by "adiñ = before", proceded by the Participle; *e.g. Priusquam ipse veniat, ego abibo* = to yeuñčea adiñ āuñ vetolo = before he come, I shall go".

Si = if

It is expressed *a*) either by the Conditional in -leār or *b*) by "zārtār = if", followed by the Future Contingent, or by the Past Perfect (see p. 251), if it is a pure Conditional; or by another tense, as the meaning requires, if it is not a pure Conditional (see p. 304); or also followed by a tense of the Indicative Mood; *e.g.* "*si homines bene orarent, salvarentur omnes* = mānšāniñ boreñ rāzar keleār, sākāṭ sārgār vetit = if men would pray well, all would go to heaven"; "*si hoc feceris, praemium dabo* = tuveñ yeñ keleār, āuñ tukā ināṁ ditāñ, *or* zārtār tuñ yeñ kārtai, āuñ tukā ināṁ ditāñ = if you do this, I shall give you a prize;" *c*) by "pokšek", but this last mode corresponds rather to the English "in case that" (see p. 251).

---

[1] Many Masculine Nouns ending in "ó" change "ó" into "ā", sometimes into "ŏ" in the Plural; see gleaning *parergon*, below.

Nisi

It is expressed *a*) either by the Negative form of the Conditional, or *b*) by the Participle followed by "šivāi *or* kărit = *praeter*," or *c*) very often by the Gerund Negative in "-tanañ"; *e.g.* "*Nisi poenitentiam feceritis, omnes peribitis* = prăjit kărinăñ zaleăr, săkăț yemkaṇḍănt veteleăt, *or* zărtăr tumiñ prăjit kărinănt *etc.* *or* tumiñ prăjit kellea šivāi (*or* kărit) *etc.* *or* tumiñ prăjit kărinastanañ *etc.*"

Dum = while

It may be expressed *a*) either by the Gerund in "-tanañ", *or b*) by the Participle followed by "veļăr (*or* veļa) = in time", *or c*) by "kăiñ *or* yedvăñ = when", with a tense of the Indicative; *e. g.* "*dum regnaret Canutus rex Angliae, scientiae florebant* = Kanuț Inglez răi, raspot kărtanañ, lok sikpăk teăḍl lagtălo, *or* Kanuț raspot kărčea veļăr, *or* kăiñ Kanuț raspot kartălo *etc.* = when Canute was reigning, the sciences were flourishing".

"Without"

The English "without" joined to the Participle corresponding to the Italian *senza*, to the Latin *quin*, *e. g.* "without doing this, you cannot get what you wish"; this "without", I say, is translated by the Negative Gerund in "-tanañ", or with Negative Conditional as has been said of *quin*. Often this Negative Gerund in "-tanañ" is joined to the Verb "rău"; *e.g.* "văur kărinastanañ răutăñ = I remain without working, I do not work".

If "without" is joined to a Substantive, it may be translated by "viṇe", *e. g.* "without doubt = dubăva viṇe"; or by a Compound Negative word, *e.g.* "without fault = guniăuñ-natullo".

"Unless", see *Ne* after the Verbs of *fearing*.

Dummodo, or modo = provided

It may be translated *a*) by the Conditional, *e. g.* "*dummodo tu facias quod in te est, Deus te adiuvabit* = provided you do what is on your part, God will help you = tuje hātānt assā tuveñ teñ keleār, Dēu tukā kumok kārtolo"; *b*) sometimes by the Gerund in "-tanañ", although not so exactly.

Donec, usquedum = until

It may be expressed *a*) by "moṇasār" (*or* also "pāriant") placed at the end of the sentence, and leaving the Verb in the required person with its regular and full termination, or *b*) by -sār added to the pure root (with the euphonical a or i inserted before "-sār", if required); *e. g.* "*non praeteribit generatio haec donec omnia fiant* = yeñ monšākul sārseñ-nāñ, sārvụ vāstu gāḍtāt moṇasār, *or* gāḍāsār = this generation will not pass until all these things have happened". The first form seems to be more used.

Statim ac = as soon as

It may be expressed *a*) by "uprāṇt" preceded by the Participle joined to "far *or* kšāṇ = moment", thus: "*statim ac Petrus exivit flevit amare* = Pedru bāir geleā uprānt, teāts farā tsāḍ rāḍlo = (literally) after Peter went out, in that very moment he wept bitterly"; or also *b*) by the Gerund in -un and "far" *or* "kšāṇ", as before, *e. g.* "Pedru bāir votzun teātz farā tzāḍ rāḍlo"; *or* *c*) only by the Past Perfect Participle followed by "farāk", *e. g.* "tuñ uṭụlleā farāk = as soon as you get up".

Quamvis (and *synonyms*) = although
(see above *ut*)

Utrum—an, ne—an

"*Utrum—an*, or *Ne—an* = gi—yā, or only -gi". "*Ubi est? in ecclesia an in cubiculo* = to khāiñ assā? Igārjentgī yā kuḍānt? = is he in the church or in the room?" "*Nescio utrum bene an male fecerit* = taṇeñ boreñgi vāiṭ kelāñ āuñ neṇañ = I do not know whether he has done well or wrong"; "*nescio utrum hoc sit rectum an pravum* = yeñ tzukgī sāmā āuñ neṇañ = I do not know whether this is right or wrong".

Sive—sive

"*Sive—sive* = zāuñ—zāuñ", literally corresponding to the Italian *sia—sia*; for this "zāuñ" is Subjunctive of "zatā", *e. g.* "*sive sit ex urbe, sive sit ex pago, vectigalia solvat* = šerāntlo zāuñ, gāvāntlo zāuñ kāppo dīzāi". This "zāuñ" is put after, as it is a Verb; yet sometimes it is put also before the affected word.

Si vis—si vultis (joined to some other Verb)

This may be translated *a*) literally by "kušivartāñ = I desire" put in the required tense; *b*) yet it is more common to use another form, *i. e.* "zatā" put in the Conditional Present, and preceded by the root of the principal Verb and "zāi" (inserting, if required, the usual euphonical a or i); *e. g.* "*si vis ad vitam ingredi, serva mandata* = 1) zārtār zārgār votsunk khuši assā, sambāḷ upades, *or* 2) sārgār votsazāi zaleār, sambāḷ upades"; literally it may be translated thus: "if it happens (that) you must go to heaven, keep the commandments" (see page 255).

B. Some difficult tenses in some sentences

1. "*Si breviati non fuissent dies illi* = te dis moṭve zāināñ zatit zaleār = if those days had not been shortened".

This Verb is compounded of the Adjective "moṭve = short"; "zāināñ = does not become", Present Negative; "zatit" Future Past; "zaleār" Conditional. Literally we may translate: "if it did not happen (that) those days would have become, not to become short", or better we may say: here we have the Conditional joined with Future Contingent Negative (see p. 269); or still better: "zatit zaleār" is the affirmative mixed Future Conditional (p. 269); "zāināñ zatit zaleār", the same tense but Negative.

2. *Rogate ne fuga vestra fiat in sabbato* = magā tumčeñ poḷāp sonvārā gāḍanāñ zāundi = *lit.* pray (that) your flight may not happen on Saturday".

This Verb is compounded of the Imperative Negative of "gaḍtā = happens". It is a peculiar kind of Negative Imperative (see the Paradigm of Conjugation).

3. "*Manducate quae apponuntur vobis* = khāyā jeo vāstu tanče lagiñ astit".

Here the Past Future is used, because "*apponuntur*" has this meaning in this context; in Latin we might say: *quae apposita fuerint* or also it may be considered as Contingent Future.

4. "*Vis, eamus, et eradicemus ea?* = vortautā tuji khuši amiñ votsun teñ lāunči? = *lit.* is thy will, we to go (having gone) to eradicate it?"

Here, "lāuñči" is the Infinitive Absolute governed by *voluntas*, and agrees with it.

5. "*Conveni quod darem unum denarium* = yēk poiso ditāñ móṇ kārār kelā = I made the agreement that I give a half-penny (*l.* 4 pies).

Here it is used *quod* (móṇ), although we have the *oratio directa* as in Hebrew; *dixi quod vobis dabo.*

6. "*Promittis ne te hoc non amplius facturum* = yeñ tūñ eā mukār kārsonāi móṇ utar ditāigī?"

Here the Infinitive Future Active is resolved by the Conjunction "móṇ = that", in the Future Indicative.

7. "*Spero, cum tibi probatum iri* = to tukā mānuotolo móṇ āuñ pātietāñ = I trust that you will approve this, *lit. Ille tibi placebit quod, ego confido.*" The Infinitive Future Passive is resolved as the Active Infinitive Future.

8. "*Nec quisquam rex Persarum potest esse, qui non ante Magorum disciplinam perceperit* (*Cic.*) = nor can any one be king of the Persians who has not first learnt the discipline of the Magi = ani kōṇ Perśiāntso rāi zāināñ, zotiśāñči vidyā neṇāñzāit zaleār."

You see the Perfect Subjunctive rendered by the compound tense of Conditional and Contingent Future.

9. "*O fortunate adolescens, qui tuae virtutis imitatores inveneris*=O fortunate youth, who hast found (*i. e.* in that thou hast found) imitators of thy virtue! = ō sukhi burgeā, zakā pāṭlaugār meḷḷe!...pāṭlaugār meḷḷeā pasun!" Here the Perfect is rendered by the Indicative or by "pasun".

10. "*Sunt qui dicant M. Crassum non ignarum esse consilii ejus*=they say M. Crassus to be no stranger to his scheme=M. Krassusāk tatso nāmuno kāḷtā móṇ moṇtāt".

Remark the omission of "they" in this and similar sentences.

11. "Pātak nāiñ-zalleā sārvụ vāstunt voḍilāñčeā utrāk paḷo dīzāi=we must obey the word of the superiors in all not sinful things".

Remark the construction according to the above rules, especially of "pātak nāiñ-zalleā sarvụ" which is like an Adjective of "vāstunt".

12. "Tuje tābent aščeañ sāmestāñči favoti zātān kār= take care of all who are under your care".

Remark, again, the collocation of words; then "sāmestāñči" double Adjective.

13. "Peleāk tačeñ boreñ nāuñ meḷaseñ kārizāi=we must cause our neighbour to have his good name restored."

Remark the use of the Imperfect Subjunctive.

14. "Peleātso mōg kār kāso tuzo=love your neighbour as yourself".

"Pelo" becomes "peleātso", because it depends on "mōg" as Genitive; "kāso" is declined and agrees with "mōg" understood. Literally in Latin we should say: *qualem amorem tui facis, (talem) amorem proximi fac.* Hence "kāso" agrees with "mōg".

15. "Māg-ṇeāñ bāir amiñ prājit kārizāi=besides prayer we must make penance".

Remark the use of "bāir".

16. "Sākrāmentāñčeañ guṇātso amkāñ vivor somzouñčeāk, Jezu Kristān yēk diṣṭi poḍči bhāili khuṇā nemsilyā=

Jesus Christ instituted an exterior visible sign to give us tc understand the effect of the Sacraments".

"Somzouñčeāk" Dative of "somzouñtso" Absolute Infinitive, from "somzāi", Causative Verb; it is Dative to show aim. "Guṇātso" Adjectival Genitive governed by "vivor". "Nemsileā" agrees with "khuṇa", as it has a passive meaning.

17. "Bāutism ghetoleāče takler udāk ghāl = pour out water upon the head of him who receives baptism".

Remark 1) the participial construction; "bāutism", governed by the Participle, precedes it; 2) the Participle "ghetolo" converted into an Adjective in -tso, because it is Genitive.

18. "Săkrāment diunčeā veḷār amiñ Jezu Kristān formaileānt tiñ utrañ moṇazāi = while giving the Sacrament we must say those words (which) have been commanded by Jesus Christ".

Remark 1) the omission of the Relative Pronoun without participial construction; "formaileānt" agrees with "utrañ"; it is 3rd Person Plural Perfect.

19. "Kumgār kāṇeizāi zaleār, mădhe rāti thāun ăn udāk gēnaye = if you want to receive holy communion, you cannot take any food or water from midnight".

Remark the form "kāṇeizāi zaleār".

20. If it is the duty of a good king to help the state, it is also the duty of good citizens *etc.* = zărtăr boreā rāyātso kāido assā stitik kumok kărunk, boreañ rāitāntso-i kāido assā" *etc.*

21. "With the exception of Plato, I am inclined to think I should be right in calling Aristotle the first philosopher of antiquity = Plato šivāi, Arisṭoṭlụ porneañ kālāntlo poilo ginăna-sodnār moḷḷo săma-señ makā distā".

Remark 1) the Konkani manner to express the quasi-diminutive notion "I am inclined to think"; here two modes are employed, *i. e.* "distā = seems", and as "distā" does not suffice, because it means "it seems *or* I think, I have the opinion", hence "-señ" is added, whereby we get the full meaning; *lit.* "it seems to be somewhat right." 2) Remark "kālāntlo" which agrees with "ginăna-sodnăr", because it is the Adjectival Genitive (see p. 52); here the Genitive is converted into an Adjective in -lo, because it means in. Remark 3) that "poilo" agrees also with "ginăna-sodnăr", because it belongs directly to this word, not to "kăl"; if it belonged to "kăl", it should be put in the oblique case (see p. 52). Remark 4) the change of "móṇ" into "moḷḷo" which moreover agrees with "ginăna-sodnăr".

22. "*Multi in parandis equis adhibent curam, in amicis eligendis negligentes sunt* = many take pains in getting horses, but are careless in choosing friends (*Cic.*) = săbăr mănis goḍe (*or* goḍeănk) kăṇeuñčeănt preyetăn kărtăt, iștănk vintsun kăḍčeănt făḍpoši zăun assăt".

Now a few examples about Participial sentences governed by Postpositions.

23. "We all like to tell our sorrow to one who after having heard, will be willing and able to have mercy on us and to help us = amkăñ ăikon amčer kăkuḷt dovorunk ani amkăñ kumok kărunk khuši ani tank assellea lăgiñ amiñ sămest amči duk săngunk khuši vartăuñ."

Remark 1) the use of the Participle "assellea" followed by a Postposition; it is preceded by "khuši ani tank", because these two words are the subject of "assellea"; they are left in the Nominative as if the Verb were in a finite mood. 2) These two words are preceded by "amčer kăkuḷt....", because these words are governed and determined by "khuši ani tank". The other words are clear.

24. "Come to me, who am your God, says our L. J. C. = tumtso Dēu zăun asselleă moje lăgiñ yeă, móṇ sangtă Somi Jezu Krist".

Remark here too the use of the Participle.

25. "Yeke băilmănšek assollo titso yekăts pŭtụ morn păulleă veḷăr Somia Jezu Kristăn tičeñ răḍneă poḷeun tičea putăk portun jivont kellea pori, to tujeñ răḍneñ poḷeun, tujea vistatso

ătmo zo taņeñ apleñ amolik răgtăčea nimāņo thembo vikraun soḍăilolo to, dubău nastanăñ portun jivont kărtolo = as our Lord Jesus Christ having seen the weeping of a woman, when her only son had died, resuscitated him; so he seeing thy weeping, will, no doubt, resuscitate the soul of thy friend, whom he redeemed by having shed even the last drop of His precious blood".

Remark 1) the long sentence governed by the Postposition "póri = as". All words governed by 'póri" precede it according to the order of dependence; hence first the Participle "kellea", then "jivont", because it is immediately governed by "kellea" and determines "kellea" (what done?), then "portun", because it determines "jivont" (which time has he given life?), then the object of "kellea", viz. "tiče putāk", because the object precedes the Verb, then "Somia poļeun," because this sentence is adverbial explaining "when Jesus Christ resuscitated", hence it must precede; and in this sentence first the Instrumental, because also in a sentence of finite mood, the Instrumental should precede (Somia Jesu Kristān poļeilăñ), then the Accusative, then the Verb; finally, in the first place the sentence "yeke...veļăr", because it is another adverbial sentence explaining the following; consequently it must precede it; in this sentence itself the subject preceded by the governed words ("yeke...putų") is put in the first place, then the Verb, ("morn...veļăr") which here has an adverbial form. Or more exactly "veļăr" might be considered as Postposition; hence, it is preceded first by the Participle, then by the subject of the Participle, with all words belonging to the subject.

Hence we see that the general rule (as said in Ch. III.) for arranging sentences is to put the explaining parts before the explained ones; if in an explaining sentence there are words or parts explaining and explained (or determining and determined), the explaining are put before the explained parts. As to the others, Postpositions are put at the end of the governed sentence, joined to the Participle; in a participial sentence the words are left nearly in the same order as in the full pronominal sentence.

26. "Altārir assellea amčea sodvondarāče hāt kurpe bārit zāun assāt = the hands of our Saviour who is on the altar are full of graces".

Remark here too the Participial sentence.

If we wish to insert all the difficult sentences, we should never come to an end, so let us finish the first Appendix here, leaving something also to private diligence and to practice.

APPENDIX II

Translation of some chapters of the Holy Bible

1. The following translation was intended for beginners; wherefore it is very literal, and here and there not well agreeing with the nature of Konkani; if it had been somewhat free, as it should be apart from such necessity, the beginners could not have found in the English translation the Konkani sentence. This aim must be kept in view in order to judge about this translation. I grant that a freer translation would have been more Konkani.

2. The words between brackets are not words of the Holy Bible but explanations inserted by me when the literal translation was not sufficient to convey a clear notion. Such explanations, together with the footnotes, have been taken either from *Menochio* or from the English *Douay* Version.

3. In the translation with Kanarese letters I introduce three new signs in order the better to express thereby the Konkani sounds. These are ಜ಼=z, ಚ಼=ts; ˘ above the consonant to express ụ or ạ (half vowel). This ˘ has been used already in such a way by the Basel Mission Press of Mangalore; see Polyglot Vocabulary, p. xv. The simple ಜ=j, ಚ=č. I use ್ for the Sanskrit "virāma", *i.e.* as a sign of the absence of any vowel or half vowel, as in Kanarese too this ್ has such a meaning.

4. For the sake of convenience I put first the Kanarese alphabet.

A. Vowels

Initial forms	Medial and final forms	Corresponding Roman Characters	Approximate Pronunciation
ಅ	‿	ă	like a in 'about' or in *adoro*
ಆ	ಾ	ā	„ a in 'far' or in *aro*
ಇ	ಿ	ĭ	„ i in 'thin' or in *aridus*
ಈ	ೀ	ī	„ i in 'police' or in *marinus*
ಉ	ು	ŭ	„ u in 'full' or in *coluber*
ಊ	ೂ	ū	„ u in 'rule' or in *rubor*
ಋ	ೃ	r̥̆	vocalized short r, nearly as r in 'centre'
ೠ	ೄ	r̥̄	„ long r
ಎ	ೆ	ĕ	like e in 'effort' or in *comedo*
ಏ	ೇ	ē	„ ea in 'swear' or as e in *terra*
ಐ	ೈ	ei	„ ei in 'height'
ಒ	ೊ	ŏ	„ o in 'not' or in *operari*
ಓ	ೋ	ō	„ o in 'vote' or in *ordine*
ಔ	ೌ	ou	„ ou in 'house' or in *laudo*

ᵕ u̯ or ą, viz. half vowel.

್ sign of the absence of a vowel (Sanskrit virāma).

ಂ ṅ nasal sound, an indistinct n.

ಃ vocalized h.

B. Consonants

Consonants with the inherent vowel ཨ a	Form and position when combined with other Consonants	Corresponding Roman Characters	Approximate Pronunciation
ཀ	ྐ	ka	like ka in 'kalendar'
ཁ	ྑ	kha	the same aspirated
ག	ྒ	ga	as ga in 'gallon'
གྷ	ྒྷ	gha	„ aspirated
ང	ྔ	ṅga	a very guttural and nasal ga
ཅ	ྕ	ča	as cha in 'chapter' or c in *cinis*
ཆ	ྖ	čha	ča aspirated
ཙ	ྩ	tsa	as z in German, viz. the sounds of [t and s combined
ཚ	ྪ	tsha	„ aspirated
ཇ	ྗ	ja	as ja in 'Japan' but thinner
ཇྷ	ྗྷ	jha	„ aspirated
ཛ	ྫ	za	as sa in 'nasal' or in *rosa*
ཛྷ	ྫྷ	zha	„ aspirated
ཉ	ྙ	gna	as nya in 'banyan' or gn in *agnus*
ཊ	ྚ	ṭa	the cerebral ta
ཋ	ྛ	ṭha	ṭa aspirated
ཌ	ྜ	ḍa	the cerebral ḍa
ཌྷ	ྜྷ	ḍha	ḍa aspirated
ཎ	ྞ	ṇa	the cerebral ṇa
ཏ	ྟ	ta	common ta
ཐ	ྠ	tha	ta aspirated
ད	ྡ	da	common da
དྷ	ྡྷ	dha	da aspirated
ན	ྣ	na	common na

Consonants with the inherent vowel ಅ a	Form and position when combined with other Consonants	Corresponding Roman Characters	Approximate Pronunciation
ಪ	್ಪ	pa	common pa
ಫ	್ಫ	pha	pa aspirated
ಬ	್ಬ	ba	common ba
ಭ	್ಭ	bha	ba aspirated
ಮ	್ಮ	ma	a common ma
ಯ	್ಯ	ya	as ya in 'yam' or as j in *ajo*.
ರ	್ರ	ra	common ra
ಲ	್ಲ	la	common la
ವ	್ವ	va	common va
ಶ	್ಶ	śa	palatal English sha
ಷ	್ಷ	ṣa	cerebral „ sha
ಸ	್ಸ	sa	as sa in 'salute'
ಹ	್ಹ	ha	as ha in 'harangue'
ಳ	್ಳ	ḷa	cerebral ḷa
ಕ್ಷ	ಕ್ಷ	kṣa	combination of ka and ṣa, Latin x

N. B. In the approximate pronunciation, and in the corresponding Roman characters I have written ka, ga *etc.*, because each of the given consonants contains a short a.

ಅ ರ ಂ ಬ್

ಅವಸ್ವರ್ I.

1 ಸುರುವೆರ್ ದೇವಾನ್ ಸರ್ಗ್
ಅನಿ ಸೌಂಸಾರ್ ರಚ್ಲೊ.
2 ಪುಣ್ ಸೌಂಸಾರಾಕ್ ರುಪ್
ಅನಿ ಜೀವಿ ವಸ್ತು ನಾತ್ಲೆಲ್ಲೊ,
ಅನಿ ಕಾಳೊಕ್ ಅಸೊಲೊ ಗುಂಡಾ
ಯೆ ವೊಯ್ರ್; ಅನಿ ದೇವಾಚೊ ಸ್ಪಿರಿತ್
ಉದ್ಕಾಂಚೆರ್ ತ್ಸಾಲ್ತಾಲೊ.
3 ಅನಿ ದೇವಾನ್ ಮೊಳೆಂ: ಉ
ಜ್ವಾಡ್[1] ಜಾಉಂಡಿ. ಅನಿ ಉಜ್ವಾಡ್
ಜಾಲೊ.
4 ಅನಿ ಉಜ್ವಾಡ್ ಬೊರೊ ಜಾ
ಉನ್ ಅಸಾ ಮೊಣ್ ದೇವಾನ್ ಪೊ
ಳ್ಯೆಲೆಂ; ಅನಿ ಉಜ್ವಾಡ್ ಕಾಳೊಕಾಂ
ತ್ಲೊ ವಿಂಗಡ್ ಕೆಲೊ.
5 ಅನಿ ಉಜ್ವಾಡಾಕ್ ದೀಸ್ ಮೊ
ಣ್ ಮೊಳೊ, ಅನಿ ಕಾಳೊಕಾಕ್ ರಾತ್
ಮೊಳಿ; ಅನಿ ಸಾಂಜ್ ಅನಿ ಸಕಾಳಿಂ
ಏಕ್ ದೀಸ್ ಜಾಲೊ.
6 ದೇವಾನ್ ತಾಚೆ ಶಿವಾಯ್ ಸಾಂ
ಗ್ಲೆಂ: ಉದ್ಕಾಂ ಮೊಡೆಂ ಮೊಳಾಬ್[2]
ಜಾಉಂಡಿ; ಅನಿ ಉದ್ಕಾಂ ಉದ್ಕಾಂ
ತ್ಲಿಂ ವಿಂಗಡ್ ಕರುಂಡಿ.
7 ಅನಿ ದೇವಾನ್ ಮೊಳಾಬ್ ಕೆ
ಲೆಂ, ಅನಿ ಮೊಳ್ಬಾ ಖಾಲ್ ಅಸ
ಲ್ಲಿಂ ಉದ್ಕಾಂ ಮೊಳ್ಬಾರ್ ಅಸ್ಲ್ಲ್ಯಾ,

ARĂMB

Avasvăr I.

1 Suruver Dēvān sărg
ani souñsăr rătslo.
2 Puṇ souñsărāk rup
ani jīvio văstu nāṭ̣lleo,
ani kāḷok asolo guṇ-
ḍāye voir; ani Dēvātso
Spirit udkāñčer tsăl-
tālo.
3 Ani Dēvān moḷeñ:
uzuăḍ[1] zăundi. Ani
uzuăḍ zālo.
4 Ani uzuăḍ boro zăun
asă móṇ Dēvān poḷei-
leñ; ani uzuăḍ kāḷo-
kāntlo viñgaḍ kelo.
5 Ani uzuăḍāk dīs móṇ
moḷo, ani kāḷokāk rāt
moḷi; ani sănz ani să-
kāḷiñ yēk dīs zālo.
6 Dēvān tače šivăi
sangleñ: udkāñ modeñ
moḷab[2] zăundi; ani ud-
kāñ udkāntliñ viñgăḍ
kărundi.
7 Ani Dēvān moḷab
keleñ, ani moḷbā khāl
asṣlliñ udkañ moḷbār

GENESIS

Chapter I.

1 In the beginning God
created heaven and earth.
2 And the earth was
void and empty, and dark-
ness was upon the face of
the deep; and the Spirit
of God moved over the
waters.
3 And God said: Be
light[1] made. And light
was made.
4 And God saw the
light that it was good;
and he divided the light
from the darkness.
5 And he called the
light Day, and the dark-
ness Night; and there
was evening and morning
one day.
6 And God said: Let
there be a firmament[2]
made amidst the waters;
and let it divide the
waters from the waters.
7 And God made a fir-
mament, and divided the
waters that were under

---

[1] "Uzuăḍ" mupčeñ: uzuăḍ zo udoun ani poḍun sănz ani. săkāḷiñ zăunk kărăp zăun asolo.—"Light", viz: light which by its rising and setting make morning and evening.

[2] "Moḷab" mupčeñ: buiñ ani bhou ubăr noketrāñ modeñ assolle zăgo.—"Firmament", viz: the space between the earth and the highest stars.

ಉದ್ಕಾಂತ್ಲಿಂ ವಿಂಗಡ್ ಕೆಲ್ಯಾಂತ್;
ಅನಿ ಅಸೆಂ ಜಾಲೆಂ.

8 ಅನಿ ದೇವಾನ್ ಮೊಳ್ಬಾಕ್ ಸ
ರ್ಗ್ ಮೊಳೆಂ; ಅನಿ ಸಾಂಜ್ ಅನಿ
ಸಕಾಳಿಂ ದುಸ್ರೊ ದಿಸ್ ಜಾಲೊ.

9 ಅನಿ ದೇವಾನ್ ಸಾಂಗ್ಲೆಂ:
ಸರ್ಗಾ ಖಾಲ್ ಅಸ್ಲಿಂ ಉದ್ಕಾಂ
ಯೆಕೆ ಸುವಾತೆರ್ ಮೆಳುಂದಿತ್; ಅನಿ
ಸುಕೊ ಜಾಗೊ ದಿಸುಂದಿ. ಅನಿ ಅಸೆಂ
ಜಾಲೆಂ.

10 ಅನಿ ದೇವಾನ್ ಸುಕ್ಯಾ ಜಾ
ಗ್ಯಾಕ್ ಬುಯಿಂ ಮೊಣ್ ಮೊಳಿ, ಅನಿ
ಉದ್ಕಾಂಚ್ಯಾ ಜೊಮ್ಯಾಕ್ ದರ್ಯೊ.
ಅನಿ ಯೆಂ ಬೊರೆಂ ಜಾವುನ್ ಅಸಾ
ಮೊಣ್ ದೇವಾನ್ ಪೊಳೆಲೆಂ.

11 ಅನಿ ಸಾಂಗ್ಲೆಂ: ಬುಯಿಂ ಉ
ಬ್ಜೊಂದಿ ತರ್ನೆಂ ತಣ್ ಅನಿ ಬಿಯಿಂ
ಕರ್ಚೆಂ ಅಪ್ಲ್ಯಾ ತರಾ ಪರ್ಮಾಣೆ, ಅ
ನಿ (ಉಬ್ಜೊಂದಿ) ಫೊಳಾದಿಕ್ ರುಕ್ ಅ
ಪ್ಲ್ಯಾ ತರಾ ಪರ್ಮಾಣೆ ಫೊಳ್ ದಿವುಂ
ಚೊ, ಜಾಚೆಂ ಬಿಯಿಂ ತಾಚೆ ಬಿತರ್ ಅ
ಸುಂ ಬುಯಿಂಚೆರ್. ಅನಿ ಅಸೆಂ ಜಾಲೆಂ.

12 ಅನಿ ಬುಯಿಂನ್ ಉಬ್ಜೈಲೆಂ
ತಣ್ ತರ್ನೆಂ, ಅನಿ ಫೊಳ್ ದಿವುಂಚೆಂ
ಅಪ್ಲ್ಯಾ ತರಾ ಪರ್ಮಾಣೆ, ಅನಿ ರುಕ್
ಫೊಳಾದಿಕ್, ಹರ್ಯೆಕ್ಲ್ಯಾಕ್ ಅಸುನ್
ಬಿಯಿಂ ಅಪ್ಲ್ಯಾ ತರಾ ಪರ್ಮಾಣೆ. ಅನಿ
ಯೆಂ ಬೊರೆಂ ಮೊಣ್ ದೇವಾನ್ ಪೊ
ಳೆಲೆಂ.

asallea udkāntliñ viñgāḍ keliñ; ani aseñ zāleñ.

8 Aņi Dēvān moḷbāk sărg moḷeñ; ani sānz ani săkāḷiñ dusro dīs zālo.

9 Ani Dēvān sañgleñ: sărgā khāl asaliñ udkañ yēke suāter meḷundit; ani suko zāgo disundi. Ani aseñ zāleñ.

10 Ani Dēvān sukeā zāgeāk buiñ móṇ moḷi, ani udkānčeā zomeāk dărio. Ani yeñ boreñ zaun asā móṇ Dēvān poḷeileñ.

11 Ani sañgleñ: buiñ ubzoundi tărneñ tāṇ ani bīñ kārčeñ aplea tārā pārmāṇe, ani (ubzoundi) foḷadik ruk aplea tārā pārmāṇe foḷ diuñtso, začeñ bīñ tače bitār asuñ buiñčer. Ani ăseñ zāleñ.

12 Ani buiñn ubzaileñ tāṇ tărneñ, ani foḷ diuñčeñ aplea tārā pārmāṇe, ani ruk foḷādik, hāryekleāk asun bīñ aplea tārā pārmāṇe. Ani yeñ boreñ móṇ Dēvān poḷeileñ.

the firmament, from those that were above the firmament; and it was so.

8 And God called the firmament, heaven; and the evening and morning were the second day.

9 God also said: let the waters that are under the heaven, be gathered together into one place; and let the dry land appear. And it was so done.

10 And God called the dry land, earth, and the gathering together of the waters, he called seas. And God saw that it was good.

11 And he said: let the earth bring forth the green herb, and such as may have seed, and the fruit-tree yielding fruit after its kind, which may have seed in itself upon the earth. And it was so done.

12 And the earth brought forth the green herb, and such as yieldeth seed according to its kind, and the tree that beareth fruit having seed each one according to its kind. And God saw that it was good.

13 ಆನಿ ಸಾಂಜ್ ಆನಿ ಸಕಾಳಿಂ ತಿಸ್ರೊ ದೀಸ್ ಜಾಲೊ.	13 Ani sānz ani săkāḷiñ tisro dīs zālo.	13 And the evening and the morning were the third day.
14 ಆನಿ ದೇವಾನ್ ಸಾಂಗ್ಲೆಂ: ಉಜ್ವಾಡಿಕ್ ವಸ್ತು ಜಾಂವುಂದಿತ್ ಸರ್ಗಿಂಚ್ಯಾ ಮೊಳ್ಬಾರ್, ಆನಿ ದಿಸಾಂತ್ಲಿ ರಾತ್ ವಿಂಗಡ್ ಕರುಂದಿತ್, ಆನಿ ಗುರ್ತು ಅಸುಂದಿತ್ (ದಾಕೌಂಕ್) ವೇಳ್ ಆನಿ ದೀಸ್ ಆನಿ ವರ್ಸಾಂ:	14 Ani Dēvān sañgleñ: uzuāḍik vāstu zāundit sărgiñčeā moḷbār, ani disāntli rāt viñgāḍ kărundit, ani gurtụ asundit (dākounk) vēḷ ani dīs ani vărsāñ:	14 And God said: let there be lights made in the firmament of heaven, to divide the day and the night, and let them be for signs, and for seasons, and for days and years:
15 ತೆಂ ಸರ್ಗಿಂಚ್ಯಾ ಮೊಳ್ಬಾರ್ ಪರ್ಜಳುಂದಿತ್, ಆನಿ ಬುಯಿಂಕ್ ಉಜ್ವಾಡ್ ದಿಉಂದಿತ್; ಆನಿ ಅಸೆಂ ಜಾಲೆಂ.	15 Teo sărgiñčeā moḷbār părzāḷundit, ani buiñk uzuāḍ diundit. Ani aseñ zāleñ.	15 To shine in the firmament of heaven, and to give light upon the earth. And it was so done.
16 ಆನಿ ದೇವಾನ್ ದೋನ್ ವೋಡ್ ಉಜ್ವಾಡಿಕ್ ವಸ್ತು[1] ಕೆಲ್ಯೊ: ಏಕ್ ವೋಡ್ ದಿಸಾಚೆರ್, ಆನಿ ಏಕ್ ಲಾನ್ ರಾತಿಚೆರ್ ರಾಜ್ವಟ್ಕಾಯ್ ಕರಿಸ್ಯೊ, ಆನಿ ನೆಕೆತ್ರಾಂ.	16 Ani Dēvān dón vóḍ uzuāḍik vāstu[1] keleo: yēk vóḍ disāčer, ani yēk lān rātičer rāzvoṭkāi kărisio, ani neketrañ.	16 And God made two great lights[1]: a greater light to rule the day, and a lesser light to rule the night, and the stars.
17 ಆನಿ ತಾಂಕಾಂ ಸರ್ಗಿಂಚ್ಯಾ ಮೊಳ್ಬಾರ್ ಗಾಲಿಂ ಬುಯಿಂಕ್ ಉಜ್ವಾಡ್ ದಿಉಂಕ್,	17 Ani tankāñ sărgiñčeā moḷbār galiñ buiñk uzuāḍ diunk,	17 And he set them in the firmament of heaven to shine upon the earth,
18 ಆನಿ ದಿಸಾಚೆರ್ ಆನಿ ರಾತಿಚೆರ್ ರಾಜ್ವಟ್ಕಾಯ್ ಕರುಂಕ್ ಆನಿ ಉಜ್ವಾಡ್ ಆನಿ ಕಾಳೋಕ್ ವಿಂಗಡ್ ಕರುಂಕ್. ಆನಿ ತೆಂ ಬೊರೆಂ ಮೊಣ್ ದೇವಾನ್ ಪೊಳೆಲೆಂ.	18 Ani disāčer ani rātičer rāzvoṭkāi kărunk ani uzuāḍ ani kāḷok viñgāḍ kărunk. Ani teñ boreñ móṇ Dēvān poḷeileñ.	18 And to rule the day and the night, and to divide the light and the darkness. And God saw that it was good.
19 ಆನಿ ಸಾಂಜ್ ಆನಿ ಸಕಾಳಿಂ ಚೌತೊ ದೀಸ್ ಜಾಲೊ.	19 Ani sānz ani săkāḷiñ tsouto dīs zālo.	19 And the evening and morning were the fourth day.
20 ಆನಿ ದೇವಾನ್ ಸಾಂಗ್ಲೆಂ: ಉದ್ಕಾಂ ಉಬ್ಜೌಂದಿತ್ ಜಿಉದಾಚ್ ಜಿವ್ಯಾ ಆತ್ಮ್ಯಾಚಿ ಆನಿ ಸು	20 Ani Dēvān sañgleñ: udkañ ubzoundit jiudād jiveā ātmeāči	20 God also said: let the waters bring forth the creeping creature

ಕ್ಣಿಂ ಬುಯ್ಂಚೆರ್ ಸರ್ಗಿಂಚ್ಯಾ ಮೊಳ್ಬಾ ಖಾಲ್.	ani sukṇiñ buiñčer sārgiñčeā mōḷbā khāl.	having life, and the fowl that may fly over the earth under the firmament of heaven.
21 ಅನಿ ದೇವಾನ್ ರಚ್ಲ್ಯೊ ವೊದ್ ಮಾಸ್ಳ್ಯೊ ಅನಿ ಸರ್ವ ಜಿಉಜಾತ್ (ಜಿ ಉದ್ಕಾಂತ್ ಜಿಯೆತಾ) ಜಾಂಕಾಂ ಉದ್ಕಾನಿಂ ಉಬ್ಜೈಲ್ಲ್ಯೊ ಅಪ್ಲ್ಯಾ ತರಾ ಪರ್ಮಾಣೆ, ಅನಿ (ರಚ್ಲಿಂ) ಸರ್ವ ಸುಕ್ಣಿಂ ಅಪ್ಲ್ಯಾ ತರಾ ಪರ್ಮಾಣೆ. ಅನಿ ತೆಂ ಬೊರೆಂ ಮೊಣ್ ದೇವಾನ್ ಪೊಳೈಲೆಂ.	21 Ani Dēvān rătzlo vóḍ māsḷeo ani sārvų jiuzāt (ji udkānt jietā) zankā udkāniñ ubzailleo aplea tārā pārmāṇe, ani (rătzliñ) sārvų sukṇiñ aplea tārā pārmāṇe. Ani teñ boreā móṇ Dēvān poḷeileñ.	21 And God created the great whales, and every living and moving creature, which the waters brought forth, according to their kinds, and every winged fowl according to its kind. And God saw that it was good.
22 ಅನಿ ದೇವಾನ್ ತಾಂಕಾಂ ಆಶಿರ್ವಾದ್ ದಿಲೆಂ ಸಾಂಗುನ್: ವಾಡಾ ಅನಿ ಚಡಾ ಅನಿ ದರ್ಯಾಚಿಂ ಉದ್ಕಾಂ ಬೊರಾ, ಅನಿ ಸುಕ್ಣಿಂ ಬುಯ್ಂಚೆರ್ ಚಡುಂದಿತ್.	22 Ani Dēvān tankāñ āširvād dileñ sāngun: vāḍā ani tsāḍā ani dariāčiñ udkaā borā, ani sukṇiñ buiñčer tsāḍundit.	22 And He blessed them saying: Increase and multiply, and fill the waters of the sea, and let the birds be multiplied upon the earth.
23 ಅನಿ ಸಾಂಜ್ ಅನಿ ಸಕಾಳಿಂ ಪಾಂಚ್ವೊ ದೀಸ್ ಜಾಲೊ.	23 Ani sānz ani sākāḷiñ pāntsvo dīs zālo.	23 And the evening and the morning were the fifth day.
24 ತಾಚೆ ಶಿವಾಯ್ ದೇವಾನ್ ಸಾಂಗ್ಲೆಂ: ಬುಯ್ಂ ಜಿವ್ಯಾಂ ಮೊನ್ಜಾತಿಂಕ್ ಉಬ್ಜೊವುಂದಿ ಅಪ್ಲ್ಯಾ ತರಾ ಪರ್ಮಾಣೆ, ಸಾದ್ಯಾಂ ಮೊನ್ಜಾತಿಂಕ್, ಜಿಉದಾದಿಂಕ್, ರಾನ್ವೊಟ್ ಮೊನ್ಜಾತಿಂಕ್ ಅಪ್ಲ್ಯಾ ತರಾ ಪರ್ಮಾಣೆ. ಅನಿ ಅಸೆಂ ಜಾಲೆಂ.	24 Tače šivāi Dēvān sangleñ: buiñ jiveāñ monzātink ubzoundi aplea tārā pārmāṇe sādeañ monzātink, jiudādink, rānvoṭ monzātink apleā tārā pārmāṇe. Ani taseñ zāleñ.	24 And God said: let the earth bring forth the living creature in its kind, cattle and creeping things and beasts of the earth, according to their kinds. And it was so done.
25 ಅನಿ ದೇವಾನ್ ಬುಯ್ಂಚ್ಯಾ ಮೊನ್ಜಾತಿಂಕ್ ಕೆಲ್ಯೊ ತಾಂಚ್ಯಾ ತರಾ ಪರ್ಮಾಣೆ ಅನಿ ಸಾದೆ ಮೊನ್ಜಾತಿಂಕ್ ಅನಿ ಸರ್ವ ಜಿಉದಾದಿಕ್ ಬುಯ್ಂಚೆ	25 Ani Dēvān buiñčeā monzātink keleo tančeā tārā pārmāṇe ani sade monzātink ani	25 And God made the beasts of the earth according to their kinds, and cattle, and every

ಜಾತ್ಯಾ ತರಾ ಪರಮಾಣೆಂ. ಅನಿ ತೆಂ ಬರೆಂ ಮೊಣ್ ದೇವಾನ್ ಪೊಳೆಲೆಂ.

sărvụ jiudādik buiñče tačeā tārā pārmāṇe. Ani teñ boreñ móṇ Dēvān poḷeileñ.

thing that creepeth on the earth after its kind. And God saw that it was good.

26 ಅನಿ ಸಾಂಗ್ಲೆಂ: ಮನ್ಶ್ಯಾಕ್ ಕರಿಯಾಂ ಅಮ್ಚೆ ಬರಿ ಅನಿ ಅಮ್ಚ್ಯಾ ಸಾರ್ಕ್ಯಾಟ್ಸೊ[1]: ಅನಿ ತೊ ಮಾಸ್ಳ್ಯಾಂಚೆರ್ ದರಿಯಾಚ್ಯಾ ಅನಿ ಸುಕ್ಣ್ಯಾಂಚೆರ್ ಅನಿ ಮೊನ್ಜಾತಿಂಚೆರ್ ಅನಿ ಸಗ್ಳ್ಯಾ ಬುಯಿಂಚೆರ್ ಅನಿ ಸರ್ವ ಬುಯಿಂತ್ ತರ್ತೆಲೆ ಜಿವಾಳಿಂಚೆರ್ ರಾಜ್ವೊಟ್ ಕರುಂದಿ.

26 Ani sangleñ: mănšāk kāriāñ amče bāri ani amčeā sărkeātso[1]: ani to māsḷiānčer dăriăčeā, ani sukṇeāñčer ani monzātiñčer ani săgḷea buiñčer ani sărvụ buint tsărtele jivāḷičer rāzvoṭ kărundi.

26 And he said: let us make man to our image[1] and likeness; and let him have dominion over the fishes of the sea, and the fowls of the air, and the beasts, and the whole earth, and every creeping creature that moveth upon the earth.

27 ಅನಿ ದೇವಾನ್ ಮನ್ಶ್ಯಾಕ್ ಕೆಲೊ ಅಪ್ಲ್ಯಾ ಸಾರ್ಕ್ಯಾಟ್ಸೊ: ದೇವಾಚ್ಯಾ ಸಾರ್ಕ್ಯಾಕ್ ತಾಕಾ ರಚ್ಲೊ, ದಾದ್ಲೊ ಅನಿ ಅಸ್ತ್ರಿ ತಾಂಕಾಂ ರಚ್ಲ್ಯಾಂತ್.

27 Ani Dēvān mănšāk kelo aplea sărkeātso: Dēvāčea sărkeāk takā rătzlo, dādlo ani ăstri tankāñ rătzliñ.

27 And God created man to his own image: to the image of God he created him, male and female he created them.

28 ಅನಿ ದೇವಾನ್ ತಾಂಕಾಂ ಆಶಿರ್ವಾದ್ ದಿಉನ್ ಸಾಂಗ್ಲೆಂ: ವಾಡಾ, ಅನಿ ತ್ಸಾಡಾ[2], ಅನಿ ಬುಯಿಂ ಭೊರಾ ಅನಿ ತಿಕಾ ಖಾಲ್ತಿ ಕರಾ, ಅನಿ ದರಿಯಾಚೆ ಮಾಸ್ಳ್ಯಾಂಚೆರ್ ಅನಿ ಸಮೆಸ್ತಾಂ ಬುಯಿಂಚೆರ್ ಹಾಲ್ತೆಲ್ಯಾಂ ಮೊನ್ಜಾತಿಂಚೆರ್ ರಾಜ್ವೊಟ್ ಕರಾ.

28 Ani Dēvān tankāñ āširvād diun sangleñ: vāḍā, ani tsāḍā[2], ani buiñ bhorā ani tikā khālti kārā, ani dăriăče māsḷiānčer ani sămestañ buiñčer hălteleañ monzātiñčer rāzvoṭ kārā.

28 And God blessed them, saying: Increase and multiply[2] and fill the earth, and subdue it, and rule over the fishes of the sea, and the fowls of the air, and all living creatures that move upon the earth.

29 ಅನಿ ದೇವಾನ್ ಸಾಂಗ್ಲೆಂ: ಪೊಳೆಯಾ, ಆವೆಂ ತುಮ್ಕಾಂ ಸರ್ವ ತಾಣ್ ದಿಲಾಂ ಬಿಂ ದಿಂವ್ಚೆಂ ಬುಯಿಂ

29 Ani Dēvān sangleñ: poḷeyā, āuveñ tumkāñ sărvụ tāṇ dilāñ, biñ

29 And God said: Behold I have given you every herb bearing seed

1) "Amčeā sărkeātso": Dēvāčeñ sarkeñ ătmeānt asā; kiteāk ătmo morn natullo ani spirit zāun asā dekun.—"To our image": This image of God is in the soul, which is immortal and spiritual.

2) "Vāḍā ani tsāḍā": I hukum naiñ, bogār fōḷ ubsounčeñ āširvād.—"Increase and multiply": This is not a precept, but a blessing rendering them fruitful.

ಚೆರ್, ಅನಿ ಸಮೆಸ್ತ್ ರುಕ್ ಅಪ್ಲ್ಯಾ ಬಿತರ್ ಬೀಂ ಅಸುನ್ ತುಮ್ಕಾಂ ಖಾಣಾಕ್ ಜ್ಹಾಯ್ಸೆಂ:

diuñčeñ buiñčer, ani sămest ruk aplea bităr bīñ asun tumkāñ khāṇāk zāiseñ:

upon the earth, and all trees that have in themselves seed of their own kind, to be your meat:

30 ಅನಿ (ಆವೆಂ ಯೆಂ ದಿಲಾಂ) ಸಮೆಸ್ತಾಂ ಬ್ಯುಂಚ್ಯಾಂ ಮೊಂಜ್ಹಾತಿಂಕ್, ಅನಿ ಸಮೆಸ್ತಾಂ ಸುಕ್ಣ್ಯಾಂಕ್ ಮೊಳ್ಬಾಚ್ಯಾ, ಅನಿ ಸಮೆಸ್ತಾಂ ಬ್ಯುಂಚೆರ್ ಹಾಲ್ತೆಲ್ಯಾಂಕ್, ಜಾಂಕಾಂ ಜಿವ್ ಅಸಾ, ತಾಂಕಾಂ ಖಾಉಂಕ್ ಅಸಾಸೆಂ. ಅನಿ ಅಸೆಂ ಜಾಲೆಂ.

30 Ani (āveñ yeñ dilāñ) sămestañ buiñčeāñ monzātink, ani sămestañ sukṇeānk moḷbāčea, ani sămestañ buiñčer hălteleānk, zankāñ jiv asā, tankāñ khāunk asāseñ. Ani aseñ zāleñ.

30 And to all beasts of the earth, and to every fowl of the air, and to all that move upon the earth, and wherein there is life, that they may have to feed upon. And it was so done.

31 ಅನಿ ದೇವಾನ್ ಸಮೆಸ್ತ್ ಅಪ್ಣೆಂ ಕೆಲ್ಲಿಯೊ ವಸ್ತು ಪೊಳೆಲ್ಯೊ, ಅನಿ ಭೊವು ಬೊರೆಯೊ ಅಸಲ್ಲ್ಯೊ; ಅನಿ ಸಾಂಜ್ ಅನಿ ಸಕಾಳಿಂ ಸೊವೊ ದಿಸ್ ಜಾಲೊ.

31 Ani Dēvān sămest apṇeñ kellio văstu poḷeileo, ani bhou boreo asạlleo; ani sānz ani săkāḷiñ sovo dīs zālo.

31 And God saw all the things that He had made, and they were very good. And the evening and morning were the sixth day.

ಅವಸ್ವರ್ II.

Avasvār II.

Chapter II.

1 ತರ್ ಸರ್ಗ್ ಅನಿ ಬ್ಯುಂ ಅನಿ ಸರ್ವ್ ತಾಂಟ್ಸೊ ಸುರುಂಗಾರ್ ಸಂಪೂರ್ಣ್ ಜಾಲೊ.

1 Tăr sărg ani buiñ ani sărvụ tāntso suruñgār sămpūrṇ zālo.

1 So the heavens and the earth were finished, and all the furniture of them.

2 ಅನಿ ದೇವಾನ್ ಸಾತ್ವೊ ದಿಸ್ ಅಪ್ಣೆಂ ಕೆಲ್ಲೊ ವಾಉರ್ ಪುರ್ತೊ ತಿರ್ಸಿಲೊ; ಅನಿ ಸಾತ್ವೊ ದಿಸ್, ಸರ್ವ್ ವಾಉರ್ ಮನ್ನ ಕರ್ನ್ ಸೌಕಾಸಾಯ್ ಕಾಣ್ಯೆಲ್ಯಾಂ.

2 Ani Dēvān sātvo dīs apṇeñ kello vāur purto tirsilo; ani sātvo dīs sărvụ vāur mănna kărn soukāsāi kāṇeileā.[4]

2 And on the seventh day God ended His work which He had made: and He rested on the seventh day from all His work which He had done.

3 ಅನಿ ಸಾತ್ವ್ಯಾ ದಿಸಾಕ್ ಆಶಿರ್ವಾದ್ ದಿಲೆಂ ಅನಿ ತಾಕಾ ಪವಿತ್ರ್ ಕೆಲೊ; ತ್ಯಾ ದಿಸಾ ಸರ್ವ್ ಅಪ್ಲ್ಯಾ

3 Ani sātveā disāk āširvād dileñ ani takā păvitrạ kelo: tea disā

3 And He blessed the seventh day, and sanctified it; because in it He

[4] "Soukāsāi kāṇeileā", mupčeñ: ani dusreāñ tărāñčeo văstu kărunknānt.—"Rested", viz: He ceased to make new kinds of things.

[illegible]	sărvų apleõ văstu răt-sun ani kărn răulo de-kun.	had rested from all His work which God created and made.
4 [illegible]	4 Vo sărgiñtso ani bu-iñtso ărămb: aseñ Dē-vān tankăñ rătsleănt.[1]	4 These are the generations of the heaven and the earth, when they were created, in the day that the Lord God made the heaven and the earth:
5 [illegible]	5 Ani aseñ Dēvān răts-liñ săkăḍ setañ gădeăñ-čiñ ubzounčeā ădiñ, ani săkăḍ tăṇañ gāunčiñ kirlouñčeā ădiñ[1]: kite-āk moḷeăr Somia Dēvān pāus dăḍlunk natullo buiñčer, ani buiñ besăi kărtso mănis natullo.	5 And every plant of the field before it sprung up in the earth, and every herb of the ground before it grew: for the Lord God had not rained upon the earth; and there was not a man to till the earth.
6 [illegible]	6 Puņ yēk zăr măti-entli băir sărtăli săgḷea buiñčeā melbhăgăk u-dăk simpči.	6 But a spring rose out of the earth, watering all the surface of the earth.
7 [illegible]	7 Tăr Dēvān mănšăk kelo mătiečeā ubrān: a-ni tačeā toṇḍănt jivătso usuăs funklo, ani aseñ mănis ătmeān jivo zălo.	7 And the Lord God formed man of the slime of the earth: and breathed into his face the breath of life, and man became a living soul.
8 [illegible]	8 Ani Somia Dēvān khušălăyečeñ văiñkuṭ suruvent găḍųlleñ, ani thăiñ apṇeñ kellea măn-šăk gălo.	8 And the Lord God had planted a paradise of pleasure from the beginning, wherein He placed man whom He had formed.

[1] *Lit.* In this way God has created them.

[2] *Lit.* Thus God created all plants of the field before they germinated, and all herbs of the country before the germination.

[illegible]	9 Ani Dēvāu ubzăilo mătientleăn sărvu ta-rānče ruk, disṭik sobit ani rutsik suădik, ani vaiñkuṭă modeñ jiṇietso ruk[1] ani bore ani văiṭ zăṇvăiyetso ruk.[2]	9 And the Lord God brought forth of the ground all manner of trees, fair to behold, and pleasant to eat of: the tree of life[1] also in the midst of paradise, and the tree of knowledge[2] of good and evil.
[illegible]	10 Ani yēk năiñ khu-śălāyeče suătentli băir sărtāli văiñkuṭăk udăk simpunk, zače, thăiñ thăun, čăr vāṇṭe zatăt.	10 And a river went out of the place of plea-sure to water paradise, which from thence is di-vided into four heads.
[illegible]	11 Yēkăčeñ năuñ Phi-zon: ti săgḷea Hevilăth moḷḷea găvăñ boun-tăṇiñ văută, thăin ban-găr zată.	11 The name of the one is Phison: that is it which compasseth all the land of Hevilath, where gold groweth.
[illegible]	12 Teă găuñčeñ ban-găr bhou boreñ: thăiñ bdell ani onikin fător meḷtă.	12 And the gold of that land is very good: there is found bdellium and the onyx stone.
[illegible]	13 Ani dusre năiñčeñ năuñ Gehon: ti săgḷea Etiopiă moḷḷea găvăñ bountăṇiñ văută.	13 And the name of the second river is Gehon: the same is it that com-passeth all the land of Ethiopia.
[illegible]	14 Tisre năiñčeñ nă-uñ Tigris: ti Assiriă	14 And the name of the third river is Tigris: the

[1] "Jiṇietso ruk", munčeñ: tačiñ foḷañ bolăiki dităliñ.—"Tree of life", i. e. its fruits had the power of preserving in a constant state of health.

[2] "Zăṇvăietso ruk" = tačiñ foḷăñ zăṇvăi dităliñ, sorpăn fōṭ sangleă părmăṇe.—"Tree of knowledge", i. e. its fruits had the power of giving a superior kind of knowledge, be-yond that which God was pleased to give, as the deceitful serpent had said.

[illegible]	isileān vāutā: Ani tsonti nāiñ Euphrāt.	same passeth along by the Assyrians. And the fourth river is Euphrates.
15 [illegible]	15 Tār, Dēvān mānšāk kāṇeun takā khušālāyečeā vāiñkuṭānt galo, teñ besāi kārunk ani rākunk.	15 And the Lord God took man, and put him into the paradise of pleasure, to dress it and to keep it.
16 [illegible]	16 Ani takā[1] hukum dili sāngun: sārvụ vāiñkuṭāčeañ rukānčeañ foḷāntliñ khāuyet:	16 And he commanded him[1] saying: of every tree of paradise thou shalt eat:
17 [illegible]	17 Puṇ bore ani vāiṭ zāṇvāyečeā rukāčeañ foḷāntliñ khāinakā. Khā ši zaleār, teāts disā morn mortoloi.	17 But of the tree of knowledge of good and evil, thou shalt not eat. For in what day soever thou shalt eat of it, thou shalt die the death.
18 [illegible]	18 Somia Dēvān ani sangleñ: Mānis yeklātz aso boro nāiñ: amiñ takā yēk kumok kārči sangātiṇ tače sarki kāriāñ.	18 And the Lord God said: It is not good for man to be alone: let us make him a help like unto himself.
19 [illegible]	19 Tār, sākāḍ mātientleāñ monzātink ani sākāḍ moḷbāčeañ sukṇeānk Dēvān ubrān kārtātz, tankāñ Adāuñ mukār galiñ, poḷeunk kāso tankāñ ulo kārtā móṇ: kiteāgi moḷeār, kāsāleñ Adāun jiuzātink ulo kelo tāsāleñ tančeñ nāuñ.	19 And the Lord God having formed out of the ground all the beasts of the earth, and all the fowls of the air, brought them to Adam to see what he would call them: for whatsoever Adam called any living creature the same is its name.

[1] "Takā" mhuṇčeñ: tankāñ.—"He commanded him", i. e. the singular is used for the plural; for the precept has been given to both, Adam and Eve.

20 ಅನಿ ಅದಾಉನ್ ಸಮೆಸ್ತಾಂ ಜಿಉಜಾತಿಂಕ್, ಸಮೆಸ್ತಾಂ ಸುಕ್ಣ್ಯಾಂಕ್ ಮೊಳ್ಬಾಚ್ಯಾಂ ಅನಿ ಸಮೆಸ್ತಾಂ ಬುಇಂಚ್ಯಾಂ ಮೊಂಜಾತಿಂಕ್ ತಾಂಚಿಂ ನಾವಾಂ ಮೆಳಿಂ. ಪುಣ್ ಅದಾಉಂಕ್ ಏಕ್ ಸಾರ್ಕಿ ಸಾಂಗಾತಿಣ್ ಮೆಳ್ನಾತ್ಲಿ.

20 Ani Adāun sāmestañ jiuzātink, sāmestañ sukṇeānk moḷbā čeañ ani sāmestañ buiñčeañ monzātink tānčiṅ nāvañ moḷiṅ. Puṇ Adāunk yēk sarki sangātiṇ meḷnatulli.

20 And Adam called all the beasts by their names, and all the fowls of the air, and all the cattle of the field: but for Adam there was not found a helper like himself.

21 ತೊವೊಳ್ ದೇವಾನ್ ಅದಾಉಂಕ್ ಏಕ್ ನೀದ್ ಪೊಡಾಇಲಿ ಅನಿ ತಾಕಾ ನೀದ್ ಪೊಡ್ತಾಚ್, ಬೊರ್ಯಾಂತ್ಲಿ ಏಕ್ ಕಾಡ್ನ್, ಮಾಸಾನ್ ತಾಚೆ ಬಾಡ್ಲಾಕ್ ಬುರಾಕ್ ಭೊರ್ಲೊ.

21 Tovoḷ Dēvān Adāunk yēk nīd poḍāili ani takā nid poḍtats, boreantli yēk kāḍn, māsān tače bādlāk burāk bhorlo.

21 Then the Lord God cast a deep sleep upon Adam: and when he was fast asleep, he took one of his ribs, and filled up flesh for it.

22 ಅನಿ ದೇವಾನ್ ಅದಾಉಂತ್ಲಿ ಕಾಡ್ಲ್ಲಿ ಬೊರ್ ಅಸ್ತ್ರಿ ಕೆಲಿ: ಅನಿ ತಿಕಾ ಅದಾಉಂ ಮುಕಾರ್ ವೆಲಿ.

22 Ani Dēvān Adāuñtli kāḍulli bor āstri keli: ani tikā Adāuñ mukār veli.

22 And the Lord God built the rib which he took from Adam into a woman: and brought her to Adam.

23 ಅನಿ ಅದಾಉನ್ ಸಾಂಗ್ಲೆಂ: ಏಂ ಹಾಡ್ ಮೊಜ್ಯಾಂ ಹಾಡಾಂತ್ಲೆಂ ಅನಿ ಏಂ ಮಾಸ್ ಮೊಜ್ಯಾ ಮಾಸಾಂತ್ಲೆಂ; ತಿಚೆಂ ನಾಉಂ ಮಾನ್ಶಾ ಥಾಉನ್ ಆಇಲಿ ಅಸ್ತೆಲೆಂ, ಮಾನ್ಶಾ ಥಾಉನ್ ಆಇಲಿ ದೆಕುನ್.

23 Ani Adāun sangleñ: yeñ hāḍ mojeañ hāḍāntleñ ani yeñ mās mojea māsāntleñ; tičeñ nāuñ mānšā thāun āili asteleñ, mānšā thāun āili dekun.

23 And Adam said: This now is bone of my bones, and flesh of my flesh; she shall be called woman, because she was taken out of man.

24 ತ್ಯಾ ಪಾಸುನ್ ದಾದ್ಲೊ ಆಪ್ಲ್ಯಾ ಬಾಪಾಕ್ ಅನಿ ಆವೊಯ್ಕ್ ಸೊಡ್ನ್, ಆಪ್ಲೆ ಅಸ್ತ್ರಿಯೆಕ್ ಲಾಗ್ತೊಲೊ, ಅನಿ ಏಕಾಟ್ ಮಾಸಾಂತ್ ದೊಗಾಂ ಅಸ್ತೆಲಿಂ.

24 Tea pāsun dadlo apleā bāpāk ani āuoik soḍn, aple āstriek lāgtolo, ani yekāts māsānt dogāñ asteliñ.

24 Wherefore a man shall leave father and mother, and shall cleave to his wife: and they shall be two in one flesh.

25 ಅನಿ ತಿಂ, ಮೊಳ್ಯಾರ್ ಅದಾಉಂ ಅನಿ ಏವ್, ವಿಂಗ್ಗಿಂ ಅಸ್ಲಿಂ, ಅನಿ ಲಾಜನಾತ್ಲ್ಲಿಂ.

25 Ani tiñ, móḷeār Adāuñ ani Yev, viṇgiñ asḷiñ, ani lāzanātḷliñ.

25 And they were both naked: to wit, Adam and his wife: and were not ashamed.

ಅವಸ್ವರ್ III.	Avasvar III.	Chapter III.
1 [illegible]	1 Puṇ sorop sămestañ Dēvān kelleañ monzā-tiñ prās nāḍgo. Taṇeñ ăstrie kāḍe sangleñ: kiteāk Dēvān tumkāñ aḍvarlāñ, kăsăleiñ vāiñ-kuṭāčea rukāčea foḷā-ntleñ khāunk?	1 Now the serpent was more subtle than any of the beasts of the earth which the Lord God had made. And he said to the woman: Why hath God commanded you, that you should not eat of every tree of paradise?
2 [illegible]	2 Takā ăstrien zāb diun sangleñ: vāiñku-ṭānt asạlleañ foḷantliñ amiñ khātāuñ:	2 And the woman answered him saying: Of the fruit of the trees that are in paradise we do eat:
3 [illegible]	3 Puṇ vāiñkuṭā mo-deñ asạllea rukāčeā foḷāntleñ khāunk ani hāt gālunk, morana zāunk Dēvān aḍvarlāñ.	3 But of the fruit of the tree which is in the midst of paradise, God hath commanded us that we should not eat, and that we should not touch it, lest perhaps we die.
4 [illegible]	4 Tovoḷ sorpān ăstrie kāḍe sangleñ: dubāu-nāstanañ tumiñ morn morčinānt.	4 And the serpent said to the woman: No, you shall not die the death.
5 [illegible]	5 Kiteāk moḷeār Dēu zaṇā ki khellea disā tumče doḷe ukte zātele ani Dēvā bări zāteleāt, boreñ ani vāiṭ zaṇā-zāun.	5 For God doth know that in what day soever you shall eat thereof, your eyes shall be opened: and you shall be as gods, knowing good and evil.
6 [illegible]	6 Dekun, foḷ boreñ khāuñčeāk, ani sobit disṭik, ani khušālāye-čeñ poḷeuñčeāk asā mōṇ	6 And the woman saw that the tree was good to eat, and fair to the eyes, and delightful to

ನ್, ಕಾಡ್ಲೆಂ ತಾಚೆಂ ಫೊಳ್, ಆನಿ
ಖೆಲೆಂ ಆನಿ ಆಪ್ಲ್ಯಾ ದಾದ್ಲ್ಯಾಕ್
ದಿಲೆಂ ಆನಿ ತಾಣೆಂ ಖೆಲೆಂ.

7 ಆನಿ ದೊಗಾಂಚೆ ದೊಳೆ ಉಕ್ತೆ
ಜಾಲೆ [1]: ಆನಿ ಆಪ್ಣಾಂಕ್ ವಿಂಗೆಂ ಮೊ
ಣ್ ಪೊಳೆಉನ್, ಅಂಜುರಾಚ್ಯಾ ಖೊ
ಲಿಯೊ ಸಿವೊನ್ ಆಪ್ಣಾಂಕ್ ನೆಸೊಣ್
ಕೆಲಿ.

8 ಆನಿ ಸೊಮಿಯಾ ದೆವಾಚೊ
ತಾಳೊ ಆಯ್ಕುನ್ ಜೊ ವೈಂಕುಟಾಂತ್
ದಣ್ಪಾರಾ ಉಪ್ರಾಂತ್ ವಾರ್‍ಯಾಕ್ ಬೌಂ
ತಾಲೊ, ಆದಾಉಂ ಆನಿ ತಾಚಿ ಅಸ್ತ್ರಿ
ಲಿಪ್ಲಿಂ ಸೊಮಿಯಾ ದೇವಾ ಮುಕಾರ್
ವೈಂಕುಟಾಚ್ಯಾಂ ರುಕಾಂ ಮೊಡೆಂ.

9 ಆನಿ ಸೊಮಿಯಾ ದೇವಾನ್
ಆದಾಉಂಕ್ ಆಪೊಉನ್ ತಾಕಾ ಸಾಂ
ಗ್ಲೆಂ: ಖೈಂ ಆಸಾಯ್?

10 ತಾಣೆಂ ಸಾಂಗ್ಲೆಂ: ತುಜೊ ತಾ
ಳೊ ಆಯ್ಕಲಾ ವೈಂಕುಟಾಂತ್ ಆನಿ
ಮಾಕಾ ಭೆಂ ದಿಸ್ಲಾಂ ವಿಂಗೊ ಆಸಾಂ
ದೆಕುನ್ ಆನಿ ಲಿಪ್ಲಾಂ.

11 ತಾಣೆಂ ಸಾಂಗ್ಲೆಂ: ಕೊಣೆಂ
ತುಕಾ ದಾಕೈಲೆಂ, ವಿಂಗೊ ಆಸಾಯ್ ಮೊ
ಣ್, ಆವೆಂ ಆಡ್ವಾರ್ಲೆಲೆಂ ಫೊಳ್
ತುವೆಂ ಖೆಲ್ಲ್ಯಾ ಶಿವಾಯ್?

ăstrien poḷeun, kăḍleñ tačeñ foḷ, ani kheleñ ani aplea dadleăk dileñ ani taṇeñ kheleñ.

7 Ani dogăñče doḷe ukte zăle [1]: ani apṇănk viṇgiñ móṇ poḷeun, anjurăčeo kholio sivon apṇănk nesoṇ keli.

8 Ani Somia Dēvătso tăḷo aikun zo văiñkuṭănt dănpară uprănt văreăk bountălo Adăuñ ani tači ăstri lipliñ Somia Dēvă mukăr vaiñkuṭăčeañ rukăñ modeñ.

9 Ani Somia Dēvăn Adăunk ăpoun takă sangleñ: khăiñ asăi?

10 Tăṇeñ sangleñ: tuzo tăḷo aikală văiñkuṭănt ani makă bheñ dislăñ viṇgo asăñ dekun ani liplăñ.

11 Taṇeñ sangleñ: koṇeñ tukă dakăileñ viṇgo asăi móṇ, ăveñ aḍvarleleñ foḷ tuveñ khellea šivăi?

behold: and she took of the fruit thereof and did eat, and gave to her husband who did eat.

7 And the eyes of them both were opened [1]: and when they perceived themselves to be naked, they sewed together fig-leaves, and made themselves aprons.

8 And when they heard the voice of the Lord God walking in the paradise at the afternoon air, Adam and his wife hid themselves from the face of the Lord God, amidst the trees of paradise.

9 And the Lord God called Adam, and said to him: Where art thou?

10 And he said: I heard thy voice in paradise; and I was afraid, because I was naked, and I hid myself.

11 And he said to him: Who hath told thee that thou wast naked, unless thou hast eaten of the fruit of the forbidden tree?

---

[1] "Ukte zăle", mupŏeñ: tiñ volkaliñ apli tsuk.—"And the eyes *etc.*" viz. they got aware of the committed sin; *i. e.* they made the unhappy experience of having lost the good of original grace etc.

12 ಅನಿ ಆದಾಉನ್ ಸಾಂಗ್ಲೆಂ:
ತುವೆಂ ಮಕಾ ದಿಲ್ಲೆ ಅಸ್ತ್ರಿಯೆನ್
ಮಕಾ ಫೊಳ್ ದಿಉನ್, ಆವೆಂ
ಖೆಲೆಂ.

13 ಅನಿ ಸೊಮಿಯಾ ದೇವಾನ್
ಅಸ್ತ್ರಿಯೆಕ್ ಸಾಂಗ್ಲೆಂ: ಕಿತ್ಯಾಕ್ ಯೆಂ
ಕೆಲ್ಯಾಂ? ತಿಣೆಂ ಜಾಬ್ ದಿಉನ್
ಸಾಂಗ್ಲೆಂ: ಸೊರ್ಪಾನ್ ಮಕಾ ಫೊ
ಟೈಲ್ಯಾಂ ಅನಿ ಆವೆಂ ಖೆಲೆಂ.

14 ಅನಿ ಸೊಮಿಯಾ ದೇವಾನ್
ಸೊರ್ಪಾಕ್ ಸಾಂಗ್ಲೆಂ: ಯೆಂ ಕೆಲ್ಲ್ಯಾ
ಪಾಸ್ವೊತ್ ಸಾಮೆಸ್ತಾಂ ಜಿಉಜಾತಿಂ,
(ಅನಿ) ಮೊಂಜಾತಿಂ ಬಿತರ್ ತುಕಾ ಸಿ
ರಾಪ್ ಪೊಡುಂ: ತುಜಾ ಹರ್ದ್ಯಾನ್
ತ್ಸರ್ತೊಲೊಯ್ ಅನಿ ಸಮೆಸ್ತಾಂ ತುಜ್ಯಾ
ಜಿಣಿಯೆಚ್ಯಾ ವರ್ಸಾನಿಂ ಮಾತಿ ಖಾ
ತೊಲೊಯ್.

15 ಆಉಂ ದುಸ್ಮಾನ್ಕಾಯ್ ಗಾ
ಲ್ತೊಲೊಂ ತುಜೆ ಅನಿ ಅಸ್ತ್ರಿಯೆ ಬಿತರ್,
ತುಜ್ಯಾ ಬಿಯಾ ಅನಿ ತಿಚ್ಯಾ ಬಿಯಾ
ಬಿತರ್: ತಿ ತುಜೆಂ ಮೊಸ್ತಕ್ ಮೊಸ್ತಿ
ತೆಲಿ ಅನಿ ತುಂ ತಿಚೆ ಖೊಟೆಕ್ ನಾಡಿ
ಕರ್ತೊಲೊಯ್.

16 ಅನಿ ಅಸ್ತ್ರಿಯೆಕ್ ಸಾಂಗ್ಲೆಂ:
ಆಉಂ ತುಜೆ ಗುರ್ವಾರ್ಪೊಣಾಚೆ ಕಷ್ಟ
ತ್ಸಾಡೈತೊಲೊಂ: ದುಕಿನ್ ಪುತಾಂಕ್
ಪುರ್ಸುತ್ ಜಾತೆಲಿ, ಅನಿ ದಾದ್ಲ್ಯಾ
ಖಾಲ್ ಅಸ್ತೆಲಿ, ಅನಿ ತೊ ತು
ಜೊ ಧನಿ ಜಾಉನ್ ಅಸ್ತೊಲೊ.

12 Ani Ādaun sang-
leñ: tuveñ makā dille
ăstrien makā foḷ diun,
āveñ kheleñ.

13 Ani Somia Dēvān
ăstriek sangleñ: kiteāk
yeñ kelāiñ? Tiṇeñ zāb
diun sangleñ: Sorpān-
makā foṭeiliñ ani āveñ
kheleñ.

14 Ani Somia Dēvān
sorpāk sangleñ: yeñ
kellea pasvot sămestañ
jiuzātiñ, (ani) monzātiñ
bităr tukā sirāp poḍuñ:
tujā hărdeān tsărtoloi
ani sămestañ tujeā ji-
ṇiečeā vărsāniñ māti
khātoloi.

15 Āuñ dusmānkāi
găltoloñ tuje ani ăstrie
bităr, tujeā biā ani ti-
čeā biā bităr: ti tujeñ
mostak mostiteli ani
tuñ tiče khoṭek nāḍi
kărtoloi.

16 Ani ăstriek sang-
leñ: āuñ tujea gurvăr-
poṇāče kăšṭ tzăḍăito-
loñ: dukin putānk pur-
sut zatelī, ani dadleā
khāl astelī, ani to tuzo
dhăni zāun astolo.

12 And Adam said:
The woman, whom thou
gavest me to be my com-
panion, gave me of the
tree, and I did eat.

13 And the Lord God
said to the woman: Why
hast thou done this? and
she answered: The ser-
pent deceived me, and I
did eat.

14 And the Lord God
said to the serpent: Be-
cause thou hast done this
thing, thou art cursed
among all cattle and
beasts of the earth: upon
thy breast shalt thou go,
and earth shalt thou eat
all the days of thy life.

15 I will put enmities
between thee and the
woman, and thy seed and
her seed: she shall crush
thy head, and thou shalt
lie in wait for her heel.

16 To the woman also
he said: I will multiply
thy sorrows, and thy con-
ceptions: in sorrow shalt
thou bring forth children,
and thou shalt be under
thy husband's power, and
he shall have dominion
over thee.

17 ಆನಿ ಆದಾಂವುಂಕ್ ಸಾಂಗ್ಲೆಂ ತುಜೆ ಅಸ್ತ್ರಿಯೆಚೆಂ ಉತರ್ ಐಕಲ್ಲ್ಯಾ ಪಾಸುನ್ ಆನಿ ಅದ್ವಾರ್ಲೆಲ್ಯಾ ರುಕಾಚೆಂ ಫೊಳ್ ಖೆಲ್ಲ್ಯಾ ಪಾಸ್ವೊತ್ ಆನಿ ತುವೆಂ ಯೆಂ ಅದಾರ್ಲೆಲ್ಯಾ ಪಾಸ್ವೊತ್ ಬುಯ್ಂಕ್ ಶಿರಾಪ್ ಪೊಡುಂ: ವಾವುರ್ ಕರ್ನ್ ತಾಂತ್ಲೆಂ ಖಾವುಂಕ್ ಘೆತೊಲ್ಯೊ ಸಮೆಸ್ತಾಂ ತುಜೆ ಜಿಣಿಯೆಚ್ಯಾಂ ದಿಸಾನಿಂ.	17 Ani Adāunk sangleñ: tuje ăstriyečeñ utar aikalleā pasun ani aḍvarleleā rukāčeñ foḷ khelleā pasvot, ani tuveñ yeñ adārleleā pasvot, buink širāp poḍuñ: vāur kărn tantleñ khāunk ghetoloi sămestañ tuje jiṇiečeañ ḍisāniñ.	17 And to Adam he said: Because thou hast hearkened to the voice of thy wife, and hast eaten of the tree, whereof I commanded thee, that thou shouldst not eat, cursed is the earth in thy work: with labour and toil shalt thou eat thereof all the days of thy life.
18 ತಿ ತುಕಾ ಕಾಂಟೆ ಆನಿ ಖುಂಟೆ ಉಬ್ಜಾಯ್ತೆಲಿ ಆನಿ ಬುಯ್ಂತ್ಲೆಂ ತಾಣ್ ಖಾತೊಲ್ಯೊ.	18 Ti tukā kaṇṭe ani khuṇṭe ubzāiteli ani buintleñ tăṇ khātoloi.	18 Thorns and thistles shall it bring forth to thee; and thou shalt eat the herbs of the earth.
19 ಕಪಾಲ್ ಗಾಮೆಉನ್ ಜೀವೊನ್ ಕರ್ತೊಲ್ಯೊ, ತುಕಾ ಕಾಡ್ಲೆಲಿ ಮಾತಿ ಪೊರ್ತುನ್ ಜಾತಾಯ್ ಮೊಣಸರ್, ಕಿತ್ಯಾಕ್ ಮೊಳ್ಯಾಫ್ ಮಾತಿಯೆತ್ಸೊ ಜಾಉನ್ ವೊರ್ತಉತಾಯ್ ಆನಿ ಮಾತಿ ಜಾತೊಲ್ಯೊ.	19 Kăpāl gāmeun jivon kărtoloi, tukā kāḍleli māti portun zātāi moṇasăr, kiteăk moḷeāf matietso zāun vortautāi ani māti zătoloi.	19 In the sweat of thy face shalt thou eat bread till thou return to the earth, out of which thou wast taken: for dust thou art, and into dust thou shalt return.
20 ಆನಿ ಆದಾಉನ್ ಆಪ್ಲೆ ಅಸ್ತ್ರಿಯೆಕ್ ಎವ್ ಮೊಣ ಮೊಳಿ, ತಿ ಸಮೆಸ್ತಾಂ ಜಿವ್ಯಾಂಚಿ ಆವೊಯ್ ಜಾಉನ್ ವೊರ್ತಉತಾ ದೆಕುನ್	20 Ani Adāun aple ăstriek Yev móṇ moḷi, ti sămestañ jiveānči āuoi zāun vortautā dekun.	20 And Adam called the name of his wife Eve: because she was the mother of all the living.
21 ಆನಿ ದೇವಾನ್ ಆದಾಉಂಕ್ ಆನಿ ತಾಚೆ ಅಸ್ತ್ರಿಯೆಕ್ ಚಾಂಬ್ಡ್ಯಾಚ್ಯೊ ನೆಸೊಣ್ಯೊ ಕೆಲ್ಯೊ ಆನಿ ತಾಂಕಾಂ ಗಾಲ್ಯೊ.	21 Ani Dēvān Adāunk ani tače ăstriek tsambḍeāčeo nesoṇio keleo ani tankāñ gāleo.	21 And the Lord God made for Adam and his wife garments of skins, and clothed them.
22 ಆನಿ ಸಾಂಗ್ಲೆಂ: ಪೊಳೆ, ಆದಾಉಂ[1] ಆಮ್ಚ್ಯಾಂತ್ಲ್ಯಾ ಎಕ್ಲ್ಯಾ ಬರಿ ಜಾಲೊ ಬೊರೆಂ ಆನಿ ವ್ಯಾಟ್ ಜಾಣಾ	22 Ani sangleñ: poḷe, Adāuñ[1] amčeāntleă yeklea· bāri zālo boreñ	22 And he said: Behold Adam[1] is become as one of us, knowing good and

[1] "Pole, Adāuñ": iñ utrañ Dēvān sangleānt bestāuñčeāk. — "Behold Adam": This was spoken by way of reproaching.

[illegible]

23 [illegible]

24 [illegible]

ani vāiṭ zaṇazāun: tăr, atāñ (amiñ takā aḍkāḷ kărizāi), hāt gāln jiṇiečeñ foḷ kāḍčeāntlo ani khāun sădānts jieunčeāntlo.

23 Ani Somia Dēvān takā khušālāyečeā văiñkuṭāntlo bāir gālo takā kāḍleli buiñ besāi kărunk.

24 Ani Adāunk bāir gālo ani khušālāyečea vāiñkuṭa mukār kerubimānk ani ujeāči ani hăryeke kusin hālči talvār jiṇiečea rukātso mārog rākunk dovorli.

evil: now, therefore, lest perhaps he put forth his hand, and take also of the tree of life, and eat, and live for ever.

23 And the Lord God sent him out of the paradise of pleasure, to till the earth from which he was taken.

24 And he cast out Adam; and placed before the paradise of pleasure Cherubims, and a flaming sword, turning every way to keep the way of the tree of life.

ಗಾದಿ.

ಅವಸ್ವರ್ I.

1 [illegible]

2 [illegible]

3 [illegible]

4 [illegible]

GĀDI

Avasvăr I.

1 Gādi Sālmāučeo, zo Dāvidātso put, Izrāyelātso rāi.

2 (Ye kāide asāt) bud ani zāṇvāi sikūnk:

3 Tanče vorviñ mānšāk budičiñ utrañ somzatāt, ani zāṇvāyečeñ sikap, nīt ani somzikāy ani nāy meḷtā.

4 Sādeānk bud, tărnāṭeānk zāṇvāy ani gineān labtā.

PROVERBS

Chapter I.

1 The parables of Solomon, the son of David king of Israel.

2 To know wisdom, and instruction:

3 To understand the words of prudence: and to receive the instruction of doctrine, justice, and judgment, and equity.

4 To give subtilty to little ones, to the young man knowledge and understanding.

5 ಬುದಿವೊಂತ್ ಐಕುನ್ ಅಧಿಕ್ ಬುದಿವೊಂತ್ ಜಾತೊಲೊ; ಆನಿ ಸೊಮ್ಜೊಣಿ ತ್ಸಾಲೌಂಚಿ ಸಾಮಾರ್ಥಿ ಭೊಗ್ತೊಲೊ.	5 Budivont aikun, ădhik budivont zătolo; ani somzoṇi tsălounči sāmărthi bhogtolo.	5 A wise man shall hear and shall be wiser: and he that understandeth, shall possess governments.
6 ವೊಪಾರ್ ಆನಿ ತಿತ್ಸೊ ಅರ್ಥ್, ಬುದಿವೊಂತಾಚಿಂ ಉತ್ರಾಂ ಆನಿ ತಾಂಚೆ ಗುಟ್ ಸೊಮ್ಜಾತೊಲೊ.	6 Vopăr ani titso ărth, budivontăčiñ utrañ ani tānče guṭ somzatolo.	6 He shall understand a parable, and the interpretation, the words of the wise, and their mysterious sayings.
7 ದೇವಾಚಿ ಭಿರಾಂತ್ ಬುದಿತ್ಸೊ ಆರಂಭ್. ನೆಣಾರ್ ಬುದ್ ಆನಿ ಸಿಕಾಪ್ ಬೆಪಾರ್ವೊ ಕರ್ತಾತ್.	7 Dēvāči bhirānt buditso ărămbh. Neṇār bud ani sikap bepārvo kărtăt.	7 The fear of the Lord is the beginning of wisdom. Fools despise wisdom and instruction.
8 ಐಕ್, ಮೊಜ್ಯಾ ಬುರ್ಗ್ಯಾ, ತುಜ್ಯಾ ಬಾಪಾಚ್ಯಾ ಸಿಕೊಣ್ಯಾ, ಆನಿ ತುಜೆ ಆವೈಚೆ ಉಪದೇಸ್ ಸೊಡಿನಾಕಾ;	8 Āik, mojea burgeā, tujea bāpāčeo sikoṇeo, ani tujo āvoiče upadēs soḍinakū:	8. My son, hear the instruction of thy father, and forsake not the law of thy mother:
9 ಮೆಳೊಂಕ್ ಸೊಬಿತಾಯ್ ತುಜ್ಯಾ ಮೊಸ್ತಕಾಕ್, ಆನಿ ನೆಟೊನ್ ತುಜ್ಯಾ ಗಳ್ಯಾಕ್.	9 Meḷonk sobitāi tujeā mostăkāk, ani neṭon tujeā găḷeāk.	9 That grace may be added to thy head, and a chain of gold to thy neck.
10 ಮೊಜ್ಯಾ ಪುತಾ, ಪಾತ್ಕ್ಯಾಂನಿಂ ತುಕಾ ಫುಸ್ಲಾಯ್ಲ್ಯಾರ್, ತಾಂಕಾಂ ಐಕಾನಾಕಾ.	10 Mojea putā, pātkiāniñ tukā fuslāileār, tankāñ aikānakā.	10 My son, if sinners shall entice thee, consent not to them.
11 ತಾಣಿಂ ಸಾಂಗ್ಲ್ಯಾರ್: ಆಮ್ಚೆ ಸಾಂಗಾತಾ ಯೆ, ರಗತ್ ವಾವೊಉಂಕ್ ನಾಡಿ ಕರ್ಯಾಂ, ಗುಣ್ಯಾಉಂ ನಾತ್ಲೆಲ್ಯಾಕ್ ಬೆಸ್ತೆಂ ಮೋಸ್ ಕರ್ಯಾಂ:	11 Taṇiñ sangleār: amče sangatā ye, rāgat vāvounk nāḍi kāriāñ, guniāuñ-natullеāk besṭeñ mōs kăriāñ:	11 If they shall say: Come with us, let us lie in wait for blood, let us hide snares for the innocent without cause:
12 ತಾಕಾ ಜೀವೊ ಗಿಳ್ಯಾಂ, ಯೆಮ್ಕೊಂಡಾ ಬರಿ, ಆನಿ (ತಾಕಾ) ಸಗ್ಳೊ (ಗಿಳ್ಯಾಂ) ಎಕಾ ತಳ್ಯಾಂತ್ ಬುಡ್ಚ್ಯಾ ಬರಿ.	12 Takā jīvo giḷiāñ; yemkóṇḍā bări, ani (takā) săgḷo (giḷiāñ) yekā tăḷeānt buḍčeā bări.	12 Let us swallow him up alive like hell, and whole as one that goeth down into the pit.

13 [illegible]	13 Amkāñ (tači) sāgḷi moḷādik āst meḷteli, amčiñ gārañ luṭin bhorteleāuñ.	13 We shall find all precious substance, we shall fill our houses with spoils.
14 [illegible]	14 Amče sangatā yeāpār. kār, yekāts poti amkāñ asundi.	14 Cast in thy lot with us: let us all have one purse.
15 [illegible]	15 Mojea putā, tanče sangatā tsāl nakā, tuzo pāi tančeā pāivāṭentlo pois kāḍ.	15 My son, walk not thou with them, restrain thy foot from their paths.
16 [illegible]	16 Kiteāk moḷeār, tānče pāi vāiṭāk tsāltāt; ani rāgat vāvounk ausārtāt.	16 For their feet run to evil, and make haste to shed blood.
17 [illegible]	17 Puṇ besṭeñ sukṇeāñ mukār zaḷañ galtāt.	17 But a net is spread in vain before the eyes of them that have wings.
18 [illegible]	18 Te aplea jīvāki nāḍi kārtāt, ani apleañ ātmeānk mōs kārtāt.	18 And they themselves lie in wait for their own blood, and practise deceits against their own souls.
19 [illegible]	19 Asents sāmestañ surātiānčeo vāṭo bhogtoleānče ātme bāsmitāt.	19 So the ways of every covetous man destroy the souls of the possessors.
20 [illegible]	20 Bud bāir bōb mārn ulāitā; bīdint aplo tāḷo aikāso kārtā.	20 Wisdom preacheth abroad, she uttereth her voice in the streets.
21 [illegible]	21 Ti porjānčea sabhāñ modeñ apṇāk pārgāṭ kārtā, paṭṇāñčea bāglañ kāḍe apliñ utrañ utsārtā sangun:	21 At the head of multitudes she crieth out, in the entrance of the gates of the city she uttereth her words, saying:

22 [illegible]	22 Kedóḷ pāriant, burgeānu, neṇārpoṇātso mōg kārtāt, ani neṇār luksānāk poḍtāt, teo vāstu aša kārtele, ani bud-nāṭulle zāṇvāi kanṭāḷtele?	22 O children, how long will you love childishness, and fools covet those things which are hurtful to themselves, and the unwise hate knowledge?
23 [illegible]	23 Āuñ tumkāñ bešṭaitanañ, bore zayā: poḷeyā, āuñ moje motint čintāñ teñ tumkāñ ugteñ kārteliñ ani mojiñ utrañ tumkāñ dākeiteliñ.	23 Turn ye at my reproof: behold I will utter my spirit to you, and will shew you my words.
24 [illegible]	24 Kiteāk moḷeār, āveñ (tumkāñ) apoileāt ani tumiñ inkār kelāñ, āveñ mozo hāt vistārlā ani koṇeñ poḷeunknāñ.	24 Because I called, and you refused: I stretched out my hand, and there was none that regarded.
25 [illegible]	25 (Āveñ tumkāñ dille) sāgḷe buditso tumiñ bepārvo kelā ani mojea besṭauṇeāk lakša kārunknāñ.	25 You have despised all my counsel, and have neglected my reprehensions.
26 [illegible]	26 Āuiñ tumčea bosmačeā veḷār hasteliñ, ani tumči česṭai kārteliñ tumiñ bhiyetāt teñ tumčer poḍčea veḷār.	26 I also will laugh in your destruction, and will mock when that shall come to you which you feared.
27 [illegible]	27 Aučit ākānt kāšṭaitanañ ani nāš vādāḷā bāri lagiñ pāutanañ, tumčer dāgd ani vign yetanañ:	27 When sudden calamity shall fall on you, and destruction, as a tempest, shall be at hand, when tribulation and distress shall come upon you:

28 [illegible]	28 Tovōḷ te makā apoitele ani āuñ aikuntsonāñ: phanteār uṭṭele ani āuñ tankañ meḷtsonāñ:	28 Then shall they call upon me, and I will not hear: they shall rise in the morning and shall not find me:
29 [illegible]	29 Sikap kāṇṭāḷḷelea pasun ani Dēvāči bhirānt kaṇeṇatullea pasvot,	29 Because they have hated instruction, and received not the fear of the Lord,
30 [illegible]	30 Ani moji bud inkār kellea pasvot ani sāmestañ āveñ dillea budinče višiānt vāiṭ ulāilleañ pasvot.	30 Nor consented to my counsel, but despised all my reproof.
31 [illegible]	31 Dokun, te apleā vāṭečiñ foḷañ khātele, ani aple hikmatiniñ dados zātele.	31 Therefore they shall eat the fruit of their own way, and shall be filled with their own devices.
32 [illegible]	32 Burgeānčeo tauki tankāñ jivsiñ mārteleo, ani neṇārānčeñ borepoṇ tankāñ naś kārteleñ.	32 The turning away of little ones shall kill them, and the prosperity of fools shall destroy them.
33 [illegible]	33 Puṇ zo kōṇ makā aikat zaleār, bheñ nastanāñ soukāsāi kāṇeitolo ani sompurṇai bhogtolo, vāiṭānčeñ bheñ nāstanañ.	33 But he that shall hear me, shall rest without terror, and shall enjoy abundance, without fear of evils.
ಅವಸ್ವರ್ II.	Avasvār II.	Chapter II.
1 [illegible]	1 Mojea burgeā (tukā titleñ borepoṇ meḷte-	1 My son, if thou wilt receive my words, and

[illegible]	leñ) tūñ mojiñ utrañ kaṇeśi zaleār, ani moje upādēs tuje kāḍe sāmbāḷn dovorśi zaleār,	wilt hide my commandments with thee,
2 [illegible]	2 (Āseñ) tuje kān bud aikatele: tujeñ kāḷiz vondai bud sikčeāk.	2 That thy ear may hearken to wisdom: incline thy heart to know prudence.
3 [illegible]	3 Kiteāk moḷeār tuveñ bud māgleār ani tujeñ kāḷiz zāṇvāyek vondaileār:	3 For if thou shalt call for wisdom, and incline thy heart to prudence:
4 [illegible]	4 Tuveñ tikā duḍuā bāri sodleār, ani bāugārā bāri tikā konḍleār,	4 If thou shalt seek her as money, and shall dig for her as for a treasure:
5 [illegible]	5 Tovoḷ Dēvāči bhirānt somzotoloi, ani Dēvāči zāṇvāi tukā meḷteli.	5 Then shalt thou understand the fear of the Lord and shalt find the knowledge of God:
6 [illegible]	6 Kiteāk moḷeār Dēu bud ditā, ani tačeā tonḍāntli bud ani zāṇvāi (yeta).	6 Because the Lord giveth wisdom: and out of His mouth cometh prudence and knowledge.
7 [illegible]	7 Sāma tsālteleānči bolāiki rāktolo, ani sādepoṇān tsālteleānk sambāḷtolo,	7 He will keep the salvation of the righteous, and protect them that walk in simplicity,
8 [illegible]	8 Nītičeo vāṭo ani bāgevontāntso mārog rākun.	8 Keeping the paths of justice, and guarding the ways of saints.
9 [illegible]	9 Tovoḷ nīt ani somzikāi ani nāi ani sārvụ bori vāṭ somzotoloi.	9 Then shalt thou understand justice, and judgment and equity, and every good path.

10 [illegible]	10 Bud tujea monănt riglеăr, ani zăṇvăi tujeă ătmeăk mănuoleăr:	10 If wisdom shall enter into thy heart, and knowledge please thy soul:
11 [illegible]	11 Bud ani zăṇvăi tukă răkteli,	11 Counsel shall keep thee, and prudence shall preserve thee,
12 [illegible]	12 Văiṭ văṭentlo ani văiṭ ulounčeă mănšăntlo tukă soḍounk:	12 That thou mayest be delivered from the evil way, and from the man that speaketh perverse things:
13 [illegible]	13 Te (văiṭ mănis) nīṭ mărog tsuktăt ani kăḷokăčeă mărgăr tsăltăt:	13 Who leave the right way, and walk by dark ways:
14 [illegible]	14 Te, văiṭ ădărn, santos bhogtăt, ani bhou văiṭ văstuñ thăiñ ulăs bhogtăt.	14 Who are glad when they have done evil, and rejoice in most wicked things:
15 [illegible]	15 Tănčeo văṭo khoṭeo, tănčeñ năḍteñ lăjisṭ.	15 Whose ways are perverse, and their steps infamous.
16 [illegible]	16 (Buḍin) dusre ani năiñzălle ăstriek, tsukon ghetoloi, ti (ăstri) apleăñ utrăniñ fuslaită;	16 That thou mayest be delivered from the strange woman, and from the stranger, who softeneth her words;
17 [illegible]	17 Ani dăkṭe pirăyer tika meḷḷeă dădleăk soḍtă;	17 And forsaketh the guide of her youth;
18 [illegible]	18 Ani Dēvăčisomorth visărtă; tičeñ (văiṭ ăstriečeñ) găr morṇăk bă-	18 And hath forgotten the covenant of her God; for her house inclineth

[illegible]	gotā, āni tičiñ meṭāñ yemkóṇḍā isileān vortāt.	unto death, and her paths to hell.
19 [illegible]	19 Tiče kāḍe vetele, pāṭi yeunčenānt ani jiṇiečeāñ vāṭāniñ rigčenānt.	19 None that go in *unto* her, shall return again, neither shall they take hold of the paths of life.
20 [illegible]	20 Tăr, bore vāṭer tsāl ani nītivāntāntso mārog soḍinakā.	20 That thou mayest walk in a good way: and mayest keep the paths of the just.
21 [illegible]	21 Kiteāk moḷeār zokōṇ nītivānt zāun vortautā, to souñsārānt sukh bhogtolo, ani sāde thaiñ tāktele.	21 For they that are upright, shall dwell in the earth: and the simple shall continue in it.
22 [illegible]	22 Puṇ khoṭe souñsārāntle nāpāintz zātele, ani zokoṇ khoṭepoṇānt rāutā, souñsārānt urtsonāñ.	22 But the wicked shall be destroyed from the earth: and they that do unjustly shall be taken away from it.
ಅವಸ್ವರ್ III.	**Avasvār III.**	**Chapter III.**
1 [illegible]	1 Mojea burgeā, moje upādēs ani mojiñ formānañ tujeñ kāḷiz sāmbāḷundi.	1 My son, forget not my law, and let thy heart keep my commandments.
2 [illegible]	2 Kiteāk moḷeār, āče vorviñ sābār pirāi ani jiṇiečiñ vārsañ, ani soukāsāi tukā meḷteli.	2 For they shall add to thee length of days, and years of life and peace.
3 [illegible]	3 Kākuḷt ani sāt kedints sōḍinakā; tankāñ gāḷeānt gāl ani tujeā kaḷzānt borāi:	3 Let not mercy and truth leave thee, put them about thy neck, and write them in the tables of thy heart:

4 [illegible]	4 Ani Dēvā ani mănšāñ mukār tukā kurpā ani somzikāi meḷteli.	4 And thou shalt find grace and good understanding before God and men.
5 [illegible]	5 Săgḷeā kaḷzān Dēvăčer pătie: ani tuje budičer pătienakā.	5 Have confidence in the Lord with all thy heart, and lean not upon thy own prudence.
6 [illegible]	6 Sămestañ văstuñ thăiñ takā (Dēvăk) čint, ani to tuji jiṇi tsalăitolo.	6 In all thy ways think on Him, and He will direct thy steps.
7 [illegible]	7 Tuje motint budivănt zăun asai móṇ čintun rāvanakā: Dēvăk bhiye, ani văiṭ tsukăi;	7 Be not wise in thy own conceit: fear God, and depart from evil:
8 [illegible]	8 Kiteăk moḷeăr, ṭuje kuḍik bolăiki ăsteli, ani tujeañ hăḍăñ bităr yēk bolăikitso rós rigtolo.	8 For it shall be health to thy navel, and moistening to thy bones.
9 [illegible]	9 Dēvăk măn dī tuje ăstin, ani takā (dī) sămestañ poiliñ foḷañ:	9 Honour the Lord with thy substance, and give Him of the first of all thy fruits:
10 [illegible]	10 Aní tujiñ tupiñ born zateliñ, ani tuje găṇe soreăn sămpūrṇ zătele.	10 And thy barns shall be filled with abundance, and thy presses shall run over with wine.
11 [illegible]	11 Dēvăn dăḍleli šikša inkăr kărnakā, ani to tukā săma kărčeā veḷăr takā sōḍinakā:	11 My son, reject not the correction of the Lord: and do not faint when thou art chastised by Him:
12 [illegible]	12 Kiteăk moḷeăr, Dēu koṇătso mōg kărtā, ta-	12 For whom the Lord loveth, He chastiseth: and

ತೊ ಶಿಕ್ಷಾ ದಿತಾ: ಆನಿ ಬಾಪಾ ಬರಿ
ಅಪ್ಲ್ಯಾ ಬುರ್ಗ್ಯಾಕ್ ಥಾಯಿಂ ಸಂತೊಸ್
ಪಾವತಾ.

kā to šikšā ditā: ani
bāpā bāri apleā bur-
geā thāiñ sāntos pautā.

as a Father in the son He
pleaseth himself.

13 ಭಾಗೆವೊಂತ್ ತೊ ಮನಿಸ್,
ಜೊಕಾ ಜಾಣ್ವಾಯ್ ಮೆಳ್ತಾ ಆನಿ ಬುದಿ
ನ್ ಭೊರ್ತಾ:

13 Bhāgevoṅt to mā-
nis, zakā zāṇvāi meḷtā
ani budin bòrtā:

13 Blessed is the man
that findeth wisdom and
is rich in prudence:

14 ತಿ ಭೊಗ್ಚಿ ರುಪಿಯಾನಿಂ ವ್ಯಾ
ಪಾರ್ ಕರ್ಚ್ಯಾ ಪ್ರಸ್ ಬೊರಿ, ಆನಿ
ತಿಚೆಂ ಫೊಳ್ ಭೌ ನಿತಳ್ ಆನಿ ಪೊಯ್ಲ್ಯಾ
ಬಾಂಗಾರಾ ಪ್ರಸ್ (ಬೊರೆಂ).

14 Tī bhogči rupiāniñ
veāpār kārčeā prās bo-
ri, ani tičeñ fòḷ bhou
nitāḷ ani poileā bāngā-
rā prās (boreñ).

14 The purchasing
thereof is better than the
merchandise of silver,
and her fruit than the
chiefest and purest gold:

15 ಸಮೆಸ್ತಾಂ ಆಸ್ತ್ಯಾಂ ಪ್ರಸ್
ಮೊಲಾದಿಕ್; ಆನಿ ಸರ್ವ್ ಖುಶೆಚ್ಯೊ
ವಸ್ತು ತಿಕಾ ಸರ್ ಕರುಂಕ್ ನೊಜೊ.

15 Sāmestañ āstiāñ
prās molādik āni sārvu
khušečeo vāstu tikā sār
karunk nozo.

15 She is more precious
than all riches: and all
the things that are de-
sired, are not to be com-
pared with her.

16 ತಿಚ್ಯಾ ಉಜ್ವ್ಯಾ ಹಾತಾಂತ್
ಲಾಂಬ್ ಜಿಣಿ, ಆನಿ ತಿಚ್ಯಾ ದಾವ್ಯಾ
ಹಾತಾಂತ್ ಗ್ರೆಸ್ತ್ಕಾಯ್ ಆನಿ ಆನಂದ್.

16 Tičeā uzveā hā-
tānt lāmb jiṇi, ani tičeā
dāveā hātānt grestkāi
ani ānānd.

16 Length of days is in
her right hand, and in
her left hand riches and
glory.

17 ತಿಚೆ ಮಾರಗ್ ಸುಂದರ್ ಆ
ನಿ ಸಕಡ್ ತಿಚ್ಯೊ ವಾಟೊ ಸೌಕಾಸಾ
ಯೆಚ್ಯೊ.

17 Tiče mārāg sundār
ani sākāḍ tičeo vāṭo
soukāsāyečeo.

17 Her ways are beauti-
ful ways, and all her
paths are peaceable.

18 ಜೊ ಕೊಣ್ ತಿಕಾ ಭೊಗಿತ್
ಜಾಲ್ಯಾರ್, (ಬುದ್) ತಾಕಾ ಜಿಣಿಯೆ
ಚ್ಯಾ ರುಕಾ ಬರಿ ಜಾತಾ, ಆನಿ ಜೊ
ಕೊಣ್ ತಿಚೆ ಸಾಂಗಾತಾ ರಾವಾತ್
ಜಾಲ್ಯಾರ್, ಭಾಗೆವಂತ್.

18 Zo kōṇ tikā bhogit
zaleār, (bud) takā jiṇi-
ečea ruka bāri zatā, ani
zo kōṇ tiče sangātā rā-
vat zaleār, bhāgevānt.

18 She is a tree of life
to them that lay hold on
her: and he that shall
retain her is blessed.

19 ದೇವಾನ್ ಜಾಣ್ವಾಯೆನ್
ಸೌಂಸಾರ್ ಗಡ್ಲೊ, ಬುದಿನ್ ಮೊಳಾ
ಬ್ ಗಟ್ ಕೆಲೆಂ.

19 Dēvān zāṇvāyen
soufisār gāḍlo, budin
moḷāb gāṭ keleñ.

19 The Lord by wisdom
hath founded the earth,
hath established the
heavens by prudence.

20 ತಾಚೆ ಜಾಣ್ವಾಯೆನ್, ಗುಂ
ಡಾಯೊ ಜಾಲ್ಯೊ ಆನಿ ಕುಪಾಂ ಉ
ಬೆನ್ ಭೊರ್ತಾತ್.

20 Tāče zāṇvāyen
guṇḍāyo zāleo ani ku-
pañ uben bòrtāt.

20 By His wisdom the
depths have broken out,
and the clouds grow
thick with dew.

21 [illegible]	21 Mojea burgeā, yiñ (utrañ) visārnakā, upadēs ani bud sāmbāḷ:	21 My son, let not these things depart from thy eyes: keep the law and counsel:
22 [illegible]	22 Ani tujea ātmeāk jiṇi ani tujeā gāḷeāk yēk neṭon meḷteli.	22 And there shall be life to thy soul, and grace to thy mouth.
23 [illegible]	23 Tovoḷ dhāirān tsāltoloi, ani tujea pāyāk fātor lagtsonāñ.	23 Then shalt thou walk confidently in thy way, and thy foot shall not stumble.
24 [illegible]	24 Nidtanañ bhiyetsonāi, soukāsāi bhogtoloi ani tuji nid bori zateli.	24 If thou sleep, thou shalt not fear: thou shalt rest, and thy sleep shall be sweet.
25 [illegible]	25 Aučit bhyāk ani tujer poḍčeañ khoṭeāñčeñ podviek bhiyenakā.	25 Be not afraid of sudden fear, nor of the power of the wicked falling upon thee.
26 [illegible]	26 Kitcāk moḷeār, Dēu tuje kāḍe astolo ani tuje pāi sāmbāḷtolo, nādint poḍanāñ zāunk.	26 For the Lord will be at thy side, and will keep thy foot that thou be not taken.
27 [illegible]	27 Upkār kārunk khuši vortāleāk aḍāi nakā: tānk asleār, tuñi upkār kār.	27 Do not withhold him from doing good, who is able; if thou art able, do good thyself also.
28 [illegible]	28 Tujeā išṭā kāḍe sānginakā: vots ani portun ye: fāleā ditoloñ moṇ: zārtār teāts farā diunk tanktā.	28 Say not to thy friend: Go, and come again: and to-morrow I will give to thee: when thou canst give at present.
29 [illegible]	29 Tujeā išṭāčer naḍi kārnakā, kiteāgāi moḷeār to tujer pātiyetā.	29 Practise not evil against thy friend, when he hath confidence in thee.

Kannada	Transliteration	English
30 [illegible]	30 Yekā mānšā kāḍe kāraṇ nāstanāñ zāgḍā nakā, kiteāk moḷeār tāṇeñ tukā kāiñ vāiṭ kārunknāñ.	30 Strive not against a man without cause, when he hath done thee no evil.
31 [illegible]	31 Nīt nātullea mānšātso mosor kārnakā, ani tačeā mārgār tsālnakā:	31 Envy not the unjust man, and do not follow his ways:
32 [illegible]	32 Kiteāk moḷeār haryekā yeḍḍaitoleāk Dēu kaṇṭaḷtā, ani Dēvāči sālgi sādeāñ kāḍe.	32 For every mocker is an abomination to the Lord, and his communication is with the simple.
33 [illegible]	33 Dēvā thāun koṭeānčeā garāñ bitār durbaḷkāi rigteli; puṇ boreānčeāñ gārānk āširvād lābhteleñ.	33 Want is from the Lord in the house of the wicked: but the habitations of the just shall be blessed.
34 [illegible]	34 Dusreānk čestāi kārteleānči, (Dēu) kebdai kārtolo, ani boḷeānk (Dēu) kurpā ditolo.	34 He shall scorn the scorners, and to the meek He will give grace.
35 [illegible]	35 Budivānt bud bhogtele: nēṇārāntso mān lāz.	35 The wise shall possess glory: the promotion of fools is disgrace.
ಅವಸ್ವರ್ IV.	Avasvār IV.	Chapter IV.
1 [illegible]	1 Putrāno, bāpāčeo sikoṇeo aikā, ani mòn diā bud sikonk.	1 Hear, ye children, the instruction of a father, and attend that you may know prudence.
2 [illegible]	2 Āuñ boreñ deṇeñ tumkāñ ditoloñ, moje upadēs sōḍinakāt.	2 I will give you a good gift, forsake not my law.
3 [illegible]	3 Kiteāk moḷeār, āuñi mojea bāpātso put zāun	3 For I also was my father's son, tender and

Kannada	Transliteration	English
[illegible]	asulloñ̄ zāgrutāyen makā vāḍāilloñ[1] ani yekāts burgeā bāri moje āuoi mukār.	as an only son in the sight of my mother.
4 [illegible]	4 Ani to makā sikāitālo ani sangtālo: tujeñ kāḷiz mojiñ utrañ kāṇeundi, mojiñ formanañ sambāḷ ani jiṇi jietoloi.	4 And he taught me, and said: Let thy heart receive my words keep my commandments, and thou shalt live.
5 [illegible]	5 Zaṇvāi bhōg, bud bhōg: mojea toṇḍāčiñ utrañ visār nakā, ani tiñ tsukāi nakā.	5 Get wisdom, get prudence: forget not, neither decline from the words of my mouth.
6 [illegible]	6 Tikā (bud) sóḍinakā, ani ti tukā rākteli: titso mōg kār, ani ti tukā sambāḷn dovorteli.	6 Forsake her not, and she shall keep thee: love her, and she shall preserve thee.
7 [illegible]	7 Zāṇvāyeči suru (i), zaṇvāi bhōg, ani sāgḷe asti prās bud zōḍ.	7 The beginning of wisdom, get wisdom, and with all thy possessions purchase prudence.
8 [illegible]	8 Tikā dhār ani ti tukā vorniteli: ani tikā poṭlun geši zaleār, tiče thāun tukā ānānd yetolo.	8 Take hold on her, and she shall exalt thee: thou shalt be glorified by her, when thou shalt embrace her.
9 [illegible]	9 Ti tujeā mostakāk tsāḍ kurpā diteli, pārzālik mukutān tukā sambāḷteli.	9 She shall give to thy head increase of graces, and protect thee with a noble crown.
10 [illegible]	10 Āik, mojea burgeā, ani mojiñ utrañ kāṇge tukā jiṇiečiñ vārsāñ tzāḍāsiñ.	10 Hear, O my son, and receive my words, that years of life may be multiplied to thee.

[1] *Lit.* I have been educated with care.

11 [illegible]	11 Āuñ tukā zāṇvāyeči vāṭ dākāitoloñ: nītičea mārgār tukā tsālāitoloñ:	11 I will shew thee the way of wisdom, I will lead thee by the paths of equity:
12 [illegible]	12 Teā mārgār pāi gāln, tuje pāi kūsṭān tsālčenānt ani dauntanañ āḍkaḷ meḷčināñ.	12 Which when thou shalt have entered, thy steps shall not be straitened, and when thou runnest thou shalt not meet a stumbling block.
13 [illegible]	13 Sikāp sambāḷ, teñ soḍinakā: teñ rāk, tuji jiṇi zāun asā dekun.	13 Take hold on instruction, leave it not: keep it, because it is thy life.
14 [illegible]	14 Khoṭeānčea mārgā thāiñ sāntos pāvānakā, ani khoṭeānči vāṭ tukā manuonāñ zāundi.	14 Be not delighted in the paths of the wicked, neither let the way of evil men please thee.
15 [illegible]	15 Ti (vāṭ) tsukāi; teṇeñ votsanākā: poisileān vots, ani ti sōḍ.	15 Flee from it, pass not by it: go aside, and forsake it.
16 [illegible]	16 Kiteāk moḷeār vāiṭ kelleā šivāi te nidanānt ani tankāñ nīd poḍanāñ mōs kellea šivāi.	16 For they sleep not except they have done evil: and their sleep is taken away unless they have made some to fall.
17 [illegible]	17 Khoṭepoṇātso unḍo khātāt ani vāiṭpoṇātso soro piyetāt.	17 They eat the bread of wickedness, and drink the wine of iniquity.
18 [illegible]	18 Puṇ boreānči vāṭ pārzāḷik uzuāḍā bāri mukār tsāltā ani tsāḍtā sāmpūrṇ dīs pāriant.	18 But the path of the just, as a shining light, goeth forwards and increaseth even to perfect day.
19 [illegible]	19 Khoṭeānče vāṭ kāḷokānt: khāiñ poḍtāt mōṇ tankāñ kāḷanāñ.	19 The way of the wicked is darksome: they know not where they fall.

20 [illegible]	20 Mojeā burgeā, mojiñ utrañ āik, ani mojeā ulouṇeāk kān dī.	20 My son, hearken to my words, and incline thy ear to my saying.
21 [illegible]	21 Tujeañ doḷeāñ thāun pois votsānāñ zāundit; tujeā kaḷzā modeñ tiñ sambāḷ:	21 Let them not depart from thy eyes, keep them in the midst of thy heart:
22 [illegible]	22 Kiteāk moḷeār tiñ meḷteleānk jiṇiek ani sāmestañ mānšānk voktāk poḍtāt.	22 For they are life to those that find them, and health to all flesh.
23 [illegible]	23 Tsāḍ zāgrutāyen tujeñ kāḷiz sambāḷ, tantleān jiṇ ubzātā dekun.	23 With all watchfulness keep thy heart, because life issueth out from it.
24 [illegible]	24 Tuje sārsileñ vāiṭ tonḍ kāḍ: peleātso mān kāḍče vonṭ tuje pois kār.	24 Remove from thee a froward mouth, and let detracting lips be far from thee.
25 [illegible]	25 Tuje doḷe sāma poḷeundit, ani tsāltanañ mukār dišṭ gāl.	25 Let thy eyes look straight on, and let eyelids go before thy steps.
26 [illegible]	26 Tujeāñ pāyānk nīṭ mārog kār, ani sākāḍ tujeo vāṭo gāṭ zāteleo.	26 Make straight the path for thy feet, and all thy ways shall be established.
27 [illegible]	27 Ujvea hātāki dāvea hātāki tsukon vots nakā: tujiñ meṭañ vāiṭā thāun pois kār. Kiteāk moḷeār ujveā hātāk asḷleo vāṭo Dēu zāṇā, ani dāvea hātāk asḷleo vāṭo vāiṭ. To tujeo vāṭo	27 Decline not to the right hand nor to the left: turn away thy foot from evil. For the Lord knoweth the ways that are on the right hand: but those are perverse which are on the left hand. But He

ಲೊ ಅನಿ ತುಕಾ ಪೊಣ್ಯಾಂತ್ ಸೌಕಾ ಸಾಯೊನ್ ಚಲ್ಯತೊಲೊ.	sāma kārtolo, ani tukā poiṇānt soukāsāyon tsālāitolo.	will make thy courses straight, He will bring forward thy ways in peace.
ಅವಸ್ವರ್ V.	**Avasvār V.**	**Chapter V.**
1 ಮೊಜ್ಯಾ ಬುರ್ಗ್ಯಾ, ಮೊಜಿ ಸಿಕೊಣ್ ಆಯ್ಕ್, ಅನಿ ಮೊಜೆ ಬುದಿಕ್ ಕಾನ್ ದಿ.	1 Mojea burgeā, moji sikoṇ āik, ani moje budik kān dī.	1 My son, attend to my wisdom, and incline thy ear to my prudence.
2 ತುಜಿ ಚಿಂತ್ನಾ ರಾಕುಂಕ್, ಅನಿ ತುಜ್ಯಾಂ ವೊಂಟಾನಿಂ ಅಪ್ಲೆ ಕ್ಯಾದೆ ಸಾಂಬಾಳುಂಕ್, ಅಸ್ತ್ರಿಯೆಚ್ಯಾ ಮೊಸಾಕ್ ಕಾನ್ ದೀನಾಕಾ.	2 (Tuji) čintna rākunk, ani tujeañ voṇṭāniñ aple kāide sambāḷunk. Astriečeā mosāk kān dī nakā.	2 That thou mayest keep thoughts, and thy lips may preserve instruction. Mind not the deceit of a woman.
3 ಕಿತ್ಯಾಕ್ ಮೊಳ್ಯಾರ್ ವ್ಹಾಟ್ ಅಸ್ತ್ರಿಯೆಚೆ ವೊಂಟ್ ಮೊವಾ ಬರಿ ಸ್ವಾದಿಕ್, ಅನಿ ತಿಚಿಂ ಉತ್ರಾಂ ತೆಲಾ ಪ್ರಸ್ ಮೊವಾಳ್;	3 Kiteāk moḷeār vāiṭ āstrieče voṇṭ movā bāri suādik, ani tičiñ utrañ telā prās movāḷ;	3 For the lips of a harlot are like a honeycomb dropping, and her throat is smoother than oil.
4 ಪುಣ್ ತಿಚೆಂ ನಿಮಾಣೆಂ ವಸ್ತು ಕಾಜ್ರ್ಯಾ ಬರಿ ಕೊಡು, ಅನಿ ದೊನ್ ಧಾರಿ ಅಸ್ಲೆ ತಾಲ್ವಾರಿ ಬರಿ ದೊಂಸಾಚೆಂ.	4 Puṇ tičeo nimāṇeo vāstu kazreā bāri koḍu, ani dón dhari asḷlle tālvāri bāri domsāčeo.	4 But her end is bitter as wormwood, and sharp as a two-edged sword.
5 ತಿಚೆ ಪಾಯ್ ಮೊರ್ನಾ ಥೈಂ ಚಲ್ತಾತ್; ಅನಿ ತಿಚಿಂ ಮೆಟಾಂ ಯೆಂಕೊಂಡಾಂತ್ ರಿಗ್ತಾತ್.	5 Tiče pāi mornā thāiñ tsāltāt; ani tičiñ meṭañ yemkóṇḍānt rigtāt.	5 Her feet go down into death, and her steps go in as far as hell.
6 ತಿ ಜಿಣಿಯೆಚ್ಯಾ ಮಾರ್ಗಾರ್ ಚಲನಾಂ; ತಿಚೆಂ ವಾಟೊ ದುಬಾವಾಚೆಂ ಅನಿ ಸಾಂಗುಂಕ್ ನೊಜೊ ಅಸಲ್ಲೆಂ.	6 Ti jiṇiečeā mārgār tsālanāñ; tičeo vāṭo dubāvāčeo ani sāñgunk nozo asḷlleo.	6 They walk not by the path of life, her steps are wandering, and unaccountable.
7 ತರ್ ಅತಾಂ ಮಕಾ ಆಯ್ಕ್, ಬುರ್ಗ್ಯಾ, ಅನಿ ಮೊಜ್ಯಾ ತೊಂಡಾಚಿಂ ಉತ್ರಾಂ ಸೊಡಿನಾಕಾ.	7 Tār atañ makā āik, burgeā, ani mojea toṇḍāčiñ utrañ sōḍinakā.	7 Now therefore, my son, hear me, and depart not from the words of my mouth.
8 ತುಜಿ ವಾಟ್ ತಿಚೆ ಥಾಉನ್	8 Tuji vāṭ tiče thāun	8 Remove thy way far

[illegible]	pois aşundi, ani tičea garāčeā bāglā lagiñ votsanakā.	from her, and come not nigh the doors of her house.
9 [illegible]	9 Tuzo mān dusreānk ani tuzo jīv niṣṭureāk dīnakā.	9 Give not thy honour to strangers, and thy years to the cruel.
10 [illegible]	10 Tuji bolāiki dusreāniñ pāḍ kārināñ zāunčea pasvot ani tuji āst dusreānčeā gārāk poḍanāñ zāunčea pasvot[1],	10 Lest strangers be filled with thy strength, and thy labours be in another man's house,
11 [illegible]	11 Tuzo mān dusreānk dileār kaḍek rāḍši, jedvañ tujeñ mās ani tuji kuḍ nāš zāit ani sāngši:	11 And thou mourn at the last, when thou shalt have spent thy flesh and thy body, and say:
12 [illegible]	12 Kiteāk āveñ sikoṇ kāṇṭāḷḷi, ani besṭauṇeñ mojeā kaḷzān aikunknāñ,	12 Why have I hated instruction, and my heart consented not to reproof,
13 [illegible]	13 Ani makā sikāiteleānčeñ utār āikunknāñ, ani upadesink kān diunknā?	13 And have not heard the voice of them that taught me, and have not inclined my ear to masters?
14 [illegible]	14 Lāgiñ lāgiñ sārvuṇ vāiṭānt poḍlāñ; igārječe ani sabhečc modeñ astanāñi[2].	14 I have almost been in all evil, in the midst of the church and of the congregation.
15 [illegible]	15 Tuje bāintleñ ani tuje zāričeā vāuñčeñ udāk piye.	15 Drink water of thy own cistern, and the streams of thy own well:

[1] *Lit.* In order that your health may not be spoiled by others, and your property may not fall to another.

[2] In the middle of so many good men I was so ashamed to commit so many sins.

16 ತುಜಿ ಜರ್ ಬ್ಯಾರ್ ದಿಸಾ ಜ್ಯಾ, ಆನಿ ತುಜಿಂ ಉದ್ಕಾಂ ಬಿದಿಂತ್ ವಾಂಟ್.	16 Tuji zār bāir disazāi, ani tujiñ udkañ bidiut vāṇṭ.	16 Let thy fountains be conveyed abroad, and in the streets divide thy waters.
17 ತಿಂ ತುಂಚ್ ಭೋಗ್, ಆನಿ ದುಸ್ರ್ಯಾಂ ಮನ್ಶಾಂಕ್ ತಾಂಚೆ ವಾಂಟೆ ಮೆಳಾನಾಂ ಜಾಉಂದಿತ್.	17 Tiñ tunts bhōg, ani dusreañ mānšānk tānče vāṇṭe meḷanāñ zāundit.	17 Keep them to thyself alone, neither let strangers be partakers with thee.
18 ತುಜೆ ಜರಿಕ್ ಆಶೀರ್ವಾದ್ ಮೆಳುಂದಿ, ಆನಿ ತುಜ್ಯಾ ತರ್ನಾಟ್ಯಾ ಪಿರಾಯೆರ್ (ತುಕಾ ಮೆಳ್ಳೆ[1]) ಅಸ್ತ್ರಿಯೆ ಕಡೆ ಸೌಕಾಸ್ಯಾ ಭೋಗ್.	18 Tujo zārik āšīrvād meḷundi, ani tujcā tārnāṭeā pirāyer (tukā meḷḷe[1]) āstrye kāḍe soukāsāi bhōg.	18 Let thy vein be blessed, and rejoice with the wife of thy youth:
19 ತಿ ಮೆರ್ವಾ ಬರಿ ಮೊಗಾಳ್ ಆನಿ ಮೆರ್ವಾಚ್ಯಾ ಪಿಲಾ ಬರಿ ಪ್ರೀತಿಚಿ ಜಾಉನ್ ಆಸುಂದಿ: ತಿಚೆಂ ಫೊಳ್ ಸೌಕಾಸಾಯೆನ್ ಭೋಗ್ ಆನಿ ತಿಚೊ ಮೋಗ್ ಕರ್ನ್ ಸದಾಂತ್ ಸಂತೋಸ್ ಪಾವ್.	19 Ti meruā bāri mogāḷ ani meruāčeā pilā bāri prītiči zāun asundi: tičeñ fōḷ soukāsāyen bhōg ani titso mōg kārn sadānts sāntōs pāu.	19 Let her be thy dearest hind, and most agreeable fawn: let her breasts inebriate thee at all times, be thou delighted continually with her love.
20 ಕಿತ್ಯಾಕ್, ಮೊಜ್ಯಾ ಬುರ್ಗ್ಯಾ, ದುಸ್ರೆ ಅಸ್ತ್ರಿಯೆ ವೊರ್ವಿಂ ಫೊಟ್ವೊತ್ಯಾ ಆನಿ ದುಸ್ರ್ಯಾಚ್ಯಾ ಉಸ್ಕ್ಯಾಂತ್ ಸೌಕಾಸ್ಯಾ ಕಾಂಗ್ತ್ಯಾ?	20 Kiteāk, mojea burgeā, dusre āstrie vorviñ foṭuotāi ani dusreačeā uskeānt soukāsāi kāṇgetāi?	20 Why art thou seduced, my son, by a strange woman, and art cherished in the bosom of another?
21 ದೇವು ಮನ್ಶಾಚೆ ವಾಟೊ ಪೊಳ್ತಾ, ಆನಿ ತಾಚಿಂ ಸಮೆಸ್ತ್ ಮೆಟಾಂ ಮೆಜ್ತಾ.	21 Deu mānšāčeo vāṭo poḷāitā, ani tačiñ sāmest meṭañ meztā.	21 The Lord beholdeth the ways of man, and considereth all his steps.
22 ಖೊಟೊ ಮನಿಸ್ ಆಪ್ಲ್ಯಾ ಖೊಟೆಪೊಣಾನ್ ಸಾಂಪ್ಡ್ತಾ, ಆಪ್ಲಾ ಪಾತ್ಕಾಂಚ್ಯಾ ಬಾಂದ್ಪಾಸಾಂತ್ ಪಡ್ತಾ.	22 Khoṭo mānis apleā khoṭepoṇān sāmpoḍtā, aplea pātkānčeā bāndpāsānt poḍtā.	22 His own iniquities catch the wicked, and he is fast bound with the ropes of his own sins.
23 ತೊ ಮೊರ್ತೊಲೊ, ಬುದ್ ತಾಕಾ ನಾತ್ಲ್ಲಿ ದೆಕುನ್; ಆನಿ	23 To mortolo, bud takā nātulli dekun; ani	23 He shall die, because he hath not re-

[1] Whom you married.

ಆಪ್ಲ್ಯಾ ಸಬಾರ್ ಪಿಸ್ಯಾಪೊಣಾನ್ ನಾಡಿಂತ್ ಪೊಡ್ತೊಲೊ.	apleā săbār piseāpoṇān nāḍlint poḍtolo.	ceived instruction, and in the multitude of his folly he shall be deceived.
ಅವಸ್ವರ್ VI.	**Avasvăr VI.**	**Chapter VI.**
1 ಮೊಜ್ಯಾ ಬುರ್ಗ್ಯಾ, ತುಜ್ಯಾ ಇಷ್ಟಾ ಬದ್ಲಾಕ್ ಉತರ್ ದಿಶಿ ಜಾಲ್ಯಾರ್, ಪಾರ್ಕ್ಯಾ ಕಡೆ ಹಾತ್ ದಿಲ್ಯಾ; ತುಜ್ಯಾ ತೊಂಡಾಚ್ಯಾಂ ಉತ್ರಾನಿಂ ಸಾಂಪಡ್ಲ್ಯಾ.	1 Mojea burgeā, tujea iṣṭā bădlāk utar diśi zaleār, părkiā kăḍe hāt dilāi; tujea tonḍāčeaṅ utrāniṅ sāmpăḍlāi.	1 My son, if thou be surety for thy friend, thou hast engaged fast thy hand to a stranger.
2 ತುಜ್ಯಾ ತೊಂಡಾಚ್ಯಾ ಉತ್ರಾಂನಿಂ ಸಾಂಪಡ್ಲ್ಯೊ, ಆನಿ ತುಜ್ಯಾಂ ಸಬ್ದಾನಿಂ ಬಾಂದ್ಲೆಲ್ಲೊ ಜಾಉನ್ ವೊರ್ತಉತಲ್ಯೊ.	2 Tujea tonḍāčea utrāṅniṅ sāmpaḍloi, ani tujeaṅ săbdāniṅ bāndullo zāun vortautaloi.	2 Thou art ensnared with the words of thy mouth, and caught with thy own words.
3 ತರ್, ಮೊಜ್ಯಾ ಬುರ್ಗ್ಯಾ, ಆಉಂ ಸಾಂಗ್ತಾಂ ತೆಂ ಕರ್, ಆನಿ ತುಕಾತ್ಸ್ ಚುಕೊನ್ ಘೆ: ತುಜ್ಯಾ ಪೆಲ್ಯಾಚ್ಯಾ ಹಾತಾಂತ್ ಪೊಡ್ಲ್ಯೊ ದೆಕುನ್. ದಾಉಂ ಆಉಂಸರ್, ತುಜ್ಯಾ ಇಷ್ಟಾಕ್ ಉಟ್ಯ:	3 Tăr, mojea burgeā, āuṅ sangtāṅ teṅ kăr, ani tukāts tsukon ghe: tujeā peleāčeā hātāṅt poḍuloi dekun. Dāuṅ, auṅsăr, tujea iṣṭāk uṭāi:	3 Do therefore, my son, what I say, and deliver thyself: because thou art fallen into the hand of thy neighbour. Run about, make haste, stir up thy friend:
4 ದೊಳೆ ದಾಂಪಿನಾಕಾ, ನೀದ್ ಪೊಡಾನಾಂ ಜಾಉಂದಿ.	4 Doḷe dāmpinakā, nīd poḍanāṅ zāundi.	4 Give not sleep to thy eyes, neither let thy eyelids slumber.
5 ಚಿತಾಳಾ ಬರಿ ಪೋಳ್, ಆನಿ ಸುಕ್ಣ್ಯಾ ಬರಿ ಸಿಕಾರೆಗಾರಾಚ್ಯಾ ಹಾತಾಂತ್ಲೊ ಚುಕೊನ್ ಘೆ.	5 Čitāḷā bări pōḷ, ani sukṇeā bări sikāregārāčea hātāntlo tsukon ghe.	5 Deliver thyself as a doe from the hand, and as a bird from the hand of the fowler.
6 ಮುಯೆ ಕಡೆ ವೊಚ್, ಆಳ್ಷಿ ಮಾಣ್ಸಾ, ಆನಿ ತಚ್ಯೊ ವಾಟೊ ಪೊಳೆ ಆನಿ ಬುದ್ ಸಿಕ್:	6 Muye kăḍe vots, ālsi mănšā, ani tačeo vāṭo poḷe ani bud sik:	6 Go to the ant, O sluggard, and consider her ways, and learn wisdom:
7 ತಿ, ಮೊಸ್ತಕ್ ಆನಿ ಉಪದೇಸಿ ಆನಿ ರಾಯ್ ನಸ್ತಾನಾಂ,	7 Ti, mostak ani upă-dēsi ani rāi nastanaṅ,	7 Which, although she hath no guide, nor master, nor captain,

8 [illegible]	8 Gimāčeā veḷār apṇāk khāṇ tāyār kārtā, ani beḷeāčeā veḷār ahār rūs kārtā.	8 Provideth her meat for herself in the summer, and gathereth her food in the harvest.
9 [illegible]	9 Kodoḷ pāriant, ālsiā, nidtāi? Kāiñ nidontlo uṭši?	9 How long wilt thou sleep, O sluggard? when wilt thou rise out of thy sleep?
10 [illegible]	10 Illeñ nidtoloi, illi nīd poḍteli, illeñ hāt zodtoloi soukāsāi kāṇeunk:	10 Thou wilt sleep a little, thou wilt slumber a little, thou wilt fold thy hands a little to sleep:
11 [illegible]	11 Ani durbāḷkāi, poiṇāriā bāri ani akānt hatiārañ asalleā mānšā bāri pāuteli. Puṇ tsurk zāun asleār, zāri bāri tujeñ beḷeñ yeteleñ, ani durbāḷkāi tuje lāgsili veteli.	11 And want shall come upon thee as a traveller, and poverty as a man armed. But if thou be diligent, thy harvest shall come as a fountain, and want shall flee far from thee.
12 [illegible]	12 Dēvāk soḍtolo, upkārāk poḍanātullo mānis, kāpāṭān tsāltā.	12 A man that is an apostate, an unprofitable man walketh with a perverse mouth.
13 [illegible]	13 Doḷe moḍn hiāāre ditā, pāy boḍāitā, boṭān ulāitā.	13 He winketh with the eyes, presseth with the foot, speaketh with the finger.
14 [illegible]	14 Vāiṭ monān vāiṭ činttā ani sādānts nyāi kārāitā.	14 With a wicked heart he deviseth evil, and at all times he soweth discord.
15 [illegible]	15 To yekāts farā nāš zātolo, yekāts farā bhos-	15 To such a one his destruction shall present-

[illegible]	motolo-ani tăče mukăr takă vokăt asčeññăñ.	ly come, and he shall suddenly be destroyed, and shall no longer have any remedy.
16 [illegible]	16 Dēu kanṭăltă teo văstu să ani sătvi văstụ ăḷšiketă.	16 Six things there are which the Lord hateth, and the seventh His soul detesteth:
17 [illegible]	17 Garvišṭ doḷe, foṭi mărči jīb, guniăuñ nătụlleñ ragat văuoitolo hăt,	17 Haughty eyes, a lying tongue, hands that shed innocent blood,
18 [illegible]	18 Văiṭ čiñtna band-čeñ mòn, văiṭăk sompeñ tsăltele păy,	18 A heart that deviseth wicked plots, feet that are swift to run into mischief,
19 [illegible]	19 Foṭi utsărtolo, foṭkiro săkšigăr, ani băvăñ bităr bebănău kărtolo.	19 A deceitful witness that uttereth lies, and him that soweth discord among brethren.
20 [illegible]	20 Mojea burgeă, băpăče upădēs sămbăḷn dovor, ani tujeă măyeči somort sōḍinakă.	20 My son, keep the commandments of thy father, and forsake not the law of thy mother.
21 [illegible]	21 Te monă bităr dămp, ani găḷeănt găl.	21 Bind them in thy heart continually, and put them about thy neck.
22 [illegible]	22 Tuñ tsăltanañ te tuje săngată tsălundit, tuñ nidtanañ, te tukă răkundit, ani zăgo zătanañ tănče kăḍe ulăi.	22 When thou walkest, let them go with thee: when thou sleepest, let them keep thee, and when thou awakest talk with them.
23 [illegible]	23 Kiteăk moḷeăr formăn yěk divo, ani upă-	23 Because the commandment is a lamp, and

[illegible]	dēs yēk uzuāḍ, ani jiṇieči vāṭ besṭaunči sikoṇ:	the law a light, and reproofs of instruction are the way of life:
24 [illegible]	24 Tukā vāiṭ āstrientlo, părkiā fuslāunče jibentlo rakčeā pāsun.	24 That they may keep thee from the evil woman, and from the flattering tongue of the stranger.
25 [illegible]	25 Tujeñ mòn tiči sobitāieči āšā kărinān zāundi, ani tičeā hišārānče nāḍint poḍanakā:	25 Let not thy heart covet her beauty, be not caught with her winks:
26 [illegible]	26 Kiteāk moḷeār vāiṭ āstriečeñ moḷ kāšṭān yēk uṇḍo: puṇ āstri mānšātso molādik ătmo sāmpaḍāitā.	26 For the price of a harlot is scarce one loaf: but the woman catcheth the precious soul of a man.
27 [illegible]	27 Uzo apleā hărdeānt, nesoṇ lāsanāstanañ, mānšān lipāyetgī?	27 Can a man hide fire in his bosom, and his garments not burn?
28 [illegible]	28 Yā keṇḍānčer pāi lāsanāstanañ tsāliyetgī?	28 Or can he walk upon hot coals, and his feet not be burnt?
29 [illegible]	29 Tāsents apleā peleāčeā āstrie kāḍe tsāltolo, tikā apoḍleleā veḷār nitāḷ nāiñ.	29 So he that goeth unto his neighbour's wife, shall not be clean when he shall touch her.
30 [illegible]	30 Tsorčeñ bhou vāiṭ pātak nāiñ[1]; kiteāk moḷeār bhukello jīv dādos kărunk tsortā.	30 The fault is not so great when a man hath stolen; for he stealeth to fill his hungry soul:
31 [illegible]	31 Ani to sāmpḍat zaleār, sāt pāuṭi tzāḍ vāpas ditolo[2]: ani apleā gărāči sāgḷi āst ditolo.	31 And if he be taken, he shall restore sevenfold, and shall give up all the substance of his house.

[1] "Bhou vāiṭ pātak nāiñ" muṇčeā: produāra mukār.—"The fault is not so great" viz. compared with adultery.

[2] *Cf.* Exodus, Ch. 22.

32 [illegible]	32 Puṇ produvāri apleā monāčeā piseapoṇān aplo ātmo hogḍāitā:	32 But he that is an adulterer, for the folly of his heart, shall destroy his own soul:
33 [illegible]	33 To apṇāk akmān ani lāz rās kărtā, ani tātso beābru urtolo.	33 He gathered to himself shame and dishonour, and his reproach shall not be blotted out.
34 [illegible]	34 Kitcāk moḷcār dādleātso mosor ani krōdh fārikpoṇāčeā disā māf kărtsonāñ.	34 Because the jealousy and rage of the husband will not spare in the day of revenge.
35 [illegible]	35 Ani koṇeñi māgleāri aikuntsonāñ, ani fārikpoṇāk săbār kaṇkeoi kāṇeuntsonāñ.	35 Nor will he yield to any man's prayers, nor will he accept for satisfaction ever so many gifts.

ಸಾಂ ಲುಕಾಚೆಂ ಪುಸ್ತಕ್	**SAÑ LUKĀČEÑ PUSTAK**	**St. LUKE**
ಅವಸ್ವರ್ I.	Avasvăr I.	Chapter I.
1 [illegible]	1 Săbăr mānšāniñ amče bitār gaḍulleañ văstunči katā sāngunk prāyătān kărtāts;	1 Forasmuch as many have taken in hand to set forth in order a narration of the things that have been accomplished among us;
2 [illegible]	2 Zāseñ amkāñ sikăilāñ sākš zāun poḷeleāñ šāstrā-muniāryāniñ:	2 According as they have delivered them unto us, who from the beginning were eye-witnesses and ministers of the word:
3 [illegible]	3 Săkăḍ văstu suruver thāun tsătrāyen ani krāmān tukā sāngunk,	3 It seemed good to me also, having diligently attained to all things

ಥಿಯೊಫಿಲಾ, ಮಕಾಕಾ ಬೊರೆಂ ದಿಸ್ಲೆಂ,	bhou boreā Theophilā, makāi boreṅ dislen,	from the beginning, to write to thee in order, most excellent Theophilus
4 ತುಂ ಸಿಕ್ಲೆಂ ಸತ್ ಖರೆಂ ಮೊಣ್ ಸೊಮ್ಜಸೆಂ.	4 Tuṅ sikullen sāt khāren móṇ somzasen.	4 That thou mayest know the verity of those words in which thou hast been instructed.
5 ಹೆರೊದ್ ಮೊಳ್ಳ್ಯಾ ಜುದೆಯಾಚ್ಯಾ ರಾಯಾಚ್ಯಾ ದಿಸಾನಿಂ ಆಮ್ಕೊ ಸಾಸೆರ್ದೊತ್ ಅಸುಲ್ಲೊ, ಜಾಚೆಂ ನಾಉಂ ಜಕಾರಿಅಸ್, ಅಬಿಅಚ್ಯಾ ಕುಟ್ಮಾತ್ಸೊ: ತಾಚಿ ಅಸ್ತ್ರಿ ಆರೊನಾಚ್ಯಾಂ ದುವಾಂತ್ಲಿ, ಆನಿ ತಿಚೆಂ ನಾಉಂ ಎಲಿಜಾಬೆತ್.	5 Herod moḷḷeā Judeyāčeā rāyāčeā disāniṅ āmko sāserdot asullo, začen nāuṅ Zakāriās, Abiāčea kuṭmātso: tači āstri Aaronāčeān duvāntli, ani tičen nāuṅ Elizābet.	5 There was in the days of Herod, the king of Judea, a certain priest named Zachary, of the course of Abia: and his wife was of the daughters of Aaron, and her name Elizabeth.
6 ದೊಗಾಂಇ ದೇವಾ ಮುಕಾರ್ ನೀತಿವಂತ್ ಜಾಉನ್ ವೊರ್ತಾವುತಾಲಿಂ, ಆನಿ ದೇವಾಚೆ ಸಕಡ್ ಉಪದೇಸ್ ಆನಿ ದೇವಾಚಿ ಸೊಮೊರ್ತ್ ಚುಕಾನಾಸ್ತಾನಾಂ ಸಾಂಬಾಳ್ತಾಲಿಂ.	6 Dogāṅi Dēvā mukār nītivānt zāun vortautāliṅ, ani Dēvāče sākāḍ upādēs ani Dēvāči somort tsukanāstanaṅ sambāḷtāliṅ.	6 And they were both just before God, walking in all the commandments and justifications of the Lord without blame.
7 ಪುಣ್ ತಾಂಕಾಂ ಬುರ್ಗಿಂ ನಾತ್ಲ್ಲಿಂ, ಎಲಿಜಾಬೆತ್ ವಾಂಜ್ ಆನಿ ದೊಗಾಂಇ ಮಾತಾರಿಂ ಜಾಉನ್ ಅಸ್ಲ್ಲಿಂ ದೆಕುನ್.	7 Puṇ tankāṅ burgiṅ nātulliṅ, Elizābet vānz ani dogaṅi mātāriṅ zāun asalliṅ dekun.	7 And they had no son, for that Elizabeth was barren, and they both were well advanced in years.
8 ಆನಿ ತೊ ಶಾಸ್ತ್ರಾಚೆ ಕಾಯ್ದೆ ತಾಕಾ ನೆಮ್ಸಿಲ್ಯಾ ವೆಳಾರ್ ಪಾಳ್ತಾನಾಂ,	8 Ani to šāstrāče kāide takā nemsileā veḷār pāḷtanaṅ,	8 And it came to pass, when he executed the priestly function in the order of his course before God,
9 ಸಾಸೆರ್ದೊತಿಚೆ ದಸ್ತುರಿ ಪರ್ಮಾಣೆ, ಸರ್ತಿನ್ ಬಾಯ್ರ್ ಸರ್ನ್ ದೇವಾಚ್ಯಾ ಗಾರಾಂತ್ ರಿಗ್ಲೊ ಧುಂಪೊಉಂಕ್;	9 Sāserdotiče dāsturi pārmāṇe, sārtin bāir sārn dēvāčeā gārānt riglo dhumpounk;	9 According to the custom of the priestly office, it was his lot to offer incense, going into the temple of the Lord;

10 ಆನಿ ಸೆಗ್ಳೊ ಜೋಮೊ ಧುಂಪೌಂಚ್ಯಾ ವೆಳಾರ್ ಮಾಗ್ಣೆಂ ಕರ್ನ್ ಬ್ಯಾರ್ ಅಸುಲ್ಲೊ.	10 Ani săgḷo zomo dhumpounčea veḷār māgṇeñ kărn bāir asullo.	10 And all the multitude of the people was praying without at the hour of incense.
11 ಆನಿ ದೇವಾಚೊ ಬೊಡ್ವೊ ಧುಂಪಾಚೆ ಅಲ್ತಾರಿಚ್ಯಾ ಉಜ್ವ್ಯಾ ದಿಕ್ಕಾನ್ ತಾಕಾ ದಿಷ್ಟಿ ಪೊಡ್ಲೊ.	11 Ani Dēvātso boḍvo dhumpāčea altāričeā uzveā dikkān takā diṣṭi poḍlo.	11 And there appeared to him an Angel of the Lord, standing on the right side of the altar of incense.
12 ಜಾಕಾರಿಆಸ್ ಪೊಳೆಉನ್ ಭಿಯೆಲೊ ಆನಿ ಕಾಂಪ್ಲೊ.	12 Zakāriās poḷeün bhiyelo ani kāmplo.	12 And Zachary seeing him was troubled, and fear fell upon him.
13 ಆನಿ ಬೊಡ್ವ್ಯಾನ್ ತಾಕಾ ಸಾಂಗ್ಲೆಂ: ಭಿಯೆನಾಕಾ, ಜಾಕಾರಿಆಸಾ, ಕಿತ್ಯಾಕ್ ಮೊಳ್ಯಾರ್ (ದೇವಾನ್) ತುಜೆಂ ಮಾಗ್ಣೆಂ ಆಯ್ಕಲಾಂ: ಆನಿ ತುಜಿ ಅಸ್ತ್ರಿ ಎಲಿಜಾಬೆತ್ ತುಕಾ ಎಕಾ ಬುರ್ಗ್ಯಾಕ್ ಪರ್ಸುತ್ ಜಾತೆಲಿ, ಆನಿ ತಾಕಾ ಜುವಾಉಂ ಮೊಣ್ ನಾಉಂ ದೊವೊರ್ತೊಲೊಯಿ:	13 Ani boḍveān takā sangleñ: Bhiyenakā, Zakāriāsā, kiteāk moḷeār (Dēvān) tujeñ māgṇeñ aikalāñ: ani tuji ăstri Elizābet tukā yekā burgeāk părsut zāteli, ani takā Juāuñ móṇ nāuñ dovortoloi:	13 But the Angel said to him: Fear not Zachary, for thy prayer is heard; and thy wife Elizabeth shall bear thee a son, and thou shalt call his name John:
14 ಆನಿ ತೊ ತುಕಾ ಸಂತೋಸ್ ಆನಿ ಉಲಾಸ್ ದಿತೊಲೊ, ಆನಿ ಸಬಾರ್ ಲೋಕ್ ತಾಚ್ಯಾ ಜಲ್ಮಾಕ್ ಸಂತೋಸ್ ಪಾಉತೊಲೊ.	14 Ani to tukā santōs ani ulās ditolo, ani săbār lōk tačeā zălmāk santōs pāutolo.	14 And thou shalt have joy and gladness, and many shall rejoice in his nativity.
15 ಕಿತ್ಯಾಕ್ ಮೊಳ್ಯಾರ್ ತೊ ವೋಡ್ ದೇವಾ ಮುಕಾರ್, ಆನಿ ಸೊರೊ ಆನಿ ಅಮಲಾಚಿ ವಸ್ತು ಪಿಯೆಉಂಚೊನಾಂ, ಆನಿ ಸ್ಪಿರಿತಾ ಸಾಂತಾನ್ ಬೊರ್ನ್ ಜಾತೊಲೊ, ಮಾಯೆಚೆ ಕುಸಿಂತ್ ಅಸ್ತಾನಾಂ ಮೊಣಾಸರ್ ಸಯ್ತ್.	15 Kiteāk moḷeār to vōḍ Dēvā mukār, ani soro ani amalāči văstu piyeuntsonāñ, ani Spiritā Santān born zātolo, māyeče kusint astanāñ moṇāsăr săit.	15 For he shall be great before the Lord: and shall drink no wine nor strong drink, and he shall be filled with the Holy Ghost even from his mother's womb.
16 ಆನಿ ಸಬಾರ್ ಇಜ್ರಾಯೆಲಾಚ್ಯಾಂ ಪುತ್ರಾಂಕ್ ತಾಂಚ್ಯಾ ದೇವಾ ಥಾಂಯ್ ಪೊರ್ತಿತೊಲೊ.	16 Ani săbār Izrayelāčeañ putrānk tančeā Dēvā thāiñ portitolo.	16 And he shall convert many of the children of Israel to the Lord their God.

17 [illegible]	17 Ani to Eliā bări tače mukār votolo; bāpānčiñ kāḷzañ putrāñ thāiñ ani anbāvāḍtiānk nītivontānče budik portounk, Somiāk sămpūrṇ zomo tăyār kărunk.	17 And he shall go before him in the spirit and power of Elias; that he may turn the hearts of the fathers unto the children, and the incredulous to the wisdom of the just, to prepare unto the Lord a perfect people.
18 [illegible]	18 Ani Zakāriāsān Boḍveā kăḍe moḷeñ: yeñ kăseñ āveñ zāṇā zāunčeñ? kitoāk moḷeār, āuñ mātāro ani moje ăstriek săbār pirāi asā.	18 And Zachary said to the Angel: Whereby shall I know this? for I am an old man, and my wife is advanced in years.
19 [illegible]	19 Ani Boḍveān zāb diun săngleñ: āuñ Dēvā mukār rāuntso Gābriel; ani (Dēvān) makā dhāḍlāñ tuje găḍe ulounk ani yeñ tukā pārgăṭ kărunk.	19 And the Angel answering, said to him: I am Gabriel who stand before God; and am sent to speak to thee, and to bring thee those good tidings.
20 [illegible]	20 Ani poḷe: mono astoloi, ani ulounk tānk asčināñ, yeo văstu zatāt moṇāsăr; āveñ tukā sangullleo văstu, jeo gaḍun yeteleo fāvoteā veḷār, sătmandunknāi dekun.	20 And behold thou shalt be dumb, and shalt not be able to speak until the day wherein these things shall come to pass; because thou hast not believed my words, which shall be fulfilled in their time.
21 [illegible]	21 Ani zomo Zakāriāsăk rākun asullo, ani ajāp zātālo to igārjent toḍou kartā môn.	21 And the people were waiting for Zachary, and they wondered that he tarried so long in the temple.

22 ಅನಿ ಬ್ಯಾರ್ ಸರ್ನ್ ತಾಚೆ ಗಡೆ ಉಲೊಂವ್ಕ್ ತಾಂಕ್ ನಾತ್ಲ್ಲಿ ಅನಿ ತಾಕಾ (ಝೊಮ್ಯಾಕ್) ಕಳಿತ್ ಝಾಲೆಂ ಕಿ ಸಾಸೆರ್ದೊತಿಕ್ ಇಗರ್ಜೆಂತ್ ಏಕ್ ದಿಷ್ಟ್ ಪೊಡ್ಲಿ ಮೊಣ್. ಅನಿ ತೊ ಲೊಕಾಕ್ ಗುರ್ತಾನಿಂ ಉಲಯ್ತಾಲೊ ಅನಿ ಮೊನೊ ರಾವ್ಲೊ.	22 Ani bāir sārn tāče gāḍe ulounk tānk nātḷli ani takā (zomeāk) kāḷit zāleñ ki sāserdotik igārjent yēk dišṭ poḍḷli móṇ. Ani to lokāk gurtāniñ ulāitālo ani mono rāulo.	22 And when he came out he could not speak to them, and they understood that he had seen a vision in the temple. And he made signs to them, and remained dumb.
23 ಅನಿ ಅಪ್ಲ್ಯಾ ಶಾಸ್ತ್ರಾಚೆಂ ಕಾಮ್ ಝಾಲ್ಯಾ ಉಪ್ರಾಂತ್ ಗರಾ ಗೆಲೊ.	23 Ani apleā šāstrāčeñ kām zāleā uprānt gārā gelo.	23 And it came to pass, after the days of his office were accomplished, he departed to his own house.
24 ತೆ ದೀಸ್ ಝಾಲ್ಯಾ ಉಪ್ರಾಂತ್ ಎಲಿಝಾಬೆತ್, ತಾಚಿ ಅಸ್ತ್ರಿ, ಗರ್ಬೆಸ್ತ್ ಝಾಲಿ ಅನಿ ಪಾಂಚ್ ಮ್ಹೈನೆ ಲಿಪ್ತಾಲಿ ಸಾಂಗುನ್:	24 Te dīs zāleā uprānt Elizābet, tači ăstri, gărbest zāli, ani pānts moine liptāli sangun:	24 And after those days Elisabeth, his wife, conceived, and hid herself five months, saying:
25 ದೇವಾನ್ ಮೊಜೆ ಥೈಂ ಯೆಂ ಕೆಲಾಂ, ಜ್ಯಾಂ ದಿಸಾನಿಂ ತಾಣೆಂ ಮಕಾ ಪೊಳೆಲಿ ಮನ್ಶ್ಯಾ ಬಿತರ್ ಮೊಜೆ ವೊಯ್ಲೊ ಅಕ್ಮಾನ್ ಕಾಡುಂಕ್.	25 Dēvān moje thāiñ yeñ kelāñ, jeañ disāniñ taṇeñ makā poḷeili mănša bitār moje voilo ăkmān kāḍunk.	25 Thus hath the Lord dealt with me in the days wherein He hath had regard to take away my reproach among men.
26 ಅನಿ ಸವ್ಯಾ ಮೊಯ್ನ್ಯಾ ದೇವಾನ್ ಗಾಬ್ರಿಯೆಲ್ ಮೊಳ್ಳ್ಯಾ ಬೊಡ್ವ್ಯಾಕ್ ಧಾಡ್ಲೊ ಗಾಲಿಲ್ಯಾಚ್ಯಾ ನಾಝರೆತ್ ಮೊಳ್ಳ್ಯಾ ಶೆರಾಂತ್, ದಾವೀದಾಚ್ಯಾ ಗರಾಣ್ಯಾಚ್ಯಾ,	26 Ani săveā moineā Dēvān Gābriel moḷḷea Boḍveāk dhāḍlo Galileāčeā Nazaret moḷḷea šerānt, Dāvīdāčea gărāṇeāčea,	26 And in the sixth month, the Angel Gabriel was sent from God into a city of Galilee, called Nazareth,
27 ಝೊಝೆ ಮೊಳ್ಳ್ಯಾ ದಾಡ್ಲ್ಯಾ ಕಾಡೆ ಕಾಝಾರ್ ಝಾಲ್ಲೆ ಅಂಕ್ವಾರಿ ಲಾಗಿಂ; ಅನಿ ಅಂಕ್ವಾರಿಚೆಂ ನಾಉಂ ಮಾರಿ.	27 Zoze moḷḷea dādleā kāḍe kāzār zālle ankuāri lāgiñ; ani ankuāričeñ nāuñ Māri.	27 To a virgin espoused to a man whose name was Joseph, of the house of David; and the virgin's name was Mary.
28 ಅನಿ ಬೊಡ್ವ್ಯಾನ್ ತಿಚೆ ಕಡೆ ವೊಚುನ್ ಸಾಂಗ್ಲೆಂ: ನಮಾನ್, ಕುರ್ಪೆನ್ ಭೊರ್ಲೆಲಿ, ಸೊಮಿ ದೇವು	28 Ani Boḍveān tiče kāḍe votsun sangleñ: Namān, kurpen bhorlele,	28 And the Angel being come in, said unto her: Hail, full of grace, the

ತುಜೆ ಥ್ಯಂ ಅಸಾ; ಅಸ್ತ್ರಿಯಾಂ ಬಿತರ್ ತುಂ ಸದೆಉಂ.	Somi Dēu tuje thāiñ asā; āstreāñ bitār tuñ sādeuñ.	Lord is with thee: blessed art thou among women.
29 ತಿ ಆಯ್ಕುನ್, ತ್ಯಾ ಸಾಂಗ್ಣ್ಯಾ ಪಾಸುನ್ ಭಿಯೆಲಿ; ಅನಿ ಚಿಂತಾಲಿ ಕಸಲೊ ನಮಸ್ಕಾರ್ ಮೊಣ್.	29 Ti āikun, tea sangņeā pasun bhiyeli; ani čintāli kasalo namaskār móņ.	29 Who having heard, was troubled at his saying, and thought within herself what manner of salutation this should be.
30 ಅನಿ ಬೊಡ್ವ್ಯಾನ್ ತಿಕಾ ಸಾಂಗ್ಲೆಂ: ಭಿಯೆನಾಕಾ, ಮಾರಿಯೆ, ತುಕಾ ದೇವಾ ಮುಕಾರ್ ಕುರ್ಪಾ ಮೆಳ್ಳ್ಯಾ ದೆಕುನ್.	30 Ani Boḍveān tikā sangleñ: Bhiyenakā, Māriye, tukā Dēvā mukār kurpā meḷḷeā dekun.	30 And the Angel said to her: Fear not, Mary, for thou hast found grace with God.
31 ಪೊಳೆ: ಗರ್ಬೆಸ್ತ್ ಜಾತೆಲಿ, ಅನಿ ಯೆಕಾ ಬುರ್ಗ್ಯಾಕ್ ಪೊರ್ಸುತ್ ಜಾತೆಲಿ, ಅನಿ ತಾಕಾ ಜೆಜು ಮೊಣ್ ನಾಉಂ ದೊವೊರ್ತೆಲಿ.	31 Poḷe: gārbest zāteli, ani yekā burgeāk porsut zātelī, ani takā Jezu móņ nāuñ dovortelī.	31 Behold thou shalt conceive in thy womb, and shalt bring forth a son; and thou shalt call his name Jesus.
32 ಉವೊ ವ್ಹೊಡ್ ಜಾಉನ್ ವೊರ್ತಾಉತೊಲೊ, ಅನಿ ತಾಕಾ ಭೌ ವ್ಹೊಡ್ ದೇವಾಚೊ ಪುತ್ ಮೊಣ್ ಮೊಣ್ತೆಲೆ, ಅನಿ ದೇವು ತಾಕಾ ದಿತೊಲೊ ತಾಚ್ಯಾ ಮಾಲ್ಗಡ್ಯಾ ದಾವಿದಾಚೆಂ ಸಿಯಾಸನ್ ಅನಿ ತೊ ಜಾಕೊಬಾಚ್ಯಾ ಗರಾಣ್ಯಾಂತ್ ಸದಾಂಕಾಳ್ ರಾಜ್ವೊಟ್ಕಿ ಕರ್ತೊಲೊ.	32 Uo vōḍ zāun vortautolo, ani takā bhou vōḍ Dēvātso put móņ moņtele, ani Dēu takā ditolo tačeā mālgāḍea Dāvīdāčeñ siāsan ani to Jakobāčeā gārāņeānt sādāñkāl rāzvoṭkāi kārtolo.	32 He shall be great, and shall be called the Son of the most High, and the Lord God shall give unto him the throne of David his father: and he shall reign in the house of Jacob for ever,
33 ಅನಿ ತಾಚೆ ರಾಜ್ವೊಟ್ಕ್ಯಾಯೆಕ್ ಸೆವೊಟ್ ಅಸ್ಸೊನಾಂ.	33 Ani tače rāzvoṭkāyek sevoṭ assonāñ.	33 And of his kingdom there shall be no end.
34 ತೊವೊಳ್ ಮಾರಿಯೆನ್ ಬೊಡ್ವ್ಯಾಕ್ ಸಾಂಗ್ಲೆಂ: ಯೆಂ ಕಸೆಂ ಜಾವಿಯೆತ್? ಕಿತ್ಯಾಕ್ ಮೊಳ್ಯಾರ್ ಆಉಂ ದಾದ್ಲ್ಯಾಕ್ ವೊಳ್ಕನಾಂ.	34 Tovoḷ Mārien Boḍveāk sangleñ: Yeñ kāseñ zāviet? Kiteāk moḷeār āuñ dādleāk voḷkanāñ.	34 And Mary said to the Angel: How shall this be done? because I know not man.
35 ಅನಿ ಬೊಡ್ವ್ಯಾನ್ ಜಾಬ್ ದಿಉನ್ ಸಾಂಗ್ಲೆಂ: ಸ್ಪಿರಿತ್ ಸಾಂತ್ ತು	35 Ani Boḍveān zāb diun sangleñ: Spiritu	35 And the Angel answering, said to her:

ಜೆರ್ ದೆಉಂತೊಲೊ ಆನಿ ಭೌ ವೊಡಾಚಿ (ದೇವಾಚಿ) ಪೊಡ್ವಿ ತುಕಾ ಸಾಂಬಾಳ್ತೆಲಿ, ಆನಿ ತ್ಯಾ ಪಾಸುನ್ ತುಜೆ ಬಿತರ್ ಗರ್ಭ ಸಂಬಾಉತೊಲೊ ಭಾಗೆವೊಂತ್, ತಾಕಾ ದೇವಾಚೊ ಪುತ್ ಮೊಣ್ ಮೊಣ್ತೆಲೆ.	Sāntụ tujer deuntolo ani bhou voḍāči (Dēvāči) podvi tukā sambāḷteli, ani teā pasun tuje bitār gărb sambautolo bhāgevont, takā Dēvātso put móṇ moṇtele.	The Holy Ghost shall come upon thee, and the power of the Most High shall overshadow thee. And therefore also the Holy which shall be born of thee shall be called the Son of God.
36 ಆನಿ ಪೊಳೆ: ಎಲಿಜಾಬೆತ್ ತುಜಿ ಮಾಉಸಿ ಬೊಯ್ಣ್, ಆಪ್ಲೆ ಮಾತಾರೆ ಪಿರಾಯೆರ್ ಗರ್ಭ ಸಂಬಾಉಲ್ಯಾ, ಸ ಮೊಯ್ನ್ಯಾಂ ಥಾಉನ್;	36 Ani poḷe: Elizābet, tuji māusi boiṇ, aple mātāre pirāyer gărb sambauleā să moineañ thāun;	36 And behold thy cousin Elizabeth, she also hath conceived a son in her old age: and this is the sixth month with her, that is called barron;
37 ಕಿತ್ಯಾಕ್ ಮೊಳ್ಯಾರ್ ದೇವಾಕ್ ಕ್ಯಾಂಚ್ ಉತರ್ ಅಉಗಡ್ ನ್ಹಂ.	37 Kiteāk moḷeār Dēvāk kāiñts utar augăḍ nāiñ.	37 Because no word shall be impossible with God.
38 ಆನಿ ಮರಿಯೆನ್ ಸಾಂಗ್ಲೆಂ: ಪೊಳೆ, ಆಉಂ ದೇವಾಚಿ ಚಾಕರ್ಣ್; ಮೊಜೆ ಥ್ಯಂ ತುಜ್ಯಾಂ ಉತ್ರಾಂ ಪರ್ಮಾಣೆ ಜಾಉಂ. ಆನಿ ತಿಚೆ ಲಾಗ್ಸಿಲೊ ಬೊಡ್ವೊ ಗೆಲೊ.	38 Ani Māriyen sangleñ: poḷe, āuñ Dēvāči tsākārn; moje thāiñ tujeañ utrañ pārmāṇe zāuñ. Ani tiče lāgsilo Boḍvo gelo.	38 And Mary said: Behold the handmaid of the Lord, be it done to me according to thy word. And the Angel departed from her.
39 ಆನಿ ಮರಿ ಉಟುನ್ ತ್ಯಾಂ ದಿಸಾನಿಂ ಪರ್ವತಾಂಚ್ಯಾ ಗಾವಾಂತ್ ಅಉಸರಾನ್ ಗೆಲಿ ಜುದೆಯಾಚ್ಯಾ ಶೆರಾಂತ್.	39 Ani Māri uṭun teañ disāuiñ pārvătāñčeā gāvānt ausārān geli, Judeāčeā šerānt.	39 And Mary rising up in those days, went into the hill country with haste into a city of Juda.
40 ಆನಿ ಜಕಾರಿಅಸಾಚ್ಯಾ ಗಾರಾಂತ್ ರಿಗೊನ್, ಎಲಿಜಾಬೆತಿಕ್ ಮಾನ್ ಕೆಲೊ.	40 Ani Zakāriāsāčeā gārānt rigon Elizābetik mān kelo.	40 And she entered into the house of Zachary, and saluted Elizabeth.
41 ಆನಿ ಎಲಿಜಾಬೆತ್ ಮರಿಯೆಚೊ ನಮಸ್ಕಾರ್ ಆಯ್ಕುನ್, ಬುರ್ಗ್ಯಾನ್ ತಿಚೆ ಕುಸಿಂತ್ ಉಲಾಸ್ ಭೊಗ್ಲೊ, ಆನಿ ಎಲಿಜಾಬೆತ್ ಸ್ಪಿರಿತಾ ಸಾಂತಾನ್ ಭೊರ್ಲಿ	41 Ani Elizābet Mārietso namaskār āikun, burgeān tiče kusint ulās bhoglo, ani Elizābet Spiritā Santān bhorli:	41 And it came to pass, that when Elizabeth heard the salutation of Mary, the infant leaped in her womb. And Elisabeth was filled with the Holy Ghost:

42 ಆನಿ ಬೊಬ್ ಮಾರ್ನ್ ಸಾಂಗ್ಲೆಂ: ಅಸ್ತ್ರೆಯಾಂ ಭಿತರ್ ತುಂ ಸದೆವುಂ, ಆನಿ ಸದೆವುಂ ಫೊಳ್ ತುಜೆ ಕುಸಿಚೆಂ ಜೆಜು.

42 Ani bōb mārn sangleṅ: ăstreāñ bităr tuñ sădeuñ, ani sădeuñ fōḷ tuje kusičeñ Jezu.

42 And she cried out with a loud voice, and said: Blessed art thou among women, and blessed is the fruit of thy womb.

43 ಆನಿ ಕಸಿ ಮೊಜ್ಯಾ ದೇವಾಚಿ ಮಾಯ್ ಮೊಜೆ ಕಡೆ ಯೆವುಂಚಿ?

43 Ani kăsi mojea Dēvăči măi moje kāḍe yeunči?

43 And whence is this to me, that the mother of my Lord should come to me?

44 ಕಿತ್ಯಾಕ್ ಮೊಳ್ಯಾರ್, ಪೊಳೆ, ತುಜೊ ತಾಳೊ ಮೊಜ್ಯಾ ಕಾನಾಂತ್ ಪೊಡೊನ್, ಬುರ್ಗ್ಯಾನ್ ಮೊಜೆ ಕುಸಿಂತ್ ಉಲಾಸ್ ಭೊಗ್ಲಾ.

44 Kiteāk moḷeār, poḷe, tuzo tāḷo mojeā kănānt poḍon, burgeān moje kusint ulās bhoglā.

44 For, behold, as soon as the voice of thy salutation sounded in my ears, the infant in my womb leaped for joy.

45 ಆನಿ ಭಾಗೆವಂತ್ ತುಂ, ಸತ್ಮಂದುಲ್ಲ್ಯಾ ಪಾಸ್ವತ್; ಕಿತ್ಯಾಕ್ ಮೊಳ್ಯಾರ್ ಸೊಮಿಯಾನ್ ತುಕಾ ಸಾಂಗುಲ್ಲೆಂ, ತೆಂ ತುಜೆ ಥೈಂ ಗಡುನ್ ಯೆತೆಲೆಂ.

45 Ani bhāgevont tuñ sătmanduḷleā pasvot; kiteāk moḷeār Somiān tukā sanguḷleā, teñ tuje thăiñ găḍun yeteleñ.

45 And blessed art thou that hast believed, because those things shall be accomplished that were spoken to thee by the Lord.

46 ಆನಿ ಮರಿಯೆನ್ ಸಾಂಗ್ಲೆಂ: ಮೊಜೊ ಆತ್ಮೊ ದೇವಾಕ್ ವೊರ್ಣಿತಾ:

46 Ani Măriyen sangleṅ: Mozo ătmo Dēvāk vorṇitā:

46 And Mary said: My soul doth magnify the Lord:

47 ಆನಿ ಮೊಜೆಂ ಮೊನ್ ಸಂತೊಸ್ ಪಾವುಲೆಂ, ದೇವಾ, ಮೊಜ್ಯಾ ಸೊಡ್ವೊಣ್ದಾರಾ, ಥೈಂ.

47 Ani mojeṅ mòn santōs pāuleñ, Dēvā, mojea Soḍvoṇḍarā, thăiñ.

47 And my spirit hath rejoiced in God my Saviour.

48 ಕಿತ್ಯಾಕ್ ಮೊಳ್ಯಾರ್ ಆಪ್ಲೆ ತ್ಸಾಕಾರ್ಣಿಚಿ ಕಿರ್ಕೊಳಾಯ್ ತಾಣೆಂ ಪೊಳೆಲ್ಯಾ: ಕಿತ್ಯಾಕ್ ಮೊಳ್ಯಾರ್, ಪೊಳೆ, ಯ್ಯಾ ಮುಕಾರ್ ಸಕಡ್ ಸೊಸ್ತಿ ಮಕಾ ವೊರ್ಣಿತೆಲ್ಯೊ.

48 Kiteāk moḷeār, aple tsăkărniči kirkoḷāi tāṇeñ poḷeleā: kiteak moḷeār, poḷe, yea mukăr săkăḍ sosti makā vorṇiteleo.

48 Because He hath regarded the humility of His handmaid: for, behold, from henceforth all generations shall call me blessed.

49 ಕಿತ್ಯಾಕ್ ಮೊಳ್ಯಾರ್ ಸರ್ವ್ ಪೊಡ್ವೆದಾರಾನ್ ಮೊಜೆ ಥೈಂ ವೊಡ್ ವಸ್ತು ಕೆಲ್ಯಾತ್, ಆನಿ ತಾಚೆಂ ನಾವುಂ ಭಾಗೆವಂತ್.

49 Kiteāk moḷeār sărvụ podvedārān moje thăiñ vōḍ văstu keleāt, ani tačeñ năuñ bhāgevont.

49 Because He that is mighty hath done great things to me: and Holy is His name.

50 ಆನಿ ತಾಚಿ ಕಾಕುಳ್ತ್ ತಾಕಾ ಭಿಯೆತೆಲ್ಯಾಂಚ್ಯಾಂ ಸೊಸ್ತಿಂಕ್ ಖಳಾನಾಸ್ತಾನಾಂ ಮೆಳ್ತಾ.	50 Ani tači kākuḷt takā bhiyeteleānčeañ sostink khaḷanāstanañ meḷtā.	50 And His mercy is from generation to generations, to them that fear Him.
51 ಆಪ್ಲ್ಯಾ ಹಾತಾಚೆಂ ಬೊಳ್ ದಾಕೈಲೆಂ: ಆಪ್ಲ್ಯಾ ಮೊನಾಂತ್ ಗರ್ವು ಕರ್ತೆಲ್ಯಾಂಕ್ ಭೊಸ್ಮಿಲೆ.	51 Aplea hātāčeñ bòḷ dākāileñ: apleā monānt gārvụ kārteleānk bhosmile.	51 He hath shewed might in His arm: He hath scattered the proud in the conceit of their heart.
52 ಪೊದ್ವೆದಾರ್ ಮನ್ಶ್ಯಾಂಕ್ ತಾಂಚ್ಯಾ ಸಿಂಹಾಸನಾರ್ ಥಾವುನ್ ಕಾಡ್ನ್ ಗಾಲೆ ಆನಿ ನೆಣ್ತ್ಯಾಂಕ್ ಮಾನ್ ದಿಲೊ.	52 Podvedār mānśānk tančeā siāsanār thāun kāḍn gāle, ani neṇteānk mān dilo.	52 He hath put down the mighty from their seat, and hath exalted the humble.
53 ಭುಕೆಲ್ಲ್ಯಾಂಕ್ ಬೊರೆಪೊಣಾನ್ ಭೊರ್ಲೆಆತ್, ಆನಿ ಗ್ರೆಸ್ತಾಂಕ್ ಖಾಲಿ ಸೊಡ್ಲ್ಯಾತ್.	53 Bhukelleānk borepoṇān bhorleāt, ani grestānk khāli soḍleāt.	53 He hath filled the hungry with good things: and the rich He hath sent empty away.
54 ಇಜ್ರಾಯೆಲಾಕ್ ಆಪ್ಲ್ಯಾ ಚಾಕ್ರಾಕ್ ಕಾಣ್ಗೆಲಾ, ತಾಚಿ ಕಾಕುಳ್ತ್ ಕರ್ನ್.	54 Izrāyelāk aplea tsākrāk kāṇgelā, tāči kākuḷt kārn.	54 He hath received Israel His servant, being mindful of His mercy.
55 ಜಾಂಚೆಂ ತೊ ಆಮ್ಚ್ಯಾಂ ಬಾಪಾಂಚ್ಯಾಂ, ಅಬ್ರಾಹಾಮಾ ಆನಿ ತಾಚೆ ಸಂತತಿ ಕಡೆ ಉಲೈಲೊ ಸದಾಂಕಾಳಾಕ್.	55 Zātso to amčeañ bāpānčeañ, Abrāhāmā ani tače sāntāti kāḍe ulāilo sadāñkālāk.	55 As He spoke to our fathers, to Abraham and to his seed for ever.
56 ಆನಿ ಮರಿ ತಿಚೆ ಸಾಂಗಾತಾ ಸುಮಾರ್ ತೀನ್ ಮೊಯ್ನೆ ರಾವೊನ್, ಆಪ್ಲ್ಯಾ ಗಾರಾ ಪಾಟಿ ಆಯ್ಲಿ.	56 Ani Māri tiče sangātā sumār tīn moine rāvon, apleā gārā pāṭi āili.	56 And Mary abode with her about three months: and she returned to her own house.
57 ಆನಿ ಪೊರ್ಸುತ್ ಜಾಂವ್ಚೊ ವೇಳ್ ಪಾವೊನ್, ಎಲಿಜಾಬೆತ್ ಯೆಕಾ ಬುರ್ಗ್ಯಾಕ್ ಪೊರ್ಸುತ್ ಜಾಲಿ.	57 Ani porsut zāuntso vèḷ pāvon, Elizābet yekā burgeāk porsut zāli.	57 Now Elisabeth's full time of being delivered was come, and she brought forth a son.
58 ಆನಿ ತಿಚ್ಯಾಂ ಸೆಜಾರ್ಯಾನಿಂ ಆನಿ ಸೈರ್ಯಾನಿಂ ಆಇಕುನ್ ಕಿ ದೇವಾನ್	58 Ani tičeañ sezāreāniā ani seireāniñ āi-	58 And her neighbours and kinsfolks heard that

[illegible]	kun ki Dēvān tiči kăkuḷt keliā móṇ, tikā porāb ditāliñ.	the Lord hath shewed His great mercy towards her, and they congratulated with her.
59 [illegible]	59 Ani aṭvea disā burgeāk sirkumsizăr kărunk yeun, takā bāpāčeñ nāuñ Zakăriās móṇ dovortāliñ.	59 And it came to pass that on the eighth day they came to circumcise the child, and they called him by his father's name Zachary.
60 [illegible]	60 Ani tače āvoin zāb diun sangleñ: nakā, băgār takā Juāuñ móṇ nāuñ dovorizāi.	60 And his mother answering, said: Not so, but he shall be called John.
61 [illegible]	61 Ani sangtāle tiče kăḍe ki tujeā seireāñ bităr koṇāki tăsăleñ nāuñ nāñ móṇ.	61 And they said to her: There is none of thy kindred that is called by this name.
62 [illegible]	62 Ani tačeā bāpā kăḍe gurtāniñ vitsārtāle kăsăleñ nāuñ takā dovorizāi móṇ khuši asā.	62 And they made signs to his father, how he would have him called.
63 [illegible]	63 Ani taṇeñ yēk foḷi māgun borāileñ săngun: tačeñ nāuñ Juāuñ móṇ. Ani săkăḍ ajāp zāle.	63 And demanding a writing-table, he wrote, saying: John is his name. And they all wondered.
64 [illegible]	64 Teāts farā tačeñ tòṇḍ ani tači jīb suṭli ani Dēvāk vorṇoun ulonk laglo.	64 And immediately his mouth was opened, and his tongue loosed, and he spoke, blessing God.
65 [illegible]	65 Ani bheñ disleñ sămestañ tančeañ sezāreānk ani săgḷeā Ju-	65 And fear came upon all their neighbours; and all these things were

Kannada	Konkani	English
[illegible]	deāčeañ părvătānčer yeo văstu părgăṭ zāleo:	noised abroad over all the hill-country of Judea:
66 [illegible]	66 Ani zokōṇ aikatālo, teñ apleā monā bitār sambāḷtālo sangun: uo burgo kōṇ zāit? kiteāk moḷeār Dēu tače sangātā asullo.	66 And all they that had heard them laid them up in their heart, saying: What an one, think ye, shall this child be? For the hand of the Lord was with him.
67 [illegible]	67 Ani Zakāriās, tātso bāpui, Spiritā Santān bhórlo, aṇi mukār gaḍčeo văstu săngleo, săngun:	67 And Zachary his father was filled with the Holy Ghost: and he prophesied saying:
68 [illegible]	68 Izrāelātso Dēu sădeuñ, kiteāk moḷeār to beṭlā, ani tāṇeñ soḍvoṇ kelea aple părječi.	68 Blessed be the Lord God of Israel: because He hath visited and wrought the redemption of His people:
69 [illegible]	69 Ani tāṇeñ amkāñ yekā podvedār soḍvoṇdārāk dilā, Dāvidā apleā tsākrāčea gărānt,	69 And hath raised up an horn of salvation to us, in the house of David His servant.
70 [illegible]	70 Zatso to ulāilo bhāgevontañ prophetāñ vorviñ, je gelleā kālānt asạlle.	70 As He spoke by the mouth of His holy prophets, who are from the beginning.
71 [illegible]	71 Amkāñ amčeāñ dusmānāntle ani amtso mosor kărteleāntle soḍāileāt:	71 Salvation from our enemies, and from the hand of all that hate us:

[1]) Latin bāsen: "soḍvoṇičeñ" *Sing.* muṇčeñ: "podvedār soḍvon".—According to the Latin: "horn of salvation", i. e. "powerful salvation".

72 [illegible]	72 (Tāṇeñ Soḍvoṇdārāk dilā) amčeāñ bāpānči kākuḷt kärunk ani (tanče kāḍe kelleā) kärärätso ugḍās kärunk.	72 To perform mercy to our fathers, and to remember His holy testament.
73 [illegible]	73 Pārmāṇātso (ugḍās kärunk) jeñ tāṇeñ amčeā bāpā Abrahāmā kāḍe keleñ (moṇčeñ) ki to amkāñ (titli kurpā) ditolo mòṇ,	73 The oath which He swore to Abraham our father, that He would grant to us,
74 [illegible]	74 Aseñ ki amiñ amčeā dusmānāntle soḍāitāts, bheñ nastanañ tači tsākri kāruñ,	74 That being delivered from the hand of our enemies, we may serve Him without fear,
75 [illegible]	75 Bhāgevontpoṇān ani nītin tače mukār amče sāmestañ jiṇiyečeāñ disāniñ.	75 In holiness and justice before Him, all our days.
76 [illegible]	76 Ani tukā, burgeā, bhou vòḍ Dēvātso prophet mòṇ nāuñ zateleñ, kiteāk moḷeār Dēvā mukār vetoloi vāṭ tāyār kärunk.	76 And thou, child, shalt be called the prophet of the Highest: for thou shalt go before the face of the Lord to prepare His ways.
77 [illegible]	77 Soḍvoṇiči zāṇvāi sikounk tače pārjek pātkānčeñ bogsaṇeñ meḷāseñ:	77 To give knowledge of salvation to His people, unto the remission of their sins:
78 [illegible]	78 (Yeñ bogsaṇeñ meḷtā) amčeā Dēvāče kākuḷtin, je kākuḷtin unts thāun udeuntso suryo amkāñ beṭlā,	78 Through the bowels of the mercy of our God, in which the Orient, from on high, hath visited us,

79 (ತುಂ ಮುಕಾರ್ ವೆತೊಲೊಯ್) ಮೊರ್ಣಾಚ್ಯಾ ಕಾಳೊಕಾಂತ್ ಆನಿ ಸಾವುಳೆಂತ್ ನಿದ್ಲ್ಯಾಂಕ್ ಉಜ್ವಾಡ್ ದಿವುಂಕ್, ಆನಿ ಅಮ್ಚೆ ಪಾಯ್ ಸೌಕಾಸಾಯೆಚ್ಯಾ ಮಾರ್ಗಾರ್ ಚಲೊವುಂಕ್.

79 (Tuñ mukār vetoloi) morṇāčeā kāḷokānt ani sāuḷent nidḷlleāṅk uzvāḍ diunk, ani amče pāi soukāsāyečeā mārgār tsālounk.

79 To enlighten them that sit in darkness, and in the shadow of death: to direct our feet into the way of peace.

80 ಆನಿ ಬುರ್ಗೊ ವಾಡ್ತಾಲೊ ಆನಿ ಗಾಟ್ ಜಾತಾಲೊ ಆತ್ಮ್ಯಾಂ ಥೈಂ ಆನಿ ರಾನಾಂತ್ ಅಸ್ಲ್ಲೊ ತೊ ಆಪ್ಣಾಕ್ ಇಸ್ರಾಯೆಲಾಕ್ ದಾಕಯ್ತಾ ಮೊಣಸರ್.

80 Ani burgo vāḍtālo ani gāṭ zatālo ātmeā thāiñ ani rānānt asḷllo to apṇāk Izrāelāk dākāitā moṇasār.

80 And the child grew, and was strengthened in spirit: and was in the deserts until the day of his manifestation to Israel.

GLEANING AND CLEANING, ΠΑΡΕΡΓΟΝ.

PART I.

I premise as the foundation of this Chapter, that from the very beginning of this Grammar, I intended 1) to write a Grammar to be circulated privately only among my brethren of the Society who know Latin, other Grammars etc.; 2) to omit all niceties, although required by exactness, especially as regards spelling, in which point I did not follow the Kanarese but the Roman alphabet. Hence many things are to be found, which are not exact, if we judge of them according to the full science of Grammar. But there is a rule of common sense to judge of such works, not bad in themselves, according to the intention of the author. In order to judge about other things, *e.g.*, order, style etc., consider that this Grammar has been composed within a few months. As to Gleaning, I must limit myself to the most necessary things, leaving many other things to the Dictionary, and omitting others in order not to increase too much the size of this book. As to Cleaning, I do not correct things which depend on the extraordinary circumstances, in which this book has been composed, *e. g.* order, style, exercises, foreign words *etc.* Some Cleaning will be left to the Dictionary, for the above reason.

PART I. Chapt. I. 1) The explanation of the vowels and consonants is only approximate; strictly we should distinguish four a (see p. 191); hence short vowels too can have the stress of the voice as "tzăḍ=much" (see *l. c.* and p. 231, para. 8, *d.*). 2) What I say of the Kanarese manner of writing etc. must be understood not of the Kanarese language, but of the Kanarese letters, used also for Tuḷu by the Basel Mission Press in Mangalore. This regards especially the ‘ which in Kanarese very seldom occurs and even then shows absence of a vowel; in

Tuḷu it occurs at every step as a sign of a half vowel. 3) Some principles laid down in this Chapter are not strictly adhered to, first on account of having changed my plan, then on account of great hurry, finally on account of the state of Konkani still quite unsettled: I myself became aware of a more correct mode only after a great part of the Grammar had been printed; many things have been omitted purposely, in order to make the matters easier. 4) According to the Mahrātti I should have written ă in many cases in which it has been omitted, and so other similar things. The reason is because I do not adapt Konkani to Mahrātti, which would be ridiculous, but to the common pronunciation, which pronunciation and not the Mahrātti is to be considered as the rule.—For the same reason I have written some words not as the Kanarese words of a similar root.

Page 2, *line* 10. "A short *o*" viz. closed o, if the accent does not fall upon ă. In Kanarese this closed o (ă) is written ಅ, viz. short a which has some gradations to be learnt by practice.

Line 8, *et seq. a fine.* These words are said only on the supposition that a kind of half vowel be pronounced at the end of every word ending in a consonant; but as this is not the case, as I say in the note, hence whenever a word is written with a pure consonant at the end, pronounce it without the half vowel, keeping this sound for ạ or ụ. As regards ạ, and ụ, *omnibus consideratis*, it seems better to use only ụ for both sounds, although between them there is some difference which can be left to be learnt by practice. The reason of this is, because the things are more simple in this way, and for the Kanarese alphabet I introduced only one sign for both viz. ᵕ. This half vowel occurs often in the middle of words.

Page 3, *para.* 1. Add to these cerebral letters also ḷ, ṇ, as on p. 5, 6, and ṣ̌, as on p. 191. The difference between š and ṣ̌ is this: š is palatal, ṣ̌ is cerebral.

Para. 2. Add h to the letters which can be aspirated. In Kanarese only the above letters have a peculiar sign: yet the aspirated **h** can occur also after other consonants (see p. 194). The Konkani aspiration is less strong than the English one.

Page 4, *para*. 4. **Ts** would better render the sharp **s**, expressed by the Kanarese ಚ and Mahrātti च. Hence **ts** and **tš** could be put aside, for the sake of simplicity also. This **ts** can be aspirated as in Kanarese and in Mahrātti; then it should be written **tsh**, as the aspirated **z** becomes **zh**.

About the hard **s** see, however, p. 105, *note* 1. This hard **s** is not so rare. The soft **z** is like **s** in *misery*.

Para. 6. Also in the middle I write often **ñ**. The nasal sound by itself sounds sometimes **n**, sometimes **m**; yet **ñ** might express, by convention, both sounds.

Page 5. The common **a** is pronounced somewhat open, not very slowly, or very quickly. In Kanarese we have no proper sign for it. See p. 191.

Page 6. Closed **o** is as o in *note*, open **o** is as o in *not*. No need to say that **kš** differs from **ks**.

Both **u̥** and **v** are called nearly **u**, but they differ: **u̥** is nearly **u**, because it is half vowel; **v** is nearly **u**, because often it is pronounced between **v** and **u** or also like an **u**; *e. g.* "uzvāḍ = uzuāḍ".

Para. 1, of the note, is premature.

Page 7. *g*) "Aha" perhaps is, in its origin, not vulgar, but correct, because it comes from the Mahrātti "आहे = I am".

2. **Ts** is expressed by ಚ which sounds also **č**.

Chapter II. In many words the accent upon the last syllable is so slight that you cannot perceive distinctly whether it is upon the last or upon the penultimate; *e. g.* "gāli."

Besides the principal accent there is a secondary accent upon a preceding syllable, especially in compound words which have a secondary accent upon the last syllable of the first word.

As to the diphthongs see some completion of this rule on p. 195. Perhaps we can make it clearer and more complete by saying that mostly the true (*i. e.* pronounced as one sound) final diphthongs formed: 1) by a as first vowel and another true vowel, and 2) by e combined with i and u, 3) by o combined with i and u, have the accent upon the first vowel (ai, ao, au, ei, eu, oi, ou, *not* ayo, ayi, avu *etc.*). The other true or apparent (as, "ia = ya" etc.) diphthongs have more commonly the accent upon the second vowel (as ea, eo, ie, io, iu, ua, ui, ue, uo). The combinations ae, ao, ie, *etc.* which result from the addition of the termination of the Declension to the Original, have the accent upon the last vowel (see p. 195). In Kanarese they would be written, usually, with y *or* v between the two vowels, thus eye, iye, avu *etc.*, and so they would not even appear as diphthongs. The most usual combinations of two vowels are these (omitting the combination of a vowel with itself): 1) ae, *ai*, *ao*, *au;* 2) ea, *ei*, eo, *eu;* 3) ia, ie, io, iu; 4) oa, oe, *oi*, *ou;* 5) ua, ue, ui, uo. The diphthongs in Italics have usually the accent upon the first. Compare, however, the rule of the text.

Pronounce y (or the corresponding i) *distinctly* as a consonant: hence make the pause of the voice before y: "vidya = vid-ya".

Page 8, *para.* 1. ....not only low but also some of high castes pronounce "bā″ra" *etc.;* "rā″ja = king"; "rǎjā′ = leave."

Para. 2. "saḍe = ½" used with numerals, properly has only half accent, because the second word has the principal accent; yet it seems to differ from other compounds, because it has the secondary accent not upon the last but upon the penultimate syllable: "saḍe-tīn = 3½."

Appendix. Many things could be said here, if time would allow, about the change of quantity.

PART II. Chapter I. Page 9, *line* 13. Assemblage of dialects, viz. apparently: see p. 317. A *common* language in *potentia* at least is there; dialects almost *actu.*

Page 10, *line* 7. Characteristic, *i. e.* distinguishing; I do not mean to say that we will call this case characteristic, although it could be called so.

Page 11, *line* 13, *et seq.* Strictly, the pure Adjectives used as Adjectives have no proper form for the Original; yet they have it, if used as Pronouns.

Page 12, *line* 17, *et seq.* This rule does not hold good for all cases.

Page 12, *line* 24, *et seq.* This must not be taken as unexceptional, because few Postpositions do not govern the Original, as I say in Chapter VI.

Line 3, *a fine.* What is said hereafter on p. 13, compared with p. 14, *n.* 3, can be considered as a general rule on this point.

Page 13, *line* 12. "In the same way", *i.e.* the same terminations of the singular; but in the Vocative usually the affix nu or no must be added. Perhaps somebody might consider nu not as affix but as an essential part of the termination of the Vocative.

Line 20, *et seq.* There are some exceptions to this rule; see Dictionary.

Page 13, *line* 17, *et seq.* This construction usually does not take place, if the Noun, not contracted, would have as many syllables in the oblique cases, as in the Nominative; hence no contraction in the 3rd declension. A similar contraction takes place also in Verbs; *e.g.* "utrun", instead of "utarun = having crossed".

Page 14, *n.* 1. In Greek, Grammarians call a contraction not only the fusion of two vowels into one, but also the omission of one vowel; hence we can call this omission simply and properly contraction.

Note 6. To, ti, teñ are sometimes used really and properly as Articles. (See p. 235.)

Line 29, *et seq.* Some of these rules are premature.

Line 8, *a fine.* This must be understood only of the obsolete Postposition "antụ". See p. 41, para. 3.

Para. 2. "antụ" is still really used in Mahrātti as a Postposition (आंत).

Page 15, *para.* 4. Cf. Ch. VI. and Part IV. Ch. II. Art. 6. At least two Postpositions govern the Nominative.

Para. 7. It should be put in the 1st Declension. Moreover some at least of such Nouns in a can have a Plural form in some cases, *e.g.* in the Dative.

Page 16, *line* 1. "krupa", see page 20, *n.* 2, its approximately right spelling.

Para. 8. More simply say that the Nominative is du. Yet in Mahrātti it is "dhuv".

Para. 9. In some rare cases the preceding Nouns are left in the Nominative.

B. In the following five paragraphs only Common Nouns are treated of.

Page 17, *para.* 1. Besides these two Nouns there are some others which, usually, are not of Feminine Gender.

Add as 5) Abstract Nouns in sāṇ may follow this Declension; *e.g.* "koḍsāṇ = bitterness", or the 4th; as also 6) the Feminine Nouns and Diminutive Nouns derived both from the Masculine by changing o into i; *e.g.* "bokḍi, goḍi, guḷi" *etc.*

Page 18, *line* 2. To "use the Original" add "or sometimes the Nominative or Dative".

Line 13. "Nominative yo". This happens especially with some Nouns in a used also in the Plural, and also with some other Nouns; *e.g.* "kărn, -e", "khuši, -e, *or* -še"; in the Plural "kărneo, khušeo". In such cases y is kept also in the oblique cases. Some of such Nouns can have -e, or -ie in the Original.

Page 19, *line* 2. "Rāṇiāno". The suffix must be always added. This must be applied to the following Declensions too.

Page 20, *note* 2. This note is useless, if we write with Kanarese letters or also with Roman letters, but adhering strictly to the Kanarese.

Page 20, *line* 12. "sikša *or* šikša".

Page 21, *line* 1. *et seq.* It is better to omit the Verb "assā".

Line 10, *et seq.* After further inquiring it seems that

"kurāḍ" is of the 4th Declension: kul, -a, is *n.*, kuli, -e is *f.*: both ways can be used.

Page 22, *para.* 3. Also Masculine or Neuter Nouns in au or ou usually are of the 2nd Declension: the spelling "āuñ *or* āu" is better than "ao *or* āoñ".

Page 23, *line* 4, *a fine.* "Kăšţ" is better used as Masculine.

Page 24, *para.* 4. This rule only hinted at, can be perfected by saying that all or nearly all Masculine Nouns of this Declension ending in ó change it into ă or, seldom, into ò, in the Plural; *e.g.* "poṇós = jack-fruit", "kolós = cupola (?)", "soróp = snake", "māróg = way", "koróḍ = 100 lakhs", "fātór = stone", "pormóḷ = smell", "hātór = bamboo-mat", "dārvónd = door-frame", "korvónt = saw", "ḍongór = mountain", "rākkós = monster", "voṇók = cocoanut-shell", "bikóṇ = bug", "ḍukór = pig", "róng = colour"; all these have ă in the Plural. "Fóḍ = boil", "dór = rope of plantain-tree", "sór = necklace", "kāsou = small tortoise", "fóṇḍ = grave", "rós = juice",: . . . have ò in the Plural. Hence instead of ă we cannot write o.

Masculine Nouns ending in é change it into è; but I cannot say as yet, that this change of é into è is so extended as the change of o. Of many Masculine Nouns having é in the last syllable, up to this I could not find any one against this rule.

Line 3, *a fine.* "Bāpai *or* pāpā", strictly "pāpā"; "bāpai" is another form.

Page 25, *line* 2. "Kāḷiz" strictly means "liver"; yet usually it is taken for "heart".

Page 26, *para.* 2. "Burgeānu" belongs to para. 1.

Page 29, *para.* 1. There are some Nouns which take ia not ea; *e.g.* "bheñ, bhiā = fear". If a Noun ends in io or yo or uo, euphony requires only a not ea to be added; *e.g.* "surio *or* suryo = sun", "suriāk = to the sun". If we write yo and vo, we might say yea, vea *etc.*

Page 32, *para.* 4. "Ākānt" does not suit well, because more commonly it is declined according to the 2nd Declension.

Page 34, *note* 3. More commonly "boiṇ" is of the 4th Declension also in the Plural.

Line 3. Viz. this nasal sound sounds more distinctly than the nasal sound of the Plural; *e.g.* "burgeānk": exactly "burgeāñ-k", pronounced however as "burgeānk"; but ñ of such Nouns must sound distinctly a pure ñ.

Page 36, *Ex.* 1. "Guru" is used by some also for priests of the Old Testament.

Page 37, *line* 10, *a fine.* "Săkăṭ", some say "săkăḍ" oblique cases "săgḍā".

Page 38, *b.* Names of girls take a Neuter termination also in the Nominative, if possible; hence "Mărieñ = Mary" (girl): Mări (woman).

Page 39, *note.* Premature.

Page 41, *para.* 2. Premature.

Page 42, *para.* 4. "Lók" can be used in the Plural as in Latin *populus.*

b): "Mănis", used for a woman, follows the 1st Declension in the Singular, the 2nd Neuter in the Plural.

c): "Dāg" is often used also in the Singular.

Page 43, *line* 5. The form "bāpai" is more used in addressing.

Page 44, *line* 1. Only few consider small children as Neuter.

Feminine: a) This exception is to be limited to certain fixed cases; usually younger female relatives (not the wife by the husband), and women in much lower condition are considered as Neuter both in speaking to and about them; in other cases the Neuter Gender seldom occurs; hence the beginner will better employ the Feminine Gender.

Page 45. Add to *Feminine:* Abstract Nouns in "sāṇ" are Feminine; *e.g.* "koḍsāṇ = bitterness".

Page 46, *lines* 6-7, *a fine.* This difficulty can be considerably diminished so: Nouns of the 2nd Declension ending in a syllable with ó or é, are mostly or always Masculine (see

p. 400, *note* on p. 24); Nouns of the 2nd Declension having ò or è in the Nominative Singular are mostly Neuter; *e.g.* "mòṇ, pòṭ, lèk".

Page 47. The names of male animals ending in o, have often, the Feminine ending in i.

Page 48, *line* 10, *a fine.* There are some exceptions; *e.g.* "fāvo = due", is not declinable; some Adjectives ending in a consonant can sometimes take the terminations o, i, eñ. But these two exceptions are very rare.

Page 49, *lines* 1, 2. If the Adjective is predicate, it does not occur, usually, in the oblique cases.

Line 16. Some Adjectives ending in a consonant take a in the oblique cases for all Genders.

Note 1. Such use is not very extended.

Lines 13, 9, *a fine.* Yet Adjectives having a termination which is found also in Substantives, *e.g.* i, can be declined especially if used as Nouns; *e. g.* "gărvi = proud", "gărveañ mănšānk *or* gărveānk = to proud men".

Page 50, *b*): "boreo ăstrio", better "boreo ăstreo", as in the oblique cases too, e is used: still better "ăstryo".

Page 51, *line* 17. "săkṭe" is derived from "săkăṭ" by dropping the vowel a, because often in the Adjectives too happens what has been remarked on p. 13.

§ 2. Perhaps this and the following paragraphs might have been put more properly under Art. II.

Page 52, *para.* 1. Premature. Remark however that the rule here hinted at, holds good also when there are many subordinate Adjectives. (See an example in para. 5, page 53.) Moreover the Adjective accompanying the Adjectival Genitive, follows, in concord, this Adjective, not the principal Noun: "bore jiṇiečiñ vărsañ = years of good life".

Line 5, *a fine.* "sămestañ" can also be Nominative Neuter; better put this example: "săkṭañ gărānče fātăr = stones of all the houses". Here it appears as an oblique case. At any rate the last part of this first observation is not obligatory.

Page 53, *para.* 3. In such a case there would be a composition; hence it would be better to put a hyphen: "Dēvā-kurpa."

Para. 4. According to para 1, p. 52, only "Somia Jezu Kristāčea kāḷzāčeñ fest" is right. By way of composition, we might say: "...Krista-kāḷzāčeñ fest". People say: "Somia Jezu kāḷzāčeñ fest".

To these subordinate Adjectives the rule of para. 1 is to be applied. The parallel Adjectives seem to agree directly with their Noun; *e.g.* "bangārāčiñ ani rupeāučiñ gārañ = houses of gold and silver".

Para. 5. The use of ea for e, of e for ea, seems to be not very correct theoretically; yet in some cases, *e.g.* "bāpāče nāviñ", there is universal use which has the force of a rule; those cases must be kept.

Page 54, § III. Premature.

Page 55. An is the termination of the Instrumental; hence it implies the meaning "through". (See Syntax.)

Line 5. The example is not very suitable.

Line 14. In conformity with the explanation it means "you who are far, go". "Poisilo" is better.

Line 12, *a fine.* "Foḷ" for "fruit," properly is *n.*, and ò, if figuratively, more commonly, is *m.*, and ó.

Line 5, *a fine.* "moṭṭo = very fat"; "moṭo = fat".

Page 57, *line* 4. The last sentence is to be understood in conformity with the definition of the Church.

Art. II. As only numerals have been put, another title might have been better.

No. 2. "doni, dogi," they are declined just as "dōn, dōg", to which you add i; hence "dogañ-i" *etc.*

No. 7. "Sāt (pronounced quickly)"; as there are two long a, as I said in Ch. IX. P. III., this a seems to be the less long one.

Page 58, *No.* 43. "tečāḷis *or* tevečāḷis"; the 2nd form is more correct.

Page 59, *No.* 100. "Señ"; some pronounce "šeñ, šembor": this 2nd form agrees with the Mahrātti.

Page 59, *No.* 160. Some say also "yekšeñ ani sāṭ".

Para. 1. The first manner of counting is vulgar.

Page 61, *line* 1. Some do not use the second form for irrational animals; yet this form seems to be more common.

Para. 3. *Cf.* 231, *para.* 8.

Para. 4. Strictly speaking "săvāi" does not mean $1\frac{1}{4}$, but is a general particle, in Mahrātti "săvā", meaning "having a fourth more, *or* more by a fourth"; hence it is the proper form to express $1\frac{1}{4}$, $2\frac{1}{4}$, $3\frac{1}{4}$, *etc.;* in this way "săvāi dōn = $2\frac{1}{4}$", "săvāi tīn = $3\frac{1}{4}$" *etc.* To say $1\frac{1}{4}$, "yēk" is understood, and can reasonably be understood according to the above meaning. For facilitating this point, I put together those fractional or mixed numbers:

"$\frac{1}{4}$ = pāu, *or* kāldo"; "$\frac{1}{2}$ = ărdho"; "$\frac{3}{4}$ = pāuṇo, *or* mukāl"; "$1\frac{1}{4}$ = săvāi"; "$1\frac{1}{2}$ = dēḍ"; "$1\frac{3}{4}$ = pāuṇeñ dōn"; "$2\frac{1}{4}$ = săvāi dōn" (and so $3\frac{1}{4}$, $4\frac{1}{4}$....); "$2\frac{1}{2}$ = eḍets *or* eḍez"; "$2\frac{3}{4}$ = pāuṇeñ tīn" (in a similar way $3\frac{3}{4}$ *etc.*); "$3\frac{1}{2}$ = saḍe tīn, "$4\frac{1}{2}$ = saḍe-čār" *etc.* For fractions lower than $\frac{1}{4}$ see p. 244 *n.* 1.

Page 62. § II. Add also "čouto = fourth" as irregular; moreover from 19 upwards insert a before adding vo; *e.g.* "yekuṇisāvo, visāvo, yēk-visāvo, tisāvo" *etc.*

§ IV. The distributive numbers can be used for the multiple numbers, because the distributive notion contains also a multiple notion; *e.g.* "čačār rupoi dovor = put the Rupees four by four"; hence you must have either 8 or 12 *etc.*; but the prevailing notion is distributive, and properly it cannot be used for multiple numbers. The last mode in some contexts cannot be used exactly; *e. g.* having received four rupees and desiring to have four more, I cannot say: "dōn pāuṭi tsāḍ di", because this would mean 8 more (12). Instead of "dōn pāuṭi tsāḍ" sometimes it would be better to repeat the number; *e.g.* "dōn pāuṭi čār = twice four".

Page 63. § VI. Few persons use "dāñ" (Mahrātti दां) instead of "pāuṭi": Add moreover: to say "first, secondly..", they say "poile suāter, dusre suāter", *lit.* "in the first place, in the second place". The form "poileañ, dusreañ" *etc.* as in Mahrätti, can be also used, yet it would rather mean: "by the first, by the second."

Page 64, *line* 4. "šeär": more commonly "šer"; in any case it must be pronounced quickly with the accent upon a.

Line 10. Better "kitlo-temp zäi," at the end.

Line 14. "Deḍsea" is better.

Page 66, *line* 4. "Säma" can also be used, *e.g.* "Pedru Pauläk säma assä = Peter is equal to Paul". If the comparison is in particular, then "säma" does not seem very suitable.

Line 3, *a fine.* "assä" better "zäun assä".

Page 67, *line* 4. "bhägivänt": some say "bhägevont".

Page 68, *line* 4. Perhaps "uttim" has the same origin as the Italian "*ottimo*" and the Latin "*optimus*". It is used also in Kanarese, Mahrätti, and Sanskrit.

These comparative and superlatives, except "tsäḍ", might perhaps be considered as independent words, which can express also the comparative and superlative meaning of these Adjectives.

Line 18. "tikeñ": "čikeñ" is more common.

Add the termination -so. (See Part III. Ch. II.) In some cases by -leñ some diminutives can be formed; *e.g.* "ghāṇṭleñ = small bell".

Page 69, *line* 8-10. Among these modes I mention here another, viz. the doubling of the consonant, by which augmentative or superlative meaning is produced; *e.g.* "voḍoḷ = lately, just now"; "voḍḍoḷ = some time ago"; "moṭo = fat", "moṭṭo = very fat". I cannot say how far this last mode can be used.

Exercise: "dhäiryavont", some say "dhäiravont *or* dhäirivont".

"Sukh". According to Max Müller (Sanskrit Grammar for Beginners, ch. II. § 116), final aspirate letters lose their aspiration, in Sanskrit; it seems that in the niece of Sanskrit, we should follow the same rule; hence either we should write "sukhụ *or* suk". This remark regards other words too. Yet throughout the Grammar I did not observe strictly this point, nor is it, perhaps, to be taken into consideration.

Page 70. § 1. Better "āveñ *or* ăueñ.

"Amāñ" is an old Original of "amiñ", *e.g.* "amāñ pasun vināti kăr = pray for us".

Page 72, *para.* 1. "*amore tui* = out of love to you".

Para. 2. viz. if the Postpositions govern the Original; for if it governs the Dative or Nominative, then the pure Dative or Nominative is used.

Para. 4. *Cf.* Part IV. Chapter I.

Para. 5. "Chiefly"; this kind of Instrumental is as well used for the Nouns etc.

Page 73, *line* 4, *a fine.* "tintso": this by analogy with "titso" is right, but used by very few; instead of it, "tāntso" is used.

Page 74. In the table, before "tanče", insert:

"....*pl. m. pd. sn.* tantso, tanči, tančeñ."

Page 75, *lines* 4-6. Such derivation is not probable.

Line 10. They can be used as well also as masculine or feminine.

Page 78, *para.* 3. In this example "koṇ" is not an Interrogative Pronoun.

Page 79, *line* 18. "Koṇ to" is not used commonly as a Pronoun in the oblique cases; as an Adjective, it becomes "koṇ-tea".

§ 6. 1. These can be called Pronouns also in Latin.

b) "*quilibet* = any one".

Line 8, *a. f.* "yeyēklo *or* yēkyēklo".

Page 80, *line* 11. "*aliquis* = somebody"; "*nemo* = nobody".

Line 18. "*aliquis* = somebody".

Page 82, *line* 19. "....seems to be out of place" viz. to Europeans, but in itself it is elegant. The exclusive meaning ("only") probably is the emphatic meaning which in some contexts takes naturally an exclusive meaning. Whatever it may be, this -ts can be translated often by "only".

Page 82. § 9. *qualis...talis* = as...as, *quot...tot* = as many...as many, *quantus...tantus* = how great...as great, *qui...is* = who...he, *quicumque...is* = whosoever...he.

Page 83, *para.* 9, see Syntax Ch. II. Art. III.

Page 84, *line* 20. "rāk = keep, *i. e.* guard".

Line 11, *a fine.* "sărgăr", better "sărg"; or if you put "sărgăr", add "assă".

Line 7, *a fine.* "tinčiñ": more common "tančiñ".

Page 85, *line* 8. "apuṇ", better "apuṇạts". "Apuṇ" in the 2nd person usually does not sound well.

Line 15. "Kontso išṭ": better use the Accusative.

Line 13, *a fine.* Some say and pronounce "dătărn"; yet more common and more philological is "dótórn".

Line 10, *a fine.* "Kăssăloi" means here "of any quality", not only *any*.

Page 86, *line* 8. Some say "Rupoi, rupia": this is more correct.

Page 87. The beginners can read observation 7, p. 118, and the last part of observation 26, p. 125, from line 7, *a fine*, before reading the Paradigm.

As a general rule all compound forms can be conjugated fully also in their elements, if the elementary forms are liable to conjugation; so, *e.g.*, "geleăuñ asleăuñ", "veteăleuñ asleăuñ", *etc.*; this must be kept in view, in order to be dispensed with repeating it many times. (See p. 123, *l.* 17.)

The conjugation of the Regular Verbs can be simplified, as regards the more common tenses of the affirmative form in this way (root: 2nd Person Imperative):

1) -tă is the fundamental termination of the Present Indicative.
2) -lo (-lă) is the fundamental termination of the Past Tenses ("-lolo *or* -ụllo" in the Past Perfect).
3) -tălo (Present and Past joined) is the fundamental termination of the Imperfect.

4) -tolo is the fundamental termination of the Future, *i. e.* nearly as the Imperfect.

5) -so is the fundamental termination of the Imperfect Subjunctive.

6) -tso is the fundamental termination of the Infinitive Absolute, Gerundive and Participle.

7) -uñ is the fundamental termination of the Subjunctive and Optative Present.

8) -leăr is the fundamental termination of the Imperfect Conditional and Optative.

9) -iyet (-yet) is the fundamental termination of the Potential.

10) -zăi is the fundamental termination of the Necessary Mood.

11) -an (-in) is the fundamental termination of the Contingent Future.

1. The Participles usually have the termination of the corresponding tense, except that -tolo is also Present, and -tso is Present and Future.

2. The Compound Tenses are formed by adding "zată *or* assă" to the simple form.

3. The fundamental termination moreover must be modified a little, sometimes, in the different Persons: usually the 1st and 3rd Persons Singular are equal (o or a); the 2nd ends in i (oi, ai...); the 1st Plural in uñ (auñ...); the 2nd in -at (-eat...). Sometimes this fundamental termination is not only modified in the different Persons but also in the same Person, according to the different Genders (terminations of the Adjectives).

For the sake of simplicity the periphrastic conjugation should be eliminated from the paradigm, and explained wholly separately.

Page 88, *Perfect.* The spelling -ia, instead of ea, is understood also for the Plural.

Page 89, *l.* 2 and 4. ăi, ăăt are more correct than ăi, ăăt. *Line* 2. a of an is a mean between ă and ā.

Line 8, *a fine.* "*utinam is veniret* = oh if he would come!" "*Deus faciat bonum* = God bless you!" "*utinam venisset* = oh if he would have come!"

Page 90. *Imperfect.* "Corresponding" *etc.* this is its chief not its only meaning; i is commonly inserted, not a. Sometimes the Verb kăr must be added.

Line 6, *a fine.* "sika zāleăr"; probably it must be "sikat zāleăr" (see p. 89, *l.* 5 *et seq.*)

Line last. About -iyet *cf.* p. 127.

Page 91. If you add the Past Perfect *etc.* of "zatā" *or* "assā" to the Present Potential and Necessary, you would get the Past Perfect Tense *etc.*

Page 92, *note:* Tĕi is too hard; hence ĕi, ĕeñ will do, and so in other similar cases.

Page 93, *line* 4, *a fine.* Some prefer the form "natlo" *etc.* to "natullo" *etc.*

Page 94, *line* 11. Better "natallo": I would prefer to say "natullo, natulli" *etc.* as in the Imperfect.

Line 19, *et seq.* Not all make this distinction.

Line last. The insertion of the euphonical vowel is to be understood also of the 2nd Person Singular and Plural.

Page 95, C. "Not commonly used"; it is not rare.

Line 6, *a fine.* "If you like", *i. e.* if you like exactness. (See § 5.)

Page 97. "Zatā" is irregular as the Verbs ending in a vowel, not as kăr, *etc.* (See § 7.)

To "zatā" and "assā" must be applied the remarks to be made on the 1st and 2nd Future Negative, Conditional and Conditionatum Negative of nid (see notes on pp. 112, 113, 114).

Page 100, *line* 12, *et seq.* Some say "zaisonāñ" *etc.*

Line 19. "As explained above", *i. e.* on p. 94.

Page 101, D. The full conjugation of "zatonāñ" is this: *Singular:* 1. 2. as given; 3) zatonāñ, zatināñ, zatenāñ. *Plural:* 1) zatenāuñ, 2) zatināṅt, 3) zatenāṅt, zateonāṅt, zatināṅt.

H. Better "zăunknatullo (*two* l).

Note 1. This note is to be put after "assă", p. 107.

Page 102, *Note* 1. Notwithstanding this reason, now I would write "asă".

Page 104, G. "aš-ci...." the hyphen is used only to show the reader the change of sound of s.

II. "niñ", better "năiñ". The full form "assanăñ" *etc.* occurs also.

Page 109, *line* 1. This seems to be the common form of 2nd Future; *e.g.* "when you will come I shall have finished".

D. The 2nd Conditional "nidlo" (*ex.* nidullo) must be conjugated as the Past Perfect.

Page 110, *line* 3, "nidtoñ" is used also absolutely in the meaning of "I would sleep"; so, *e.g.* "igărjent vetoñ: puņ văļ năñ = I would go to the church, but I have no time".

E. 3) "niduñ" is vulgar.

Page 111, *line* 5, *a fine*. "nidanatuleăuñ, nidanatuleăuñ". Although it seems to be right, yet such a delicate shade is not common, nor, perhaps, quite certain.

Page 112. 1*st and* 2*nd Future*. The exact form is as given there; yet very few use the full form; more commonly in the Plural 1st Person they use only the first form (nidčenăuñ), and in 2nd Person the 3rd form (nidčinănt) or the 1st (nidčenănt). The other Persons are used, as given in the Grammar.

Page 113. C. *Imperfect*. "Nidanăñ" must be conjugated as the Present Negative Indicative.

Past. "Nidanatullo" must be conjugated as the Imperfect Negative Indicative. This remark holds good also for the Conditional.

Page 114, *line* 7, *a fine*. The Latin means "it was not to sleep".

2*nd Conditionatum*. "Nidtonăñ" must be conjugated as "zatonăñ". (See note for p. 101.)

Page 115. "Nidtsonāñ" could be used only in correlative sentences (as "-tā to"); better use "nidanaye asollo".

Page 116, *para.* 2. I is much more frequently inserted than a.

Line 9, *a fine.* Some pronounce in such a way this v that it seems to be an u; consequently for the Verbs in u or uñ no change would take place.

Page 117, *para.* 3. *b*) There may be some exception required, especially by euphony; *e.g.* "sik" has "sikan", "zā" has "zāin". "Sik" is one of the excepted Verbs from the "kārmaṇi" construction. Perhaps these two irregularities are connected; time will clear up this point.

Page 119, *line* 8. The Future in -un (see p. 109) seems to be simply the 2nd Future. Whereas the other forms (p. 108) can be used only in some cases. (See note for p. 109.)

Para. 9. "Nidtonāñ asollo" is used commonly only as 2nd Conditionatum; "nidtonāñ asollo zāin" is not often used; hence, for practice, the 1st Negative Future can be used also as 2nd Negative Future.

Page 121, *line* 10. For practice, keep only "nidtonāñ" as 1st Negative Conditional, and "nidtonāñ asollo" as Past Negative Conditional.

Page 122, *line* 15. The Imperfect Subjunctive has a pure s; hence the termination -so, -si, or -señ is not included.

Page 123, *line* 5. "*Conspici potuit* = could be seen".

Line 8. "*Facturus erat* = was doing", yet in such a meaning it is not common; it is used, commonly, for *fecerit*. In the above periphrastic meaning people say rather "kārun assolo" *or* "kārtañ thāiñ assolo".

Line 18. "...in o", add: "also if o is followed by nāñ". This double conjugation takes place also in other tenses (see the preceding observations).

Para. 20. The termination je is often used, but vulgar: ze for zāi seems also, although frequently used, too dialectical.

Page 124, *line* 1. "nāñ" is not very nasal; in Mahrātti it is not nasal, so that we might be entitled, perhaps, to write nā.

Para. 23. Add "also the Masculine in the Plural changes o into e."

Page 128, *line* 5. "Khiaḷ" perhaps "khêḷ": There is a varying pronunciation.

Page 130, *line* 4. "Kiteñ āuveñ kārizāi" better: "āuveñ kiteñ kārizāi".

Page 132, § 1. Generally only āi or i is the right mood; ai or oi or ei generally is not quite correct; yet in some rare cases it may occur. Or we may say that āi seems to sound ai *or* ei, if we do not consider it carefully.

§ 2. "Yekameka" can be put also in other cases; *e. g.* "yekamekāčer kuṭ kārtāt".

Page 134, § 4. These Verbs are to be used with great circumspection.

Page 135, § 5. More exactly thus: "mārn geleñ = *lit.* the having beaten went, *i. e.* finished"; the Gerund in -un is the subject of "geleñ".

§ 6. Except the form in "-tāñ, thāiñ assā", the others are not commonly used, except in some peculiar cases.

Page 137, *para.* 8. Only "yeunk" can be considered as grammatical.

Para. 9. "Vetso *or* veso"—the first form is right.

Page 140, *para.* 12. "móṇ", better: "mhóṇ" according to the Mahrātti; some say "mhuṇ".

Para. 13. "ubzono"; as it is doubtful, so better avoid it.

Para. 14. "bosta" seems to be used for the Present, because the Perfect is used for a thing which still continues (see Syntax), yet in itself it is not Present.

Page 141. *c*) The same happens in the Supine; hence p. 142 "paloānk", or better "palvonk". Yet this point is not settled as yet.

Page 142. Add the Participle "paloaunk natullo" (*Caus.*) and "palvanaṭullo" (*Neuter*).

Page 143, *para.* 3. This is not clear, say simply: they make -antso instead of -auntso. The initial vowel of the termination (a or i of an in...) is omitted, if it is the same as the last vowel of the root.

Para. 4. Add: This i is omitted also in the Imperative, *e.g.* "ubzăundi", from "ubzăi".

Page 144, *last line.* "Pedrun", right grammatically, but not common; they would say: "Pedru vorviñ kărtăñ = I do through Peter".

Page 145, *line* 13. More common "aplea itleăk mărn ghetălo".

Line 3, *a fine of the text.* "aplea....jietăñ"—more common: "yeklăts jietăñ".

Page 146, *lines* 3, 4. "kăṇ"; as correct form use "kăṇeun".

Line 14. Better "melăgi?"

Line 4, *a fine of the text.* "siktoloñ astoloñ"; more common: "siktăñ thăiñ astoloñ".

Line 3, *a fine of the text.* "kăṇeuñso assă", more common: "kăṇeizăi".

Page 147. 1. *a*) "poisilo" better than "poislo".
"săklo", say better "săkăilo".
"tea kusilo", better "tea kušitso", and so the other compounds.

Page 148. *b*) "disă"dis...*or* disăñdis, disăñdisătso".
"vegiñso": seldom used.
"măgirtso" better than "măgirlo".
"yedôḷ păriant", Adjective "yedôḷ păriantḷo".
Add: "yedôḷ = up to this", "yedôḷi = even up to this".
"sekiñ": "sekintso".
"phuḍe", *Adj.* "phuḍlo".
"ăprupătso" better than "ăpruptso".
c) "čikeñ" more common than "tikeñ".
"sumărso", better: "sumărătso".

Page 149. *d*) "säsäräyetso" *or* "säsär".
"kapäs *or* kapäz".
"soukäsäyetso" is more correct.

Page 150. "niñ", better say: "näiñ".

Page 152. "vesleän", better: "issileän".

Para. 3. "-nt" now is not a Postposition.

Page 153, *para.* 6. "särgäränt", see about it Part. IV. Ch. II. Art VI.

Page 154, *line* 7, *a fine*. "maldisäoñ", better put it in the beginning of the sentence.

Page 155. The English *or* in sentences like "does he come or not" is omitted, and the negative particle only suffices: "to yetägï näñ?"

Line 16. "Mòṇ", some say "muṇ"; better: "mhòṇ *or* mhuṇ".

Line 2, *a fine*. Not correct, the form "-leär" with "zärtär". (See p. 251.)

Page 157. "Synetymology": Some might not approve of this new word. I could not find a better single word. In two words we could have said "General Etymology". See, however the new words used by Max Müller, and you will either blame, together with me, also Max Müller, or let such a title pass. I grant, however, that the things spoken of here, I would have put in Part I., II., IV., if I could have done so; but this part had arisen while printing, when it was too late to insert these things in Part I. and II.; after all, this division is the same *quoad substantiam*, as the division of Etymology in particular and general, which division is no doubt right. Moreover it seems to contribute to clearness to collect into one place things distinct from Syntax and Etymology. I grant also that I have anticipated some things of Part III. in Parts I. and II., because from the very beginning of printing I thought to put in Part I. and II., the most necessary things treated of here.

Page 158, *para.* 4. -re is used sometimes also for men, and -go also for women, especially by elder relatives towards younger ones.

Page 161. *c*) Some pronounce nearly -ši, -šeñ; it is better -si, -señ.

Para 5. "I" has sometimes an emphatic meaning when joined to the negative particle, similar to the Latin *ne quidem*, *nullus omnino* etc.; see an example p. 165, *l.* 9, *a fine.*

Page 162, *Chapter III.* The last example can be better explained in another way. (See p. 241, *note*).

Page 163, *Art* 1. Instead of a, sometimes au or similar forms are used.

Page 164, *line* 3. This is the common mode of making a Substantive negative.

a): This is the common mode of making an Adjective negative.

d): "năiñ assalo" can be changed, *e. g.*, into "năiñ astanañ".

Page 167, Ch. V. It seems that as we have Causative Verbs, so we can have derived Causative Nouns; viz. if the Noun has a causative meaning, it must insert some letters (especially o or ă); but this is not quite certain, althougth it is certain of some Participial Adjectives; *e.g.* "dukountso, dukitso". Hence from Causative Verbs are derived, in this supposition, Causative Nouns, from non-causative Verbs non-causative Nouns.

Page 168, *line* 11, *a fine.* "Băir-gălneñ" does not sound well.

Last line. Add: Instead of -ni *or* -neñ, they use sometimes -na; *e.g.* "sŏd = seek", "sodna = inquisition".

Page 169, *line* 1. "Sărkeñ" is an elegant but not much used termination. Sometimes the termination -poņ, -ap *etc.* have the same meaning.

Line 14. "Sermăvist", not a common word.

Line 11, *a fine.* "čeḍuñ" is rather derived from "čeḍo", etymologically, although, as to the meaning, it is used for girls, as "burgo" for boys.

Page 169, *line* 10, *a fine*. "pāḍi" is formed regularly. The termination ṅa or ṅ is used especially with Nouns ending in a consonant, (in ar, in the first place) i is used with Nouns ending in o.

Page 170, *para*. 1. -lo is added also to Adverbs or Postpositions; *e. g*. "voir, voilo; "mukār, mukāvelo". Moreover its meaning is, sometimes, not exactly, "coming out". Strictly it is the 1st Locative adjectivized; the meaning "out of" must be rendered by some other word, *e. g*. "bāir", or by the context.

Page 172, *para*. 5. This holds good also for the Negative Adjectives. The Noun prefixed is Singular or Plural as the meaning requires; *e. g*. "cloudy sky = kupaṅ (*pl.*) asallẽñ moḷāb".

Para. 6. Better "dik".

Page 176, *para*. 2. In some cases to the Adverb in -eñ the Gerund of -kār (-kārn) is added.

Page 177, *line* 1, *et seq*. "zāuñ = *lit*. by being or becoming or by having been or become"; hence to know whether this form can be used, substitute this literal translation, and see whether then it is suitable.

Page 180, *line* 1. "reunion", say better: "college".

Page 181, *Ch. VII*. Perhaps the rules about ñ could be simplified, especially in compounds; viz. ñ might be omitted in some of the indicated cases, although strictly speaking there should be ñ.

Page 182, *e*) There are some exceptions; *e. g*. "paṭlāu".

Page 183, *line* 4. But Pronouns have ñ also in the Instrumental, and the Pronouns of 1st and 2nd Person also in the Nominative Singular and Plural.

c) This never or almost never happens.

Page 185, *line* 8, *a fine*, *et seq*. Although this is true, yet for the sake of simplicity, let us distinguish only what is absolutely required, *i. e*. s, ts, č, leaving the other shades to practice.

Page 186, *line* 3. "...into tŏ", in order to simplify, let us say "into ŏ".

Line 9. ಮನುಷ್ಯ is a Kanarese word, ("mănuša = man") not a Konkani word written with Kanarese letters.

Line 20. *e. g.* "porza, porze = people": yet some say "porje".

Line 22. *e.g.* "māz, mazā = centre".

Page 188, *line* 11. "...to the Canarese ˒," *i.e.* this sign of the Kanarese Alphabet is used as a sign of half vowel in some languages, *e.g.* in Tuḷu; in Kanarese it is a sign of an absent vowel. (See note on Part I.)

Page 189, *line* 1. As I did not pay great attention to this point, especially to its spelling, so this rule has not much value.

At all events, as I said, let us keep only ų as a sign of half vowel.

Line 4. *a fine.* Add the change of ó into ă or ŏ. (See notes on 2nd Declension.)

The sound of ą or ų can be approximately perceived in pronouncing, *e.g.* "et", by removing suddenly the tongue from the roof of the mouth after having pronounced t.

Page 190, *line* 4, *et seq.* This rule requires further consideration: it is however true that euphony seems to require the indicated changes.

Page 191, *line* 7, *a fine.* "šĕḷ", some pronounce "šel".

Page 192, *line* 7. "throat", *add* "and nose".

Line 17, *et seq.* This letter is called vocalized r by the author of the Polyglot Vocabulary, most appropriately, as far as I can judge in this delicate matter, which is rather foreign to my subject: it never or very seldom occurs in Konkani.

Page 193, *line* 15, *a fine.* It seems better to use ˒ for the "virāma", ˘ for ų.

Page 194, *line* 15. Hodson says that it is a vowel or a consonant according to the position.

Page 196, *line* 12, 13. It is more common to let the word agree with the Masculine in preference to the Feminine (as I remarked in line 10-12) instead of using the Neuter. The same holds good for Verbs.

Page 197, *line* 6. In Mahrātti the Neuter Plural in such case is used: but after having written this page, I came to know, that commonly the daughter-in-law, speaking about the mother-in-law, and the wife of a younger brother, speaking about the wife of an elder brother, use the Plural Neuter; in other cases such a use is not common.

The Verbs compounded of a Noun and an Adjective sometimes are considered, as to concord, as simple Verbs; *e.g.* "nāš kăr, inkār kăr", which consequently govern the Accusative, although etymologically they should govern other cases.

Note 1. Probably it is a mistake; at any rate it seems better to avoid such a use.

Page 198, *para.* 6. Not seldom the adjectival Genitive seems to follow, as to concord, the rules of Nouns rather than the rules of Adjectives.

Line 7, *a fine*. *Cf.* note to p. 240.

Page 199, *para* 9. It can be reduced to *para*. 6; because in the full sentence we should say "zakā ukto kelā".

Para. 10. Time will clear this point: some say that "vord" means only "news", and even in a meaning of contempt: the Noun should be "vordegār".

Page 200, *line* 17. If the Neuter is used, in some cases it is better to add "kărn".

Page 201, *Exercises*, *line* 1. "Koṇ" better "koṇ-i (Indefinite).

Exercises, *line* 7. "ismāl", perhaps better: "ismāl *or* ismól": at any rate it is a foreign word.

Exercises, *line* 10. "astit", better: "assāt".

Page 203, *line* 12, *a fine*. The termination -neṅ is not in common use, except for few Nouns.

Page 205, *line* 14. "keḷambo", some say "keḷạmbo".

B. "Omitting" *etc.* this remark regards not only the Nominative but also the other cases and other parts of speech. The things clear by themselves or common also to Latin or English are often omitted.

§ 1. 1. Materially is Nominative, but philosophically is Accusative in a different form and so also 2. When the English Noun is or can be preceded by "as", that Noun is put in the Nominative followed by "móṇ" (*or* "moḷḷo" *etc.*)

Page 206, *Exerc.*, *line* 1. "mēlnītidār", better add "kärn".

§. 2, *line* 6. "Author of the..." *i.e.* of the Grammar which has the title "The Student's Manual of the Mahrātti Grammar". Whenever I mention Mahrātti Grammar, I intend to quote this Grammar.

Line 5, *a fine.* "-unčeāk", add: "or only -čeāk".

Page 207, *line last.* "but....", viz. etymologically; yet use can prevail over etymology.

Remark about Dative as also about Accusative *etc.* that there are other cases in which Dative (or Accusative *etc.*:) must be used; *e.g.* "te šikšek tärtärtāñ=I tremble at that punishment".

Page 209, *line* 7. "kirkoḷi": compound of "kirkoḷ" and 'i.'

Line 9. "seguṇā thāiñ" seems to be better than "seguṇāniñ"; this second form does not express exactly the meaning of "thāiñ"; yet "seguṇāniñ" is more common.

Line 10. "sälgi": some think that "sälgi" cannot be used in a good meaning as here; such opinion comes from the abuse of "sälgi" for bad things; yet in itself it is a good word and used also in a good meaning; see in the Mahrātti Dictionary of Bābā Padmānji, its meaning agreeing with the Konkani meaning. What is the good thing of which no abuse can be made?

Page 211, *note* 1. Perhaps better "vidye-sāl, *or* pāṭa-sāl".

Page 212, *line* 9, *a fine.* "poisleān", better "poisileān".

Para. 7. Adjectives in -ntlo and -lo are different; *e.g.* "šerāntlo....voilo".

Page 213, *para.* 9. Such form in -čeān *or* -jeān is sometimes used also with the Potential. (See P. IV. Ch. III.)

Para. 9, *last line.* "thāiñ" and "tantleān" probably have a different root; moreover the meaning differs somewhat.

Page 214, *line* 10. The meaning is: "It is not required to go through the town of Goa, although you pass near to Goa".

Line 11. Some say "Rupiā" *etc.* in the oblique cases, instead of "Rupoiā".

Page 215, *para.* 1. I said elsewhere that this -nt comes from the Mahrātti -ānt, still used in that language as a special word, but not in Konkani.

Page 216, *line* 10. "dhu". In Mahrātti it is aspirated; yet in Konkani it seems to sound not aspirated.

Para 4. We can say also "Devāk satmand" *etc.*

Page 217, *line last of the text.* viz. That author says (p. 17) that the Vocative is the crude form.

Page 218, *para.* 3. In such case there would be a composition; hence hyphen, and would coincide with para. 4.

Page 220, *line* 2. There seems to be a slight difference of meaning between using the Dative and the Communicative.

Exercises, line 4. In this example it is better to use "thāiñ", not "kāḍe".

Page 223, *line* 2. "Drāšṭāntāk" perhaps not in common use.

Page 224, *para.* 7. Sometimes such a Substantive must be put in the Plural, and then the Noun converted into an Adjective (Genitive) should agree with it also in number, (although we find examples in which that Adjective does not agree in Number); *e. g.* "dusreānčeo česṭāio kār = mock others". Moreover there are some Verbs of this kind which cannot govern the Genitive, although etymologically the Genitive should be used, *e.g.* "nāš kār".

Page 225, *line* 14. What is said about -lo, must be understood of the Adjectives in -ntlo; for the others may not be according to this explanation. Sometimes the Adjective in -ṅtlo means "....out of..."

Page 226, *line* 4. "tirzāun" is not a real Adverb.

b) "....*et memorari* ..... = and to remember his Holy Testament the oath which he swore". Remark that "ugḍās" is masculine; yet -jeñ agreeing with "pārmāṇ".

Page 229, *line* 2. The Postposition must be used, but with the required changes, *e. g.* with a full relative sentence or with a participial sentence.

Page 231, *line* 1. Better "an answer to be given by them became impossible".

Para. 7. You find many of these Adjectives in the Dictionary. Usually it is better to resolve them into a Finite Mood, or at least not to use them as a predicate (p. 190, *l.* 7-4, *a. f.*)

Para. 8, *d*) "....short but slowly", viz: closed and slowly.

Page 233. *a*) and *b*) are elegant but not common modes.

Page 234. § 1. This is a gleaning of Part II.

§ 2, *a.* "....usually are not", say "not often are...".

Pgae 235. *d*) Better say that "to is like an article"; then we could say: "o to mānis = this is the man", *or* "manis...... o = (the) man.....this".

Line 2, *a fine*. If we do not consider "tintso" (as I noted when gleaning the Pronouns), then we must take away 12 combinations, 6 of "-tintso", 6 of "-intso".

Page 237. *a*) In such sentences "tasolo" is often used in the second part.

Page 238, *line* 13, *a fine*, *et seq*. Yet instead of "jintso" people use "zantso"; hence only 18 combinations.

Page 240, *line* 13, *et seq*. It seems that if there is no word in the Nominative with which they should agree, they are put in the Neuter Singular. Perhaps the rule of the Mahrātti Grammar can be useful here, viz.: These declinable Adverbs are put in the Neuter Singular, *a*) when the subject of the Intransitive Verb is omitted: *b*) when such a subject is inflected: *c*) when both subject and object of the Transitive Verb are inflected.

Page 242. *b*) Some say "khāintso" instead of "kontso"; I think however that "khāintso" and "kontso" are two different Pronouns. We may add "kāintso" derived from "kāiñ=when". These Pronouns can be also non-interrogative.

Page 245, *para.* 3, 4. About Past and Perfect we might perhaps follow this simple rule: Use the Perfect to express that an action has been very recently completed or that an action has been completed in past time, yet the state of things brought about continues up to the present, for other past actions use the Past or the Past Perfect.

Para. 5. I doubt about the correctness of using the Past Perfect for the Imperfect.

Page 247, *para.* 7. In some cases the form in an (or in) can be properly used as 2nd Future. (See p. 273, *note.*)

See the note on this point, in the 2nd Part, viz. on page 109.

Add: This mood is used for the Future when this contains something Imperative; *e. g.* "make peace, then you will offer your offering to God".

Page 249, *para.* 2, *line* 6. "Only" is not exact, if we take "only" rigorously, (see page 266, *line* 9, *a fine.*)

Page 250, *line* 8, *et seq.* The form in "sarko" probably means also suitableness, as I said of the Adjectives compounded with "sarko".

Page 254, *line* 6. The form in -toñ can also be used in this meaning; *e.g.* "āuñ itsārtoñ=I should like to ask".

Line 15, "see below". This has been explained already.

Page 263, *line* 5, *a fine.* "yetanañ", better: "yeun *or* aileā uprānt." The Latin means: "and the rest I will set in order when I come".

Page 268, *line* 1. "astāñ *etc.*=I am habitually".

Page 273, *para.* 12. 2) In this meaning it is not often used.

Para. 14. "Vātsunk tanktā" seems to be improperly used for "*licet legere*".

Page 273-274, *and alibi.* Some of the Latin sentences are rather Konkani-Latin than pure Latin, in order to show more distinctly the things.

Page 274, *line* 12. "above mentioned", "uprānt" excepted.

Page 276, *line* 21, to "-un" add "and -unk".

Page 279, *para.* 6. Some take these Verbs as Neuter; yet after careful inquiry, I can say that many take them also really as passive, if the vowel is open; much more, that this is in conformity with Sanskrit, the grandmother of Konkani.

Page 280. See another mode by pāu in the I. Appendix, p. 331, which however is low. It corresponds nearly to the Hindustāni "jānā", and Mahrātti "jāṇeñ = to go", whereby the passive voice is expressed sometimes in those languages.

Page 286, § 7, *line last.* Better: "yekamekāčer"; else it is doubtful.

Page 288, *line* 3, *et seq.* The given example doẹs not suit the Latin expression well; we should take a compound Verb, one element of which expresses something more vague and undetermined; *e. g.* "āpoun āḍ *or* tzālun vetā". Notwithstanding, the given example can be made suitable by modifying somewhat the explanation. I need not say that I do not intend to find in this kind of Verbs a perfect similarity to the famous *materia* and *forma*, as the particle "as" of the text shows; I intend only to imprint in the mind this unknown point by a known similar point.

Page 296, *para.* 2. "moṇsār", variety of "moṇāsār".

Page 297, *line* 2. "phuḍa", some say: "phudār;" probably they are two Nouns.

Para 9. "Khāl" occurs also in a proper meaning, and for material things: "taḷa", properly, according to the Mahrātti, should mean "at the bottom of".

Page 298, *line* 8, 7, 6, *a fine*, belong to para. 11.

Page 300, *para.* 22. Often "kaḍtso" is used for "thāun" viz. if for "from" we could substitute literally "being near or from being near"; yet an exact literal translation of "kaḍtso" is not easy. (See p. 298, para. 10.)

Page 301, *para.* 25. "Magčeā vorviñ", better "māg-ṇeñ kārčeā vorviñ", *or* "Dēvā lāgiñ māgčeā vorviñ".

"Khālinastanañ," better: "khālanastanañ" *or* "khālnastanañ".

Para. 26. By accident "šivāi" has not been put in the example: it should be "...sosullea šivāi".

Page 306. *a*) In such cases the Accusative usually is not omitted, as it can be omitted in Latin; *e.g.* "I have been educated = *educatus sum*, makā vāḍāilā".

c) Some do not say "takā khāviet"; yet it is not wrong.

e) This remark holds good also for the Negative form.

Very few persons do not follow this rule; they say: *e. g.* "tuveñ mojiñ utrañ āikaliñgi?": yet the almost universal use must prevail over the use of a few persons. They will say: the Verb must agree with the object. I answer: universal use is a stronger rule on this point, than the rule of concord. At any rate time will clear up this point.

Page 307. *f*) If these Verbs are made Causative, they follow the "kārmāṇi" construction.

Page 308, *line* 1. The same participial sentences are used also when an English secondary sentence is translated by a Konkani Postposition; because this governs the Participle. The only change to be made is of the Verb into the Participle. (See some examples p. 339.)

Page 310, § 1. In interrogative sentences it is not required, as a general rule, to put the subject after the Verb.

Page 311. If there are two or more subordinate sentences, that which governs follows the governed one.

Page 312. As regards the sequence of tenses, nearly the same rule of the English holds good, except that very often the Indicative is used for the Subjunctive.

When the secondary sentence does not imply any *oratio indirecta*, then it cannot be resolved into a *directa oratio*, but the rule of the sequence of tenses is observed; *e.g.* "he saw that the bear was excited = asvel utsamboḷ zāun assạleñ móṇ taṇeñ poḷeilāñ". Yet sometimes Konkani uses the Present instead of the Imperfect or Past; *e.g.* "to Igārjent toḍou kārtā móṇ poḷeun ajap zāle = having seen that he remained long time in the church, they were astonished".

Page 313. From this change of the *oratio obliqua* into *oratio directa* derives the frequent use of Present Tense instead of Past Tense. Yet this change is not obligatory.

An English *oratio indirecta* (at least in *potentia*), can be translated 1) by changing it entirely into an *oratio directa*, retaining however "móṇ": "he prays God to forgive = bogos móṇ . . ."; 2) by putting only the Verb in the tense required by the *oratio directa*: "Let us pray God to extend His hand over us = Dēvā lāgiñ māgiāñ, to āplo hāt lambāi móṇ amče voir"; 3) by putting the Verb in the Mood or Tense, but not in the Person, required by the *oratio indirecta*: "Saserdot māgtā Spirita Santā lāgiñ to tumče voir yeundi móṇ = the priest prays the Holy Ghost to come in you".

Page 314, *Art I.* In North Kanara many speak also Konkani, but as I am informed, so different in some places from the Konkani of South Kanara, that it approaches to the Goanese branch, if it is not the really Goanese branch, which is considerably different from our branch both in rules and words, as I have seen by comparing some words and sentences of that country with ours.

Page 315, *line* 21. "etc." Among these other languages hinted at, I mention especially Hindusthāni.

Line 2, *a fine.* If this book should happen to fall into the hands of learned philologists, I admonish them beforehand that I do not insist much upon the words *Dravidian*, *Gaurian*, *Turenian etc.*

Page 317. *b*) In order not to contradict what I said on p. 316, we must understand these things thus: *actu* Konkani is almost a collection of dialects; *in potentia* there are common forms, which although apparently different, however by diligent consideration may appear *in the main* also *actu* common. Hence we can say that Konkani is on the way to become a formed language.

Page 318. The purists of Konkani, instead of begging at every step from Mahrätti or Sanskrit, should try to express the notions with Konkani words, avoiding however too vulgar modes of speaking; this is certainly a very difficult but useful task. I do not however deny that in some cases we may borrow some words from those languages.

Page 319, *para.* 3. Not only composition, but derivation also should be employed, and what is more important, inquiring which existing words in Konkani could render properly or metaphorically, the Latin or English word, although the words are not commonly used in such a way.

One of the many things to be done, not mentioned there, would be to try to have some uniformity both in rules and words, in order to make a cultivated language above so many varieties. If some of the rules of this Grammar and some words of the Dictionary are found not well founded or not suitable, others should be substituted as more fit; but we should stop then at some.

Page 324, *para.* 7, *line* 4. "Negative form", add "of Verbs"; yet such mode is perhaps not vulgar.

Page 325, *para.* 1, *et seq.* Only a small number of the different senses of these Verbs has been given.

We may add out of many other things, as a peculiarity of Konkani, the frequent use of converting into Adjectives, Adverbs or Postpositions.

APPENDIX I.

As the title shows, it is not my intention to put down all the difficult modes of speaking, nor do I intend to put down only really difficult modes; but to gather out of a number some modes ot speaking, which *passim* have been hinted at throughout Grammar, or have not been put at all.

Page 330, *last line.* "bôḷ karinastana", better say "āḍ-aileā šivāi".

Page 331, *ac si* ..."paullea bări", is too vulgar; better: "....mărleleā bări".

Quippe qui. "gratsăr" means "fortune, *i.e.* fate".

Page 332, *line* 8. "sarlea", better "bāir-sărleā", *or* "gelcā".

Page 334, *Donec. a*) With "moṇāsăr" it is more common to put the Verb in the 3rd Person Singular of the Present Indicative (also for Past Tenses); *e.g.* "te (tuñ, āmiñ) yetā moṇāsăr".

Page 334, *line* 18. "tsăḍ", better "zaḷān = *lit.* with burning (sorrow)".

APPENDIX II.

1. In writing Konkani with Kanarese letters I have followed the principle of similarity, *i. e.* I have written in such a way that only those letters which are pronounced and their pronunciation should be written; *e.g.* ăi is expressed not by ೈ but by ಅ್ಯ; because ă is rendered by ಅ not by ೆ. Hence I have deviated somewhat from the common way, and also from the Kanarese rules regarding writing; *e.g.* I write ಜಾಉನ್ (zāun), *not* ಜಾವುನ್ (zāvun), ದೇಉ, *not* ದೇವು *etc.* The reasons of this deviation are: *a*) because the beginners, not versed in the vernaculars, would have taken up, in doing else, a wrong pronunciation, unless I had given some other rules about this point; *b*) because in Mahrātti, which is the proper alphabet of Konkani, I found a similar manner of writing; so I found written "पाऊस् = pāus", not "pāvus", as some write[1];

[1] The same remark holds good for other deviations; *e. g.* about ್ joined to ಉ, ಊ *etc.* Yet I did not keep Mahrātti as ruling principle in every case: the ruling principle is the common usage in speaking and conformity of pronouncing with reading according to the Roman way of reading, which way more or less prevails at least as to the sound of the vowels, and has been laid down as the foundation on p. 1.

c) this manner is more simple, easier and also more scientific. This reason especially prevails when we have to settle the manner of writing. This I could do the more readily, as Kanarese is not the proper alphabet of Konkani, and nothing is settled. *d*) The rule about accent should have been changed, if I had followed the Kanarese common manner.

2. As regards the translation, I have used some foreign or less exact words, although there is the pure or exact Konkani word, for the reason stated in P. IV. Ch. III.; so, *e.g.*, to say "Gospel" there is a beautiful Konkani word used also in Sanskrit, Mahrātti, Kanarese and Tulu.

3. Although I tried to adhere to the Latin text, for the reasons stated above, yet in some cases it was rather difficult without losing too much of Konkani propriety; hence in some rare cases the translation is not quite literal. Moreover while translating into Konkani I had under my eyes, not the English, but the Latin Vulgate with the Notes of Menochio and the French paraphrase of Carrières; hence some sentences literally agree with the Latin, not with the English translation.

4. We need not remark on some imperfections owing partly to the literal translation, partly to the great hurry with which this has been done. Hence, no doubt, a better translation could have been made in other circumstances; consequently I limit myself to remark on only these more striking points.

Page 360, *v.* 3, *et alibi.* "somzikāy", better "somzon".

Page 369, *v.* 19, "gāṭ", better "tir".

Page 370, *v.* 28, "iṣṭa kāḍe", better "iṣṭāk".

Page 376, *v.* 13. Some decline "upādēsi", according to the 2nd Declension; yet this is not so correct.

PART II.

This 2nd part is at the same time a kind of "Errata-Corrige" and reduction to uniformity. Nobody can be surprised at the following list; for 1) a perfectly correct mode of writing throughout, was beyond my aim (see pp. 2, 6, 295); 2) many things can be written and are pronounced in many ways; hence sometimes I have written the same word in one way, sometimes in another way: here, for the sake of simplicity, I choose one of these modes, viz., what I judge to be more correct; 3) nothing is settled in this language; hence although I established the signs to be used from the very beginning, yet, owing to the state of Konkani, on the way I saw that something could have been better put in another way; hence also, the variety in writing the same word. Therefore the many corrections often are rather only a reduction to uniformity. However I do not intend to correct every thing which perhaps could be mentioned, because about some points I am not sure, especially as regards the aspirated and cerebral sound. Many of these correct modes of writing have been hinted at in Grammar. Here I put them together.

A. General Corrections.

1. Complexive Corrections.

1. "So", termination of the Adjectival Genitive and of some Participles should always be written -tso (see p. 122, para. 15).

2. ja, ča, termination of some words of the 3rd Declension, should be written jea, čea (see p. 26, *et seq.*).

3. 2nd person singular of Contingent Future ši for či, and 2nd person plural šāt for čāt.

4. Past Participle in compound tenses with two l ("-lolo -yllo, -llo"), and so also all Past Participle in lo used as Adjectives (see p. 262).

5. Ts, always ts (see pp. 193, 397).
Tó either ts or pure ċ.
6. Sometimes the euphonical vowel has been omitted.
7. Imperfect Subjunctive should be written with one s.
8. Causative Verbs in ăi or i only.
9. Na should be always nasal, although in Mahrātti is not nasal, and in Konkani too it is not very much nasal.
10. -nt of the Locative is -ñt: and so often ñ has been written n, when there was no necessity to write ñ.
11. The Past Tenses should have ụ instead of ă.
12. Whenever an Adjective or Participle has o in the penultimate, it is changed into e (sometimes ụ) when the last syllable has not the vowel o (see p. 187).

2. Single words which often occur.

Errata—Corrige.

ăḍ...hăḍ[1] (var. aḍ)
aḍăr...adăr
aḷtsi... alsi; some make it cerebral, in Mahrātti it is not cerebral.
ărdo...ărdho (var. ărdo)
ăriyeklo...hăryeklo
ātmo... ătmo (although in Kanarese ā-)
bāgivont...bhāgivont
bair...bhāir (var. bāir)
băš...bhăš (var. băš)
bau...bhău (brother) (var. [bău)
beñ...bheñ, bhya
benjer...benjar
beṭ...bheṭ (var. beṭ)
beṭai...bheṭai (var. beṭăi)
bitor...bităr

Errata—Corrige.

bógăr...băgăr (var. băgăr, bógăr)
bor...bhor (var. bor)
čo (*in compounds*)...čou
daḍlo...dadlo
dik (*direction*)..dikkụ
dosmānkai...dusmānkăi
duḍḍu...duḍu
duv...du
găl...ghāl (var. găl)
găr...ghăr (many say also "găr")
ge...ghe (var. ge)
hanga...ánga
kălto...khălto
kăi... kaiñ
kai... kaiñ (if it means "where": khăiñ)

[1] What is said of the original form, must be said of its derivations.

Errata—Corrige.

kakult...kākuḷt
kassolo (kosso), tassolo (tasso), assolo (asso), zasso — with one s *i. e.* "kasolo" *etc.*
keḷ...kheḷ
koṭṭo ... khoṭo
kumzār...kumsār
kuši...khuši (var. kuši)
lukšān...luksān
maṭouñ...māṭou
māuñ..māu (=scar; father-in-law=māuñ)
moḷaba...moḷba
moḷḷeār...moḷeār
monis...mănis
nilso...niḷtso
pānz...pānts
păriănt...păriant
paṭlauñ...paṭlau
phaḍe...phuḍeñ
-pon (termination of Abstract Nouns)...-poṇ

Errata—Corrige.

răng (*sing.*)... róng (*sing.*) răng (*plur.*)
sarti...săḍti
soḷḷo...sollo
sotrai...tsătrai
tāmḍo...tāmbḍo
taniñ, taneñ *etc.* ... taṇiñ, taṇeñ *etc.* (and so similar terminations)
tala...taḷa
tăr (*kind*)...thăr (although not aspirated in Kanarese)
thăr (*therefore*)...tăr
ui"...voi"
uttar...utar
upkār *n.*...upkār *m.* (hence *Pl. Nom.* upkār, not upkārañ)
vors...văra
vorvi...vorviñ
yemkaṇḍ.. yemkăṇḍ *or* yemkóṇḍ

B. Particular Corrections

Errata	*Corrige*
P. 2, *l.* 7. farō	farò.
„ „ *l.* 10. short	closed.
„ „ *l.* 7, *a f.* this	this half vowel
„ 4, *l.* 9, *a f.* m̲. n̲.	m. n
„ 5, *l.* 12. hăs-čeñ	hās-čeñ
„ „ *l.* 6. tai	thăiñ
„ 10, *l.* 8. je	ye

Errata	*Corrige*
P. 13, *l. last.* vonad, vondi	voṇāt (*or* voṇót), voṇti
„ 14, *l.* 6. animate	inanimate
„ „ *Para.* 6. hac	*haec*
„ „ *l.* 22. There	7. There
„ „ *l.* 26. that that "gér" is a corruption	that "ger" is an abbreviation
„ „ *l.* 8. *a f.* bāpāvorvi	bāpā vorviñ
„ 15, *para.* 4, *l.* 4. Few others govern the Dative Singular Postpositions.	Few others govern the Dative. See Postpositions
„ 15, *l.* 2, *a f.* if the meaning is Plural	*omit these words*
„ 20, *l.* 13. sobit = necessary	sobit = nice
„ 21, *l.* 1. assā	zāun assā
„ 22, *l.* 4. dudiñ, -ṇ	dudiñ, *n.*
„ 25, *l.* 13, *a f.* dis assā	dis zāun asā
„ 26, *l.* 1. confrier	confrère
„ „ *l.* 2. kurouñ	kurou
„ 31, *l.* 6. sāddāntz	sādānts (and so elsewhere)
„ 35, *throughout*, 4th	*read* 5th
„ 37; *ll.* 7, 8. văstu	văstụ
„ 39, *l.* 17. Šesar	Sezār
„ „ *l.* 4, *a f.* Indiānt	Indient
„ „ *l.* 3, *a f.* on the Himalaya	on the Himalayas
„ 41, *last l.* yēkavorsā	yēka vārsā
„ 42, *para.* 4. kārkār	karkar
„ „ „ māḷi	māḷie
„ 48, *l.* 11, *a f.* man	men
„ 50. *c.* balseñ	baḷseñ
„ 51, *l.* 11, *a f.* Appendix *etc.*	Part III.
„ 52, *last l.* koṭṭepoṇāñso	khoṭeāntso
„ 53, *l.* 19. Kristāčeñ	Kristāčea
„ 54, § 3. tāun	*omit it*

Errata	*Corrige*
P. 54, *l.* 19. tāun	thāun (and so elsewhere) (var. tāun)
„ 55, *l.* 10, *a f.* nilso	niḷtso (in Mar. not cerebral)
„ „ *l.* 8, „ ălduvo	ăḷduvo
„ 56, *l.* 9. Moje	Mojeñ
„ „ *l.* 4, *a f.* Sezāričea	Sezāryăčea
„ 57, *No.* 17. sotra	sătra
„ 26. sovis	săvis
„ 27. sattāvis	satāvis
„ 29. yēkuṇtis	*better:* yēkuṇeñtis "uṇeñ" *should be always nasal.*
„ 58, *last l.* yeksăsṭ	yeksašṭ (and so in the following numbers)
„ 59, *l.* 7, *a f.* so	să
„ „ *l.* 5, „ 26	21
„ 60, *l.* 2. can count	cannot count
„ 64, *l.* 5. bokši	bogsi (and so elsewhere)
„ „ *l.* 9. kitleñ	kitliñ
„ „ *l.* 12, *a f.* assulo	zāun assullo
„ „ *l.* 10, „ Pončisvea	Ponpončisvea
„ 67, *l.* 3, *a f.* bhās	bhāš
„ 68, *l.* 9. *libriceino*	*libriccino*
„ „ *l.* 8, *a f.* rāuḷ (*m.*)	rāuḷ (*n.*)
„ 76, *l.* 6. guṇāzo	guṇātso
„ 77, *l.* 5, *a f.* apṇānzo	apṇāntso
„ 79, *l.* 22. irregularity	irregularities
„ „ *l.* 6, *a f.* ei	ai
„ 84, *l.* 4. aḍar = commit (*v.*)	aḍar = commit
„ „ *l.* 15. kāints nā	*better:* khaintsa-nāñ
„ „ *l.* 21. bāpui. Tāso	bāpui: tātso
„ 85, *l.* 6, *a f.* assā?	assā.
„ 86, *l.* 2. sărgārtāun	sărgār thāun
„ 87. *Imperfecte*	*Imperfect*

Errata	*Corrige*
P. 90, *l.* 6, *a f.* assă	zată
„ 93, *l.* 1. -ta	-tañ
„ 95, *l.* 17. zăun	zăuñ
„ 111, II. *nondormiebam*	*non dormiebam*
„ „ *l.* 5, *a f.* nid-natąleaoñ	nid-a-natąleaoñ
„ 119, *l.* 9, *a f.* nidteteñ	nidteleñ
„ 122, *l.* 12. This 16th	This 15th
„ 123, *l.* 8. *erit*	*erat*
„ „ *last l.* be	become
„ 126, *l.* 5. Art.	Chapt.
„ 128, *l.* 10. lačil	laččil
„ „ *l.* 11. sár	băir sár
„ „ *l.* 14. game	ghame (var. game)
„ 129, *l.* 3. paisăvănt	paišavănt
„ „ *l.* 13. Koinča	Kăinčea
„ „ *l.* 8-9, *a f.* Săkor	Săkăr
„ 130, *l.* 11. bog	bhog (var. bog)
„ „ *l.* 3, *a f.* vago	văgo *or* vógo
„ 131, *l.* 6, *a f.* assąleañ	assąlleañ
„ „ „ „ dileñ	dilleñ
„ „ *l.* 3, „ moje	mozo
„ 132, *l.* 2. mojăn	amčeăn
„ „ *l.* 11. poḍṇañ	poḍanañ
„ „ *l.* 3, *a f.* ai	ăi
„ „ *l.* 2. por-tañ	portatăñ
„ 133, *l.* 15. § 6.	§ 7.
„ „ *l.* 16. not Causative	non-causative
„ 134, *l.* 14. suḍlo	suṭlo
„ „ *l.* 15. fuḍlo	fuṭlo
„ „ „ suḍtă	suṭṭă
„ „ *l.* 16. fuḍtă	fuṭṭă
„ 135, *l.* 10. to beat him	after having beaten him
„ 144, § 8. Defective Verb	Defective Verbs
„ 146, *l.* 6. aḍli	adli

Errata	*Corrige*
P. 148, *l.* 20. kaḍieso	kaḍetso
„ 150, *l.* 2, *a f.* tzärlo	särlo
„ 151, *l.* 1. tintz	tinạts
„ „ *l.* 9. käṇeitoleānk	käṇeiteleānk
„ „ „ čiț	čit
„ 152, *l.* 18. bäuntaṇeñ	bäuntäṇiñ
„ „ *l.* 3, *a f.* emkaṇḍāntlo	yemkăṇḍāntlo
„ 154, *l.* 12, *a f.* vitzärnakāt	visarnakāt
„ 167, *l.* 10, *a f.* niškāl	niskăl
„ 170, *l.* 4, *a f.* boreṇ	boroñ
„ 171, *l.* 6. as "at	"as at
„ „ *l.* 7. as the	as at the
„ 173, *para.* 9. "fit to do. ."	"fit to. . ."
„ 175, *l.* 12, *a f.* kātär	kātär
„ 176, *l.* 10. Substantive	Substantive or Adjective
„ 178, *l.* 17, 18. that -un.	that in -un
„ 184, *l.* 9. ĕ and z, into	ĕ, and z into
„ 194, *l.* 19. dukhụ	duhkụ *or* duhkhụ
„ 198, *l.* 13, *a f.* burgāčeā	burgeāčeā
„ 200, *l.* 4. thing	things
„ 206, *l.* 6, *a f.* javaṇāk	jeuṇāk
„ 209, *l.* 2, *a f.* of the grammar	of Grammar
„ 211, *Exerc. l.* 4. sāngnakā	sānganakā
„ 213, „ *l.* 3. sukoi	tsukăi
„ 214, *l.* 4. Kristāči	Kristāčeñ
„ „ *l.* 5. papsilā	papsilāñ
„ „ § 5, *l.* 3. distinction	perspicuity
„ 217, *Exerc. l.* 3. Dāñparā	Danpār
„ 220, *l.* 10. mātrụ āuñ. . uleināñ	āuñ. . . uleināñ mātrụ
„ „ *l.* 14. beṭāitoloi	*better:* bheṭai
„ 222, *Exercise, l.* 5. sākor	sākār
„ 223, *last l.* father	house

Errata	*Corrige*
P. 224, *l*. 14, *a f*. dis	dis-a
" 227, *l*. 9. Postposition	Postpositions
" 228, *l*. 19, 20. hurdle	screen
" 233, *Exercise*. *l*. 2. tzălti	tsălto
" 235, *l*. 14. lăsleño	lasleñ ò
" 240, *l*. 8, *a f*. dhaḍlă	dhaḍlăñ
" " *l*. 2, *a f*. correspond	corresponds
" 244, *last line*. "the date"	*add* "of months"
" 251, *l*. 7. tuveñ	tuñ
" 263, *l*. 13, *a f*. be	being
" 269, *l*. 5. is	were
" " *l*. 10, *a f*. vănčasonăñ	văntsatsonăñ
" 275, *l*. 16. ăuveñ	ăuñ
" " *l*. 4, *a f*. as far it	as far as it
" 279, *l*. 13. khălto astolo	khălto kello astolo
" 280, *l*. 14, *a f*. "tuṭ	"suṭ
" 283, *l*. 5, *a f*. poḷeitats	poḷeităñts
" 284, *l*. 11. ălsai	ălsai
" " *l*. 22. kătăr	kătăr
" " *l*. 3, *a f*. by a blow	by blowing
" 286, *l*. 2. " "	" "
" 294, *l*. 6. (As....)	(As to the insertion of "gi" see p. 241.)
" 297, *l*. 3-4. is immediately after	is after
" 304, *l*. 1. tiṇeñ	ti
" 320, *l*. 4. viz.	is
" 330, *l*. 10. beată	beatăñ
" 336, *para*. 7. *cum*	*eum*
" 348, *v*. 16. [1]	*omit* [1]
" 349, *v*. 21, *l*. 1. ratzlo	ratsleo
" 351, *v*. 31, *l*. 5. sovo	săvo
" 355, *v*. 21, *l*. 3. boreantli	borintli
" 358, *v*. 18, *l*. 3. kelăiñ	keleiñ

Errata	*Corrige*
P. 358, *v.* 13, *l.* 5. foţeiliñ	foţeileñ
„ 364, *v.* 28, *ll.* 3. 5. -tso-	-či-
„ 369, *v.* 15, *l.* 1. astiañ	astiñ
„ 369, *v.* 19. gắţ	ghắţ (var. gắţ)
„ 377, *v.* 20, *l.* 3. dusreăčeă	dusrečea
„ 378, *v.* 1. tujea..sāmpaḍlāi	*omit it*
„ „ *v.* 2, *l.* 4. vortautaloi	vortauloi
„ 385, *v.* 20, *l.* 3. zatāt	zatā
„ 396, *l.* 16. this closed	this nearly closed
„ 409, *l.* 20. the	a
„ 415, *l.* 10, *a f.* had	has

N. B. 1. On *page* 432, *line* 2, *a f.* instead of „ „ *l.* 6, *read:* „ 7, *l.* 4, *a f.*

2. *a f.* means that the pages must be counted from the bottom to the top.

3. "var." means variety (of pronunciation). The pronunciation within brackets seems to be less correct, although perhaps more common than the other.

The kind reader can make by himself some other little corrections, *if there be any more*, either with the aid of the rules laid down in Grammar, or with his own good judgment. The Kanarese text of the Bible has not been corrected at all; for, the middle column is mostly, a sufficient help for what little mistakes there may be: see however what is said about this point in the Preface. Generally, the manner of writing in the fourth part is more correct than that of the other parts; because then I had made up my mind to pay some attention also to spelling. In making the above corrections I tried to follow the common pronunciation; consequently I have written some words differently from the similar Mahrātti words (see

p. 396); yet as I do not pretend to know perfectly the common pronunciation, it may be that some corrections are the expression of a peculiar pronunciation, not of the common one, notwithstanding my efforts to distinguish one from the other. In this case, *i. e.* if there is a variety among the natives themselves, I would rather follow the manner which agrees more with Mahrātti. Accordingly, some words, especially those which deviate from the Mahrātti may be found later on as needful of correction. But the reader in his good sense will understand that in the present state of Konkani it is thoroughly impossible to be perfectly accurate in these niceties, if it is difficult, not to say impossible, to be quite accurate in the most essential points. Hence I omit, out of many, some other more prominent remarks which I had to make about some points; we must be content with what we have until the Konkani language has reached a more settled state.